DEFENDING

LIFE

2019

FROM CONCEPTION TO NATURAL DEATH

AMERICANS
UNITED
FOR LIFE

AUL.org

Catherine Glenn Foster, M.A., J.D.
PRESIDENT & CEO

EDITOR-IN-CHIEF:

Steven H. Aden, J.D.
CHIEF LEGAL OFFICER & GENERAL COUNSEL

ASSOCIATE EDITORS:

Evangeline J. Bartz, M.A., J.D.
CORPORATE COUNSEL & VICE PRESIDENT OF OPERATIONS

Bradley N. Kehr, J.D.
GOVERNMENT AFFAIRS COUNSEL

Rachel N. Busick, J.D.
STAFF COUNSEL

Natalie M. Hejran, J.D.
STAFF COUNSEL

CONTRIBUTING EDITORS:

Thomas A. Shakely
CHIEF ENGAGEMENT OFFICER

Clarke D. Forsythe, M.A., J.D.
SENIOR COUNSEL

Praise for Defending Life

AUL'S 2019 LEGAL GUIDE BEING USED ACROSS THE COUNTRY

"Americans United for Life has a long and successful history of fighting to protect our most vulnerable — the unborn. I share that passion for protecting life and have seen the benefits of AUL's efforts both during my time as a Congressman and as the Governor of the State of Indiana. I have long believed that a society will be judged by the way it treats its most vulnerable, and I am proud that Indiana is one of the most pro-life states in the country."

MICHAEL R. PENCE *Vice President of the United States and former Governor of Indiana*

"I believe every life is sacred and that life begins at conception. Throughout my career in public service I've maintained a 100 percent pro-life record. As governor I have been proud to sign the pro-life legislation that has come to my desk. I will continue to defend the life of the unborn, and I appreciate the efforts of Americans United for Life to provide lawmakers with the tools they need to craft strong pro-life bills."

MARY FALLIN *Governor of Oklahoma*

"The 'sanctity of life' is not a campaign slogan or a marketing jingle. It is the recognition that the value of human life is not assigned by our governments, philosophers, or neighbors; it is the corner-stone of civilization... In Arkansas, we used resources provided by Americans United for Life and, with bipartisan majorities, enacted and strengthened existing protections for the unborn and their mothers. I am... thankful that Americans United for Life's model legislation is already saving lives in my state and elsewhere."

ASA HUTCHINSON *Governor of Arkansas*

TABLE OF CONTENTS

From the President

CATHERINE GLENN FOSTER, M.A., J.D. / PRESIDENT & CEO

The historic Duke Ellington Bridge in Washington D.C. (below), near the Americans United for Life office, spans a picturesque stretch of the Rock Creek Parkway. Stately and tall, it's been considered a landmark of neoclassical architecture since it was built in 1934. Unfortunately, in modern times it also gained a reputation as a "jumper's bridge" – a bridge with easy access to the 12-story precipice, high enough to virtually ensure death. Thankfully, after the city installed a six-foot-high anti-suicide fence in January 1986, at the behest of a grieving father whose daughter had jumped from the bridge, the Ellington Bridge has seen far fewer deaths.[1] And despite predictions by some mental

The historic Duke Ellington Bridge near the Americans United for Life office in Washington D.C.

health professionals and others opposed to the fence, the nearby and similarly situated Taft Bridge did not become the location of preference for the desperate and depressed, as suicides there did not appreciably rise – even though the Taft Bridge is barely a tenth of a mile from the Ellington Bridge and has no safety barriers.

What lessons can we learn from the Ellington Bridge, now restored to its proper place as a historic landmark, critical connector at the heart of our nation, and lovely masterwork of architecture?

Experts have long known, and good research shows, that barriers are highly effective at halting suicides, according to Jill Harkavy-Friedman of the American Foundation for Suicide Prevention. In an interview with the Washington Post, Harkavy-Friedman noted that intervention often makes the difference in the lives of persons contemplating suicide. "Suicides are impulsive acts, and the people who commit them are not thinking clearly, have trouble solving problems, have difficulty shifting gears, and weigh risks differently," she said. "They're going to grab whatever is available. They don't change gears if that is thwarted, because they have rigid thinking in that moment.... If they get to the bridge and there is a barrier, they're not going to shift gears. It's as simple as that."[2]

Such efforts are therefore critical in battling America's crisis-level epidemic of suicide, with the most recent figures from the U.S. Centers for Disease Control & Prevention (CDC) tallying nearly 45,000 suicides in 2016.[3] Yet even in the midst of this crisis, with tens of thousands of irreparable losses – and as life advocates urgently work to promote lifelong mental health and well-being, preserve

understanding of the unique value of each human being, and protect every life – anti-life activists have managed to pass medicalized suicide in six states and the District of Columbia under the deceptive banner of "Death with Dignity."

At Americans United for Life, we fight hard against efforts to enact so-called "assisted suicide" regimes because they are simply legally endorsed suicide by another name. The push for a "right to die" with the help of a physician is being ushered in under the guise of "compassion," "dignity," and "control," but the truth is that the legalization of such suicide, stripped of its euphemistic pretensions, is really only a doctor's legal right to prescribe a massive overdose of barbiturates – sleeping pills, essentially – for a person under his care and thereby to secure a "safe" and "reliable" death for her (although it often fails to deliver even that) with no repercussions to himself.

Tellingly, suicide advocates like "Compassion and Choices" (formerly the "Hemlock Society") don't advocate for a "right" to kill oneself by just any means – jumping from a bridge, shooting oneself, or guessing how many pills it would take to do the job – because these methods are shocking, abhorrent, and untrustworthy. Instead, they insist on the "right" to a medicalized death at the hands of a doctor, who alone controls the legal authority to prescribe death-dealing drugs. Thus, the path to legally endorsed suicide, like abortion, depends upon securing the assistance of a medical professional, the very trusted leaders whose training has taught them to respect life and to "do no harm." And just as we're seeing the demand for "abortion access" give rise to an insistence that doctors and nurses participate in destroying life in the womb, we're also seeing a growing threat to healthcare rights of conscience in states that have legalized suicide by physician.

The answer to the problem of suicide is the same, whether it's a desperate desire to jump from a bridge or a more societally respectable decision for "death with dignity" by prescription suicide. We know that when a person considering suicide gets help from caring family, friends, and professionals and learns that their life has meaning and value, most find hope and choose life. That's true for a depressed and overwhelmed teenager, a patient who's received a diagnosis of a terminal illness, or a senior with debilitating health. That's the message of musician Logic's inspiring song "1-800-273-8255," featuring Alessia Cara and Khalid – the title of the song is the phone number for the National Suicide Prevention Lifeline – which Logic has called the "most important song" he has ever written, as calls and outreach to the Lifeline have surged since the track's release. Like the suicide barriers on "jumper's bridges," it's people who care enough to intervene who make the difference in others' lives.

That's why Americans United for Life is about protecting precious human beings at every age of life, from conception through natural death. Every person should be embraced in the human family, and nothing can justify a failure to protect any innocent human life. From life-affirming pregnancy centers to conscientious doctors and nurses to caring friends and family members who are willing to intervene in the life of a depressed individual, we must be willing to serve as the safety nets to catch people slipping through the cracks, to "be the bridges" that build critical connections from

person to person, lift people up, and inspire hope. We must be trusted bulwarks against the storms and provide the path that will guard human life from destruction.

And that's why I'm privileged and delighted to serve as the President and CEO of Americans United for Life, America's pro-life legal advocacy organization. We formed in 1971 as the first national pro-life organization to proactively promote life and well-being and to push back against the efforts of anti-life activists to legalize abortion and the destruction of human life. Together, we are making the difference. In the past year, we've worked with advocates for life from coast to coast to put a stop to "suicide by physician" in state after state.

And we've achieved notable gains against abortion in the last several years; the CDC just issued its "Abortion Surveillance Report," and it adds to the proof that women are choosing to live without abortion.[4] Although CDC data is late and tends to be incomplete, the report documents a drop of 2% in the abortion rate nationwide between 2014 and 2015 – a total of nearly fifteen thousand innocent lives saved. The CDC continues to document the historic plummet in demand for abortion in the last twenty-five years, which has left the U.S. abortion rate at the same place it was in 1972 – the year before *Roe v. Wade* was decided. It's as if the easy availability of abortion on demand that *Roe* ushered in has ultimately made no difference to America's refusal to accept abortion as a "normal" part of the fabric of our society forty-five years later. But sadly, the CDC report is not all good news. It is also a very sobering reminder that abortion remains, as the title of Americans United for Life's groundbreaking investigative exposé calls it, *Unsafe*;[5] for 2014, the CDC documented six known cases of maternal abortion deaths – all of them attributed to so-called "safe and legal abortion."

Yet with every election, legislative vote, and Supreme Court case, Planned Parenthood and the abortion industry bombard young women with ominous warnings of how overturning *Roe* will negatively impact their ability to define their education, their careers, and their dreams for the future. With our national conference *Women Speak 2018,* Americans United for Life broke new ground in rebutting this tired argument, using fresh research to show how women can, and will, flourish in a society that does not constitutionalize abortion on demand. We're already looking forward to *Women Speak 2019*, and we hope you'll be able to join us in Washington D.C. for what promises to be a thought-provoking and compelling experience of hearing from highly successful women – scholars, doctors, journalists, and policy advocates from across the political spectrum – as they document why women can live and flourish without abortion.

And I'm very pleased to offer a feature article by Americans United for Life's Senior Counsel, Clarke D. Forsythe, "A New Supreme Court with New Challenges," which highlights new opportunities for advancing the cause of life with a pro-life Supreme Court majority. Our lawyers are working with states in courts across the country, engaging our legal strategy to overturn *Roe v. Wade* and once again empower the states to defend human life.

As we move forward together into 2019 as a movement for life, it's important to take stock of the advances we're making together. That's why for this first time in this edition, you'll find two new features that spotlight the progress we've made over the past year in enacting life-saving state legislation and securing pro-life victories in the courts. First, in recognition of the strides we've making in federal and state courts, and the new pro-life majority in the U.S. Supreme Court, we've added a new component to the State Reports, "The Day After *Roe*." This feature assesses where each of the 50 states and the District of Columbia will stand the day after the Supreme Court overturns the key holding of *Roe v. Wade* that there is a "fundamental right" under the federal Constitution to access abortion. Americans United for Life's Chief Legal Officer, Steven H. Aden, introduces this new feature by analyzing recent changes to the Court's personnel and offering an analysis of what they might portend for *Roe's* reversal.

Second, we've included a "State of the States" analysis of 2018 policy gains by Americans United for Life's Government Affairs Counsel, Bradley N. Kehr. This new feature is a state-by-state recap of the key developments in life-related legislation, from new protections for infants in the womb to patient-protective developments for those most in need of our protection and support, as well as strengthened safeguards for the rights of conscience of healthcare professionals. The "State of the States Report" will enable legislators and policy advocates to see at a glance the gains other states are making in defending life through law as they consider new opportunities in their own and at the federal level.

One of Americans United for Life's top legislative priorities for 2019 is our *Abortion Reporting Act*,

AUL CEO Catherine Glenn Foster at the *Gosnell* premier with real-life detective James Wood, who led the Gosnell investigation.

updated this year to incorporate research conducted by our friends at Charlotte Lozier Institute (CLI). Masked by inaccurate and incomplete data on abortion's safety and efficacy, the true dangers of abortion remain underreported and all too often ignored, as our publication *Unsafe: America's Abortion Industry Endangers Women* documents. In the summer of 2015, CLI undertook a review of state abortion reporting laws, examining statutes and published reports and talking with state officials about their practices regarding gathering and publishing information.[6] This comprehensive examination showed what many of us already recognized: as a result of our nation's deficient abortion reporting system, American abortion data is inaccurate and often misleading. A significant number of abortions go unreported, and the deaths of and injuries to countless women who have had abortions are effectively swept under the rug. As the author of a leading abortion textbook acknowledges, "[T]here are few surgical procedures given so little attention and so underrated in its potential hazard as abortion."[7]

The dangers these scofflaw abortionists pose to women and children were yet again revealed to all of us recently with the murder trial and conviction of Philadelphia abortionist Kermit Gosnell. AUL team members were in the courtroom for that trial, promoting transparency and accountability for the atrocities that occurred behind those now-closed clinic doors. And last fall, I was privileged to attend the premiere of the film Gosnell: The Trial of America's Biggest Serial Killer in Los Angeles. (Americans United for Life CEO Catherine Glenn Foster at the Gosnell premiere with real-life detective James Wood, who led the Gosnell investigation.) We all owe a debt of thanks to the Philadelphia police department and investigators who uncovered the horrors of Gosnell's abortion facility, and to the Gosnell filmmakers for reminding us both that the sunlight of exposure is the best antiseptic for dangerous and substandard abortionists and that good data is the currency of these investigations.

Pro-life advocates in Indiana attest to the importance of sound abortion data from their own experience. Cathie Humbarger of Indiana Right to Life used public records requests to unearth documentation that notorious abortionist Ulrich Klopfer was endangering women and refusing to obey laws requiring the reporting of child sex abuse at his three abortion centers in Fort Wayne, South Bend, and Gary, Indiana. "The termination of pregnancy reports and abortion facility inspection reports that are available through public information requests gave us what we needed to hold abortionist Klopfer accountable to the good laws and regulations already enacted," Humbarger says. "We filed over 2,000 complaints, which ultimately led to the closure of three abortion facilities and the suspension of abortionist Klopfer's license to practice medicine in Indiana." And this past spring, Indiana's legislature passed and Governor Eric Holcomb signed into law enhanced reporting requirements based on Americans United for Life's *Abortion Reporting Act*, giving the Hoosier State even better information on how other abortionists ignore or skirt the law at the risk of women's health and infants' lives.

And we've seen tremendous gains for the right of conscience as well. This past spring, the U.S. Supreme Court gave pro-life pregnancy centers a major victory when it ruled in *NIFLA v. Becerra* that California cannot force centers to promote the state's message of free abortions. And this year also has pro-abortion forces retreating from their nationwide campaign to force pro-life healthcare professionals to assist with abortions or dispense abortion-causing drugs. One presidential official declared the Office of Civil Rights at the U.S. Department of Health and Human Services "open for business" for pro-life doctors, nurses, pharmacists, and others facing threats for their conscientious commitments. Of course, there remains an urgent need for each state to enact Americans United for Life's Healthcare Freedom of Conscience Act, which protects all participants

in the healthcare industry from threats and coercion for their pro-life convictions, and we're working with lawmakers across the country to accomplish that goal.

I hope you are as inspired as I am by all the progress we are making together, and by the brighter horizon of protection for all life that beckons in 2019 and beyond. Thank you for all you're doing to fight for every precious human life. Let's keep working – together – toward the day when everyone is welcomed in life and protected in law.

[1] Linda Wheeler, *Duke Ellington Bridge Suicides Decline Since Installation of Fence*, Wash Post, Mar. 23, 1987.

[2] Lenny Bernstein, *Why Suicide Barriers Work, Especially at Magnets Like the Golden Gate Bridge*, Wash Post, Mar. 27, 2014.

[3] Nell Greenfieldboyce, *CDC: U.S. Suicide Rates have Risen Dramatically*, Nat'l Pub. Radio (Jun. 7, 2018). If someone you know has thoughts of suicide, please contact the National Suicide Prevention Lifeline, 1 (800) 273-TALK (8255), En Español 1 (888) 628-9454, Deaf and Hard of Hearing 1 (800) 799-4889, or the Crisis Text Line by texting 741741.

[4] U.S. Ctrs. for Disease Control and Prevention, Abortion Surveillance – United States, 2015 (2018), https://www.cdc.gov/mmwr/volumes/67/ss/ss6713a1.htm?s_cid=ss6713a1_e.

[5] For a copy of Unsafe: America's Abortion Industry Endangers Women (2018 ed.), visit Americans United for Life's website at https://aul.org/publications/unsafe/.

[6] Charles A. Donovan & Rebecca Gonzales, Charlotte Lozier Inst., Abortion Reporting: Toward a Better National Standard, (2016) at https://lozierinstitute.org/wp-content/uploads/2016/08/Abortion-Reporting-Toward-a-Better-National-Standard-FINAL.pdf.

[7] Warren M. Hern, Abortion Practice 101 (1990).

A New Supreme Court with New Challenges

CLARKE D. FORSYTHE, J.D., SENIOR COUNSEL

In Abraham Lincoln's "House Divided" speech at Springfield, Illinois in June 1858, which launched his U.S. Senate campaign, he told the convention: "If we could first know where we are, and whither we are tending, we could then better judge what to do, and how to do it."

When Justice Anthony Kennedy announced his retirement from the Supreme Court on June 27, 2018, the campaign to overturn *Roe v. Wade* entered a new stage. Justice Kennedy was the essential fifth Supreme Court vote to perpetuate *Roe* since Justice Sandra Day O'Connor's retirement in 2006, and there is now, for the first time in 25 years, no majority on the Supreme Court that is emotionally invested in *Roe* as part of their judicial legacy.

With the recent confirmations of Justices Brett Kavanaugh and Neil Gorsuch, it's time to take stock of the campaign to overturn *Roe*. What have we accomplished thus far? How would a test case strategy be likely to play out? And what should be the state legislative priorities for 2019?

KEEPING *ROE* UNSETTLED, UNWORKABLE, & OBSOLETE

One of the great, unheralded achievements of the cause for life in America has been keeping *Roe* unsettled over the 45 years since it was decided, despite ferocious hostility from powerful forces and cultural elites.

Keeping *Roe* unsettled has been extremely important because when the Supreme Court considers whether to retain or overturn precedent, it looks at six factors of *stare decisis* (the law of precedent): (1) Whether the precedent is settled; (2) Whether it was wrongly decided; (3) Whether it is workable; (4) Factual changes that have eroded the precedent; (5) Legal changes that have eroded the precedent; and (6) Whether the "reliance interests"—how much the precedent has been depended upon—are substantial. In short, did the Court err, how big was the error, and what's the cost of correcting the error? These factors not only tell us how the Court might look at *Roe* in a future test case, they also provide a political and legislative road map for challenging *Roe*.

The media frenzy about *Roe* during the Kavanaugh confirmation process demonstrates that *Roe* is clearly far from "settled" as precedent. Numerous pro-life initiatives have contributed to keeping *Roe* unsettled since *Planned Parenthood v. Casey*, including the growing political strength in the states and legislative successes. These successes include the following achievements in the States since *Roe*:

- 21 states have passed limits on abortions after 20 weeks, and 18 remain in effect despite legal challenges;

- 40 states now limit abortion practice to physicians only;

- 32 states and the District of Columbia follow the taxpayer funding limitations of the federal Hyde Amendment;

- 33 states have enforceable informed consent laws, and 27 of these include a mandated reflection period;

- 44 states have passed parental involvement laws, and 40 remain in effect despite court challenges;

- 48 states have passed laws to protect rights of conscience;

- 35 states have enacted abortion clinic regulations, and 29 remain enforceable in spite of court challenges;

- 24 states have enacted ultrasound requirements;

- 38 states have fetal homicide laws, and these are operable from conception in 30 states and;

- 41 states allow civil suits for the wrongful death of an unborn child.

To keep *Roe* unsettled, advocates will need to continue to challenge *Roe* through state and federal legislation and by electing public officials who oppose *Roe*. To show that *Roe* was wrongly decided, scholarly and judicial criticism of *Roe* have mounted over the years, and must continue. *Roe* is best shown to be unworkable by the various abortion cases that the U.S. Supreme Court has decided since *Roe* and the numerous changes in the rules that the Court has jerry-rigged to decide those abortion cases. And research and data showing the negative impact of abortion on women must continue to be conducted and widely disseminated.

TEST CASES

Since there will be numerous opportunities for the justices to hear legal issues involving abortion in the next few years, we may not have to wait long to see various signals from the Court. In the October 2018 Term, for example, the Supreme Court has been asked by two states to decide whether states have the authority to defund abortion providers in their Medicaid programs. AUL filed "friend of the court" briefs in support of both states—including one on behalf of 90 Members of Congress—urging the Court to review the cases, recognize the sovereign authority of states, and decide that states can not be forced to use their limited public funds to subsidize abortion businesses. Other prospective cases include litigation over abortion non-discrimination (including on the basis of Down Syndrome) and fetal remains disposition laws. A fetal remains disposal law may present a case in which the statute can be upheld within the Court's current doctrine and yet further the state's interest in unborn human life. Additionally, there are at least five cases involving dismemberment abortion bans in the courts.

SIGNALS FROM THE NEW MAJORITY

It seems reasonable to expect that the new Supreme Court majority will proceed slowly with abortion cases and that they will put off any early showdown over the validity of *Roe* itself. It is more likely that the new majority will, in the short term, review cases in which abortion limits can be upheld within the Court's current doctrine.

One critically important factor to watch with the new majority will be the case selection the justices employ. There has long been an urban legend among political activists that the justices can be "forced" to hear a case. The reality, in fact, is that the justices have virtually absolute discretion as to when, whether, and how they address legal issues in cases. The justices hear on the merits only about 1% of the appeals that are filed annually in the Supreme Court. Thankfully, the substitution of Kavanaugh for Kennedy means that the risk that the Court will agree to hear an abortion case so as to reinforce *Roe/Casey*, as in *Whole Woman's Health v. Hellerstedt* in 2016, is virtually gone. It diminishes the power of the four pro-abortion justices; they can no longer count on a fifth justice to join a majority as Kennedy did in *Hellerstedt*. There

should be some degree of confidence that the new Roberts Court majority will select the better abortion cases, will look for cases with a good evidentiary record, and will decline to hear weaker cases or cases that will force the majority to go farther than they are ready to go in the short term.

Another signal to look for will be the cues the justices sometimes send about legal issues they are interested in. For example, in 2013, four pro-abortion justices indicated in an opinion that they were interested in hearing a challenge to an admitting privileges law from Texas. This was two years before the *Hellerstedt* decision, in which the Court by a 5-4 margin—with the four pro-abortion Justices and Justice Kennedy—threw out a Texas admitting privileges law.

CHIEF JUSTICE ROBERTS AS THE "MAN IN THE MIDDLE"

Particular attention should be given to Chief Justice John Roberts. Justice Kennedy's influence was shown by the number of times over the past decade that he was the decisive vote in 5-4 decisions. Roberts may now play that role, and observers have noted that this is the first time that a chief justice has been in the ideological middle in decades. Roberts will likely play a larger role in determining which abortion cases the Court reviews in the future and how narrowly or broadly they are decided. In addition to his "tie-breaking" power, the chief justice has special power to shape the agenda of the Supreme Court through his prioritization of cases, as he initiates and distributes a "discuss list" of cases before the justices' weekly conference. And he has the power of assigning opinions when he is in the majority, as he did in 2006 in his first abortion case, *Ayotte v. Planned Parenthood*, when he assigned the opinion of a unanimous Court to Justice O'Connor.

Roberts has expressed a goal of "greater consensus on the Court and minimalism—a preference for narrow decision making." In a speech during his first term as chief justice, he said,

> "If it is not necessary to decide more to a case, then in my view it is necessary not to decide more to a case. Division should not be artificially suppressed, but the rule of law benefits from a broader agreement. The broader the agreement among the justices, the more likely it is a decision on the narrowest possible grounds."

As the *Wall Street Journal* recently observed, Roberts "has shown an affinity in many circumstances for narrow, incremental rulings that pick up more votes, and legal observers say his strong sense of stewardship means he won't want the court to be seen as a partisan body that decides all of the nation's big legal issues on 5-4 votes." On the other hand, as liberal Supreme Court reporter Marcia Coyle observed in her 2013 book, *The Roberts Court*, Roberts "is unafraid to deliver a major 'jolt' to the system if he disagrees with the law's direction." Examples include the 2010 *Citizens United v. Federal Election Commission* decision and the 2018 *Janus v. AFSCME* decision, both of which overturned years of longstanding precedent in their respective areas.

LEGISLATIVE PRIORITIES FOR THE STATES

Future Supreme Court abortion cases will be shaped by the legislation that states enact. As many past abortion decisions by the Supreme Court show, it is imperative for the states to enact abortion legislation with a solid medical and factual record supporting the life of the unborn child and maternal health, and the legislation needs to be well-defended by the state attorney general. States should incorporate detailed legislative findings in their bills or they are at a distinct disadvantage in defending abortion laws in court.

AUL's annual edition of *Defending Life* contains specific recommendations for each state. States should prioritize legislation that defunds the abortion industry and provides affirmative legal protection for unborn child in non-abortion circumstances. Protecting women from abortion and reducing the number of abortions is also important.

State legislators who wish to sponsor clinic regulations and admitting privileges should consult AUL's 2018 groundbreaking investigative report, *Unsafe: How the Public Health Crisis in America's Abortion Clinics Endangers Women*, on the risks to women from substandard conditions and personnel in abortion facilities.

States also need to prevent erosion in the protection of human life in other bioethical areas, including assisted suicide. One good example was Iowa's 2018 enactment of a bill (SF 2418, sec. 118) to prohibit both wrongful birth and wrongful life causes of action in Iowa and overturn the Iowa Supreme

Court's decision in *Plowman v. Fort Madison Community Hospital*, [896 N.W.2d 393 (Iowa 2017)], which created a wrongful birth cause of action. Another is the 2018 law passed by Arizona which treats human embryos as human beings and directs that they be treated as children during custodial disputes between parents.

TWENTY-WEEK LIMITS

We continue to believe that 20 week (five month) limits uniquely challenge a key pillar of *Roe*, the viability rule, and do so by protecting *both* of the primary state interests that *Roe* recognized: the life of the unborn child and maternal health. As of July 2018, 21 states have enacted a 20 week limit since 2010. Most are in effect. States should not support or reinforce the viability rule through state legislation. The viability rule is arbitrary, but twenty-week limits are provisional. That is a critical difference. Twenty-week limits are an important public rebuke to the Supreme Court's viability rule and they are based upon, and highlight, the greatly increased risk to women from abortion after 20 weeks. Twenty weeks is the point at which we have the best evidence of fetal pain and the greatly increased risk of late term abortions. And while 20 weeks may be technically before viability, the Court's acknowledgment in *Webster v. Reproductive Health Services*, that there is often a 2–4 week margin of error in dating the pregnancy, may support a 20-week bill if challenged.

With the substitution of Kavanaugh for Kennedy, one of the major objections to these laws—that Kennedy might vote to reaffirm the viability rule and strike down such limits—is now obsolete.

The danger that the Court might invalidate these laws is virtually eliminated, though the risk that the Court might refuse to hear a case involving a 20 week limit—and leave a negative lower court decision standing—still exists, at least in the short-term.

THE STATUS OF THE "RELIANCE INTERESTS": MAKING THE CASE THAT ABORTION IS BAD FOR BOTH

The *Casey* Court in 1992 based its reaffirmation of *Roe* on the proposition that women have come to rely on abortion for equal opportunity in American society. That rationale was shared by a majority of justices before Kennedy's retirement and it is a powerful sentiment in contemporary American culture. It is a steady drumbeat in the media.

To counter this cultural paradigm, the cause for life needs to consistently and persistently make the case that abortion is bad for women and that that women will flourish after *Roe* is overturned. In June 2013, Americans United for Life co-sponsored with the Heritage Foundation a conference, Women Speak 2018, to make that case.

States should continue to emphasize the negative impact of abortion on women (in the courts, at the Supreme Court, in the states, and in the media) to underscore the harmful impact of abortion on women and raise understanding of abortion's risks to women, which is necessary to change public opinion and judicial opinion. Women do not need abortion to be successful.

MAINTAINING POLITICAL SUPPORT
FOR OVERTURNING *ROE*

The "seventh" factor of stare decisis—unofficial, informal, and rarely expressed, but important nonetheless—is political support for retaining or overturning the precedent. Rarely has the Supreme Court retained or overturned an important precedent in the face of substantial contrary political opposition. And Chief Justice Roberts has shown an interest in avoiding such clashes with public opinion. In addition, the political controversy surrounding the Kavanaugh confirmation will need to be answered by pro-life political wins in federal and state elections.

Pro-life leaders need to think in terms of a six-justice majority to overturn *Roe*. A 5-4 overruling would be inherently unstable—subject to being overturned with a change in the presidency and a Supreme Court retirement.

We need to keep the presidency and the Senate in order to create a six-justice majority. Continuing to elect a president and a Senate that are pro-life, maintaining pro-life majorities in 30+ states, keeping pro-life citizens mobilized, educating public opinion about the real implications—all will be necessary parts of a successful political strategy to overturn *Roe*.

The Day After Roe

STEVEN H. ADEN, J.D., CHIEF LEGAL OFFICER & GENERAL COUNSEL

The question whether Brett Kavanaugh would supply the deciding vote to overturn the holding in *Roe v. Wade* that women possess a constitutional right to abortion wasn't exactly the "elephant in the room" at his confirmation hearing last fall, since no one was ignoring it, but it did have that kind of heft in the debate over now-Justice Kavanaugh's nomination. Everyone seemed to be asking it and offering a variety of answers, ranging from the pedestrian to the hysterical. Perhaps the most extreme example, outside of Planned Parenthood's media statements, was a headline in the *Washington Examiner* that declared, "Brett Kavanaugh poised to take first step in overturning *Roe vs. Wade*."

The charge has been leveled at every Republican nominee in modern times, including those who have later voted to uphold *Roe* and abortion rights – Justices David Souter, Sandra Day O'Connor and Anthony Kennedy, to name three, who made up the famous "plurality" of justices who voted to uphold *Roe* in 1992 in *Planned Parenthood v. Casey*. In keeping with the tactic employed by modern Supreme Court nominees to refrain from commenting on cases that may come before the High Court, Justice Kavanaugh declined to comment on *Roe*. Because of this unwillingness to debate *Roe* on its own

terms, confirmation hearings have become a form of debate-by-proxy, in which a nominee's judicial philosophy is read for indications that auger one way or another how they would vote on the *Roe* question.

In the end, the pro-life movement favored Justice Kavanaugh's nomination not because the movement thought he was a sure bet to overturn *Roe*, but because his judicial philosophy is in stark contrast to the results-driven judicial activism that gave us *Roe*. Even many liberals, including Justice Ruth Bader Ginsburg, have criticized *Roe's* reasoning as sloppy and outcome-driven. If Justice Byron White was correct in declaring in his dissent in Roe that the majority's opinion finding a "fundamental right to abortion" was "an exercise in raw judicial power" — and we believe he was — the path to correcting this abuse lies in laying down the proper, historical lines of constitutional analysis based on firm facts and powerful jurisprudential arguments. For his entire career on the federal bench, Justice Kavanaugh's highest loyalty has been to the meaning of the Constitution as it was originally written, not his own personal views of what it should mean. That point of view makes Kavanaugh the avowed enemy of judicial activism

IF *ROE V. WADE* IS OVERTURNED TODAY, WILL ABORTION BE ILLEGAL IN MY STATE?

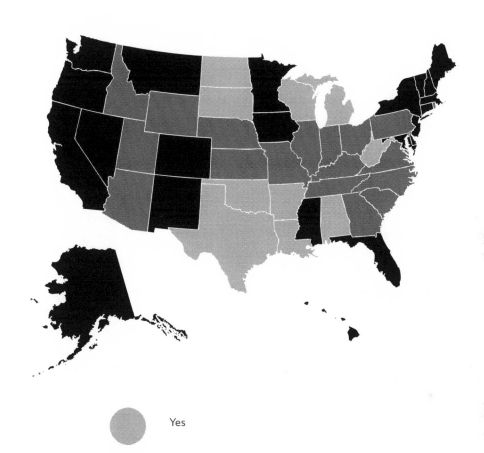

 Yes

Yes, but only after 20 weeks gestation

No

– and perhaps the best friend the Constitution and unborn children ever had.

We should also remember that, even if Justice Kavanaugh does supply the deciding vote to overturn *Roe*, the debate over abortion won't end there.

Roe's repeal would not make abortion illegal nationwide overnight, as abortion activists suggest. Abortion would be left to the states to regulate, as it was before 1973, and consigned to the realm of politics, where the electoral system offers direct accountability to the people for legislative decisions.

The fact is, if *Roe* were overturned today, only ten states would have enforceable prohibitions on the books before 20 weeks, or viability. Another eighteen states and the District of Columbia would have enforceable prohibitions only after 20 weeks. The balance, twenty-two states, would continue to have abortion on demand throughout pregnancy.

Here's a map of the U.S. showing these three categories of states, which Americans United for Life has made available as an interactive graphic on our website.

That's why Americans United for Life's "state-by-state strategy" is so critically important for the long-term fight for Life. When states enact well-crafted model legislation that protects mothers and infants and defend those laws through inevitable court challenges, they create precedents that serve as an example and an encouragement to other states. And they supply judges with sound reasons to criticize the legal straightjacket the Supreme Court put states in

with the *Roe* decision; criticism which Americans United for Life's Senior Counsel, Clarke Forsythe, has catalogued in his influential article published this year by the Georgetown Journal of Law & Public Policy, *A Draft Opinion Overruling Roe v. Wade* (available on the AUL website). Because of the growing momentum in the states and courts toward re-assessing the Supreme Court's commitment to *Roe*, and the opportunity to do so the addition of new Justices affords, AUL has added a new feature to the State Reports and Recommendations section of Defending Life — an explanation of the impact that *Roe's* overturn would have on the state's abortion laws.

2018
Rankings
& Report Cards

A Year of Pro-Life Progress Across the Country

BRADLEY N. KEHR, J.D., GOVERNMENT AFFAIRS COUNSEL

The year 2018 proved to be another year of strong pro-life engagement and progress in the states. Legislatures across the country continued to press forward to ensure that mothers are well informed about the risks of abortion, the public has valuable statistics on the realities of abortion and its complications, and public resources are no longer flowing to the abortion industry. Americans United for Life was privileged to provide the model language or legal support for nineteen new pro-life laws and two pro-life resolutions, as well as assist in defeating eight anti-life measures.

Overall, the states passed forty-five life-affirming abortion-related measures in the past year. In response to recent judicial actions including, the Supreme Court's 2016 decision in *Whole Women's Health v. Hellerstedt,* and because of a desire to ensure mothers are fully informed about their decision, states have taken an increased interest in the data underlying abortions, such as demographics of women who choose abortion and abortion-related complications. Indiana, Idaho, and Arizona enacted the next generation of abortion reporting requirements, based on AUL's

Abortion Reporting Act (see pages 382–391 *infra*) requiring that all abortion-related complications, whether presented at the abortion facility or elsewhere, be reported so as to give a true picture of the consequences of abortions to mothers. Other states, led by Ohio, sought to protect unborn children with Down syndrome and other genetic anomalies. Many other states are enacting prohibitions on abortion at five months gestation, safeguarding dignity for fetal remains, and supporting crisis pregnancy centers.

On the other hand, opponents continued to pressure states to reverse protections for mothers and their unborn children. At least sixteen states considered measures undermining existing life-affirming laws or supporting a so-called "right" to abortion. Ultimately, they enacted two bills mandating insurance coverage for elective abortion, passed restrictions on crisis pregnancy centers, and passed a resolution marking the 45th anniversary of *Roe v. Wade.* However, with the help of AUL's legal and policy experts, Rhode Island's "Reproductive Health Care Act" and New York's "Reproductive Health Act" were defeated. These bills would have codified *Roe* in state law by granting expansive legal protection to abortion and invalidating all current and future protective abortion restrictions. And while activists pushed measures to legalize suicide by prescription in over a dozen states, AUL helped allies in Connecticut, New York, and Rhode Island defeat these dangerous bills, and suicide by physician lost in every state except Hawaii.

2018 STATE LEGISLATIVE HIGHLIGHTS

In 2018, forty-five states considered 398 measures related to either abortion or suicide. A comprehensive review of the 2018 state legislative sessions is available on the AUL website, including a chart of all life-related state legislation considered in the past year. Below are highlights of state actions around the country:

Alabama enacted HB 98, placing a constitutional amendment on the November 2018 ballot to declare that there is no right to abortion under the state constitution—which voters adopted by a 22 point margin. The Alabama Senate adopted a resolution (SR 59) based on AUL model language, recognizing the contributions of pregnancy resource centers; and the state House and Senate adopted a resolution (SR 109) condemning U.S. Senator Doug Jones' vote against the Pain-Capable Unborn Child Act.

Arizona enacted SB 1393, requiring courts to grant custody of *in vitro* human embryos to the spouse who intends to allow the embryos to develop to birth.

Arkansas enacted budgetary language prohibiting state funds from being used for abortion referrals in public schools or for abortion services.

California enacted SB 743, prohibiting MediCal from excluding any provider that provides family planning services. The California Assembly and Senate both passed resolutions commemorating the 45th Anniversary of *Roe v. Wade* and asking the President and the United States Congress to support a "fundamental right to abortion" and access to those services provided by Planned Parenthood.

Connecticut enacted HB 5148, allowing a pregnant medical patient to indicate clearly on her living will that she desires life support if it would allow for her unborn child to reach live birth.

Florida enacted HB 41, creating a grant program to provide assistance for pregnancy support organizations.

Hawaii enacted HB 2739, allowing suicide by physician, and SB 501, requiring limited service pregnancy centers to disclose the availability of and enrollment information for reproductive health services.

Idaho enacted SB 1243, requiring that a woman who receives a chemical abortion be notified that there is a chance to reverse the procedure if she changes her mind before completing the drug regimen.

LIFE-RELATED MEASURES CONSIDERED IN 2018

PRO-LIFE ISSUES CONSIDERED

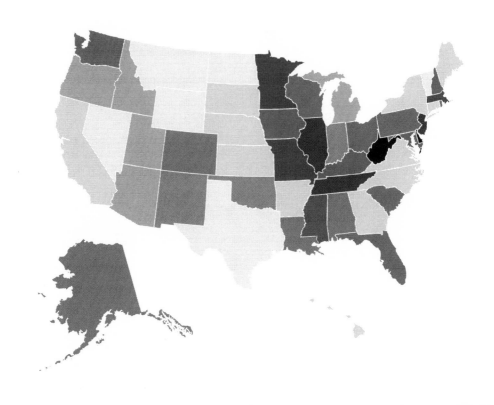

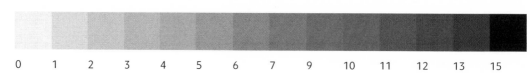

| 0 | 1 | 2 | 3 | 4 | 5 | 6 | 7 | 9 | 10 | 11 | 12 | 13 | 15 |

ANTI-LIFE ISSUES CONSIDERED

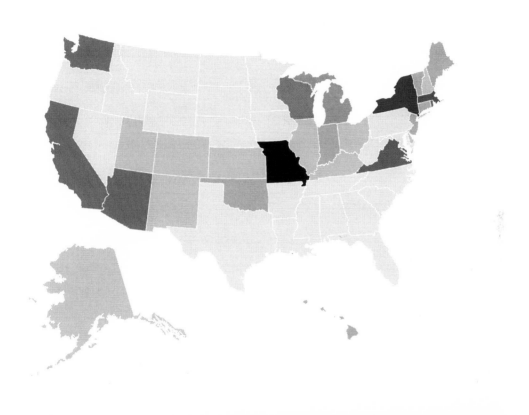

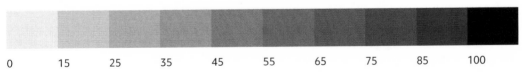

| 0 | 15 | 25 | 35 | 45 | 55 | 65 | 75 | 85 | 100 |

Illinois enacted HB 40, allowing coverage for elective abortions and reproductive health care to be included in the State Employees Group Insurance and the state's medical assistance program.

Indiana enacted SB 203, changing the state's fetal homicide law to protect the unborn at any stage of development instead of only after viability.

Iowa enacted SB 359, requiring that fetal remains be treated with dignity through burial or cremation, in line with AUL's Unborn Infants Dignity Act, and prohibiting abortions once a fetal heartbeat is present.

Kentucky enacted HB 454, prohibiting dismemberment abortions after 10 weeks post-fertilization. The state House and Senate adopted a resolution (HCR 152) to recognize the contributions of pregnancy resource centers, based on AUL model language. The House and Senate also adopted resolutions (HR 96 and SR 108) memorializing the 45 years since the *Roe v. Wade* decision and the consequences it has had, including the sixty million dead unborn, the childless homes waiting to adopt, and the decisions' severe disrespect for life.

Louisiana also enacted a series of laws (HB 273, HB 287, SB 325, and HB 891) to strengthen existing laws in regard to fetal remains, informed consent, prohibitions on abortions due to genetic anomalies, and state funding for abortion providers in response to court actions on related laws. Louisiana also enacted HB 449, requiring information on adoption agencies be posted online

on the state website; SB 181, prohibiting abortions 15 weeks post-conception (effective depending on the outcome of a lawsuit against Mississippi's similar 15-week ban); and SB 534, defining abortion and feticide as crimes of violence for the purpose of criminal prosecutions. The House and Senate also adopted a resolution (HCR 26) recognizing "Pro-Life Day" and commending pregnancy resource centers, adoption agencies, social services, and pro-life organizations and citizens.

Minnesota Governor Mark Dayton vetoed a measure that would have allowed women to see the ultrasound of their baby prior to an abortion.

Mississippi enacted HB 1510, prohibiting abortions after 15 weeks gestation.

Nebraska added language to its budget act, L 944, prohibiting Title X funds from going to organizations that perform or refer for abortions.

Ohio enacted HB 214, reflecting language in AUL's Prenatal Nondiscrimination Act, prohibiting abortions where the reason for abortion is a fetal diagnosis of Down syndrome or other genetic anomaly.

Oklahoma's House adopted a resolution (HR 1022) recognizing Rose Day and the sanctity of human life.

Pennsylvania Governor Tom Wolf vetoed a measure that would have prohibited abortions after 20 weeks—the point at which an unborn child can feel pain—and would have prohibited dismemberment abortions.

South Dakota enacted SB 110, bolstering an existing law requiring consultation with a registered pregnancy center before an abortion and finding that Planned Parenthood was intentionally undermining informed consent laws.

Tennessee enacted HB 2251 to clarify that it is the state's policy to favor childbirth and require the state to pursue a waiver to exclude elective abortion providers from TennCare—Tennessee's Medicaid program. Tennessee also enacted HB 108, requiring that reports on abortions include whether or not a heartbeat was detected if an ultrasound was performed; HB 2381 to provide for the establishment of a state monument to unborn children; and SB 2494, codifying a prioritization of family planning funds first to public entities and then to private entities that provide comprehensive care before being made available to limited service family planning providers such as Planned Parenthood.

Utah enacted SB 118, requiring that abortions be performed in an abortion clinic or hospital, enhancing requirements for what information must be provided to women prior to an abortion, and requiring that the state maintain a website with this information.

Virginia's House and Senate adopted a resolution (HJR 254) commending the March for Life and the unification of groups around the pro-life message.

Washington enacted SB 6219, requiring health insurance plans that cover maternity care to provide equivalent coverage for abortion services.

West Virginia enacted SJR 12, proposing an amendment to the state constitution for the November 2018 ballot. It was approved by voters and makes it clear that there is no right to abortion under the state constitution and nothing requires the funding of an abortion.

10

BEST AND WORST STATES FOR LIFE

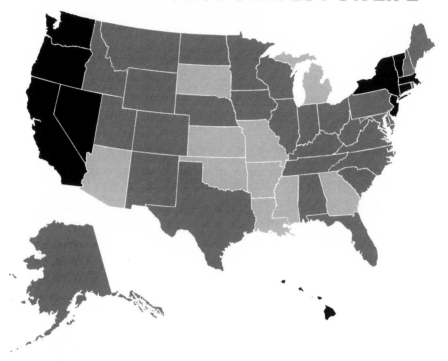

MOST PROTECTIVE STATES		LEAST PROTECTIVE STATES	
1	Arizona	50	Washington
2	Arkansas	49	California
3	Louisiana	48	Vermont
4	Oklahoma	47	New Jersey
5	Kansas	46	Hawaii
6	South Dakota	45	Oregon
7	Mississippi	44	Nevada
8	Georgia	43	New York
9	Michigan	42	Connecticut
10	Nebraska	41	Massachusetts

AUL'S 2019 STATE RANKINGS

1	Arizona	26	Florida
2	Arkansas	27	West Virginia
3	Louisiana	28	Rhode Island
4	Oklahoma	29	Minnesota
5	Kansas	30	Colorado
6	South Dakota	31	Iowa
7	Mississippi	32	Delaware
8	Georgia	33	New Hampshire
9	Michigan	34	Alaska
10	Nebraska	35	Wyoming
11	Missouri	36	Maine
12	Pennsylvania	37	Illinois
13	Texas	38	Maryland
14	Indiana	39	New Mexico
15	Alabama	40	Montana
16	North Dakota	41	Massachusetts
17	Ohio	42	Connecticut
18	Tennessee	43	New York
19	Kentucky	44	Nevada
20	Virginia	45	Oregon
21	Idaho	46	Hawaii
22	South Carolina	47	New Jersey
23	North Carolina	48	Vermont
24	Wisconsin	49	California
25	Utah	50	Washington

Alabama | RANKING: 15

Alabama has made progress in protecting women from the harms of abortion. It requires informed consent and parental consent before abortion, and it has prohibited abortion coverage in the state health insurance exchanges (as required under the federal healthcare law). However, Alabama maintains no laws regarding human cloning, destructive embryo research, or healthcare freedom of conscience.

ABORTION

- Alabama prohibits abortion at or after 5 months (i.e., 20 weeks) on the basis of the pain experienced by unborn children.

- Alabama follows the federal standard for Medicaid funding for abortions, only permitting the use of federal or state matching Medicaid funds for abortions necessary to preserve the life of the woman or when the pregnancy is the result of rape or incest.

- Alabama prohibits the dismemberment abortion procedure. The law is enjoined and in ongoing litigation.

- Alabama requires that a woman be given a 48-hour reflection period before a physician may perform an abortion and requires that she be informed of the risks of and alternatives to abortion, the probable gestational age of her unborn child, and the probable anatomical and physiological characteristics of the child at his/her current stage of development.

- Alabama also requires an abortion provider to give a woman the opportunity to review a state-sponsored videotape and written materials detailing sources of public and private support, adoption agencies, fetal development, abortion methods, and the father's legal responsibilities.

- It also requires an abortion provider to perform an ultrasound prior to an abortion and to provide a woman with an opportunity to view the ultrasound.

- Alabama requires abortion providers to explain in printed materials that it is illegal for someone to coerce a woman into having an abortion.

- A physician may not perform an abortion on an unemancipated minor under the age of 18 without first obtaining the written consent of one parent or a legal guardian unless there is a medical emergency or the minor obtains a court order. Alabama requires proof of relationship between the parent and the minor seeking an abortion and prohibits a parent, legal guardian, custodian, or any other person from coercing a minor to have an abortion. Other procedural aspects of the judicial bypass process are enjoined and in ongoing litigation.

- Abortion facilities must meet the same health and safety standards as facilities performing other out-patient surgeries.

- A law requiring the state Department of Health to not issue or renew a health center license for an abortion clinic located within 2,000 feet of a K-8 public school was declared unconstitutional.

- Alabama's requirement for abortion providers to maintain hospital admitting privileges was declared unconstitutional.

- Only a physician licensed by the state to practice medicine or osteopathy may perform an abortion.

- Alabama has an enforceable abortion reporting law but does not require the reporting of information to the Centers for Disease Control and Prevention (CDC). The measure requires abortion providers to report short-term complications.

- Abortion facilities are required to report suspected child abuse.

- Alabama requires that drug-induced abortion be administered by a physician and mandates that the physician examine the woman before providing the drugs.

- The Alabama Office of Women's Health may not advocate, promote, or otherwise advance abortion or drug-induced abortion.

- Alabama prohibits abortion coverage in the state health insurance Exchanges (required under the federal healthcare law) except in cases of life endangerment, rape, incest, or ectopic pregnancy. Further, Alabama voters approved a constitutional amendment that "prohibit[s] any person, employer, or health care provider from being compelled to participate in any health care system."

- Alabama offers "Choose Life" license plates, the proceeds of which benefit pregnancy resource centers and/or other organizations providing abortion alternatives.

LEGAL RECOGNITION OF THE UNBORN AND NEWLY BORN

- Alabama defines a "person" under its homicide laws to include the unborn child in utero at any stage of development.

- Alabama also defines a nonfatal assault on an unborn child as a criminal offense.

- It allows a wrongful death (civil) action when an unborn child at any stage of development is killed through a negligent or criminal act.

- Alabama has created a specific affirmative duty for physicians to provide medical care and treatment to infants born alive at any stage of development.

- Alabama has enacted a "Baby Moses" law under which a mother or legal guardian who is unable to care for a newborn infant may anonymously and safely leave the infant in the care of a responsible person at a hospital, police station, fire station, or other prescribed location.

- Alabama enacted the Unborn Infants Dignity Act, based on AUL model language, providing parents an option for a dignified final disposition of the bodily remains of deceased unborn infants and prohibiting the sale or other unlawful disposition of the bodily remains of a deceased unborn infant.

BIOETHICS LAWS

- Alabama maintains no laws regarding human cloning, destructive embryo research, or human egg harvesting, and it does not promote ethical forms of research.

- It maintains laws regarding the parentage of children conceived through assisted reproductive technologies.

PATIENT PROTECTION LAWS

- Alabama prohibits suicide by physician.

HEALTHCARE FREEDOM OF CONSCIENCE

PARTICIPATION IN ABORTION

- Alabama currently provides no protection for the freedom of conscience of healthcare providers.

PARTICIPATION IN RESEARCH HARMFUL TO HUMAN LIFE

- Alabama currently provides protection for the rights of healthcare providers who conscientiously object to participation in medical procedures that violate a provider's moral or religious beliefs.

DID YOU KNOW?

- In 2018, Alabama passed a resolution recognizing the life-affirming contributions that pregnancy care centers have made, and encouraging Congress to give assistance for medical equipment and abstinence education.

- Also in 2018, Alabama voters approved a state constitution amendment affirming "it is the public policy of this state to recognize and support the sanctity of unborn life and the rights of unborn children, most importantly the right to life..."

WHAT HAPPENS AFTER *ROE* IS OVERTURNED?

- Abortion will be legal up to 20 weeks of pregnancy and possibly throughout pregnancy based on existing law with undefined "health" exceptions enacted before *Roe*.

RECOMMENDATIONS
for Alabama

WOMEN'S PROTECTION PROJECT PRIORITIES

- Enhanced penalties and enforcement mechanisms for the state's abortion laws
- Drug-Induced Abortion Information and Reporting Act
- Additional components of the Parental Involvement Enhancement Act
- Components of the Child Protection Act related to evidence retention and remedies for third-party interference with parental rights

INFANTS' PROTECTION PROJECT PRIORITIES

- Partial-Birth Abortion Ban Act
- Prenatal Nondiscrimination Act
- Perinatal Hospice Information Act

PATIENT PROTECTION ACT PRIORITIES

- Joint Resolution Opposing Suicide by Physician
- Charlie Gard Act (formerly the Life Sustaining Care Act)
- Pain Medicine Education Act

ADDITIONAL PRIORITIES

ABORTION

- Defunding the Abortion Industry and Advancing Women's Health Act

LEGAL RECOGNITION AND PROTECTION FOR THE UNBORN

- Statutory prohibition on wrongful birth lawsuits
- Pregnant Woman's Protection Act

BIOETHICS

- Prohibition on Public Funding for Human Cloning and Destructive Embryo Research Act
- Human Cloning Prohibition Act

Alaska | RANKING: 34

Alaska maintains few legal protections for women seeking abortion. The Alaska Supreme Court has determined that the state constitution provides a broader right to abortion than that interpreted in the U.S. Constitution and, using this reasoning, recently struck down the state's parental notice law. Moreover, it maintains no laws regulating emerging biotechnologies.

ABORTION

- The Alaska Supreme Court has determined that the Alaska Constitution provides for a broader right to abortion than that interpreted in the U.S. Constitution.

- Alaska maintains an abortion information website and requires that a woman seeking an abortion certify in writing that a physician provided her with information on the following: fetal development, various abortion procedures, possible risks and complications associated with abortion and childbirth, eligibility requirements for medical assistance benefits, child support orders, and contraceptive options.

- It includes information about the abortion-breast cancer link in the educational materials a woman must receive prior to an abortion.

- Alaska requires a parent be notified before a minor under the age of 18 obtains an abortion unless the minor is the victim of abuse by a parent or legal guardian, there is a medical emergency, or the minor obtains a court order. The law is permanently enjoined.

- Alaska limits the performance of abortions to licensed physicians. However, the Alaska Attorney General has issued opinions that laws requiring that only licensed physicians perform abortions and imposing minimal health and safety regulations on abortion clinics are unconstitutional and unenforceable.

- Alaska has an enforceable abortion reporting law but does not require the reporting of information to the Centers for Disease Control and Prevention (CDC). The measure applies to both surgical and nonsurgical abortions.

- In 2014, Alaska enacted a law prohibiting state taxpayer dollars under its state Medicaid program to pay for abortion services unless the abortion is a "medically necessary abortion" or the pregnancy was the result of rape or incest. "Medically necessary abortion" is defined as an abortion "performed to avoid a threat of serious risk to the life or physical health of a woman." The law is enjoined and in ongoing litigation. With the law enjoined, Alaska is required to fund abortions "necessary to prevent the death or disability of the woman, or to ameliorate a condition harmful to the woman's physical or psychological health."

- Alaska offers "Choose Life" specialty license plates. The proceeds from the sale of the plates benefit pregnancy resource centers.

LEGAL RECOGNITION AND PROTECTION OF THE UNBORN AND NEWLY BORN

- Under Alaska criminal law, an unborn child at any stage of development may be considered a victim of murder, manslaughter, and criminally negligent homicide.

- Alaska also criminalizes nonfatal assaults on the unborn.

- Alaska provides a wrongful death (civil) cause of action when an unborn child at any stage of development is killed through a negligent or criminal act.

- Alaska maintains a "Baby Moses" law, which provides immunity for a parent who leaves an unharmed infant, no more than 21 days old, with police, medical personnel, hospital employees, emergency services personnel, or any person the parent believes will act in the infant's best interest.

- Alaska requires healthcare professionals to report suspicions of drug use during pregnancy.

- In the case of a stillbirth, Alaska law requires that the mother and the father (if present) must be advised that they may request the preparation of a Certificate of Birth Resulting in Stillbirth.

BIOETHICS LAWS

- Alaska maintains no laws regarding human cloning, destructive embryo research, fetal experimentation, human egg harvesting, or assisted reproductive technologies, and it does not promote ethical research alternatives.

PATIENT PROTECTION LAWS

- Alaska law specifically prohibits suicide by physician, classifying it as manslaughter.

HEALTHCARE FREEDOM OF CONSCIENCE

PARTICIPATION IN ABORTION

- Alaska law provides that no person or hospital may be required to participate in an abortion.

- Recent court decisions have narrowed the legal protection for hospitals. Currently, non-sectarian hospitals built or operated with public funds may not refuse to offer or provide abortions.

PARTICIPATION IN RESEARCH HARMFUL TO HUMAN LIFE

- Alaska currently provides no protection for the conscience rights of healthcare providers who conscientiously object to participation in human cloning, destructive embryo research, or other forms of medical research that violate a provider's moral or religious beliefs.

DID YOU KNOW?

- Alaska law allows for telemedicine abortion if all other abortion requirements be met, including that the abortion provider be in the room.

- In 2018, Alaska considered a bill that would require the physician terminating a pregnancy to use a method that would provide an opportunity for the child to survive. as well as a constitutional amendment clarifying the state constitution does not prohibit parental notice and consent before a minor's pregnancy.

- AUL submitted written testimony against a bill that would legalize suicide by physician.

WHAT HAPPENS AFTER *ROE* IS OVERTURNED?

- Abortion will be legal throughout pregnancy due to a state court decision.

RECOMMENDATIONS
for Alaska

WOMEN'S PROTECTION PROJECT PRIORITIES

- Enhanced penalties and enforcement mechanisms for the state's abortion-related laws
- 24-hour reflection period for abortion
- Coercive Abuse Against Mothers Prevention Act
- Women's Health Protection Act (abortion clinic regulations)
- Drug-Induced Abortion Information and Reporting Act
- Components of the Child Protection Act related to mandatory reporting of abuse and remedies for third-party interference with parental rights

INFANTS' PROTECTION PROJECT PRIORITIES

- Unborn Infants Dignity Act
- Perinatal Hospice Information Act
- Prenatal Nondiscrimination Act
- Born-Alive Infants' Protection Act

PATIENT PROTECTION ACT PRIORITIES

- Joint Resolution Opposing Suicide by Physician
- Charlie Gard Act (formerly the Life Sustaining Care Act)
- Pain Medicine Education Act

ADDITIONAL PRIORITIES

ABORTION

- State Constitutional Amendment (providing that there is no state constitutional right to abortion)
- Defunding the Abortion Industry and Advancing Women's Health Act
- Federal Abortion-Mandate Opt-Out Act

LEGAL RECOGNITION AND PROTECTION FOR THE UNBORN

- Pregnant Woman's Protection Act

BIOETHICS

- Prohibition on Public Funding of Human Cloning and Destructive Embryo Research Act

HEALTHCARE FREEDOM OF CONSCIENCE

- Healthcare Freedom of Conscience Act

Arizona | RANKING: 1

Over the last several years, Arizona has garnered national attention for its efforts to protect women from the well-documented harms inherent in abortion and from the substandard care given at some abortion clinics.

ABORTION

- The Arizona Supreme Court has suggested that equal protection issues that involve abortion may be subjected to strict scrutiny, but stopped short of holding that a fundamental "right" to abortion exists under the state constitution.

- Arizona's Women's Health Defense Act, limiting abortion at or after 5 months (i.e., 20 weeks) gestation and predicated on the significant risks of later-term abortions to maternal health (and also concerns for fetal pain) is permanently enjoined.

- In 2002, the Arizona Supreme Court concluded that state taxpayers must fund "medically necessary" abortions for women eligible for public assistance, suggesting but not holding that a broader state constitutional right to abortion may exist than that interpreted in the U.S. Constitution. However, a law passed in 2010 prohibits state funds from being used to pay or provide coverage for abortion, unless it is necessary to avoid "irreversible impairment of a major bodily function" or save the life of the mother.

- One parent must provide written, notarized consent before a physician may perform an abortion on a minor under the age of 18, unless the minor is the victim of incest by someone in her home, there is a medical emergency, or she obtains a court order. Arizona prohibits a third party from interfering with parental rights and assisting a minor in obtaining an abortion without the requisite parental consent.

- Arizona prohibits partial-birth abortion.

- Arizona makes it a felony to perform an abortion knowing that the abortion is sought based on the sex or race of the child or the race of a parent. Further, it is a felony to use force or the threat of force to intentionally injure or intimidate any person for the purpose of coercing a sex-selection or race-based abortion.

- At least 24 hours prior to an abortion, a woman must receive information about the nature of the procedure, the immediate and long-term risks of abortion, the risks of childbirth, alternatives to abortion, and the probable gestational age and anatomical and physiological characteristics of her unborn child. She must also receive information about medical assistance benefits, the father's liability for child support, and the public and private agencies available to assist her. Arizona also requires abortion providers to inform women about alternatives to abortion.

- Arizona requires that an ultrasound be performed at least 24 hours prior to an abortion.

- A woman who is seeking abortion because of fetal anomalies must be informed about perinatal hospice programs.

- A woman considering an abortion must be informed that it is illegal for a person to intimidate or coerce her into having an abortion.

- Arizona law requires that if a woman has not yet taken the second drug in the abortion regimen and consults an abortion clinic questioning her decision to abort or seeking information regarding the health of her fetus or the effectiveness of the abortion drug regimen, abortion clinic staff shall inform her that the use of mifepristone (the first drug in the RU-486 regime) alone to end a pregnancy is not always effective and that she should immediately consult a physician if she would like more information.

- Arizona has comprehensive licensing requirements for abortion clinics, including regulations related to administration, incident reporting, personnel qualifications and records, staffing requirements, patient rights, abortion procedures, patient transfer and discharge, medications and controlled substances, medical records, and environmental and safety standards. Arizona allows unannounced inspections of abortion facilities to ensure compliance with state abortion laws and regulations. Two provisions, one regulating the minimum equipment standards for abortions performed at 20 weeks or more and one requiring medication abortions to comply with FDA protocol, are permanently enjoined.

- Only licensed physicians may perform surgical abortions. Physicians who perform abortions must maintain admitting privileges at a local hospital and must submit verification that they have the requisite admitting privileges. Further, a physician assistant may not prescribe, dispense, or administer prescription medicine to induce an abortion, and the state board of nursing may not decree that the scope of practice for registered nurse practitioners includes performing abortions.

- Arizona has an enforceable abortion reporting law but does not require the reporting of information to the Centers for Disease Control and Prevention (CDC). The measure applies to both surgical and nonsurgical abortions and requires abortion providers to report short-term complications as well as any abortions that result in live birth. In 2018, Arizona amended the law to require abortion providers include specific information about the reason for obtaining the abortion, known medical complications as a result of the abortion, how the patient was admitted to the clinic or hospital, and other important information.

- Arizona requires that Medicaid providers cover family planning services that do not include abortion or abortion counseling.

- Arizona prohibits public funding for training to perform abortions or the use of "monies paid by students as part of tuition or fees to a state university or a community college" for abortions.

- Organizations that receive state funds through Women's Services programs may not use those funds to provide abortions or abortion referrals, and grantees cannot provide the grant money to entities that promote, refer, or perform abortions.

- A state statute permitting a tax credit for voluntary cash contributions by a taxpayer or on a taxpayer's behalf to charitable organizations does not permit donations to qualify for the credits if the beneficiary organizations provide, pay for, promote, provide coverage of, or provide referrals for abortion or financially support any other entity that does so.

- A woman may not obtain an abortion at any university facility under the jurisdiction of the Arizona Board of Regents unless the procedure is necessary to save her life.

- Arizona prohibits insurance companies from offering abortion coverage within state insurance Exchanges established pursuant to the federal healthcare law, except in cases involving rape, incest, or threats to a woman's life or health.

- Arizona further prohibits the use of state funds "directly or indirectly to pay the costs, premiums or charges associated with a health insurance policy, contract or plan that provides coverage, benefits or services related to the performance of any abortion" except in cases of life endangerment or substantial and irreversible impairment of a major bodily function.

- Arizona offers "Choose Life" license plates. The proceeds from the sale of the plates benefit organizations providing abortion alternatives.

LEGAL RECOGNITION AND PROTECTION OF THE UNBORN AND NEWLY BORN

- Arizona law defines the killing of an unborn child at any stage of development as manslaughter.

- It defines a nonfatal assault on an unborn child as a criminal offense.

- Arizona provides enhanced sentencing for domestic violence offenses when the victim is pregnant.

- Arizona allows a wrongful death (civil) action when a viable unborn child is killed through a negligent or criminal act.

- Arizona has created a specific affirmative duty of physicians to provide medical care and treatment to infants born alive at any stage of development.

- Arizona maintains a Dangerous Crimes Against Children Act which allows for the prosecution of a woman for prenatal drug use or abuse that causes harm or injury to her unborn child. Under the law, the woman can be charged with child abuse and/or drug transfer to a minor under 12 years of age. It further requires healthcare professionals to report suspected prenatal drug exposure.

- Arizona prohibits the use of an aborted human fetus or embryo in animal or human research, experimentation on a fetus or embryo intended to be aborted, offering or performing an abortion solely for the purpose of research, and the sale of body parts of deceased infants.

BIOETHICS LAWS

- Arizona prohibits destructive embryo research, human cloning, and the creation, transfer, and transportation of human-animal hybrids.

- It also prohibits taxpayer funding of human cloning and denies special tax credits to entities engaged in destructive embryo research.

- Arizona requires healthcare professionals to notify patients in the second trimester of pregnancy of post-delivery options related to stem cells contained in umbilical cord blood and options for their donation or storage in a family donor banking program.

- It also requires that women providing eggs receive information on the risks of human egg harvesting and prohibits payment for human eggs when the eggs are to be used for research purposes.

- Arizona passed a law that establishes custody of in vitro human embryos in the case of dissolution of marriage.

PATIENT PROTECTION LAWS

- In Arizona, suicide by physician is considered manslaughter.

HEALTHCARE FREEDOM OF CONSCIENCE

PARTICIPATION IN ABORTION AND CONTRACEPTION

- Arizona law protects healthcare providers who conscientiously object to participation in abortions. Under the law, healthcare providers must object in writing, and objections must be based on moral or religious beliefs.

- A pharmacy, hospital, or healthcare professional is not required to participate in or provide an abortion, abortion medication, "emergency contraception," or any medicine or device intended to inhibit or prevent implantation of a fertilized egg.

- Arizona also allows a "religiously-affiliated employer" to offer a health plan that does not cover contraceptives based on the religious beliefs of the employer or a beneficiary. "Religiously-affiliated employer" is defined as either a non-profit that primarily employs and serves individuals who share the non-profit's religious beliefs or as an organization that has incorporating documents that clearly state that religious beliefs are "central to the organization's operating principles."

PARTICIPATION IN RESEARCH HARMFUL TO HUMAN LIFE

- Arizona currently provides no protection for the rights of healthcare providers who conscientiously object to participation in human cloning, destructive embryo research, or other forms of medical research that violate a provider's moral or religious beliefs.

DID YOU KNOW?

- In 2018, Arizona amended its Abortion Reporting Act to include information on the reason for the abortion, the fetal health diagnosis that led to the abortion, and known medical complications resulting from the abortion. The bill also added requirements for the physician to submit information on the number of abortions performed as the result of a medical emergency and the number of women for whom the physician or another qualified person performed an ultrasound.

- Arizona also rejected a bill that would have legalized suicide by physician.

WHAT HAPPENS AFTER *ROE* IS OVERTURNED?

- Abortion will not be legal based on existing law enacted before *Roe*.

RECOMMENDATIONS
for Arizona

WOMEN'S PROTECTION PROJECT PRIORITIES

- Enhanced penalties and enforcement mechanisms for the state's abortion laws
- Components of the Drug-Induced Abortion Information & Reporting Act
- Components of the Parental Involvement Enhancement Act
- Child Protection Act

INFANTS' PROTECTION PROJECT PRIORITIES

- Unborn Wrongful Death Act (for a pre-viable child)

PATIENT PROTECTION ACT PRIORITIES

- Joint Resolution Opposing Suicide by Physician
- Charlie Gard Act (formerly the Life Sustaining Care Act)
- Pain Medicine Education Act

ADDITIONAL PRIORITIES

ABORTION

- State Constitutional Amendment (affirming that there is no state constitutional right to abortion)
- Defunding the Abortion Industry and Advancing Women's Health Act

LEGAL RECOGNITION AND PROTECTION FOR THE UNBORN

- Statutory prohibition on wrongful birth lawsuits
- Pregnant Woman's Protection Act

BIOETHICS

- Assisted Reproductive Technologies Disclosure and Risk Reduction Act

HEALTHCARE FREEDOM OF CONSCIENCE

- Healthcare Freedom of Conscience Act

Arkansas | RANKING: 2

Arkansas has been a leader in implementing the mother-child strategy, enacting laws that protect both mother and child from the harms inherent in abortion. It maintains strong informed consent and parental involvement requirements, comprehensive health and safety requirements for abortion facilities, and effective limits on state taxpayer funding for abortion and abortion providers.

ABORTION

- Arkansas' policy, as explained in Amendment 68, § 2 to the state constitution, is to "protect the life of every unborn child from conception until birth, to the extent permitted by the Federal Constitution."

- Arkansas maintains an enforceable abortion prohibition should the U.S. Constitution be amended or certain U.S. Supreme Court decisions be reversed or modified.

- Arkansas also prohibits abortion at or after 5 months of development (i.e., 20 weeks) on the basis of the pain felt by unborn children.

- Arkansas enacted the Sex Discrimination by Abortion Prohibition Act, which prohibits the practice of sex-selective abortion.

- Arkansas prohibits partial-birth abortion.

- It also prohibits the dismemberment abortion procedure. The law is enjoined and in ongoing litigation.

- In 2017, Arkansas enacted the Born-Alive Infant Protection Act, which provides protections for infants born alive after an abortion attempt.

- Arkansas requires that, 48 hours prior to an abortion, a physician provide a woman with information about the proposed abortion method, the immediate and long-term risks associated with the proposed method, alternatives to abortion, the probable anatomical and physiological characteristics of the unborn child at the time the abortion is to be performed, and the medical risks associated with carrying the unborn child to term. Further, state-prepared materials must be made available to her. These materials include color photographs of the probable anatomical and physiological characteristics of the unborn child at 2-week gestational increments and a list of private and public agencies providing counseling and alternatives to abortion.

- An abortion provider must check for the unborn child's heartbeat prior to abortion and must inform the woman if a heartbeat is detected. Arkansas also requires that women considering abortion receive information about fetal pain.

- Arkansas requires that an abortion provider offer a woman the opportunity to see the ultrasound image if an ultrasound is used in preparation for the abortion.

- A woman must also be informed that a spouse, boyfriend, parent, friend, or other person cannot force her to have an abortion.

- Arkansas' informed consent requirements include a provision requiring that women be given information on the potential ability to reverse the effects of chemical abortions.

- A physician may not perform an abortion on an unemancipated minor under the age of 18 without notarized written consent or in-person consent (with photo identification) from a parent or legal guardian, unless the minor states by affidavit that she is the victim of physical or sexual abuse and her only living parent or guardian is the perpetrator, a medical emergency exists, or the minor obtains a court order. Arkansas requires a detailed consent form prior to a minor's abortion.

- Arkansas prohibits intentionally causing, aiding, abetting, or assisting a child to obtain an abortion without parental consent and requires the collection of forensic samples when an abortion is performed on a minor under the age of 14.

- It prohibits an abortion if an unborn child's heartbeat is detected and the unborn child is at 12 weeks of development or greater. The law is permanently enjoined.

- Arkansas's comprehensive abortion facility regulations apply to "any facility in which the primary function is the willful termination of pregnancy." The regulations prescribe minimum health and safety standards for the facility, staffing, and clinic administration.

- All abortion facilities performing ten or more abortions per month must be licensed by the state Department of Health.

- Only a person licensed to practice medicine in the State of Arkansas may perform an abortion.

- Arkansas has an enforceable abortion reporting law but does not require the reporting of information to the Centers for Disease Control and Prevention (CDC). The measure pertains to both surgical and nonsurgical abortions and requires abortion providers to report short-term complications.

- When an abortion is performed, an abortion provider must report information related to the post-fertilization age of the unborn child.

- Employees and volunteers at "reproductive health facilities" are included in the list of mandatory reporters of suspected sexual abuse of minors.

- Arkansas law requires that, before administering an abortion-inducing drug, a physician must first examine a woman to ensure she does not have an ectopic pregnancy. After administration of the abortion-inducing drug, the physician must schedule a follow-up visit to ensure that the abortion is completed. The physician must also have a contract with a physician who has active admitting privileges and gynecological/surgical privileges at a hospital and who agrees to handle any complications. The contracted physician requirement is enjoined and in ongoing litigation.

- The Arkansas Constitution provides that no public funds will be used to pay for any abortion, except to save the mother's life. However, Arkansas follows the federal standard for Medicaid funding for abortions, permitting the use of federal or state matching Medicaid funds for abortions necessary to preserve the life of the woman or when the pregnancy is the result of rape or incest.

- Arkansas enacted a measure prohibiting the disbursement of federal and state funds to entities that perform abortions or provide abortion referrals.

- It prohibits the use of public funds for abortions, abortion referrals, or the purchase or dispensing of drug-induced abortion in public schools.

- Arkansas prohibits abortion coverage in the state health insurance exchanges (required under the federal healthcare law), except in cases of rape, incest, or when the mother's life is in danger.

- Arkansas offers "Choose Life" license plates, directing the proceeds to organizations providing abortion alternatives.

LEGAL RECOGNITION AND PROTECTION OF THE UNBORN AND NEWLY BORN

- Under Arkansas law, the killing of an unborn child at any stage of gestation is defined as a form of homicide.

- It also criminalizes nonfatal assaults on an unborn child.

- Arkansas permits women to use force to defend their unborn children from criminal violence.

- Arkansas allows a parent or other relative to bring a wrongful death (civil) lawsuit when a viable unborn child is killed through a negligent or criminal act.

- In 2017, Arkansas passed legislation prohibiting wrongful life (civil) lawsuits when there is a claim that a child would not or should not have been born.

- In 2017, Arkansas passed legislation that requires the proper burial or cremation of remains resulting from an abortion. The law is enjoined and in ongoing litigation.

- Under the Child Maltreatment Act, "neglect" includes prenatal drug use that causes the child to be born with an illegal substance in his or her system or a drug-related health problem. Moreover, test results may be used as evidence of neglect in subsequent proceedings.

- Arkansas requires healthcare providers to report the birth of an infant who suffers from fetal alcohol syndrome.

- Arkansas allows a woman who loses a child after 5 months (i.e., 20 weeks) gestation to seek a Certificate of Birth Resulting in Stillbirth which is filed with the state registrar.

BIOETHICS LAWS

- Arkansas prohibits both cloning to produce children and cloning for biomedical research.

- However, it maintains no laws pertaining to destructive embryo research. Moreover, Arkansas' fetal experimentation statute only prohibits research on a born-alive child, allowing, with the permission of the mother, research on a child born dead (e.g., aborted).

- The Newborn Umbilical Cord Initiative Act has established a network to collect and store postnatal tissue and fluid.

- Arkansas excludes an "unborn child" from the definition of "person" in the context of assisted reproductive technologies.

- Arkansas mandates that only physicians may perform artificial insemination procedures.

- Arkansas maintains no regulations related to human egg harvesting.

PATIENT PROTECTION LAWS

- Under Arkansas law, suicide by physician is a felony.

HEALTHCARE FREEDOM OF CONSCIENCE

PARTICIPATION IN ABORTION

- No person may be required to perform or participate in a medical procedure that results in abortion and cannot be subject to civil liability or other recriminatory action for their refusal to participate in abortions.

- In addition, no hospital is required to permit an abortion within its facility and cannot be subject to civil liability or other recriminatory action for its refusal.

- Arkansas provides some protection for the conscience rights of pharmacists and pharmacies.

PARTICIPATION IN RESEARCH HARMFUL TO HUMAN LIFE

- Arkansas currently provides no protection for the rights of healthcare providers who conscientiously object to participation in human cloning, destructive embryo research, or other forms of medical research that violate a provider's moral or religious beliefs.

DID YOU KNOW?

- In 2017, Arkansas enacted the Unborn Child Protection from Dismemberment Abortion Act which prohibits the dismemberment abortion procedure.

WHAT HAPPENS AFTER *ROE* IS OVERTURNED?

- Abortion will not be legal based on existing law enacted before *Roe*.

RECOMMENDATIONS
for Arkansas

WOMEN'S PROTECTION PROJECT PRIORITIES

- Enhanced penalties and enforcement mechanisms for the state's abortion-related laws

INFANTS' PROTECTION PROJECT PRIORITIES

- Unborn Infants Dignity Act
- Prenatal Nondiscrimination Act
- Perinatal Hospice Information Act
- Unborn Wrongful Death Act (for a pre-viable child)

PATIENT PROTECTION ACT PRIORITIES

- Joint Resolution Opposing Suicide by Physician
- Charlie Gard Act (formerly the "Life Sustaining Care Act")
- Pain Medicine Education Act

ADDITIONAL PRIORITIES

ABORTION

- Defunding the Abortion Industry and Advancing Women's Health Act

BIOETHICS

- Prohibition on Public Funding of Human Cloning and Destructive Embryo Research Act

HEALTHCARE FREEDOM OF CONSCIENCE

- Healthcare Freedom of Conscience Act

California | RANKING: 49

In recent years, California has become increasingly hostile to life. Despite performing the highest volume of abortions in the nation, California attempted to force pregnancy resource centers to post and disseminate a notification about state government-funded abortions, but this law was declared unconstitutional by the Supreme Court.

ABORTION

- The California Supreme Court has found that the state constitution provides a broader right to abortion than that interpreted in the U.S. Constitution.

- California has also adopted a Freedom of Choice Act providing a right to abortion even if *Roe v. Wade* is eventually overturned and specifically providing that "[e]very woman has the fundamental right to choose to bear a child or to choose and to obtain an abortion" and "[t]he state may not deny or interfere with a woman's right to choose or obtain an abortion prior to the viability of the fetus, or when the abortion is necessary to protect the life or health of the woman."

- California requires that, prior to an abortion, a woman be informed of the nature of the abortion procedure, possible risks and complications, abortion alternatives, post-procedure medical services, and family planning information.

- California requires a physician have the consent of one parent or a court order prior to performing an abortion on a minor under the age of 18. The law is permanently enjoined.

- California requires abortion facilities to meet rudimentary standards for patient care, equipment, and staffing. In 2013, California exempted abortion facilities from many generally applicable building code standards.

- Non-physicians including nurse practitioners, certified nurse-midwives, or physician assistants may perform surgical abortions or administer drug-induced abortion.

- The California Supreme Court has mandated that taxpayers pay for "medically necessary" abortions for women eligible for state medical assistance. This requirement essentially equates to funding abortion-on-demand in light of the U.S. Supreme Court's broad definition of "health" in the context of abortion.

- Grants made by the Adolescent Family Life Program may not be expended for abortions, abortion referrals, or abortion counseling.

- Family planning grants may not be used for abortions or services ancillary to abortions.

- California occasionally makes direct funding available to pregnancy resource centers.

- California protects "freedom of access" to abortion clinics and has established procedures for investigating "anti-reproductive rights crimes" under its Reproductive Rights Law Enforcement Act.

- California has adopted a measure mandating "comprehensive sex education" which includes a provision that "instruction on pregnancy shall include an objective discussion on all legally available pregnancy outcomes including...abortion."

LEGAL RECOGNITION AND PROTECTION OF THE UNBORN AND NEWLY BORN

- Since 1970, California law has defined the killing of an unborn child after the embryonic stage (7 to 8 weeks of gestation) as a form of homicide.

- The state allows a wrongful death (civil) action only when an unborn child is born alive following a negligent or criminal act and dies thereafter.

- California imposes a specific affirmative duty on physicians to provide medical care and treatment to infants born alive at any stage of development.

- California maintains a "Baby Moses" law under which a mother or legal guardian who is unable to care for a newborn infant may anonymously and safely leave the infant in the care of a responsible person at a hospital, police station, fire station, or other prescribed location.

- California funds drug treatment programs for pregnant women and newborns.

BIOETHICS LAWS

- A California constitutional amendment funds and protects the "right" to engage in destructive embryo research and human cloning.

- California prohibits cloning to produce children, but explicitly allows cloning for biomedical research, making it a "clone-and-kill" state.

- California allows research on "fetal remains."

- California also promotes ethical forms of research, tasking the University of California with developing a plan to establish and administer an Umbilical Cord Blood Collection Program for the purpose of collecting units of umbilical cord blood for use in transplantation. It also conducts an Umbilical Cord Blood Awareness Campaign to disseminate information about cord blood banking options.

- California regulates assisted reproductive technologies including specifically requiring that a patient be provided information on embryo donation.

- It requires that any advertising for egg donors (for fertility treatments) contain a statement that "there may be risks associated with human egg donation." Moreover, no human eggs may be sold for "valuable consideration," which does not include reasonable payment for the removal, processing, disposal, preservation, quality control, and the storage of the eggs.

PATIENT PROTECTION LAWS

- Suicide by physician is now legal in California. This law is in ongoing litigation.

- California enacted a measure requiring physicians to provide end-of-life counseling to patients.

- California has amended its medical school curriculum requirements to include instruction on pain management and end-of-life issues.

HEALTHCARE FREEDOM OF CONSCIENCE

PARTICIPATION IN ABORTION AND CONTRACEPTION

- California currently provides legal protection for individual healthcare providers and private health-care institutions that conscientiously object to participating in abortions. Protection also extends to medical and nursing students. However, this protection does not apply in "medical emergencies."

- It provides some protection for the conscience rights of pharmacists and pharmacies.

- Health insurance plans that provide prescription coverage must provide coverage for contraception. This requirement includes an exemption so narrow that it precludes the ability of most employers and insurers with moral or religious objections from exercising it.

PARTICIPATION IN RESEARCH HARMFUL TO HUMAN LIFE

- California currently provides no protection for the rights of healthcare providers who conscientiously object to participation in human cloning, destructive embryo research, or other forms of medical research that violate a provider's moral or religious beliefs.

DID YOU KNOW?

- In 2018, California passed pro-abortion resolutions urging the President and Congress to "express their support for the fundamental right to abortion and bodily autonomy" and support for abortion giant Planned Parenthood.

- California passed a bill that would require the abortion pill (mifepristone) to be carried at all state universities. It was vetoed by Governor Jerry Brown. AUL submitted written testimony against this bill.

WHAT HAPPENS AFTER *ROE* IS OVERTURNED?

- Abortion will be legal throughout pregnancy due to a state court decision.

RECOMMENDATIONS
for California

WOMEN'S PROTECTION PROJECT PRIORITIES

- Enhanced penalties and enforcement mechanisms for the state's abortion-related laws
- Reflection period for abortion
- Women's Health Protection Act (abortion clinic regulations)
- Drug-Induced Abortion Information and Reporting Act
- Parental Notification for Abortion Act (or parental notice initiative)
- Child Protection Act
- Coercive Abuse Against Mothers Prevention Act

INFANTS' PROTECTION PROJECT PRIORITIES

- Unborn Infants Dignity Act
- Prenatal Nondiscrimination Act
- Unborn Wrongful Death Act

PATIENT PROTECTION ACT PRIORITIES

- Suicide by Physician Ban Act
- Joint Resolution Opposing Suicide by Physician
- Charlie Gard Act (formerly the Life Sustaining Care Act)
- Pain Medicine Education Act

ADDITIONAL PRIORITIES

ABORTION

- State Constitutional Amendment (providing that there is no state constitutional right to abortion)
- Repeal of State FOCA
- Defunding the Abortion Industry and Advancing Women's Health Act
- Federal Abortion-Mandate Opt-Out Act

LEGAL RECOGNITION AND PROTECTION FOR THE UNBORN

- Amend fetal homicide law to protect unborn from conception
- Statutory prohibition on wrongful birth and wrongful life lawsuits
- Pregnant Woman's Protection Act

BIOETHICS

- Constitutional amendment banning state funding for human cloning and destructive embryo research

PATIENT PROTECTION

- Repeal of law legalizing suicide by physician.

HEALTHCARE FREEDOM OF CONSCIENCE

- Healthcare Freedom of Conscience Act

Colorado | RANKING: 30

Colorado lacks the most basic protections for maternal health and the unborn. It does not require informed consent for abortion or that abortion facilities meet minimal health and safety standards. It is also in the minority of states that do not recognize an unborn child as a potential crime victim.

ABORTION

- A physician may not perform an abortion on a minor under the age of 18 until at least 48 hours after written notice has been given to her parents, unless the parents waive the notice requirement, the minor declares she is a victim of abuse or neglect by a party entitled to notice and the abuse has been reported by the physician, there is a medical emergency, or the minor obtains a court order. Substitute notice of a grandparent, aunt, or uncle is permitted if the minor lives with him/her.

- Only licensed physicians using accepted medical procedures may perform abortions.

- Colorado has an enforceable abortion reporting law but does not require the reporting of information to the Centers for Disease Control and Prevention (CDC). The measure applies to both surgical and nonsurgical abortions.

- The Colorado Constitution prohibits public funds from being used to pay for an abortion except when the abortion is necessary to preserve the woman's life. However, a federal court has declared this provision, along with two related statutes, in conflict with federal law. Currently, Colorado follows the federal standard for Medicaid funding for abortions, permitting the use of federal or state matching Medicaid funds for abortions necessary to preserve the life of the woman or when the pregnancy is the result of rape or incest.

- Organizations that provide abortions are prohibited from receiving state family planning funds.

- School-based health clinics cannot provide abortion services.

- The Colorado Attorney General has issued an opinion stating that group health insurance provided for state employees must exclude coverage for abortion.

LEGAL RECOGNITION AND PROTECTION OF THE UNBORN AND NEWLY BORN

- Actions by a third party designed to "intentionally, knowingly, recklessly, or with extreme indifference terminate or attempt to terminate a woman's pregnancy" are felonies. Colorado also imposes enhanced criminal penalties for an assault on a pregnant woman. However, it does not recognize an unborn child as a second (and separate) victim of a crime.

- Colorado has created a civil action for "unlawful termination of a pregnancy." However, this "one-victim" measure fails to recognize an unborn child as a separate person.

- Colorado allows a parent or other relative to bring a wrongful death (civil) lawsuit when a viable unborn child is killed through the negligent or criminal act of another.

- In its definition of "child abuse or neglect," Colorado includes instances where an infant tests positive for a controlled substance at birth. It also funds substance abuse treatment for pregnant women and prohibits the use of drug tests performed as part of prenatal care in criminal prosecutions.

- Women must be informed of the availability of stillbirth certificates and be given the option to request one following a miscarriage or stillbirth.

- Colorado requires that death certificates indicate whether a woman was pregnant at the time of her death.

BIOETHICS LAWS

- Colorado maintains no laws regarding human cloning, destructive embryo research, fetal experimentation, human egg harvesting, or assisted reproductive technologies.

- Voluntary financial contributions to the Adult Stem Cells Cure Fund may be designated on state income tax forms and an account for the proceeds has been created in the state treasury.

- Colorado has enacted legislation preventing genetic information from being used to deny access to healthcare insurance or Medicare supplement insurance coverage.

PATIENT PROTECTION LAWS

- Colorado has passed legislation legalizing suicide by physician for adults.

- Colorado protects healthcare providers from liability for manslaughter when prescribing or administering palliative care prescriptions to terminally ill patients.

- Colorado maintains a Physician Orders for Life-Sustaining Treatment (POLST) Paradigm Program.

HEALTHCARE FREEDOM OF CONSCIENCE

PARTICIPATION IN ABORTION AND CONTRACEPTION

- A hospital staff member or person associated with or employed by a hospital who objects in writing and on religious or moral grounds may not be required to participate in medical procedures that result in abortions.

- A hospital is not required to admit a woman for the purpose of performing an abortion.

- Private institutions, physicians, and their respective agents may, based upon religious or conscientious objections, refuse to provide contraceptives and information about contraceptives based upon religious or conscientious objections. In addition, county and city employees may similarly refuse to provide family planning and birth control services.

PARTICIPATION IN RESEARCH HARMFUL TO HUMAN LIFE

- Colorado currently provides no protection for the rights of healthcare providers who conscientiously object to participation in human cloning, destructive embryo research, or other forms of medical research that violate a provider's moral or religious beliefs.

DID YOU KNOW?

- In 2018, Colorado considered a bill that would have prohibited the dismemberment abortion procedure.

- Colorado also considered a Protect Human Life at Conception bill.

WHAT HAPPENS AFTER *ROE* IS OVERTURNED?

- Abortion will likely be legal throughout pregnancy based on existing law with broad exception enacted before *Roe*.

RECOMMENDATIONS
for Colorado

WOMEN'S PROTECTION PROJECT PRIORITIES

- Enhanced penalties and enforcement mechanisms for the state's abortion-related laws
- Women's Right to Know Act with reflection period
- Coercive Abuse Against Mothers Prevention Act
- Women's Health Protection Act
- Parental Consent for Abortion Act
- Parental Involvement Enhancement Act
- Drug-Induced Abortion Information and Reporting Act
- Child Protection Act

INFANTS' PROTECTION PROJECT PRIORITIES

- Unborn Infants Dignity Act
- Prenatal Nondiscrimination Act
- Perinatal Hospice Information Act
- Born-Alive Infant Protection Act
- Unborn Wrongful Death Act (for a pre-viable child)

PATIENT PROTECTION ACT PRIORITIES

- Suicide by Physician Ban Act
- Joint Resolution Opposing Suicide by Physician
- Charlie Gard Act (formerly the Life Sustaining Care Act)
- Pain Medicine Education Act

ADDITIONAL PRIORITIES

ABORTION

- Defunding the Abortion Industry and Advancing Women's Health Act
- Federal Abortion Mandate Opt-Out Act

LEGAL RECOGNITION AND PROTECTION FOR THE UNBORN

- Crimes Against the Unborn Child Act
- Pregnant Woman's Protection Act

BIOETHICS

- Human Cloning Prohibition Act
- Destructive Embryo Research Act
- Prohibition on Public Funding of Human Cloning and Destructive Embryo Research Act

HEALTHCARE FREEDOM OF CONSCIENCE

- Healthcare Freedom of Conscience Act

Connecticut | RANKING: 42

Connecticut law evinces a profound disrespect for human life, providing for a broad state constitutional "right" to abortion and failing to adequately protect unborn victims of violence. Moreover, it permits cloning for biomedical research and destructive embryo research.

ABORTION

- The Connecticut Supreme Court has determined that the state constitution protects the "right" to an abortion as a fundamental right and to a greater extent than that interpreted in the U.S. Constitution.

- Connecticut maintains a Freedom of Choice Act, mandating a legal right to abortion even if *Roe v. Wade* is eventually overturned. The Act specifically provides that "[t]he decision to terminate a pregnancy prior to the viability of the fetus shall be solely that of the pregnant woman in consultation with her physician."

- Connecticut law requires that all women considering abortion receive counseling on the type of abortion procedure to be used and the discomfort and risks involved in that procedure.

- In addition to counseling on the type of abortion procedure and its inherent risks, minors must also receive information on the alternatives to abortion and public and private agencies that can provide them with assistance. Further, a qualified counselor must discuss the possibility of the minor involving a parent or other adult in her abortion decision, but there is no parental involvement requirement.

- Connecticut mandates that abortion facilities meet rudimentary health and safety standards. The regulations prescribe minimum standards for the building or facility, patient medical testing, and the maintenance of patient records.

- Connecticut limits the performance of abortions to licensed physicians.

- It has an enforceable abortion reporting law but does not require the reporting of information to the Centers for Disease Control and Prevention (CDC). The measure applies to both surgical and nonsurgical abortions and requires abortion providers to report short-term complications.

- Connecticut taxpayers are required by court order to fund "medically necessary" abortions for women eligible for public assistance. This requirement essentially equates to funding abortion-on-demand in light of the U.S. Supreme Court's broad definition of "health" in the context of abortion.

- Connecticut offers "Choose Life" license plates, the proceeds of which benefit pregnancy resource centers and/or other organizations providing abortion alternatives.

LEGAL RECOGNITION AND PROTECTION OF THE UNBORN AND NEWLY BORN

- Connecticut defines an assault on a pregnant woman resulting in "the termination of pregnancy that does not result in live birth" as a crime. The law recognizes an affirmative defense if the defendant did not know that the victim was pregnant at the time of the assault.

- Connecticut allows a parent or other relative to bring a wrongful death (civil) lawsuit when a viable unborn child is killed through the negligent or criminal act of another.

- It funds drug treatment programs for pregnant women and newborns.

BIOETHICS LAWS

- Connecticut prohibits cloning to produce children but allows cloning for biomedical research, making it a "clone and kill" state. It also permits and funds destructive embryo research, while also permitting human cloning.

- Connecticut has appropriated at least $10 million to its Regenerative Medicine Research Fund, funding both embryonic and adult stem-cell research. It does not prohibit fetal experimentation.

- Connecticut requires a physician to provide a woman in the last trimester of pregnancy with information regarding options to bank or donate umbilical cord blood. The Connecticut Umbilical Cord Blood Collection Board has been directed to engage in public education and establish an umbilical cord blood collection program.

- Connecticut regulates assisted reproductive technologies. For example, only persons certified to practice medicine in the state may perform artificial insemination.

- Connecticut prohibits direct or indirect payment for the donation of human eggs for stem-cell research.

PATIENT PROTECTION LAWS

- Assisting a suicide constitutes manslaughter.

- Connecticut has established a Physician Orders for Life-Sustaining Treatment (POLST) Paradigm program.

- Connecticut enacted a "right to try" measure allowing certain terminally ill patients, under specified conditions, to use investigational drugs.

HEALTHCARE FREEDOM OF CONSCIENCE

PARTICIPATION IN ABORTION AND CONTRACEPTION

- Under Connecticut law, no person is required to participate in any phase of an abortion against his or her judgment or religious, moral, or philosophical beliefs.

- Health insurance plans that provide prescription coverage must also provide coverage for contraception. Certain conscience exemptions apply to religious employers or organizations.

PARTICIPATION IN RESEARCH HARMFUL TO HUMAN LIFE

- Connecticut currently provides no protection for the rights of healthcare providers who conscientiously object to participation in human cloning, destructive embryo research, or other forms of medical research that violate a provider's moral or religious beliefs.

DID YOU KNOW?

- In 2018, Connecticut passed legislation that allows pregnant women to state their intent "to accept life support systems if [their] doctor believes that doing so would allow [the] fetus to reach a live birth."

- Connecticut considered legislation that unfairly targeted pregnancy resource centers and would ban their "deceptive advertising," as well as legislation that would legalize suicide by physician. AUL gave oral and written testimony against both pieces of legislation, and both have failed.

WHAT HAPPENS AFTER *ROE* IS OVERTURNED?

- Abortion will be legal throughout pregnancy.

RECOMMENDATIONS
for Connecticut

WOMEN'S PROTECTION PROJECT PRIORITIES

- Enhanced penalties and enforcement mechanisms for the state's abortion-related laws
- Women's Right to Know Act with reflection period
- Coercive Abuse Against Mothers Prevention Act
- Women's Health Protection Act (abortion clinic regulations)
- Drug-Induced Abortion Information and Reporting Act
- Parental Notification for Abortion Act
- Child Protection Act

INFANTS' PROTECTION PROJECT PRIORITIES

- Unborn Infants Dignity Act
- Prenatal Nondiscrimination Act
- Perinatal Hospice Information Act
- Born-Alive Infant Protection Act
- Unborn Wrongful Death Act (for a pre-viable child)

PATIENT PROTECTION ACT PRIORITIES

- Joint Resolution Opposing Suicide by Physician
- Charlie Gard Act (formerly the Life Sustaining Care Act)
- Pain Medicine Education Act

ADDITIONAL PRIORITIES

ABORTION

- State Constitutional Amendment (providing that there is no state constitutional right to abortion)
- Repeal of State FOCA
- Defunding the Abortion Industry and Advancing Women's Health Act
- Federal Abortion-Mandate Opt-Out Act

LEGAL RECOGNITION AND PROTECTION FOR THE UNBORN

- Crimes Against the Unborn Child Act
- Pregnant Woman's Protection Act

BIOETHICS

- Repeal of existing laws permitting human cloning, destructive embryo research, and the funding of these practices

HEALTHCARE FREEDOM OF CONSCIENCE

- Healthcare Freedom of Conscience Act

Delaware | RANKING: 32

Delaware maintains only minimal protections for a woman considering an abortion. "Loopholes" in its parental notice law eviscerate the protection such a law normally provides, and Delaware does not require that abortion facilities meet minimal health and safety standards. Further, it does not proscribe or limit human cloning, destructive embryo research, fetal experimentation, or human egg harvesting.

ABORTION

- In 2017, Delaware passed legislation codifying *Roe v. Wade* under state law. Delaware now has no limitation on abortion prior to viability. Abortion after viability is prohibited except in cases where it is necessary to protect the woman's life or health or if there is a fetal anomaly "for which there is not a reasonable likelihood of the fetus's sustained survival outside the uterus without extraordinary medical measures."

- Delaware's informed consent law requires that a woman be informed of the probable stage of her unborn child's development, the abortion procedure to be used and its inherent risks, alternative abortion procedures, the probable effects of an abortion on future childbearing, and alternatives to abortion. The informed consent law was repealed in its entirety in 2017.

- Delaware prohibits some coerced abortions, defining "coercion" as "restraining or dominating the choice of a minor female by force, threat of force, or deprivation of food and shelter." It emancipates a minor for social assistance purposes if her parents or guardians deny financial support because of her refusal to undergo an abortion.

- Delaware prohibits a physician from performing an abortion on an unemancipated minor under the age of 16 until 24 hours after notice has been given to one parent; however, the Delaware Attorney General has issued a "Statement of Policy" providing that state officials will not prosecute abortion providers who fail to comply with this requirement. The law also permits substitute notice of a grandparent or mental health professional.

- Only licensed physicians may perform abortions.

- Delaware has an enforceable abortion reporting law but does not require the reporting of information to the Centers for Disease Control and Prevention (CDC). The measure applies to both surgical and nonsurgical abortions.

- Delaware follows the federal standard for Medicaid funding for abortions, permitting the use of federal or state matching Medicaid funds for abortions necessary to preserve the life of the woman or when the pregnancy is the result of rape or incest.

- Delaware offers "Choose Life" license plates.

LEGAL RECOGNITION AND PROTECTION OF THE UNBORN AND NEWLY BORN

- Delaware law does not provide for the prosecution of third parties who kill or injure an unborn child.

- Delaware allows a parent or other relative to bring a wrongful death (civil) lawsuit when a viable unborn child is killed through the negligent or criminal act of another.

- It has a specific affirmative duty of physicians to provide medical care to infants born alive after an abortion or attempted abortion that would be provided to an infant born alive as a result of natural birth.

BIOETHICS LAWS

- Delaware does not proscribe or limit human cloning, destructive embryo research, fetal experimentation, or human egg harvesting. It also does not promote ethical forms of research or regulate assisted reproductive technologies.

PATIENT PROTECTION LAWS

- Suicide by physician is a felony in Delaware.

- Delaware maintains a Physician Orders for Life-Sustaining Treatment (POLST) Paradigm Program.

HEALTHCARE FREEDOM OF CONSCIENCE

PARTICIPATION IN ABORTION AND CONTRACEPTION

- Delaware law provides that no person can be required to participate in any medical procedure that results in an abortion.

- Hospitals are not required to permit abortions within their facilities.

- If health insurance plans provide coverage for prescription drugs, coverage must also be provided for contraception. A conscience exemption exists for religious employers.

PARTICIPATION IN RESEARCH HARMFUL TO HUMAN LIFE

- Delaware currently provides no protection for the rights of healthcare providers who conscientiously object to participation in human cloning, destructive embryo research, or other forms of medical research that violate a provider's moral or religious beliefs.

DID YOU KNOW?

- In 2018, Delaware considered legislation that would have required the woman be offered ultrasound imaging and auscultation of fetal heart tone before the termination of the pregnancy.

- Delaware also considered the Pain-Capable Unborn Child Protection Act. AUL submitted written testimony in favor of passage.

WHAT HAPPENS AFTER *ROE* IS OVERTURNED?

- Abortion will be legal throughout pregnancy.

RECOMMENDATIONS
for Delaware

WOMEN'S PROTECTION PROJECT PRIORITIES

- Enhanced penalties and enforcement mechanisms for the state's abortion-related laws
- Women's Right to Know Act with reflection period
- Coercive Abuse Against Mothers Prevention Act
- Women's Health Protection Act (abortion clinic regulations)
- Drug-Induced Abortion Information and Reporting Act
- Parental Consent for Abortion Act
- Parental Involvement Enhancement Act
- Child Protection Act

INFANTS' PROTECTION PROJECT PRIORITIES

- Unborn Infants Dignity Act
- Prenatal Nondiscrimination Act
- Perinatal Hospice Information Act
- Unborn Wrongful Death Act (for a pre-viable child)

PATIENT PROTECTION ACT PRIORITIES

- Joint Resolution Opposing Suicide by Physician
- Charlie Gard Act (formerly the Life Sustaining Care Act)
- Pain Medicine Education Act

ADDITIONAL PRIORITIES

ABORTION

- Defunding the Abortion Industry and Advancing Women's Health Act
- Federal Abortion-Mandate Opt-Out Act

LEGAL RECOGNITION AND PROTECTION FOR THE UNBORN

- Crimes Against the Unborn Child Act
- Protection for unborn children from nonfatal assaults
- Pregnant Woman's Protection Act

BIOETHICS

- Human Cloning Prohibition Act
- Destructive Embryo Research Act
- Prohibition on Public Funding of Human Cloning and Destructive Embryo Research Act

HEALTHCARE FREEDOM OF CONSCIENCE

- Healthcare Freedom of Conscience Act

District of Columbia | NOT RANKED

The District of Columbia provides virtually no protection for human life, failing to protect women from the harms inherent in abortion, to recognize and protect unborn victims of violence, or to prohibit suicide by physician. It also fails to protect the fundamental freedom of conscience of healthcare providers.

ABORTION

- Taxpayer funds may not be used for abortions unless the abortion is necessary to preserve the woman's life or the pregnancy was the result of rape or incest.

- No abortion may be performed after viability unless it is necessary to preserve the woman's life or health.

- In the District of Columbia, abortions may only be performed under the direction of a licensed medical practitioner.

- There is no parental involvement requirement.

LEGAL RECOGNITION AND PROTECTION OF THE UNBORN AND NEWLY BORN

- The laws of the District of Columbia do not recognize an unborn child as a potential crime victim.

- The District of Columbia allows a parent or other relative to bring a wrongful death (civil) lawsuit when a viable unborn child is killed through another's negligent or criminal act.

BIOETHICS LAWS

- The District of Columbia maintains no laws related to human cloning, destructive embryo research, fetal experimentation, human egg harvesting, or assisted reproductive technologies.

PATIENT PROTECTION LAWS

- The District of Columbia enacted a measure that creates a "Medical Orders for Scope of Treatment Form" (MOST Form).

- Suicide by physician is now legal for patients who have received a terminal diagnosis of six months or less.

HEALTHCARE FREEDOM OF CONSCIENCE

PARTICIPATION IN ABORTION

- The District of Columbia currently provides no protection for the rights of healthcare providers who conscientiously object to participation in abortion.

PARTICIPATION IN RESEARCH HARMFUL TO HUMAN LIFE

- The District of Columbia currently provides no protection for the rights of healthcare providers who conscientiously object to participation in human cloning, destructive embryo research, or other forms of medical research that violate a provider's moral or religious beliefs.

DID YOU KNOW?

- In 2017, Suicide by physician became legal in the District of Columbia after Congress failed to intervene. Since this measure has been in effect only two doctors have registered to participate, only one hospital publicly allows its doctors to participate, and no patients have used it.

- The Council of the District of Columbia introduced the Abortion Provider Non-Discrimination Amendment Act of 2017, which would add abortion providers as a protected class under the D.C. Human Rights Act. AUL provided written and oral testimony against the proposed Act, explaining that it would violate the First Amendment and conscience rights of health care providers.

WHAT HAPPENS AFTER *ROE* IS OVERTURNED?

- Abortion will be legal throughout pregnancy.

Florida | RANKING: 26

Despite a Florida Supreme Court decision enunciating a broader state constitutional "right" to abortion than that interpreted in the U.S. Constitution, Florida continues to make strides in protecting women and unborn children from the harms inherent in abortion.

ABORTION

- The Florida Supreme Court has determined that the state constitution provides a broader right to abortion than that interpreted in the U.S. Constitution. Under the auspices of this decision, Florida courts have struck down prior versions of the state's informed consent and parental involvement laws.

- Florida prohibits abortions after viability.

- At least 24 hours prior to abortion, Florida requires that a woman receive in-person counseling regarding the nature and medical risks of abortion, the risks of continued pregnancy, and the gestational age of the unborn child. The law is enjoined and in ongoing litigation.

- It also requires that the woman receive printed materials discussing pregnancy services and abortion alternatives, providing a description of the unborn child, and discussing available medical benefits. The law is permanently enjoined.

- Florida requires that an ultrasound be performed and that the ultrasound be reviewed with a woman before she gives her consent for the abortion.

- Florida requires that notice be given in person, by telephone, or by mail to one parent at least 48 hours prior to performing an abortion on a minor aged 17 years old or younger, unless there is a medical emergency or the minor obtains a court order. Parents must be notified about an emergency abortion within 24 hours of the procedure.

- Florida law mandates health and safety standards for abortion facilities, including annual inspections of abortion facilities, as well as prompt investigations of credible allegations that abortions are being performed at unlicensed clinics. Under the law, abortion providers are required to have hospital admitting privileges and abortion clinics are required to have written transfer agreements (to facilitate the transfer of a patient with a medical emergency and/or abortion complication) with a local hospital. Further, the law also prohibits the sale, donation or transfer of the bodily remains of an aborted infant. Portions of the law were challenged by Planned Parenthood, and the funding restriction and inspection requirements have been preliminarily enjoined.

- Only physicians licensed by the State of Florida in medicine or osteopathy or those physicians practicing medicine or osteopathy and employed by the United States may perform abortions.

- Florida has an enforceable abortion reporting law but does not require the reporting of information to the Centers for Disease Control and Prevention (CDC). The measure requires abortion providers to report short-term complications only for post-first trimester abortions.

- Florida follows the federal standard for Medicaid funding for abortions, permitting the use of federal or state matching Medicaid funds for abortions necessary to preserve the life of the woman or when the pregnancy is the result of rape or incest.

- Florida prohibits insurance plans that cover abortions (except in cases of life endangerment, rape, or incest) from receiving federal or state subsidies through a health insurance Exchange established pursuant to the federal healthcare law.

- Florida provides direct funding to pregnancy resource centers including faith-based centers.

- In 2018, Florida passed a bill allowing the state Department of Health to contract with not-for-profit pregnancy support organizations that provide various pro-life services including pregnancy testing, education, and counseling and a 24-hour hotline so clients can contact a nearby pregnancy center, as well as wellness-related care such as high blood pressure and diabetes screening.

- Florida also offers "Choose Life" license plates, the proceeds of which benefit pregnancy resource centers and/or other organizations providing abortion alternatives.

LEGAL RECOGNITION AND PROTECTION OF THE UNBORN AND NEWLY BORN

- Florida criminalizes the killing of an unborn child at any stage of gestation.

- Any crime that results in the death of an unborn child is subject to the same penalties as a crime that causes the death of another.

- Florida allows a wrongful death (civil) action only when an unborn child is born alive following a negligent or criminal act and dies thereafter.

- An infant born alive during or immediately after an attempted abortion is entitled to the same rights, powers, and privileges as any other child born alive in the course of natural birth. Healthcare providers must take reasonable and medically appropriate measures to preserve the life and health of born-alive infants.

- Florida has enacted a "Baby Moses" law under which a mother or legal guardian who is unable to care for a newborn infant may anonymously and safely leave the infant in the care of a responsible person at a hospital, police station, fire station, or other prescribed location.

- It defines substance abuse during pregnancy as "child abuse" under civil child-welfare statutes and funds drug treatment programs for pregnant women and newborns.

BIOETHICS LAWS

- Florida does not prohibit human cloning or destructive embryo research, and its prohibition on fetal experimentation applies only to a live child (and not to an aborted child).

- Florida maintains a Public Cord Blood Tissue Bank to collect and store umbilical cord blood. Women admitted to a hospital or birthing facility may be offered the opportunity to donate umbilical cord blood to the Bank (which is a public resource).

- Florida regulates assisted reproductive technologies and includes "embryo adoption" in a statutory list of "fertility techniques."

- Only "reasonable compensation" directly related to the donation of human eggs is permitted.

PATIENT PROTECTION LAWS

- Suicide by physician is considered manslaughter.

HEALTHCARE FREEDOM OF CONSCIENCE

PARTICIPATION IN ABORTION AND CONTRACEPTION

- Under Florida law, a hospital staff member, person associated with or employed by a hospital, or physician's employee who objects on religious or moral grounds is not required to participate in any medical procedure that results in an abortion.

- Certain individuals including physicians may refuse to furnish any contraceptive or family planning service, supplies, or information because of religious objections.

- Hospitals are not required to perform abortions.

PARTICIPATION IN RESEARCH HARMFUL TO HUMAN LIFE

- Florida does not expressly protect the rights of conscience of all healthcare providers who conscientiously object to participation in procedures other than abortion, such as destructive embryo research and human cloning.

DID YOU KNOW?

- Florida's informed consent law is enjoined and in ongoing litigation.

- In 2018, Florida considered a bill that would prohibit the dismemberment abortion procedure.

WHAT HAPPENS AFTER *ROE* IS OVERTURNED?

- Abortion will be legal throughout pregnancy due to a state court decision.

RECOMMENDATIONS
for Florida

WOMEN'S PROTECTION PROJECT PRIORITIES

- Enhanced penalties and enforcement mechanisms for the state's abortion-related laws
- Drug-Induced Abortion Information and Reporting Act
- Parental Consent for Abortion Act
- Parental Involvement Enhancement Act
- Child Protection Act

INFANTS' PROTECTION PROJECT PRIORITIES

- Unborn Infants Dignity Act
- Prenatal Nondiscrimination Act
- Perinatal Hospice Information Act
- Born-Alive Infant Protection Act
- Unborn Wrongful Death Act

PATIENT PROTECTION ACT PRIORITIES

- Joint Resolution Opposing Suicide by Physician
- Charlie Gard Act (formerly the Life Sustaining Care Act)
- Pain Medicine Education Act

ADDITIONAL PRIORITIES

ABORTION

- State Constitutional Amendment (providing that there is no state constitutional right to abortion)
- Defunding the Abortion Industry and Advancing Women's Health Act

LEGAL RECOGNITION AND PROTECTION FOR THE UNBORN

- Crimes Against the Unborn Child Act (protecting a child from conception)
- Pregnant Woman's Protection Act

BIOETHICS

- Human Cloning Prohibition Act
- Destructive Embryo Research Act
- Prohibition on Public Funding of Human Cloning and Destructive Embryo Research Act

HEALTHCARE FREEDOM OF CONSCIENCE

- Healthcare Freedom of Conscience Act

Georgia | RANKING: 8

Georgia provides significant legal protections for women and unborn children including an informed consent law, a parental involvement requirement for minors considering abortions, and an ultrasound mandate.

ABORTION

- Georgia prohibits abortion at or after 5 months (i.e., 20 weeks) on the basis of the pain felt by unborn children. Further, if an abortion is performed at or after 5 months of pregnancy, the abortion provider must report the medical diagnosis that necessitated the procedure.

- Georgia requires that, 24 hours prior to an abortion, a woman receive information on the medical risks of abortion and pregnancy and the gestational age of the unborn child. A woman must also receive information on medical assistance benefits, child support, and the right to review state-prepared material on a state-sponsored website.

- In addition, a woman must be orally informed that information on fetal pain is available on the state-sponsored website.

- A woman must also be offered the opportunity to view any ultrasound performed as part of the preparation for the abortion. State-developed materials must include information on organizations that provide ultrasounds.

- A physician may not perform an abortion on an unemancipated minor under the age of 18 until at least 24 hours after notice has been given in person or over the telephone to one parent, unless notice is waived in person by the parent who also presents photo identification, there is a medical emergency, or the minor obtains a court order.

- Georgia requires the juvenile court clerk to report judicial bypass statistics.

- Georgia prohibits partial-birth abortions performed after viability.

- Georgia imposes cursory administrative requirements on abortion facilities. Further, second-and third-trimester abortions must be performed in hospitals or ambulatory surgical centers.

- Only physicians licensed to practice medicine and surgery may perform abortions.

- Georgia has an enforceable abortion reporting law but does not require the reporting of information to the Centers for Disease Control and Prevention (CDC). The measure applies to both surgical and nonsurgical abortions.

- Georgia includes "reproductive healthcare facilities" in the definition of mandatory reporters for suspected child abuse.

- Georgia includes mifepristone (i.e., RU-486) in its definition of "dangerous drugs" which may be dispensed only upon prescription by a "registered practitioner." However, "practitioner" is defined broadly to include physicians, advance practice nurses, physician assistants, and even veterinarians.

- Georgia follows the federal standard for Medicaid funding for abortions, permitting the use of federal or state matching Medicaid funds for abortions necessary to preserve the life of the woman or when the pregnancy is the result of rape or incest.

- No facility operated on public school property or operated by a public school district and no employee of any such facility acting within the scope of such person's employment may provide abortions, abortion referrals, or drug-induced abortion.

- Georgia prohibits abortion coverage in the state's health insurance Exchange (established in each state under the federal healthcare law). It also prohibits abortion coverage for state employees.

- Georgia offers "Choose Life" license plates, the proceeds of which benefit pregnancy resource centers and/or other organizations providing abortion alternatives.

LEGAL RECOGNITION AND PROTECTION OF THE UNBORN AND NEWLY BORN

- Under Georgia criminal law, the killing of an unborn child at any stage of gestation is defined as a form of homicide.

- Georgia also maintains the crime of "feticide-by-vehicle," making an unborn child at any stage of development a potential victim under the state's homicide-by-vehicle law.

- Georgia defines a nonfatal assault on an unborn child as a criminal offense.

- Georgia allows a parent or other relative to bring a wrongful death (civil) lawsuit when an unborn child is killed (after "quickening") through the negligent or criminal act of another.

- It has created a specific affirmative duty of physicians to provide medical care and treatment to infants born alive at any stage of development.

BIOETHICS LAWS

- Georgia maintains no laws regulating human cloning, destructive embryo research, fetal experimentation, human egg harvesting, or assisted reproductive technologies.

- Georgia maintains the Newborn Umbilical Cord Blood Bank for postnatal tissue and fluid, making them available for medical research and treatment. All physicians and hospitals must inform pregnant patients of the full range of options for donation of postnatal tissue and fluids.

- Georgia law provides for embryo adoption.

PATIENT PROTECTION LAWS

- Under Georgia law, assisting in another person's suicide is a felony.

- Georgia maintains a Physician Orders for Life-Sustaining Treatment (POLST) Paradigm Program.

HEALTHCARE FREEDOM OF CONSCIENCE

PARTICIPATION IN ABORTION AND CONTRACEPTION

- A person who objects in writing to participating in abortions and whose objections are based on moral or religious grounds may not be required to participate in any medical procedure that results in an abortion.

- A hospital, medical facility, or physician is not required to admit a woman for the purpose of performing an abortion.

- Georgia provides some protection for the conscience rights of pharmacists and pharmacies.

- Health insurance plans that provide prescription coverage must also provide coverage for contraception. There is no conscience exception for religious employers.

PARTICIPATION IN RESEARCH HARMFUL TO HUMAN LIFE

- Georgia currently provides no protection for the rights of healthcare providers who conscientiously object to participation in human cloning, destructive embryo research, or other forms of medical research that violate a provider's moral or religious beliefs.

DID YOU KNOW?

- In 2018, Georgia considered a bill that would create a private right of action for the mother against the abortion provider.

WHAT HAPPENS AFTER *ROE* IS OVERTURNED?

- Abortion will be legal up to 20 weeks of pregnancy.

RECOMMENDATIONS
for Georgia

WOMEN'S PROTECTION PROJECT PRIORITIES

- Enhanced penalties and enforcement mechanisms for the state's abortion-related laws
- Coercive Abuse Against Mothers Prevention Act
- Women's Health Protection Act (abortion clinic regulations)
- Drug-Induced Abortion Information and Reporting Act
- Parental Consent for Abortion Act
- Components of the Parental Involvement Enhancement Act
- Components of the Child Protection Act related to evidence retention and remedies for third-party interference with parental rights

INFANTS' PROTECTION PROJECT PRIORITIES

- Unborn Infants Dignity Act
- Prenatal Nondiscrimination Act
- Perinatal Hospice Information Act
- Unborn Wrongful Death Act (providing protection from conception)

PATIENT PROTECTION ACT PRIORITIES

- Joint Resolution Opposing Suicide by Physician
- Charlie Gard Act (formerly the Life Sustaining Care Act)
- Pain Medicine Education Act

ADDITIONAL PRIORITIES

ABORTION

- Defunding the Abortion Industry and Advancing Women's Health Act
- Legal Recognition and Protection for the Unborn
- Pregnant Woman's Protection Act

BIOETHICS

- Human Cloning Prohibition Act
- Destructive Embryo Research Act
- Prohibition on Public Funding of Human Cloning and Destructive Embryo Research Act

HEALTHCARE FREEDOM OF CONSCIENCE

- Healthcare Freedom of Conscience Act

Hawaii | RANKING: 46

Hawaii lacks the most basic protections for women and unborn children. It fails to require informed consent for abortion, to mandate parental involvement in a minor's abortion decision, or to ensure that abortion facilities meet minimum health and safety standards. It also fails to protect and recognize unborn victims of violence or to proscribe or limit destructive biotechnologies such as embryo research or human cloning.

ABORTION

- Hawaii has adopted a Freedom of Choice Act. The Act provides a "right" to abortion even if *Roe v. Wade* is eventually overturned, specifically providing that "[t]he State shall not deny or interfere with a female's right to choose or obtain an abortion of a nonviable fetus or an abortion that is necessary to protect the life or health of the female."

- Hawaii has no informed consent or parental involvement law.

- Hawaii maintains no enforceable abortion facility regulations; however, only licensed physicians or surgeons may perform abortions.

- It has an enforceable abortion reporting law but does not require the reporting of information to the Centers for Disease Control and Prevention (CDC).

- Hawaii's taxpayers are required by statute to pay for "medically necessary" abortions for women receiving state medical assistance. This requirement essentially equates to funding abortion-on-demand in light of the U.S. Supreme Court's broad definition of "health" in the context of abortion.

- Hawaii law forces pregnancy centers to inform clients and patients that there are public programs that will cover contraception and "pregnancy-related services."

- Hawaii offers "Choose Life" license plates, the proceeds of which benefit pregnancy resource centers and/or other organizations providing abortion alternatives.

LEGAL RECOGNITION AND PROTECTION OF THE UNBORN AND NEWLY BORN

- Hawaii's criminal law does not recognize or protect unborn children.

- Hawaii allows a wrongful death (civil) action when a viable unborn child is killed through a negligent or criminal act.

- Hawaii does not require that appropriate medical care be given to an infant who survives an attempted abortion.

- Hawaii has a "Baby Moses" law, which permits a person to leave an unharmed infant no more than 72-hours old at a hospital, fire station, or police station and be immune from prosecution for child abandonment. The professional receiving the child must inquire into the child's medical history and provide information on social services to the person relinquishing the infant.

BIOETHICS LAWS

- Hawaii does not prohibit or regulate human cloning, destructive embryo research, or fetal experimentation.

- It supports ethical research and treatments in a unique way by providing for a leave of absence for stem cell donors.

- Hawaii does not maintain any meaningful regulation of assisted reproductive technologies or human egg harvesting.

PATIENT PROTECTION LAWS

- In Hawaii, a person who intentionally causes another person to commit suicide is guilty of manslaughter.

- Hawaii also has a Pain Patients' Bill of Rights which directs the Hawaii State Board of Nursing to develop and implement a pain and palliative care policy.

- In 2018, Hawaii passed legislation legalizing suicide by physician.

HEALTHCARE FREEDOM OF CONSCIENCE

PARTICIPATION IN ABORTION AND CONTRACEPTION

- Under Hawaii law, no person or hospital is required to participate in abortions.

- Health insurance plans that provide prescription coverage must also provide coverage for contraception. A conscience exemption exists for religious employers.

PARTICIPATION IN RESEARCH HARMFUL TO HUMAN LIFE

- Hawaii currently provides no protection for the rights of healthcare providers who conscientiously object to participation in human cloning, destructive embryo research, or other forms of medical research that violate a provider's moral or religious beliefs.

DID YOU KNOW?

- In 2018, Hawaii's legislature passed legislation legalizing suicide by physician. They considered eight different versions of the bill.

- Hawaii also considered the Born Alive Infant Protection Act.

WHAT HAPPENS AFTER *ROE* IS OVERTURNED?

- Abortion will be legal throughout pregnancy based on existing law with broad exceptions after viability exacted before *Roe*.

RECOMMENDATIONS
for Hawaii

WOMEN'S PROTECTION PROJECT PRIORITIES

- Enhanced penalties and enforcement mechanisms for the state's abortion-related laws
- Women's Right to Know Act with reflection period
- Coercive Abuse Against Mothers Prevention Act
- Women's Health Protection Act (abortion clinic regulations)
- Drug-Induced Abortion Information and Reporting Act
- Parental Notification for Abortion Act
- Child Protection Act

INFANTS' PROTECTION PROJECT PRIORITIES

- Unborn Infants Dignity Act
- Prenatal Nondiscrimination Act
- Perinatal Hospice Information Act
- Born-Alive Infant Protection Act
- Unborn Wrongful Death Act (for a pre-viable child)

PATIENT PROTECTION ACT PRIORITIES

- Suicide by Physician Ban Act
- Joint Resolution Opposing Suicide by Physician
- Charlie Gard Act (formerly the Life Sustaining Care Act)
- Pain Medicine Education Act

ADDITIONAL PRIORITIES

ABORTION

- Repeal State FOCA
- Defunding the Abortion Industry and Advancing Women's Health Act
- Federal Abortion-Mandate Opt-Out Act

LEGAL RECOGNITION AND PROTECTION FOR THE UNBORN

- Crimes Against the Unborn Child Act
- Pregnant Woman's Protection Act

BIOETHICS

- Human Cloning Prohibition Act
- Destructive Embryo Research Act
- Prohibition on Public Funding of Human Cloning and Destructive Embryo Research Act

HEALTHCARE FREEDOM OF CONSCIENCE

- Healthcare Freedom of Conscience Act

Idaho | RANKING: 21

Idaho has made significant strides in protecting women and the unborn from abortion and maintains comprehensive legal protection for the conscience rights of healthcare providers.

ABORTION

- Idaho has adopted a legislative declaration recognizing "the fundamental importance" of Idaho's interest in preserving the lives of unborn children and declaring that it is the "public policy of this state that all state statutes, rules, and constitutional provisions shall be interpreted to prefer, by all legal means, live childbirth over abortion."

- A 1996 decision by the Idaho Supreme Court has been interpreted as creating a state constitutional right to abortion that is broader than that interpreted in the U.S. Constitution.

- A law prohibiting abortions at or after 5 months (i.e., 20 weeks) on the basis of the pain experienced by unborn children is permanently enjoined.

- Under Idaho law, a physician may not perform an abortion until 24 hours after he or she provides a woman with an "accurate and substantially complete" explanation of the abortion procedure to be used; the inherent risks and possible complications of the procedure including possible effects on future childbearing; and alternatives to abortion and the risks of those alternatives. State-prepared material on fetal development, the availability of assistance from public and private agencies, and a description of commonly used abortion procedures and their specific risks must also be made available to a woman.

- Idaho requires that, at least 24 hours prior to an abortion, a woman be informed about the option to view an ultrasound image and to hear the heart tone of her unborn child. State-prepared materials also includes a list, arranged geographically, of facilities and clinics that perform ultrasounds free of charge as well as the hours of operation and contact information for each listed facility.

- An abortion provider must offer a woman seeking an abortion the opportunity to view any ultrasound that is conducted in preparation for the procedure. Additionally, a woman has the right to ask for an ultrasound, even if the abortion provider does not routinely conduct one.

- Idaho passed legislation requiring abortion-minded women to be given information regarding the possibility of medical intervention to stop or reverse chemical abortion and encouraging her to consult a health care provider prior to taking the abortifacient.

- Idaho prohibits anyone from coercing a woman into having an abortion and allows a victim of coercive abuse to bring a civil lawsuit against her abuser.

- Idaho requires written consent from one parent, a guardian, or a conservator before an abortion is performed on an unemancipated minor under the age of 18, unless there is a medical emergency, the pregnancy is the result of rape or incest, or a judicial order is obtained.

- Only licensed physicians may perform abortions.

- Idaho has an enforceable abortion reporting law but does not require the reporting of information to the Centers for Disease Control and Prevention (CDC). The measure applies to both surgical and nonsurgical abortions. The law is in ongoing litigation.

- Idaho passed a version of AUL's model abortion reporting act. The law is in ongoing litigation.

- Idaho requires a physician to examine a woman before administering drug-induced abortion. It also provides that no drug may be prescribed through "telehealth" services for the purpose of causing an abortion.

- Idaho follows the federal standard for Medicaid funding for abortions, permitting the use of federal or state matching Medicaid funds for abortions necessary to preserve the life of the woman or when the pregnancy is the result of rape or incest.

- Idaho also provides that no funds available to the state Department of Health and Welfare, by appropriations or otherwise, may be used to pay for abortions, except when necessary to save the life of the mother or when the pregnancy is the result of rape or incest.

- Idaho prohibits insurance companies from offering abortion coverage within state insurance Exchanges established pursuant to the federal healthcare law, except in cases of life endangerment, rape, or incest.

- Idaho prohibits private insurance companies from covering abortion, except in cases of life endangerment.

LEGAL RECOGNITION AND PROTECTION OF THE UNBORN AND NEWLY BORN

- Idaho defines the killing of an unborn child at any stage of gestation as homicide.

- Idaho defines a nonfatal assault on an unborn child as a criminal offense.

- Idaho allows a wrongful death (civil) action when a viable unborn child is killed through negligent or criminal act.

- Idaho's Unborn Infants Dignity Act requires that in every instance of fetal death involving a miscarriage or stillbirth, the mother or her authorized representative is informed of the right to direct the final disposition of the unborn infant's bodily remains. The law requires consent for experimentation or research on the bodily remains of the miscarried or stillborn infant.

- The Unborn Infants Dignity Act also prohibits selling, transferring, distributing, donating, accepting, using, or attempting to use the body or bodily remains of an aborted infant. The law further prohibits experimenting or conducting research on the bodily remains of an aborted infant.

BIOETHICS LAWS

- Idaho has not enacted laws regulating human cloning, destructive embryo research, fetal experimentation, or human egg harvesting, nor does it promote ethical alternatives to such destructive research.

- Idaho mandates that only physicians may perform artificial insemination and regulates semen donation.

PATIENT PROTECTION LAWS

- In Idaho, suicide by physician is a felony.

- Idaho has implemented a Physicians Order for Life Sustaining Treatment (POLST) Paradigm Program.

- Idaho has enacted a "right to try" law allowing terminally ill patients to use investigational drugs and biological products.

HEALTHCARE FREEDOM OF CONSCIENCE

PARTICIPATION IN ABORTION

- A physician is not required to perform or assist in abortions. Idaho protects "health care professionals" (principally, licensed medical providers including pharmacists) who decline to participate in abortion or the distribution and administration of drug-induced abortion.

- Nurses, medical technicians, hospital employees, and employees of physicians who object on religious, moral, or personal grounds are not required to participate in abortions. Objections must be in writing.

- A hospital, upon an objection of its governing board, is not required to admit a woman or permit the use of its facilities for the purposes of performing an abortion.

PARTICIPATION IN RESEARCH HARMFUL TO HUMAN LIFE

- Idaho protects "health care professionals" (principally, licensed medical providers including pharmacists) who decline to participate in human cloning, embryo research, and destructive stem-cell technologies.

DID YOU KNOW?

- In 2018, Idaho passed the Abortion Complications Reporting Act based on AUL's model. This legislation is currently in litigation.

WHAT HAPPENS AFTER *ROE* IS OVERTURNED?

- Abortion will be legal up to 20 weeks of pregnancy.

RECOMMENDATIONS
for Idaho

WOMEN'S PROTECTION PROJECT PRIORITIES

- Enhanced penalties and enforcement mechanisms for the state's abortion-related laws
- Women's Health Protection Act (abortion clinic regulations)
- Parental Involvement Enhancement Act
- Drug-Induced Abortion Information and Reporting Act
- Child Protection Act

INFANTS' PROTECTION PROJECT PRIORITIES

- Prenatal Nondiscrimination Act
- Perinatal Hospice Information Act
- Born-Alive Infant Protection Act

PATIENT PROTECTION ACT PRIORITIES

- Joint Resolution Opposing Suicide by Physician
- Charlie Gard Act (formerly the Life Sustaining Care Act)
- Pain Medicine Education Act

ADDITIONAL PRIORITIES

ABORTION

- State Constitutional Amendment (providing that there is no state constitutional right to abortion)
- Defunding the Abortion Industry and Advancing Women's Health Act

LEGAL RECOGNITION AND PROTECTION FOR THE UNBORN

- Pregnant Woman's Protection Act

BIOETHICS

- Human Cloning Prohibition Act
- Destructive Embryo Research Act
- Prohibition on Public Funding of Human Cloning and Destructive Embryo Research Act

Illinois | RANKING: 37

While Illinois maintains some of the nation's strongest laws protecting unborn victims of criminal violence, it provides scant protections for women considering abortion. Further, Illinois funds and promotes unethical forms of research including destructive embryo research and human cloning. In 2017, Illinois passed legislation requiring taxpayer funds to be used to pay for abortions.

ABORTION

- Illinois requires notice to a parent or other adult family member at least 48 hours prior to a minor's abortion. The law provides exceptions in cases of rape, incest, child abuse by an adult family member, or in a medical emergency and permits a minor to seek a court order to bypass the notice requirement.

- Illinois' abortion facility regulations are not uniformly applied to all of the state's abortion clinics.

- Abortion providers must have either admitting privileges or a transfer agreement with a third-party physician to facilitate hospital admissions and continuity of care for abortion patients.

- Only physicians licensed by the State of Illinois may perform abortions. A chiropractor's 1978 challenge to this requirement was rejected.

- Illinois has an enforceable abortion reporting law but does not require the reporting of information to the Centers for Disease Control and Prevention (CDC). The measure requires abortion providers to report short-term complications.

- Illinois requires abortion providers, as well as those who provide abortion referrals, to report suspected child abuse or neglect.

- Illinois taxpayers are required by court order to fund "medically necessary" abortions for women eligible for public assistance. This requirement essentially equates to funding abortion-on-demand in light of the U.S. Supreme Court's broad definition of "health" in the context of abortion.

- Illinois Department of Children and Family Services grants may be made to non-profit agencies and organizations which do not use such grants to refer for, counsel for, or perform abortions.

- In 2017, Illinois amended its state health plan to provide coverage for all abortions.

LEGAL RECOGNITION AND PROTECTION OF THE UNBORN AND NEWLY BORN

- Under Illinois criminal law, the killing of an unborn child at any stage of gestation is defined as a form of homicide.

- Illinois defines a nonfatal assault on an unborn child as a crime.

- Illinois allows a wrongful death (civil) action when an unborn child at any stage of development is killed through a negligent or criminal act.

- It has created a specific affirmative duty of physicians to provide medical care and treatment to infants born alive at any stage of development.

- Illinois maintains an Abandoned Newborn Infant Protection Act, or "Baby Moses" law, which includes a prohibition preventing persons accepting an infant under the Act from publicly discussing the circumstances surrounding the infant's legal surrender.

- Illinois defines substance abuse during pregnancy as "child abuse" under its civil child-welfare statutes. Illinois also requires healthcare professionals to report suspected prenatal drug exposure and funds drug treatment programs for pregnant women and newborns.

BIOETHICS LAWS

- Under the Stem Cell Research and Human Cloning Prohibition Act, Illinois permits and funds destructive embryo research. While the Act prohibits cloning to produce children, it specifically allows "therapeutic cloning," making it a "clone-and-kill" state.

- The state Department of Public Health has been directed to establish a network of human cord blood banks. The Department also encourages healthcare providers to distribute a state-produced publication on umbilical cord blood banking and urges all licensed hospitals to offer pregnant women the option of donating cord blood.

- Illinois provides no meaningful regulation of assisted reproductive technologies, does not regulate human egg harvesting, and permits gestational surrogacy.

PATIENT PROTECTION LAWS

- In Illinois, assisting a suicide is a felony.

- Illinois maintains a Physicians Order for Life-Sustaining Treatment (POLST) Paradigm Program.

HEALTHCARE FREEDOM OF CONSCIENCE

PARTICIPATION IN ABORTION AND CONTRACEPTION

- By statute, Illinois protects the civil rights of all healthcare providers, whether individuals, institutions, or payers (public or private), who conscientiously object to participating in any healthcare services, including abortion. The law includes protection for medical and nursing students, counselors, and social workers.

- A state appellate court has ruled that an Illinois rule forcing pharmacists to dispense "emergency contraception" violates the Illinois Health Care Rights of Conscience Act.

- Health insurance plans that provide prescription coverage must also provide coverage for contraception. A conscience exemption is provided for religious employers.

- In 2016, Illinois amended its law protecting conscience rights to impose a new mandate forcing pro-life healthcare providers, including pregnancy resource centers, to provide information on where to obtain abortions. The law is enjoined and in ongoing litigation. AUL filed a filed a "friend of court" brief against the law on behalf of health care workers and pro-life organizations.

PARTICIPATION IN RESEARCH HARMFUL TO HUMAN LIFE

- By statute, Illinois protects the civil rights of all healthcare providers who conscientiously object to participating in procedures such as human cloning or destructive embryo research.

DID YOU KNOW?

- In 2018, Illinois considered legislation that would have prohibited abortion based on a diagnosis of Down syndrome and prohibited the dismemberment abortion process.

WHAT HAPPENS AFTER *ROE* IS OVERTURNED?

- Abortion will be legal throughout pregnancy.

RECOMMENDATIONS
for Illinois

WOMEN'S PROTECTION PROJECT PRIORITIES

- Enhanced penalties and enforcement mechanisms for the state's abortion-related laws
- Women's Right to Know Act with reflection period
- Coercive Abuse Against Mothers Prevention Act
- Women's Health Protection Act (abortion clinic regulations)
- Reporting on abortion complications
- Drug-Induced Abortion Information and Reporting Act
- Parental Involvement Enhancement Act
- Components of the Child Protection Act related to evidence retention and remedies for third-party interference with parental rights

INFANTS' PROTECTION PROJECT PRIORITIES

- Unborn Infants Dignity Act
- Prenatal Nondiscrimination Act
- Perinatal Hospice Information Act

PATIENT PROTECTION ACT PRIORITIES

- Joint Resolution Opposing Suicide by Physician
- Charlie Gard Act (formerly the Life Sustaining Care Act)
- Pain Medicine Education Act

ADDITIONAL PRIORITIES

ABORTION

- Defunding the Abortion Industry and Advancing Women's Health Act
- Federal Abortion-Mandate Opt-Out Act

LEGAL RECOGNITION AND PROTECTION FOR THE UNBORN

- Pregnant Woman's Protection Act

BIOETHICS

- Human Cloning Prohibition Act
- Destructive Embryo Research Act
- Prohibition on Public Funding of Human Cloning and Destructive Embryo Research Act

HEALTHCARE FREEDOM OF CONSCIENCE

- Repeal 2016 mandate on healthcare providers to provide information on where to obtain abortions

Indiana | RANKING: 14

Indiana has made significant strides in recent years to protect women and unborn children from the harms inherent in abortion and from substandard conditions and practices in some abortion clinics. Further, it has taken steps to regulate the rapidly growing (and generally under-regulated) biotechnologies industry, prohibiting human cloning for any purpose and encouraging the donation of umbilical cord blood to support ethical research.

ABORTION

- Abortions may be performed at or after 5 months (i.e., 20 weeks) only for "medical necessity."

- Indiana prohibits partial-birth abortion.

- Indiana prohibits abortions based solely on the baby's race, sex, or diagnosis or potential diagnosis of a disability. The law also requires that a woman be provided with information on perinatal hospice when considering an abortion because the unborn child has been diagnosed with a lethal fetal anomaly. The law is permanently enjoined and in litigation.

- Indiana law requires that, at least 18 hours before an abortion, a woman receive information about the type of abortion procedure to be used, the risks of and alternatives to that particular procedure (including the risks of chemical abortion), the probable gestational age of the unborn child, the risks associated with carrying the pregnancy to term, and the name of the physician who will perform the abortion. Further, the woman must be told about state medical assistance benefits, the father's liability for child support, and abortion alternatives.

- A 2011 state law requires that informed consent information include the fact that human physical life begins when a human ovum is fertilized by a human sperm. Further, before an abortion, women must be informed that "objective scientific information shows that a fetus can feel pain" at or before 5 months (i.e., 20 weeks) gestation, but that portion of the law has been declared invalid as applied to women in the first trimester.

- Indiana requires an ultrasound at least 18 hours before an abortion. The image must be displayed unless the woman signs a form indicating that she does not desire to see the image. Further, the auscultation of fetal heart tone must be made audible, if possible, unless the woman signs a form indicating that she does not wish to hear the heart tone. This legislation is enjoined and in ongoing litigation.

- A physician may not perform an abortion on an unemancipated minor under the age of 18 without first obtaining written consent from one parent, a legal guardian, or a custodian accompanying the minor. The adult must bring government-issued identification as well as evidence showing the relationship between the adult and the minor. The parental consent requirements do not apply in a medical emergency or with a judicial bypass. The law is enjoined and in ongoing litigation.

- If an abortion is performed on a female who is less than 14 years of age, the physician who performed the abortion must transmit an informational form to both the state Department of Health and the state Department of Child Services within a specified time period.

- A woman must be informed that she has a right to determine how the fetal remains are disposed.

- All facilities performing surgical abortions must be licensed by the state Department of Health and meet comprehensive health and safety standards. State officials are required to inspect abortion facilities once a year.

- Indiana also requires that post-first-trimester abortions be performed in a hospital or ambulatory outpatient surgical center. A law requiring facilities providing chemical abortions to meet the same standards as facilities providing surgical abortions was struck down by a federal district court.

- Only physicians licensed to practice medicine in Indiana may perform abortions. Abortion providers must have admitting privileges in the county where they provide abortions or in a contiguous county. In 2014, Indiana amended its admitting privileges requirement to remove the option of contracting with another physician who has admitting privileges and to require that each abortion provider personally maintain local admitting privileges.

- Indiana has an abortion reporting law which was updated based on AUL's model bill in 2018. It now requires the reporting of information to the Centers for Disease Control and Prevention (CDC). The measure applies to both surgical and nonsurgical abortions and requires abortion providers to report both short-term and long-term complications. The law is enjoined and in ongoing litigation.

- Abortion providers must report, among other things, the post-fertilization age (of the unborn child) and, if an abortion is performed at or after 5 months (i.e., 20 weeks), the medical reason for the abortion.

- Indiana requires that a physician examine a woman before providing drug-induced abortion, effectively preventing the dangerous practice of "webcam abortion." The law also provides that the drugs cannot be administered past nine weeks post-fertilization unless the Food & Drug Administration (FDA) has approved them for such use.

- Indiana funds abortions for women eligible for public assistance when necessary to preserve the woman's life or physical health or when the pregnancy is the result of rape or incest. It further provides that neither the state nor any political subdivision of the state may make a payment from any fund under its control for the performance of an abortion unless the abortion is necessary to preserve the life of the pregnant woman.

- The state Office of Women's Health director and employees are not permitted to advocate, promote, refer for, or otherwise advance abortion or drug-induced abortion.

- In 2011, Indiana prohibited state agencies from contracting with or making grants (of state or state-administered federal funds) to entities that perform abortions or maintain or operate facilities where abortions are performed, and cancelled existing contracts with such entities. However, the Seventh Circuit enjoined the law as applied to Medicaid funding.

- Indiana prohibits insurance companies from offering abortion coverage within the state insurance Exchanges established pursuant to the federal healthcare law, except in cases of life endangerment, substantial and irreversible impairment of a major bodily function, rape, or incest.

- Indiana prohibits insurance coverage of abortion, with exceptions protecting the mother's life, guarding against substantial threats to the mother's health, and applying in cases of rape and incest. The measure is based on AUL's Abortion Coverage Prohibition Act.

- Indiana offers "Choose Life" license plates, the proceeds of which benefit pregnancy resource centers and/or other organizations providing abortion alternatives.

LEGAL RECOGNITION AND PROTECTION OF THE UNBORN AND NEWLY BORN

- Under Indiana criminal law, the killing of an unborn child is defined as a form of homicide. In 2018, it expanded this to include the crimes of voluntary manslaughter, involuntary manslaughter, and feticide.

- A person who causes the death of a child in utero while committing murder or felony murder may be sentenced to an additional fixed term of imprisonment that is equal to the advisory sentence for murder. This provision applies at any stage of gestation.

- An assault on a viable unborn child is a prosecutable crime.

- In addition, Indiana defines criminal assaults on a pregnant woman that result in miscarriage, stillbirth, or "damage to pregnancy" as an enhanced offense for sentencing purposes.

- Indiana allows a wrongful death (civil) action only when an unborn child is born alive following a negligent or criminal act and dies thereafter.

- Indiana has created a specific affirmative duty of physicians to provide medical care and treatment to infants born alive at any stage of development.

- Indiana defines substance abuse during pregnancy as "child abuse" under civil child welfare statutes. In 2013, it allocated funds for "prenatal substance use and prevention" for pregnant women.

- The state Department of Health has been directed to develop a system of registry for stillbirth information.

- Indiana law requires that an abortion clinic or healthcare facility having possession of an aborted fetus shall provide for the final disposition of the aborted fetus by interment or cremation. The law is enjoined and in ongoing litigation.

- It is a felony to sell or unlawfully transfer fetal tissue.

- Indiana prohibits altering the timing, method, or procedure of an abortion for the purpose of obtaining or collecting fetal tissue.

BIOETHICS LAWS

- Indiana prohibits human cloning for any purpose and prohibits taxpayer funding of human cloning.

- While Indiana does not explicitly prohibit destructive embryo research, it does prohibit research on embryos created from ova initially provided for use in in vitro fertilization (IVF) procedures as well as experimentation on aborted fetuses. However, the state's prohibition on experimentation on embryos created for use in IVF explicitly excludes fetal stem-cell research from its application.

- Indiana has established a public umbilical cord-blood bank and an educational initiative to promote public awareness of the importance of donating. Participating facilities must offer patients the option of donating cord blood following delivery.

- Indiana has also directed the Board of Trustees at Indiana University to establish an adult stem-cell research center.

- Indiana prohibits the purchase or sale of human ova, but does not prohibit certain transactions between a woman and a qualified IVF clinic for certain expenses (e.g., earnings lost, travel expenses, medical expenses, or recovery time).

- It does not otherwise regulate assisted reproductive technologies, but does prohibit gestational surrogacy contracts.

PATIENT PROTECTION LAWS

- Assisting a suicide constitutes a felony.

- Indiana maintains a Physicians Order for Life Sustaining Treatment (POLST) Paradigm Program.

HEALTHCARE FREEDOM OF CONSCIENCE

PARTICIPATION IN ABORTION AND CONTRACEPTION

- A physician, hospital or facility employee, or staff member who objects on religious, moral, or ethical grounds is not required to participate in abortions.

- A private or religiously affiliated hospital is not required to permit the use of its facilities for the performance of an abortion.

- Indiana has a "contraceptive equity" law, requiring health insurance coverage for contraception. No exemption is provided for employers or insurers with a moral or religious objection to contraception.

- Indiana currently provides no protection for the rights of healthcare providers who conscientiously object to participation in human cloning, destructive embryo research, or other forms of medical research that violate a provider's moral or religious beliefs.

DID YOU KNOW?

- In 2018, Indiana passed legislation that "makes the intentional loss of a fetus a crime of murder, voluntary manslaughter, involuntary manslaughter, and feticide."

- Indiana considered legislation that would have allowed "individuals with a terminal illness [...] to make a written request [...] for medication that the individual may self-administer to end the individual's life."

- Planned Parenthood has challenged the cumulative impact of the abortion regulations in the state. Litigation is ongoing.

WHAT HAPPENS AFTER *ROE* IS OVERTURNED?

- Abortion will be legal up to 20 weeks of pregnancy

RECOMMENDATIONS
for Indiana

WOMEN'S PROTECTION PROJECT PRIORITIES

- Enhanced penalties and enforcement mechanisms for the state's abortion-related laws
- Parental Involvement Enhancement Act
- Drug-Induced Abortion Information and Reporting Act
- Components of the Child Protection Act related to evidence retention and remedies for third-party interference with parental rights

INFANTS' PROTECTION PROJECT PRIORITIES

- Unborn Wrongful Death Act

PATIENT PROTECTION ACT PRIORITIES

- Joint Resolution Opposing Suicide by Physician
- Charlie Gard Act (formerly the Life Sustaining Care Act)
- Pain Medicine Education Act

ADDITIONAL PRIORITIES

LEGAL RECOGNITION AND PROTECTION FOR THE UNBORN

- Pregnant Woman's Protection Act

BIOETHICS

- Promotion of ethical research alternatives

HEALTHCARE FREEDOM OF CONSCIENCE

- Healthcare Freedom of Conscience Act

Iowa | RANKING: 31

Iowa maintains only minimal protections for women considering abortion. The Iowa Supreme Court has impeded the state Board of Medicine's ability to enforce regulations prohibiting the use of "telemedicine" for dangerous chemical abortions. Iowa allows cloning for biomedical research and destructive embryo research, while prohibiting cloning to produce children, making it a "clone-and-kill" state. Further, it does not prohibit fetal experimentation or promote ethical forms of research.

ABORTION

- Iowa prohibits abortions at or after 5 months (i.e., 20 weeks) on the basis of the pain felt by unborn children.

- Iowa requires that before performing the abortion, the physician receive written certification from the woman that an ultrasound was performed and she was given an opportunity to view the image, hear a description, and hear the heartbeat of her unborn child 72 hours prior.

- A physician may not perform an abortion on an unmarried or never married minor under the age of 18 until at least 48 hours after written notice has been provided to a parent or grandparent. There are exceptions when the minor is the victim of rape, incest, or child abuse, there is a medical emergency, or a court order is issued.

- An abortion provider must check for the unborn child's heartbeat prior to abortion. If a heartbeat is detected, the performance of an abortion is prohibited. The law is enjoined and in ongoing litigation.

- In 2002, Iowa issued the "Information, Not Criminalization" directive. The directive purportedly makes reproductive health information, including information on family planning, abortion, and adoption, available to a woman at her request. However, the information is not mandated, and there are no penalties for failure to supply the information or to otherwise provide access to the information.

- Only physicians licensed by the State of Iowa in medicine or osteopathy may perform abortions.

- Iowa has an enforceable abortion reporting law but does not require the reporting of information to the Centers for Disease Control and Prevention (CDC). The measure applies to both surgical and nonsurgical abortions.

- The Iowa State Board of Medicine issued regulations requiring that a physician physically examine a woman and document (in her medical record) the age and location of the pregnancy prior to administering drug-induced abortion. The regulations also require the physician to be present when the drugs are dispensed. The regulations were challenged by Planned Parenthood and invalidated by the Iowa Supreme Court.

- Iowa taxpayers are required to pay for abortions for women eligible for state medical assistance if the continued pregnancy endangers the woman's life, the unborn child is physically deformed, mentally deficient, or afflicted with a congenital condition, or the pregnancy is the result of reported rape or incest.

- Iowa requires abortion providers to meet certain informed consent requirements before performing abortions for which they plan to seek reimbursement from the state.

LEGAL RECOGNITION AND PROTECTION OF THE UNBORN AND NEWLY BORN

- Iowa does not protect unborn children from criminal violence.

- Iowa law provides that an attack on a pregnant woman that results in a stillbirth or miscarriage is a criminal assault.

- In 2017, Iowa passed legislation that prohibits providing, receiving, or transferring fetal body parts.

- It also requires an investigation into a newborn's death when 1) the death is believed to have occurred during or after delivery and when the delivery was only attended by the mother; or 2) the medical examiner otherwise believes an investigation is warranted.

- Iowa allows a wrongful death (civil) action only when an unborn child is born alive following a negligent or criminal act and dies thereafter.

- Iowa has created a specific affirmative duty of physicians to provide medical care and treatment to infants born alive after viability.

- It defines substance abuse during pregnancy as "child abuse" under its civil child welfare statutes. Iowa also requires healthcare professionals to report suspected prenatal drug exposure and to test newborns for such exposure when there is suspicion of prenatal drug use or abuse.

- Iowa has authorized stillbirth certificates.

BIOETHICS LAWS

- Under the Stem Cell Research and Cures Initiative, Iowa allows cloning for biomedical research and destructive embryo research, while prohibiting cloning to produce children, making it a "clone-and-kill" state.

- It does not prohibit fetal experimentation or promote ethical forms of research.

- Iowa does not regulate assisted reproductive technologies or human egg harvesting.

PATIENT PROTECTION LAWS

- Assisting a suicide constitutes a felony.

- Iowa maintains a Physician Orders for Life-Sustaining Treatment (POLST) Paradigm Program.

- It also has a "right to try" law that allows terminally ill patients to use investigational drugs.

HEALTHCARE FREEDOM OF CONSCIENCE

PARTICIPATION IN ABORTION AND CONTRACEPTION

- An individual who objects on religious or moral grounds is not required to participate in an abortion unless that abortion constitutes "emergency medical treatment" of a serious physical condition necessary to save the woman's life.

- A private or religiously affiliated hospital is not required to perform or permit an abortion that is not necessary to save a woman's life.

- Health insurance plans that provide prescription coverage must also provide coverage for contraception. No conscience exemption is provided for religious employers.

PARTICIPATION IN RESEARCH HARMFUL TO HUMAN LIFE

- Iowa currently provides no protection for the rights of healthcare providers who conscientiously object to participation in human cloning, destructive embryo research, or other forms of medical research that violate a provider's moral or religious beliefs.

DID YOU KNOW?

- Iowa's appropriations legislation for 2017 blocked Planned Parenthood and other abortion providers in the state from receiving family planning funding.

- In 2017, Iowa considered legislation that would have recognized life as beginning from conception.

WHAT HAPPENS AFTER *ROE* IS OVERTURNED?

- Abortion will be legal up to at least 20 weeks of pregnancy due to a state court decision.

RECOMMENDATIONS
for Iowa

WOMEN'S PROTECTION PROJECT PRIORITIES

- Enhanced penalties and enforcement mechanisms for the state's abortion-related laws
- Women's Health Protection Act (abortion clinic regulations)
- Women's Right to Know Act with reflection period
- Coercive Abuse Against Mothers Prevention Act
- Drug-Induced Abortion Information and Reporting Act
- Parental Consent Act for Abortion
- Parental Involvement Enhancement Act
- Components of the Child Protection Act related to evidence retention and remedies for third-party interference with parental rights

INFANTS' PROTECTION PROJECT PRIORITIES

- Unborn Infants Dignity Act
- Prenatal Nondiscrimination Act
- Perinatal Hospice Information Act
- Unborn Wrongful Death Act (for a pre-viable child)

PATIENT PROTECTION ACT PRIORITIES

- Joint Resolution Opposing Suicide by Physician
- Charlie Gard Act (formerly the Life Sustaining Care Act)
- Pain Medicine Education Act

ADDITIONAL PRIORITIES

ABORTION

- Defunding the Abortion Industry and Advancing Women's Health Act
- Federal Abortion-Mandate Opt-Out Act

LEGAL RECOGNITION AND PROTECTION FOR THE UNBORN

- Crimes Against the Unborn Child Act
- Pregnant Woman's Protection Act

BIOETHICS

- Human Cloning Prohibition Act
- Destructive Embryo Research Act
- Prohibition on Public Funding of Human Cloning and Destructive Embryo Research Act

HEALTHCARE FREEDOM OF CONSCIENCE

- Healthcare Freedom of Conscience Act

Kansas | RANKING: 5

In recent years, Kansas has aggressively implemented a life-affirming legal strategy for protecting women and their unborn children. It has prohibited certain abortions such as those performed for sex selection, adopted protective health and safety standards for abortion facilities, and ensured that taxpayer dollars are not used to subsidize abortions or abortion providers like Planned Parenthood.

ABORTION

- The Kansas Court of Appeals held that there is a right to abortion under Kansas' constitution, but an appeal is pending before the Kansas Supreme Court.

- Kansas maintains a "delayed enforcement" provision prohibiting abortion should *Roe v. Wade* be overturned.

- Kansas prohibits abortions at or after 5 months (i.e., 20 weeks) on the basis of the pain experienced by unborn children.

- Kansas prohibits sex-selection abortions.

- Kansas prohibits partial-birth abortion.

- Kansas permits abortions after viability only when an abortion provider has a documented referral from another physician not legally or financially affiliated with the abortion provider and both physicians determine that (1) the abortion is necessary to preserve the life of the pregnant woman or (2) the continuation of the pregnancy will cause a substantial and irreversible impairment of a major bodily function of the pregnant woman. For the "medical emergency" exception to apply, the underlying condition must be physical in nature and not resulting from the woman's own behavior.

- Kansas prohibits dismemberment abortions. The law is enjoined and in ongoing litigation.

- Under Kansas law, a physician may not perform an abortion until at least 24 hours after a woman has received complete and accurate information on the proposed abortion method, the risks of the proposed method, the probable gestational age of the unborn child, the probable anatomical and physiological development of the unborn child, the medical risks of carrying the pregnancy to term, and the name of the physician who will perform the abortion. Further, a woman must be informed that "abortion will terminate the life of a whole, separate, unique, living human being" and be provided written information on medical assistance benefits, agencies offering alternatives to abortion, the father's legal liability, and the development of the unborn child. In 2013, Kansas amended the law to require information on fetal pain, the woman's right to view an ultrasound image, the increased risk of breast cancer associated with abortion, and the documented risk of subsequent pre-term births following abortions.

- In 2017, Kansas passed a law that requires that women be given information regarding the qualifications and background of the physician performing their abortion.

- Kansas requires an ultrasound evaluation for all women seeking abortions. Further, the physician or other healthcare professional must, at the request of the woman, review and explain the ultrasound results including the probable gestational age of the unborn child before the abortion procedure is performed.

- Women must also be informed that the state-mandated written materials are available online and provided with a list of organizations providing free ultrasound examinations.

- All women in "medically challenging pregnancies" must be given a list of websites for national perinatal assistance including information regarding which entities provide these services free of charge. Similarly, Kansas has authorized grants, contracts, or cooperative agreements to help a family after they learn that their child has Down syndrome or other conditions.

- Kansas requires abortion providers to state in their printed materials that it is illegal for someone to coerce a woman into having an abortion. Abortion facilities must also post signs stating that it is illegal to force a woman to have an abortion.

- A physician may not perform an abortion on an unemancipated minor under the age of 18 without the written, notarized consent of two parents, unless there is a medical emergency or the minor obtains a court order. The consent of only one parent is required when the parents are not married to each other, one cannot be found, or the minor is the victim of incest by her father (which must be reported).

- Any physician who performs an abortion on a minor under the age of 14 must retain fetal tissue extracted during the procedure and send it to the Kansas Bureau of Investigation. The tissue is to be submitted "for the purpose of DNA testing and examination" and will be used to investigate (and potentially prosecute) incidents of child rape and sexual abuse.

- Kansas enacted comprehensive health and safety regulations for abortion clinics which include a requirement that the clinic be licensed by the state. The law is enjoined and in ongoing litigation.

- Kansas requires that a physician performing abortions have admitting privileges at an accredited hospital located within 30 miles of the abortion facility.

- Kansas has an enforceable abortion reporting law but does not require the reporting of information to the Centers for Disease Control and Prevention (CDC). The measure applies to both surgical and non-surgical abortions.

- Kansas also requires reporting of the medical reasons supporting the termination of a late-term pregnancy.

- Kansas mandates that the state Department of Social and Rehabilitation Services produce and distribute a report on the number of child abuse reports received from abortion providers.

- When RU-486 or any drug is used for the purpose of inducing an abortion, the drug must be administered by a physician or in the same room and in the physical presence of the physician who prescribed, dispensed, or otherwise provided the drug to the woman.

- Kansas follows the federal standard for Medicaid funding for abortions, permitting the use of federal or state matching Medicaid funds for abortions necessary to preserve the life of the woman or when the pregnancy is the result of rape or incest.

- A Kansas law effectively preventing abortion providers from receiving federal Title X funding was upheld by the Tenth Circuit.

- No state funds may be expended for any abortion, and tax benefits for abortion or abortion providers are specifically prohibited.

- Contracts with the Kansas Department of Health and Environment's pregnancy maintenance program may not be granted to groups that promote, refer for, or educate in favor of abortion.

- Abortions may not be performed in any facility, hospital, or clinic owned, leased, or operated by the University of Kansas Hospital Authority unless necessary to preserve a woman's life or prevent "a serious risk of substantial and irreversible impairment of a major bodily function."

- Kansas prohibits abortions in state-run or state-leased facilities except when necessary to save a woman's life.

- School districts, district employees or volunteers, and educational service providers are prohibited from contracting with a school district to provide abortion services (except when necessary to save a woman's life).

- Kansas prohibits insurance companies from offering abortion coverage within state insurance Exchanges established pursuant to the federal healthcare law, except in cases of life endangerment.

- Kansas prohibits private insurance companies from covering abortion, except in cases of life endangerment. Further, the state employee health benefits plan may not provide coverage for abortion except in cases of life endangerment. Kansas has also removed any tax benefit for insurance coverage of abortion.

- Public health benefits coverage for children cannot be used for abortions or abortion coverage.

- Kansas provides direct funding to pregnancy resource centers and other organizations promoting abortion alternatives.

LEGAL RECOGNITION AND PROTECTION OF THE UNBORN AND NEWLY BORN

- Under Kansas law, an "unborn child" (from fertilization to birth) is recognized as a potential victim of murder, manslaughter, vehicular manslaughter, and battery.

- Kansas defines a criminal assault on a pregnant woman that results in miscarriage, stillbirth, or "damage to pregnancy" as an enhanced offense for sentencing purposes.

- Kansas allows a wrongful death (civil) action when a viable unborn child is killed by a negligent or criminal act.

- It prohibits wrongful birth and wrongful life lawsuits.

- Kansas law requires that an attending physician take "all reasonable steps necessary to maintain the life and health" of a child (at any stage of development) who survives an attempted abortion.

- Kansas maintains a law related to fetal death or stillborn certificates.

BIOETHICS LAWS

- Kansas maintains no laws banning human cloning, destructive embryo research, or fetal experimentation.

- Kansas has enacted a measure promoting morally responsible growth in the biotechnology industry. It has specifically indicated that the terms "bioscience," "biotechnology," and "life sciences" shall not be construed to include 1) induced human abortions or the use of cells or tissues derived therefrom and 2) any research the funding of which would be contrary to federal law. The law effectively prohibits funding of human cloning and destructive embryo research.

- Kansas has directed the state Department of Health and Environment to develop and make available education and training (for healthcare providers) in the basic procedures and requirements for collecting and maintaining umbilical cord, cord blood, amniotic fluid, and placenta donations. A healthcare provider giving health services to a pregnant woman must advise her of post-delivery options to donate the umbilical cord.

- Kansas has appropriated funds for adult stem-cell research.

- Kansas maintains no meaningful regulation of assisted reproductive technologies or human egg harvesting.

PATIENT PROTECTION LAWS

- In Kansas, assisting a suicide is a felony.

- Kansas maintains a Pain Patient's Bill of Rights, which, among other provisions, allows physicians to prescribe a dosage of opiates deemed medically necessary to relieve pain. The law does not expand the scope of medical practice to allow suicide by physician or euthanasia.

HEALTHCARE FREEDOM OF CONSCIENCE

PARTICIPATION IN ABORTION

- No person may be required to participate in medical procedures that result in abortion.

- No hospital may be required to perform abortions in its facilities.

- Kansas permits an individual or healthcare facility to refuse to perform, make referrals for, or participate in abortion services or services that the individual or facility "reasonably believes" would end a pregnancy.

- Kansas provides some protection for the conscience rights of pharmacists and pharmacies.

PARTICIPATION IN RESEARCH HARMFUL TO HUMAN LIFE

- Kansas currently provides no protection for the rights of healthcare providers who conscientiously object to participation in human cloning, destructive embryo research, or other forms of medical research that violate a provider's moral or religious beliefs.

DID YOU KNOW?

- In 2018, Kansas considered a bill that would increase the required information provided to a woman seeking an abortion, including the name of the physician, whether the physician has clinical privileges at a nearby hospital, and whether the physician has lost clinical privileges at any hospital.

WHAT HAPPENS AFTER *ROE* IS OVERTURNED?

- Abortion will be legal up to 20 weeks of pregnancy.

RECOMMENDATIONS
for Kansas

WOMEN'S PROTECTION PROJECT PRIORITIES

- Enhanced penalties and enforcement mechanisms for the state's abortion-related laws
- Parental Involvement Enhancement Act
- Drug-Induced Abortion Information and Reporting Act
- Components of the Child Protection Act related to mandatory reporters of suspected child sexual abuse and remedies for third-party interference with parental rights

INFANTS' PROTECTION PROJECT PRIORITIES

- Unborn Infants Dignity Act
- Unborn Wrongful Death Act (for a pre-viable child)

PATIENT PROTECTION ACT PRIORITIES

- Joint Resolution Opposing Suicide by Physician
- Charlie Gard Act (formerly the Life Sustaining Care Act)
- Pain Medicine Education Act

ADDITIONAL PRIORITIES

BIOETHICS

- Human Cloning Prohibition Act
- Destructive Embryo Research Act
- Prohibition on Public Funding of Human Cloning and Destructive Embryo Research Act

HEALTHCARE FREEDOM OF CONSCIENCE

- Healthcare Freedom of Conscience Act

Kentucky | RANKING: 19

Kentucky has laid the groundwork necessary to advance the goals of the Women's Protection Project and for more aggressive efforts to protect women and their unborn children. Enhancements of its informed consent law, its parental involvement requirement, and its abortion facility regulations are recommended to advance Kentucky's efforts to protect maternal health and defend unborn life. Kentucky currently has only one abortion clinic operating within the state.

ABORTION

- Kentucky's legislature has declared its opposition to abortion, stating that if the U.S. Constitution is amended or certain judicial decisions are reversed or modified, the legal recognition and protection of the lives of all human beings "regardless of their degree of biological development shall be fully restored."

- Kentucky prohibits abortion at or after 5 months (i.e., 20 weeks) on the basis of the pain felt by unborn children.

- Under Kentucky law, a physician may not perform an abortion until at least 24 hours after a woman has received information about the probable gestational age of her unborn child, the nature and risks of the proposed abortion procedure, alternatives to abortion, and the medical risks of carrying the pregnancy to term. She must also be told that state-prepared materials are available for her review, that medical assistance may be available, and that the father is liable for child support even if he offered to pay for the abortion.

- In 2017, Kentucky enacted an ultrasound requirement that includes a description of the unborn child, and mandates that ultrasound images be displayed and an audible heartbeat be provided to a woman before an abortion. The law is enjoined and in ongoing litigation.

- A physician may not perform an abortion on an unemancipated minor under the age of 18 without the written consent of one parent, unless there is a medical emergency or a court order is issued.

- Kentucky prohibits the dismemberment abortion procedure when the unborn child is 11 weeks or older. The law is in ongoing litigation.

- Kentucky requires abortion clinics to meet licensing requirements and minimum health and safety standards including maintaining written policies and procedures, conducting appropriate patient testing, ensuring proper staffing, maintaining necessary equipment and medication, and providing medically appropriate post-operative care.

- Kentucky limits the performance of abortions to licensed physicians, and all abortion providers must maintain hospital admitting privileges.

- No abortion may be performed after viability unless necessary to protect the life or health of the mother.

- Kentucky has an enforceable abortion reporting law but does not require the reporting of information to the Centers for Disease Control and Prevention (CDC). The measure applies to both surgical and nonsurgical abortions.

- Kentucky follows the federal standard for Medicaid funding for abortions, permitting the use of federal or state matching Medicaid funds for abortions necessary to preserve the life of the woman or when the pregnancy is the result of rape or incest.

- It otherwise prohibits the use of public funds for abortions unless necessary to save the life of the mother.

- Kentucky restricts the use of state-owned hospitals or healthcare facilities for the performance of abortions except to save the life of the mother.

- Kentucky prohibits school districts from operating a family resource center or a youth services center that provides abortion counseling or makes referrals to a healthcare facility for the purpose of seeking an abortion.

- Hospitals with emergency room services may not counsel victims of reported sexual offenses on abortion.

- All private health insurance contracts, plans, and policies must exclude coverage for abortion unless the procedure is necessary to preserve the woman's life.

- Kentucky also prohibits insurance coverage of abortions for public employees.

- Kentucky offers "Choose Life" license plates, the proceeds of which benefit pregnancy resource centers and/or other organizations providing abortion alternatives.

- Kentucky maintains a "tiering system" for the allocation of family planning funding including funding for which abortion providers might be eligible. Under the system, first priority for funding is given to public entities that are operated by state or local government entities. Most abortion providers fall into the lowest priority category of this system.

LEGAL RECOGNITION AND PROTECTION OF THE UNBORN AND NEWLY BORN

- The definition of "person" for purposes of Kentucky homicide laws includes "an unborn child from the moment of conception."

- Kentucky allows a parent or other relative to bring a wrongful death (civil) lawsuit when a viable unborn child is killed through a negligent or criminal act.

- Kentucky has enacted a "Baby Moses" law, under which a mother or legal guardian who is unable to care for a newborn infant may anonymously and safely leave the infant in the care of a responsible person at a hospital, police station, fire station, or other prescribed location.

- Healthcare professionals must test newborns for prenatal drug exposure when there is suspicion of maternal drug abuse.

- Kentucky has allocated $1.4 million for substance abuse prevention and treatment for pregnant women.

BIOETHICS LAWS

- Kentucky maintains no laws regarding human cloning or destructive embryo research, and it does not promote ethical alternatives to such unethical research.

- It prohibits only the sale or use of a live or viable aborted child.

- Kentucky does not regulate assisted reproductive technologies or human egg harvesting.

PATIENT PROTECTION LAWS

- In Kentucky, assisting a suicide is a felony.

- Kentucky maintains a Physician Orders for Life-Sustaining Treatment (POLST) Paradigm Program.

HEALTHCARE FREEDOM OF CONSCIENCE

PARTICIPATION IN ABORTION

- A physician, nurse, hospital staff member, or hospital employee who objects in writing, on religious, moral, or professional grounds, is not required to participate in an abortion. Kentucky law also protects medical and nursing students.

- Private healthcare facilities and hospitals are not required to permit the performance of abortions if such performance violates the established policy of that facility or hospital.

PARTICIPATION IN RESEARCH HARMFUL TO HUMAN LIFE

- Kentucky currently provides no protection for the rights of healthcare providers who conscientiously object to participation in human cloning, destructive embryo research, or other forms of medical research that violate a provider's moral or religious beliefs.

DID YOU KNOW?

- In 2018, Kentucky passed a bill that prohibits the dismemberment abortion procedure when the unborn child is 11 weeks or greater.

- Kentucky also passed a resolution, based on an AUL model, honoring pregnancy centers "for their life-saving work throughout" the U.S. and Kentucky.

WHAT HAPPENS AFTER *ROE* IS OVERTURNED?

- Abortion will be legal up to 20 weeks of pregnancy.

RECOMMENDATIONS
for Kentucky

WOMEN'S PROTECTION PROJECT PRIORITIES

- Enhanced penalties and enforcement mechanisms for the state's abortion-related laws
- Coercive Abuse Against Mothers Prevention Act
- Drug-Induced Abortion Information and Reporting Act
- Parental Involvement Enhancement Act
- Child Protection Act

INFANTS' PROTECTION PROJECT PRIORITIES

- Unborn Infants Dignity Act
- Prenatal Nondiscrimination Act
- Perinatal Hospice Information Act
- Born-Alive Infant Protection Act
- Unborn Wrongful Death Act (for a pre-viable child)

PATIENT PROTECTION ACT PRIORITIES

- Joint Resolution Opposing Suicide by Physician
- Charlie Gard Act (formerly the Life Sustaining Care Act)
- Pain Medicine Education Act

ADDITIONAL PRIORITIES

ABORTION

- Defunding the Abortion Industry and Advancing Women's Health Act
- Federal Abortion-Mandate Opt-Out Act

LEGAL RECOGNITION AND PROTECTION FOR THE UNBORN

- Pregnant Woman's Protection Act

BIOETHICS

- Human Cloning Prohibition Act
- Destructive Embryo Research Act
- Prohibition on Public Funding of Human Cloning and Destructive Embryo Research Act

HEALTHCARE FREEDOM OF CONSCIENCE

- Healthcare Freedom of Conscience Act

Louisiana | RANKING: 3

Louisiana maintains some of the nation's most comprehensive laws protecting the health and safety of women seeking abortions and providing legal recognition and protection to the unborn. It also is one of few states to effectively regulate emerging biotechnologies. Not only does the state prohibit destructive embryo research and the creation of chimeras (human-animal hybrids), but it has also established an umbilical cord-blood banking program and allows for embryo adoption.

ABORTION

- Louisiana has declared that "the unborn child is a human being from the time of conception and is, therefore, a legal person for purposes of the unborn child's right to life and is entitled to the right to life from conception under the laws and Constitution of this state."

- Louisiana has enacted a measure prohibiting abortion once *Roe v. Wade* is overturned. While the prohibition includes an exception for life endangerment, there is no exception for rape or incest.

- It prohibits abortions at or after 5 months (i.e., 20 weeks) on the basis of the pain felt by unborn children.

- Louisiana law requires that before an abortion is performed on an unborn child less than 5 months post-fertilization age, the woman must receive information about resources, programs, and services for women diagnosed with fetal genetic abnormality and for infants and children born with disabilities. The law is in ongoing litigation.

- Louisiana prohibits dismemberment abortions. The law is in ongoing litigation.

- Louisiana prohibits partial-birth abortion throughout pregnancy except when necessary to save the life of the woman. The measure creates a civil cause of action for violations of the prohibition and includes more stringent criminal penalties than the related federal law, imposing a sentence of hard labor or imprisonment for one to ten years and/or a fine of $10,000 to $100,000.

- Louisiana prohibits any person from intentionally performing an abortion on an unborn child at or after 5 months post-fertilization age, if the mother is seeking the abortion solely because of the unborn child's genetic abnormality. The law is in ongoing litigation.

- A physician may not perform an abortion until at least 72 hours after a woman has been provided information about the proposed abortion procedure, the alternatives to abortion, the probable gestational age of the unborn child, the risks associated with abortion, and the risks associated with carrying the child to term. She must also be told about available medical assistance benefits, the father's legal responsibilities, and that her consent for an abortion may be withdrawn or withheld without any loss of government benefits. Women must also be provided information on psychological risks of abortion, human trafficking, and abuse. Informed consent requirements apply to both surgical and chemical abortions. The 72-hour reflection period requirement is in ongoing litigation.

- Importantly, to ensure that informed consent information focuses on a woman's individual circumstances and that she has an adequate opportunity to ask questions, the required information must be provided to the woman individually and in a room that protects her privacy.

- Louisiana maintains a website providing the required informed consent information, as well as information on abortion alternatives. Abortion providers must give women the website's address following their first contact.

- Louisiana also provides a booklet describing the development of the unborn child; detailing abortion methods and their risks; providing a list of public and private agencies including adoption agencies that are available to provide assistance; providing information about state medical assistance benefits; and describing a physician's liability for failing to obtain a woman's informed consent prior to an abortion.

- In addition, a woman considering an abortion must receive information about fetal pain; specifically, she must be told about the availability of anesthesia or analgesics to prevent pain to the unborn child. Further, the mandatory informed consent materials state that by 5 months (i.e., 20 weeks) gestation, an unborn child can experience and respond to pain and that anesthesia is routinely administered to unborn children for prenatal surgery at 20 weeks gestation or later.

- Louisiana mandates that an ultrasound be performed before an abortion and requires that the person performing the ultrasound read a "script" that includes offering the woman a copy of the ultrasound print. In 2012, the state supplemented this requirement, mandating that the ultrasound images be displayed and an audible heartbeat be provided to a woman before an abortion.

- Printed materials must include a comprehensive list of facilities that offer obstetric ultrasounds free of charge.

- Louisiana requires abortion providers to state in their printed materials that it is illegal for someone to coerce a woman into having an abortion. A coerced abortion occurs when a person engages in or threatens physical force to compel a pregnant woman to have an abortion against her will, "whether or not the abortion procedure has been attempted or completed."

- Abortion providers must post signs declaring that "it is unlawful for anyone to make you have an abortion against your will, even if you are a minor." Clinics must also post the phone number of the National Human Trafficking Resource Center hotline.

- A woman seeking an abortion following rape or incest and using state funds to pay for the abortion must be offered the same informed consent information (without the 24-hour reflection period) as is required for other abortions.

- A physician may not perform an abortion on an unemancipated minor under the age of 18 without notarized, written consent from one parent, unless there is a medical emergency or the minor obtains a court order. In 2017, Louisiana strengthened its parental consent law by requiring proof of identity for the person giving parental consent on behalf of the minor. Louisiana also added a counseling requirement for minors seeking judicial bypass of parental consent, in order to verify that the minor is not a victim of coerced abortion or sexual trafficking.

- Further, the definition of "child abuse" includes coerced abortion. Louisiana has authorized a state court to issue a temporary restraining order prohibiting activities associated with a coerced abortion.

- Louisiana requires the licensing of abortion facilities and imposes minimum health and safety standards in a variety of areas including clinic administration, professional qualifications, patient testing, physical plant, and post-operative care.

- Louisiana law allows state officials to close an abortion clinic for any violation of state or federal law that presents a risk to patients.

- Only physicians licensed to practice medicine in Louisiana may perform abortions. Abortion providers must have admitting privileges at a hospital within 30 miles of the abortion facility, but this provision is currently in litigation. Louisiana requires that physicians performing abortions be board-certified or enrolled in obstetrics and gynecology or family medicine or, if enrolled in a residency program, they be under the direct supervision of a physician board-certified in obstetrics and gynecology or family medicine. The law is in ongoing litigation.

- Louisiana has an enforceable abortion reporting law but does not require the reporting of information to the Centers for Disease Control and Prevention (CDC). The measure requires abortion providers to report short-term complications and the name and address of the hospital or facility where treatment was provided for the complications. Drug-induced abortions and any complications arising from an abortion must be reported.

- Louisiana requires the presence of a physician when a drug-induced abortion is administered or dispensed and requires the scheduling of a follow-up appointment for the woman.

- Louisiana follows the federal standard for Medicaid funding for abortions, only permitting the use of federal or state matching Medicaid funds for abortions necessary to preserve the life of the woman or when the pregnancy is the result of rape or incest.

- Public funds may not be used "for, to assist in, or to provide facilities for an abortion, except when the abortion is medically necessary to prevent the death of the mother." In 2018, Louisiana passed a law banning the Department of Health from entering into agreements for medical funding with any health-care entity that performs or assists in the performance of abortions.

- No individual or organization that performs elective abortions (or an affiliate of that individual or organization) may provide instruction or materials in public schools.

- Louisiana prohibits insurance companies from offering abortion coverage within state insurance Exchanges established pursuant to the federal healthcare law.

- Louisiana funds programs providing direct support for groups and organizations promoting abortion alternatives.

- It also offers "Choose Life" license plates, the proceeds of which benefit pregnancy resource centers and/or other organizations providing abortion alternatives.

LEGAL RECOGNITION AND PROTECTION OF THE UNBORN AND NEWLY BORN

- Under Louisiana criminal law, the killing of an unborn child at any stage of gestation is defined as a form of homicide. In addition, an "unborn child" is a victim of a "feticide" if killed during the perpetration of certain crimes including robbery and cruelty to juveniles.

- Louisiana defines a nonfatal assault on an unborn child as a criminal offense.

- It allows a wrongful death (civil) action when an unborn child at any stage of development is killed through a negligent or criminal act.

- Louisiana has created a specific affirmative duty of physicians to provide medical care and treatment to infants born alive at any stage of development.

- Under the Louisiana Children's Code, "neglect" includes instances when a newborn is identified by a healthcare provider as having been affected by prenatal drug use or exhibiting symptoms of drug withdrawal.

- Louisiana has also expanded the definition of "prenatal neglect" to include 1) "exposure to chronic or severe use of alcohol;" 2) the use of any controlled dangerous substance "in a manner not lawfully prescribed" that results in symptoms of withdrawal to the newborn; 3) the presence of a controlled substance or related metabolite in the newborn; or 4) observable and harmful effects in the newborn's appearance or functioning.

- It also funds drug treatment programs for pregnant women and newborns.

- The Parental Rights for Disposition of Fetal Remains Act requires that, prior to the final disposition of a miscarried child, a health facility must notify the woman of her right to arrange for final disposition of the child and the availability of a chaplain or counseling services.

- Louisiana's prohibition on buying, selling, transferring, or acquiring the body parts of aborted babies for money has been challenged.

- Louisiana requires burial or cremation of remains resulting from an abortion. The law is in ongoing litigation.

BIOETHICS LAWS

- Louisiana prohibits destructive embryo research and the funding of human cloning (although it does not explicitly prohibit human cloning).

- Louisiana prohibits experimentation on live-born human beings or fetuses in utero.

- Louisiana prohibits the creation of chimeras (human-animal hybrids).

- It has established the Umbilical Cord Blood Banking Program to promote public awareness of the potential benefits of cord blood banking, to encourage research into the uses of cord blood, to facilitate pre-delivery arrangements for cord blood donations, and to promote professional education programs.

- Louisiana regulates assisted reproductive technologies and allows for embryo adoption.

- Louisiana prohibits a "gestational carrier contract" from requiring abortion for any reason, including prenatal diagnosis or reduction of multiples.

PATIENT PROTECTION LAWS

- In Louisiana, suicide by physician is a felony.

HEALTHCARE FREEDOM OF CONSCIENCE

PARTICIPATION IN ABORTION

- Any person has the right not to participate in or be required to participate in any healthcare service that violates his or her conscience (including abortion and the provision of drug-induced abortion) to the extent that "access to health care is not compromised." The person's conscientious beliefs must be in writing, and patients must be notified. The law is not to be construed as relieving any healthcare provider from providing "emergency care."

- A healthcare facility must ensure that it has sufficient staff to provide patient care in the event an employee declines to participate in any healthcare service that violates his or her conscience.

PARTICIPATION IN RESEARCH HARMFUL TO HUMAN LIFE

- Any person has the right not to participate in or be required to participate in any healthcare service that violates his or her conscience (including human embryonic stem-cell research, human embryo cloning, euthanasia, or suicide by physician) to the extent that "access to health care is not compromised." The person's conscientious beliefs must be in writing, and patients must be notified. The law is not to be construed as relieving any healthcare provider from providing "emergency care."

- A healthcare facility must ensure that it has sufficient staff to provide patient care in the event an employee declines to participate in any healthcare service that violates his or her conscience.

DID YOU KNOW?

- In 2017, Louisiana strengthened its parental consent law by requiring proof of identity for the person giving parental consent on behalf of the minor. Louisiana also added a counseling requirement for minors seeking judicial bypass of parental consent, in order to verify that the minor is not a victim of coerced abortion or sexual trafficking.

- In 2018, Louisiana passed a resolution commending the state's pro-life groups such as pregnancy centers, adoption agencies, pro-life organizations, and recognizing a Pro-Life Day at the state capitol. The resolution also noted that "abortion unjustly takes the life of an innocent human baby and forever hurts the lives of women and men involved with abortion."

- Louisiana also passed legislation prohibiting abortion after 15 weeks. However, the legislation will only go into effect if the court upholds Mississippi's 15-week ban.

- Planned Parenthood has challenged the cumulative impact of the abortion regulations in the state. Litigation is ongoing.

WHAT HAPPENS AFTER *ROE* IS OVERTURNED?

- Louisiana has a law, conditioned on Roe being overturned, that makes abortion illegal, which may be enforceable.

RECOMMENDATIONS
for Louisiana

WOMEN'S PROTECTION PROJECT PRIORITIES

- Enhanced penalties and enforcement mechanisms for the state's abortion-related laws
- Drug-Induced Abortion Information and Reporting Act
- Parental Involvement Enhancement Act
- Child Protection Act

PATIENT PROTECTION ACT PRIORITIES

- Joint Resolution Opposing Suicide by Physician
- Charlie Gard Act (formerly the Life Sustaining Care Act)
- Pain Medicine Education Act

ADDITIONAL PRIORITIES

LEGAL RECOGNITION AND PROTECTION FOR THE UNBORN

- Prohibition on wrongful birth and wrongful life lawsuits
- Pregnant Woman's Protection Act

BIOETHICS

- Human Cloning Prohibition Act
- Assisted Reproductive Technologies Disclosure and Risk Reduction Act

Maine | RANKING: 36

Maine provides only minimal protection for women seeking abortions. For example, its parental involvement law contains a major loophole, allowing abortion providers to veto a parent's right to grant or withhold consent. Further, Maine is in the minority of states, failing to provide meaningful legal recognition and protection to unborn victims of criminal violence.

ABORTION

- Maine has enacted a Freedom of Choice Act providing for a legal right to abortion even if *Roe v. Wade* is eventually overturned and stating that it is the state's public policy not to restrict access to abortion before viability.

- A physician may not perform an abortion on a woman until after advising her of the probable gestational age of her unborn child; the risks associated with continued pregnancy and the proposed abortion procedure; and, at the woman's request, alternatives to abortion and information about and a list of public and private agencies that will provide assistance if she chooses to carry her pregnancy to term.

- A physician may not perform an abortion on a minor under the age of 18 until after advising her about the alternatives to abortion, prenatal care, agencies providing assistance, and the possibility of involving her parents or other adult family members in her abortion decision. Moreover, the physician must have the written consent of one parent or an adult family member, unless he/she determines that the minor is "mentally and physically competent" to give consent or has secured a court order.

- Only physicians licensed to practice medicine or osteopathy may perform abortions. This law is in ongoing litigation.

- Maine has an enforceable abortion reporting law but does not require the reporting of information to the Centers for Disease Control and Prevention (CDC). The measure applies to both surgical and nonsurgical abortions.

- Maine follows the federal standard for Medicaid funding for abortions, permitting the use of federal or state matching Medicaid funds for abortions necessary to preserve the life of the woman or when the pregnancy is the result of rape or incest. There is ongoing litigation over whether the state must provide abortion funding under MaineCare.

LEGAL RECOGNITION AND PROTECTION OF THE UNBORN AND NEWLY BORN

- Maine does not currently recognize an unborn child as a potential victim of homicide or assault.

- Maine provides for an enhanced sentence for the homicide of a pregnant woman and has created a new crime of "elevated aggravated assault" on a pregnant woman.

- It requires healthcare providers to report all deaths of infants less than one year of age, deaths of women during pregnancy, and maternal deaths within 42 days of giving birth to the Maternal Infant Death Review Panel.

- Maine allows a wrongful death (civil) action only when an unborn child is born alive following a negligent or criminal act and dies thereafter.

- Maine has created a specific affirmative duty of physicians to provide medical care and treatment to infants born alive at any stage of development.

- Maine has a "Baby Moses" law, establishing a safe haven for mothers to legally leave their infants at designated places and ensuring that the infants receive appropriate care and protection.

- Maine requires a healthcare provider involved in the delivery or care of an infant suspected to have been exposed to drugs in utero to report the suspected exposure to the state Department of Health and Human Services.

- Maine provides for the issuance of a Certificate of Birth Resulting in Stillbirth when requested by a parent.

BIOETHICS LAWS

- Maine does not maintain laws regarding human cloning, but its prohibition on fetal experimentation applies to live fetuses either intrauterine or extrauterine. Thus, its fetal experimentation statute can be read to prohibit harmful experimentation on human embryos.

- Maine does not promote ethical forms of research.

- Maine maintains no meaningful regulation of assisted reproductive technologies or human egg harvesting.

PATIENT PROTECTION LAWS

- In Maine, suicide by physician is a felony.

- Maine enacted a "right to try" measure to provide terminally ill patients with expanded opportunities to try investigational medications that have not yet received Food & Drug Administration (FDA) approval.

HEALTHCARE FREEDOM OF CONSCIENCE

PARTICIPATION IN ABORTION AND CONTRACEPTION

- The conscientious objection of a physician, nurse, or other healthcare worker to performing or assisting in the performance of an abortion may not be the basis for civil liability, discrimination in employment or education, or other recriminatory action. Medical and nursing students are also protected.

- The conscientious objection of a hospital or other healthcare facility to permitting an abortion on its premises may not be the basis for civil liability or recriminatory action.

- Private institutions, physicians, or their agents may refuse to provide family planning services based upon religious or conscientious objections.

- Maine provides some protection for the conscience rights of pharmacists and pharmacies.

- Health insurance plans that provide prescription coverage must also provide coverage for contraception. The provision includes an exemption so narrow that it excludes the ability of most employers and insurers with moral or religious objections from exercising the exemption.

PARTICIPATION IN RESEARCH HARMFUL TO HUMAN LIFE

- Maine currently provides no protection for the rights of healthcare providers who conscientiously object to participation in human cloning, destructive embryo research, or other forms of medical research that violate a provider's moral or religious beliefs.

DID YOU KNOW?

- In 2018, Maine considered legislation that would have allowed parents to seek damages for the wrongful death of a viable unborn child.

WHAT HAPPENS AFTER *ROE* IS OVERTURNED?

- Abortion will be legal throughout pregnancy.

RECOMMENDATIONS
for Maine

WOMEN'S PROTECTION PROJECT PRIORITIES

- Enhanced penalties and enforcement mechanisms for the state's abortion-related laws
- Women's Right to Know Act with reflection period
- Coercive Abuse Against Mothers Prevention Act
- Women's Health Protection Act (abortion clinic regulations)
- Drug-Induced Abortion Information and Reporting Act
- Parental Consent for Abortion Act
- Parental Involvement Enhancement Act
- Child Protection Act

INFANTS' PROTECTION PROJECT PRIORITIES

- Unborn Infants Dignity Act
- Prenatal Nondiscrimination Act
- Perinatal Hospice Information Act
- Unborn Wrongful Death Act

PATIENT PROTECTION ACT PRIORITIES

- Joint Resolution Opposing Suicide by Physician
- Charlie Gard Act (formerly the Life Sustaining Care Act)
- Pain Medicine Education Act

ADDITIONAL PRIORITIES

ABORTION

- Repeal State FOCA
- Defunding the Abortion Industry and Advancing Women's Health Act
- Federal Abortion-Mandate Opt-Out Act

LEGAL PROTECTION AND RECOGNITION FOR THE UNBORN

- Crimes Against the Unborn Child Act
- Pregnant Woman's Protection Act

BIOETHICS

- Human Cloning Prohibition Act
- Destructive Embryo Research Act
- Prohibition on Public Funding of Human Cloning and Destructive Embryo Research Act

HEALTHCARE FREEDOM OF CONSCIENCE

- Healthcare Freedom of Conscience Act

Maryland | RANKING: 38

Maryland provides virtually no legal protection for women and unborn children. It does not have an informed consent law, its parental notice law contains a loophole that eviscerates the protection this requirement typically provides, and it does not provide meaningful legal recognition and protection to unborn victims of criminal violence. It is also one of a small number of states that permits and funds destructive embryo research.

ABORTION

- Maryland maintains a Freedom of Choice Act. The Act mandates a right to abortion even if *Roe v. Wade* is eventually overturned, specifically providing that the state may not "interfere with the decision of a woman to terminate a pregnancy... 1) before the fetus is viable, 2) if the procedure is necessary to protect the life or health of the woman, or 3) if the unborn child is afflicted by a genetic defect or serious deformity."

- Under current Maryland law, an unmarried minor under the age of 18 who lives with a parent may not undergo an abortion unless one parent has been notified by the physician. However, the law contains a significant loophole: a minor may obtain an abortion without parental notification if, in the professional judgment of the physician, notice to the parent may lead to physical or emotional abuse of the minor, the minor is mature and capable of giving informed consent to an abortion, or notice would not be in the "best interests" of the minor.

- In 2012, the state Department of Health and Mental Hygiene announced that abortion facilities will have to be licensed and meet minimum health and safety standards modeled after existing standards for outpatient surgical centers.

- Only licensed physicians may perform abortions.

- Maryland taxpayers are required by statute to pay for "medically necessary" abortions for women eligible for public assistance. This requirement essentially equates to funding abortion-on-demand in light of the U.S. Supreme Court's broad definition of "health" in the context of abortion.

- Maryland offers "Choose Life" license plates, the proceeds of which benefit pregnancy resource centers and/or other organizations providing abortion alternatives.

LEGAL RECOGNITION AND PROTECTION OF THE UNBORN AND NEWLY BORN

- Maryland recognizes a "viable fetus" as a distinct victim of murder, manslaughter, or unlawful homicide. However, the law explicitly states that its enactment should not be construed as conferring "personhood" on the unborn child.

- It allows a wrongful death (civil) action when a viable unborn child is killed through a negligent or criminal act.

- Maryland law does not require physicians to provide appropriate medical care to an infant who survives an abortion.

- Maryland has a "Baby Moses" law, establishing a safe haven for mothers to legally leave their infants up to ten days of age at designated places and ensuring that the infants receive appropriate care and protection.

- Maryland law provides that a child is not receiving proper care if he/she is born exposed to methamphetamine or if the mother tests positive for methamphetamine upon admission to the hospital for delivery of the infant. It funds drug treatment programs for pregnant women and newborns.

- A healthcare provider must report the delivery of an infant exposed to controlled substances to a local social services office. The report alone will not automatically trigger a child abuse or neglect investigation.

BIOETHICS LAWS

- Maryland prohibits cloning to produce children, but not cloning for biomedical research, making it a "clone-and-kill" state.

- Maryland maintains a Stem Cell Research Fund that allows and funds destructive embryonic research. However, funds may also be used for adult stem-cell research.

- Maryland does not prohibit fetal experimentation.

- Umbilical cord blood donation educational materials are to be distributed to all pregnant patients.

- Maryland does not regulate assisted reproductive technologies, but does maintain laws on the parentage of children conceived using such technologies.

- Maryland appears to prohibit the sale or transfer of human eggs for "valuable consideration."

- It proscribes the use of sperm or eggs from a "known donor" if the donor receives any remuneration for the donation. The prohibition does not apply to anonymous donation to a tissue or sperm bank or to a fertility clinic.

PATIENT PROTECTION LAWS

- In Maryland, suicide by physician is considered a felony.

- Maryland maintains a Physician Orders for Life-Sustaining Treatment (POLST) Paradigm program.

HEALTHCARE FREEDOM OF CONSCIENCE

PARTICIPATION IN ABORTION AND CONTRACEPTION

- Under Maryland law, no person may be required to participate in or refer to any source for medical procedures that result in an abortion.

- A hospital is not required to permit the performance of abortions within its facilities or to provide referrals for abortions.

- Health insurance plans that provide prescription coverage must also provide coverage for contraception. There is a conscience exemption for religious employers.

- Maryland currently provides no protection for the rights of healthcare providers who conscientiously object to participation in human cloning, destructive embryo research, or other forms of medical research that violate a provider's moral or religious beliefs.

DID YOU KNOW?

- In 2018, Maryland again considered legislation that would prohibit abortions at or after 5 months (i.e., 20 weeks) on the basis of the pain felt by unborn children. AUL provided oral and written testimony in favor of this bill.

- Maryland also considered legislation that would prohibit dismemberment abortions.

WHAT HAPPENS AFTER *ROE* IS OVERTURNED?

- Abortion will be legal throughout pregnancy.

RECOMMENDATIONS
for Maryland

WOMEN'S PROTECTION PROJECT PRIORITIES

- Enhanced penalties and enforcement mechanisms for the state's abortion-related laws
- Women's Right to Know Act with reflection period
- Coercive Abuse Against Mothers Prevention Act
- Women's Health Protection Act (abortion clinic regulations)
- Drug-Induced Abortion Information and Reporting Act
- Meaningful parental involvement law
- Child Protection Act

INFANTS' PROTECTION PROJECT PRIORITIES

- Unborn Infants Dignity Act
- Prenatal Nondiscrimination Act
- Perinatal Hospice Information Act
- Born-Alive Infant Protection Act
- Unborn Wrongful Death Act (for a pre-viable child)

PATIENT PROTECTION ACT PRIORITIES

- Joint Resolution Opposing Suicide by Physician
- Charlie Gard Act (formerly the Life Sustaining Care Act)
- Pain Medicine Education Act

ADDITIONAL PRIORITIES

ABORTION

- Repeal State FOCA
- Defunding the Abortion Industry and Advancing Women's Health Act
- Federal Abortion-Mandate Opt-Out Act

LEGAL RECOGNITION AND PROTECTION FOR THE UNBORN

- Crimes Against the Unborn Child Act (protecting the child from conception)
- Pregnant Woman's Protection Act

BIOETHICS

- Human Cloning Prohibition Act
- Destructive Embryo Research Act
- Prohibition on Public Funding of Human Cloning and Destructive Embryo Research Act

HEALTHCARE FREEDOM OF CONSCIENCE

- Healthcare Freedom of Conscience Act

Massachusetts | RANKING: 41

Massachusetts does not adequately protect women and the unborn from the harms inherent in abortion; rather, it recognizes a broader constitutional right to abortion than that interpreted in the U.S. Constitution. It has also failed to limit and regulate emerging biotechnologies.

ABORTION

- The Massachusetts Constitution has been interpreted as providing a broader right to abortion than that interpreted in the U.S. Constitution.

- Massachusetts' informed consent law is permanently enjoined.

- A physician may not perform an abortion on an unmarried minor under the age of 18 without the written consent of one parent unless there is a medical emergency or the minor obtains a court order.

- Massachusetts' requirement that abortions after the 12th week of pregnancy be performed in hospitals is unenforceable.

- Only physicians authorized to practice medicine in the State of Massachusetts may perform abortions.

- Any person who provides prenatal care, postnatal care, or genetic counseling to parents with an unborn child diagnosed with Down syndrome must provide up-to-date information about the condition. Mandated information includes information about physical, developmental, educational, and psychosocial outcomes; life expectancy; intellectual and functional development; treatment options; and information on educational and support groups.

- Massachusetts has an enforceable abortion reporting law but does not require the reporting of information to the Centers for Disease Control and Prevention (CDC). The measure applies to both surgical and nonsurgical abortions and requires abortion providers to report short-term complications.

- Massachusetts taxpayers are required by court order to pay for "medically necessary" abortions for women eligible for public assistance. This requirement essentially equates to funding abortion-on-demand in light of the U.S. Supreme Court's broad definition of "health" in the context of abortion.

- State employee health insurance provides coverage of abortion only when a woman's life or health is endangered or in cases of rape, incest, or fetal abnormality. Further, it may not cover partial-birth abortions.

- Health maintenance organizations (HMOs) may not be required to provide payment or referrals for abortion unless necessary to preserve the woman's life.

LEGAL RECOGNITION AND PROTECTION OF THE UNBORN AND NEWLY BORN

- The Massachusetts Supreme Court has determined that the state's homicide law applies to the killing of an unborn child who has attained viability.

- Massachusetts allows a wrongful death (civil) action when a viable unborn child is killed through a negligent or criminal act.

- It requires healthcare professionals to report suspected prenatal drug exposure.

BIOETHICS LAWS

- While Massachusetts prohibits cloning to produce children, it expressly permits cloning for biomedical research and destructive embryo research, making it a "clone-and-kill" state.

- The Massachusetts Public Health Council has reversed a rule put in place during the gubernatorial administration of Mitt Romney that prohibited scientists from creating human embryos for the purpose of destroying them for research.

- Massachusetts funds destructive embryo research and allows tax credits for "life sciences" including "stem cell research."

- Massachusetts prohibits experimentation on live fetuses and allows experimentation on dead fetuses with consent of the parents.

- Massachusetts has established an umbilical cord-blood bank for the purpose of collecting and storing umbilical cord blood and placental tissues. All licensed hospitals are required to inform pregnant patients of the opportunity to donate the umbilical cord and placental tissue following delivery.

- Massachusetts requires informed consent before a physician can harvest human eggs for purposes of assisted reproductive technologies and prohibits the purchase of human eggs for "valuable consideration."

PATIENT PROTECTION LAWS

- In Massachusetts, suicide by physician remains a common law crime.

HEALTHCARE FREEDOM OF CONSCIENCE

PARTICIPATION IN ABORTION AND CONTRACEPTION

- A physician or person associated with, employed by, or on the medical staff of a hospital or health facility who objects in writing and on religious or moral grounds is not required to participate in abortions. Medical and nursing students are also protected.

- A private hospital or health facility is not required to admit a woman for an abortion.

- Health insurance plans that provide prescription coverage must also provide coverage for contraception. The provision includes a conscience exemption so narrow it excludes the ability of most employers and insurers with moral or religious objections from exercising the exemption.

PARTICIPATION IN RESEARCH HARMFUL TO HUMAN LIFE

- Massachusetts currently provides no protection for the rights of healthcare providers who conscientiously object to participation in human cloning, destructive embryo research, or other forms of medical research that violate a provider's moral or religious beliefs.

DID YOU KNOW?

- In 2018, Massachusetts considered legislation that would have prohibited abortion solely based on the sex of the unborn child as well as legislation that would have required physicians to "obtain written informed consent prior to performing abortions."

- Massachusetts also considered legislation that would prohibit the partial-birth abortion procedure.

WHAT HAPPENS AFTER *ROE* IS OVERTURNED?

- Abortion will be legal throughout pregnancy due to a state court decision.

RECOMMENDATIONS
Massachusetts

WOMEN'S PROTECTION PROJECT PRIORITIES

- Enhanced penalties and enforcement mechanisms for the state's abortion-related laws
- Women's Right to Know Act with reflection period
- Coercive Abuse Against Mothers Prevention Act
- Women's Health Protection Act (abortion clinic regulations)
- Drug-Induced Abortion Information and Reporting Act
- Parental Involvement Enhancement Act
- Child Protection Act

INFANTS' PROTECTION PROJECT PRIORITIES

- Unborn Infants Dignity Act
- Prenatal Nondiscrimination Act
- Perinatal Hospice Information Act
- Born-Alive Infant Protection Act
- Unborn Wrongful Death Act (for a pre-viable child)

PATIENT PROTECTION ACT PRIORITIES

- Joint Resolution Opposing Suicide by Physician
- Charlie Gard Act (formerly the Life Sustaining Care Act)
- Pain Medicine Education Act

ADDITIONAL PRIORITIES

ABORTION

- State Constitutional Amendment (providing that there is no state constitutional right to abortion)
- Defunding the Abortion Industry and Advancing Women's Health Act
- Federal Abortion-Mandate Opt-Out Act

LEGAL RECOGNITION AND PROTECTION FOR THE UNBORN

- Crimes Against the Unborn Child Act (to protect an unborn child from conception)
- Pregnant Woman's Protection Act

BIOETHICS

- Human Cloning Prohibition Act
- Destructive Embryo Research Act
- Prohibition on Public Funding of Human Cloning and Destructive Embryo Research Act

PATIENT PROTECTION

- Suicide by Physician Ban Act

HEALTHCARE FREEDOM OF CONSCIENCE

- Healthcare Freedom of Conscience Act

Michigan | RANKING: 9

Michigan has a solid record of protecting women and the unborn from the harms inherent in abortion including imposing medically appropriate health and safety standards on abortion facilities, regulating the provision of chemical abortions, and limiting taxpayer funding of abortion and abortion providers. However, its record on emerging biotechnologies is disappointing. Michigan specifically allows destructive embryo research and the funding of such research.

ABORTION

- Michigan possesses an enforceable abortion prohibition should the U.S. Constitution be amended or certain U.S. Supreme Court decisions be reversed or modified.

- A physician may not perform an abortion on an unemancipated minor under the age of 18 without the written consent of one parent unless there is a medical emergency or the minor obtains a court order.

- A physician may not perform an abortion on a woman until at least 24 hours after the woman receives information on the probable gestational age of her unborn child, along with state-prepared information or other material on prenatal care and parenting, the development of the unborn child, a description of abortion procedures and their inherent complications, and assistance and services available through public agencies.

- Women must be informed of the availability of ultrasounds and be given the opportunity to view the results of an ultrasound prior to abortion.

- Michigan prohibits partial-birth abortion.

- It is a criminal offense to coerce a woman to have an abortion against her will.

- A physician is required to screen patients for coercion before performing an abortion. The Department of Community Health has been instructed to develop a notice concerning coerced abortions which will be posted in abortion facilities.

- The Michigan Attorney General has issued opinions that the state's informed consent and parental consent statutes apply both to surgical abortions and to the use of mifepristone (RU-486).

- Under Michigan law, abortion clinics (where more than 50 percent of the patients served undergo abortions) are regulated as "freestanding surgical outpatient facilities." The applicable regulations provide for minimum health and safety standards in such areas as clinic administration, staff qualifications, and physical plant. Following the Supreme Court's decision in *Whole Woman's Health v. Hellerstedt*, Planned Parenthood challenged these health and safety standards.

- Michigan limits the performance of abortions to licensed physicians.

- Michigan has an enforceable abortion reporting law but does not require the reporting of information to the Centers for Disease Control and Prevention (CDC). The measure applies to both surgical and nonsurgical abortions and requires abortion providers to report short-term complications.

- Michigan requires that a woman be examined before a chemical abortion and specifically prohibits physicians from utilizing an internet web camera for such abortions. The physician must also be physically present when the drugs are dispensed.

- Michigan follows the federal standard for Medicaid funding for abortions, permitting the use of federal or state matching Medicaid funds for abortions necessary to preserve the life of the woman or when the pregnancy is the result of rape or incest.

- Michigan prohibits organizations that receive state funds from using those funds to provide abortion counseling or to make referrals for abortion and only permits ultrasound grants if they will not be used for assisting in the performance of elective abortions.

- Family planning funds are prioritized for organizations which do not perform elective abortions within a facility owned or operated by the organization, make referrals for abortions, or have written policies which consider abortion a method of family planning.

- Insurance companies participating in the state insurance Exchanges established pursuant to the federal healthcare law cannot offer policies that provide abortion coverage.

- Michigan prohibits insurance plans from covering abortions except by optional rider.

- In 2014, Michigan allocated $800,000 for a pregnancy and parenting support services program, which must provide childbirth, alternatives to abortion, and grief counseling.

LEGAL RECOGNITION AND PROTECTION OF THE UNBORN AND NEWLY BORN

- Under Michigan law, the killing of an unborn child at any stage of gestation is defined as a form of homicide.

- Michigan defines a criminal assault on a pregnant woman that results in miscarriage, stillbirth, or "damage to pregnancy" as an enhanced offense for sentencing purposes.

- Michigan defines a nonfatal assault on an unborn child as a crime.

- Michigan has applied the affirmative defense of "defense of others" to cases where a woman uses force (including deadly force) to protect her unborn child.

- It allows a wrongful death (civil) action when an unborn child at any stage of development is killed through a negligent or criminal act.

- Michigan has created a specific affirmative duty of physicians to provide medical care and treatment to infants born alive at any stage of development.

- Michigan requires healthcare professionals to report suspected prenatal drug exposure.

BIOETHICS LAWS

- In November 2008, Michigan voters passed a Stem Cell Initiative, amending the state constitution to legalize destructive embryo research and to allow the funding of research on human embryos.

- Michigan prohibits experimentation on live fetuses, but allows research on dead fetuses with the consent of the mother.

- The Michigan Legislature has directed the establishment of a state-wide network of cord blood stem-cell banks and the promotion of public awareness and knowledge about the banks and banking options (as funds are available).

- Michigan does not maintain any meaningful regulation of assisted reproductive technologies or human egg harvesting.

PATIENT PROTECTION LAWS

- In Michigan, suicide by physician is a felony.

HEALTHCARE FREEDOM OF CONSCIENCE

PARTICIPATION IN ABORTION

- A physician, nurse, medical student, nursing student, or individual who is a member of, associated with, or employed by a hospital, institution, teaching institution, or healthcare facility who objects on religious, moral, ethical, or professional grounds is not required to participate in abortions.

- A hospital, institution, teaching institution, or healthcare facility is not required to participate in abortion, permit an abortion on its premises, or admit a woman for the purpose of performing an abortion.

PARTICIPATION IN RESEARCH HARMFUL TO HUMAN LIFE

- Michigan currently provides no protection for the rights of healthcare providers who conscientiously object to participating in human cloning, destructive embryo research, or other forms of medical research that violate a provider's moral or religious beliefs.

DID YOU KNOW?

- In 2018, Michigan considered legislation that would have required a disclosure for vaccinations that contain aborted fetal tissue.

- Michigan also considered legislation that would require all pharmacies to stock over-the-counter and prescription emergency contraception and provide it with no exception for religious or conscience objections.

WHAT HAPPENS AFTER *ROE* IS OVERTURNED?

- Abortion will not be legal, except to save the life of the mother, based on existing law enacted before *Roe*.

RECOMMENDATIONS
for Michigan

WOMEN'S PROTECTION PROJECT PRIORITIES

- Enhanced penalties and enforcement mechanisms for the state's abortion-related laws
- Drug-Induced Abortion Information and Reporting Act
- Parental Involvement Enhancement Act
- Child Protection Act

INFANTS' PROTECTION PROJECT PRIORITIES

- Unborn Infants Dignity Act
- Prenatal Nondiscrimination Act
- Perinatal Hospice Information Act

PATIENT PROTECTION ACT PRIORITIES

- Joint Resolution Opposing Suicide by Physician
- Charlie Gard Act (formerly the Life Sustaining Care Act)
- Pain Medicine Education Act

ADDITIONAL PRIORITIES

ABORTION

- Defunding the Abortion Industry and Advancing Women's Health Act
- Federal Abortion-Mandate Opt-Out Act

BIOETHICS

- Repeal of constitutional amendment permitting and funding destructive embryo research
- Promotion of ethical forms of research
- Assisted Reproductive Technologies Disclosure and Risk Reduction Act

HEALTHCARE FREEDOM OF CONSCIENCE

- Healthcare Freedom of Conscience Act

Minnesota | RANKING: 29

Although the Minnesota Constitution has been interpreted to protect abortion to a greater extent than that interpreted in the U.S. Constitution, Minnesota has made some meaningful progress toward protecting women and unborn children. For example, it requires informed consent before abortion that includes information on the abortion-breast cancer link, as well as information about perinatal hospice options for families facing life-limiting diagnoses.

ABORTION

- The Minnesota Constitution protects the "right to an abortion" as a fundamental right and to a greater extent than that interpreted in the U.S. Constitution.

- Minnesota's informed consent law requires that a woman be given information on the risks of and alternatives to abortion at least 24 hours prior to undergoing an abortion.

- Minnesota requires a physician or his or her agent to advise a woman seeking an abortion after 5 months (i.e., 20 weeks) gestation of the possibility that anesthesia will alleviate fetal pain.

- It also explicitly requires a physician to inform a woman seeking abortion of the abortion-breast cancer link.

- Minnesota maintains a law prohibiting coerced abortions, defining "coercion" as "restraining or dominating the choice of a minor female by force, threat of force, or deprivation of food and shelter." The provision is applied to older women, but only pertains only to employees in government-run social programs.

- Minnesota law provides that a physician may not perform an abortion on an unemancipated minor under the age of 18 until at least 48 hours after written notice has been delivered to both parents (except if one cannot be found after a reasonable effort) unless one of the following applies: the minor is the victim of rape, incest, or child abuse which must be reported; there is a medical emergency; or the minor obtains a court order.

- Minnesota requires that abortions after the first trimester be performed in a hospital or "abortion facility."

- Only physicians licensed to practice medicine by the State of Minnesota or physicians-in-training supervised by licensed physicians may perform abortions.

- The state has an enforceable abortion reporting law but does not require the reporting of information to the Centers for Disease Control and Prevention (CDC). The measure applies to both surgical and nonsurgical abortions and requires abortion providers to report short-term complications.

- The Minnesota Care public insurance program prohibits public funds from being used to cover abortions except when the mother's life is in danger, she faces a serious health risk, or in cases of rape or incest. However, Minnesota taxpayers are required by court order to fund "medically necessary" abortions for women eligible for public assistance. This requirement essentially equates to funding abortion-on-demand in light of the U.S. Supreme Court's broad definition of "health" in the context of abortion.

- Minnesota prohibits the award of special grants to any non-profit corporation that performs abortions. Further, grantees may not provide state funds to any non-profit corporation that performs abortions.

- Pregnancy alternative grants may not be used to encourage or affirmatively counsel a woman to have an abortion that is not necessary to prevent her death, to provide her with an abortion, or to directly refer her to an abortion provider for an abortion.

LEGAL RECOGNITION AND PROTECTION OF THE UNBORN AND NEWLY BORN

- Under Minnesota law, the killing of an unborn child at any stage of gestation is defined as a form of homicide.

- Minnesota has established a penalty for injuring an unborn child as a result of operating a motor vehicle in a grossly negligent manner or while under the influence of alcohol or drugs.

- Minnesota defines a nonfatal assault on an unborn child as a criminal offense.

- Minnesota allows a wrongful death (civil) action when a viable unborn child is killed through a negligent or criminal act.

- It has created a specific affirmative duty of physicians to provide medical care and treatment to infants born alive after attaining viability.

- Minnesota has a "Baby Moses" law allowing emergency service personnel to accept a relinquished infant who is seven days old or younger.

- A court may order a pregnant woman into an early intervention treatment program for substance abuse.

- Professionals, such as healthcare providers and law enforcement officers, must report suspected abuse of a controlled substance by pregnant women. In addition, healthcare professionals must test newborns for exposure when there is suspicion of prenatal drug use.

- Minnesota also funds drug treatment programs for pregnant women and newborns.

BIOETHICS LAWS

- Minnesota does not explicitly prohibit human cloning or destructive embryo research.

- In 2011, it allowed a former prohibition on the funding of human cloning to expire.

- Minnesota prohibits experimentation on a "living human conceptus," meaning that experimentation on an aborted fetus is not prohibited.

- Minnesota does not promote ethical alternatives to destructive embryo research.

- It maintains no meaningful regulation of assisted reproductive technologies or human egg harvesting.

PATIENT PROTECTION LAWS

- In Minnesota, suicide by physician is a felony.

HEALTHCARE FREEDOM OF CONSCIENCE

PARTICIPATION IN ABORTION

- Minnesota law provides that no person, hospital, or institution may be coerced, held liable for, or discriminated against in any way for refusing to perform, accommodate, or assist in an abortion. However, this provision has been held unconstitutional as applied to public hospitals and institutions.

- State employees may refuse to provide family planning services if contrary to their personal beliefs.

- Health plan companies and healthcare cooperatives are not required to provide abortions or coverage of abortions.

PARTICIPATION IN RESEARCH HARMFUL TO HUMAN LIFE

- Minnesota currently provides no protection for the rights of healthcare providers who conscientiously object to participation in human cloning, destructive embryo research, or other forms of medical research that violate a provider's moral or religious beliefs.

DID YOU KNOW?

- In 2017 Minnesota Governor Mark Dayton vetoed legislation that would have ended taxpayer funding of abortion in the state.

- He also vetoed legislation that would have required abortion clinics to meet basic licensing requirements before performing abortions.

- In 2018, Minnesota considered bills that would "prohibit use of aborted fetal tissue for research" and prohibit the University of Minnesota "from funding fellowships related to abortion training, advocacy, or education."

WHAT HAPPENS AFTER *ROE* IS OVERTURNED?

- Abortion will be legal throughout pregnancy due to a state court decision.

RECOMMENDATIONS
for Minnesota

WOMEN'S PROTECTION PROJECT PRIORITIES

- Enhanced penalties and enforcement mechanisms for the state's abortion-related laws
- Women's Health Protection Act (abortion clinic regulations)
- Drug-Induced Abortion Information and Reporting Act
- Parental Consent for Abortion Act
- Parental Involvement Enhancement Act
- Child Protection Act

INFANTS' PROTECTION PROJECT PRIORITIES

- Unborn Infants Dignity Act
- Prenatal Nondiscrimination Act
- Unborn Wrongful Death Act (for a pre-viable child)

PATIENT PROTECTION ACT PRIORITIES

- Joint Resolution Opposing Suicide by Physician
- Charlie Gard Act (formerly the Life Sustaining Care Act)
- Pain Medicine Education Act

ADDITIONAL PRIORITIES

ABORTION

- State Constitutional Amendment (providing that there is no state constitutional right to abortion)
- Defunding the Abortion Industry and Advancing Women's Health Act
- Federal Abortion-Mandate Opt-Out Act

LEGAL RECOGNITION AND PROTECTION FOR THE UNBORN

- Pregnant Woman's Protection Act

BIOETHICS

- Human Cloning Prohibition Act
- Destructive Embryo Research Act
- Prohibition on Public Funding of Human Cloning and Destructive Embryo Research Act

HEALTHCARE FREEDOM OF CONSCIENCE

- Healthcare Freedom of Conscience Act

Mississippi | RANKING: 7

Over the last several years, AUL has worked with Mississippi to enact numerous life-affirming laws including its ban on abortions at or after 20 weeks, its informed consent law, and comprehensive protection for Healthcare Freedom of Conscience. However, it lags behind some other states in regulating emerging biotechnologies and failing to prohibit human cloning, destructive embryo research, or fetal experimentation.

ABORTION

- In *Pro-Choice Mississippi v. Fordice*, the Mississippi Supreme Court found that the state constitution's right of privacy includes "an implicit right to have an abortion." However, the court still upheld the state's informed consent law, 24-hour reflection period before an abortion, and a two-parent consent requirement before a minor may obtain an abortion.

- Mississippi has enacted legislation prohibiting abortion (except in cases of life endangerment) should *Roe v. Wade* be overturned.

- Mississippi limits abortions at 5 months (i.e., 20 weeks), on the basis of the health risks to women caused by a later-term abortion and the pain to the unborn child.

- In 2018, Mississippi passed legislation that prohibits abortions after 15 weeks gestation "except in medical emergency and in cases of severe fetal abnormality." The law is enjoined and in ongoing litigation.

- Mississippi prohibits the dismemberment abortion procedure.

- Mississippi prohibits partial-birth abortion.

- A physician may not perform an abortion on a woman until at least 24 hours after the woman receives counseling on the medical risks of abortion including the link between abortion and breast cancer, the medical risks of carrying the pregnancy to term, the probable gestational age of the unborn child, medical assistance benefits, and the legal obligations of the child's father. Mississippi also provides written material describing the development of the unborn child, the medical risks of abortion, available state benefits, and public and private agencies offering alternatives to abortion.

- In addition, an abortion provider is required to perform an ultrasound on a woman seeking an abortion. The woman must be offered the opportunity to view the ultrasound image, receive a copy of the image, and listen to the unborn child's heartbeat. Abortion facilities must purchase ultrasound equipment.

- An abortion provider must inform a woman seeking abortion at or after 5 months (i.e., 20 week) because of her unborn child's life-limiting diagnosis of certain supportive services available to her should she decide to carry the child to term. These services include counseling and care from maternal-fetal medical specialists, obstetricians, neonatologists, anesthesia specialists, clergy, social workers, and specialty nurses who focus on alleviating fear and ensuring that the woman and her family experience the life and death of their child in a comfortable and supportive environment.

- A physician may not perform an abortion on an unemancipated minor under the age of 18 without the written consent of both parents unless there is a medical emergency, the minor is the victim of incest by her father (in such circumstances, the consent of the minor's mother is sufficient), or the minor obtains a court order. The two-parent consent requirement has been upheld by both a federal appellate court and the Mississippi Supreme Court.

- Mississippi mandates minimum health and safety regulations for abortion clinics performing more than ten abortions per month and/or more than 100 abortions per year. The regulations prescribe minimum health and safety standards for the building or facility, clinic administration, staffing, and pre-procedure medical evaluations.

- Mississippi requires that second-trimester abortions be performed in hospitals, ambulatory surgical facilities, or a licensed Level I abortion facility (as defined by state statute).

- Mississippi requires abortion providers to maintain hospital admitting privileges. The law is permanently enjoined.

- Mississippi law requires physicians to be board certified in obstetrics and gynecology.

- The Abortion Complication Reporting Act requires abortion providers to report any incident in which a woman dies or needs further medical treatment as a result of an abortion. The measure applies to both surgical and nonsurgical abortions and requires hospitals to report the number of patients treated for complications resulting from abortions.

- Mississippi also requires that deaths resulting from criminal abortions, self-induced abortions, or abortions performed because of sexual abuse be reported to the medical examiner.

- Mississippi includes "reproductive healthcare facilities" in the definition of mandatory reporters for suspected child sexual abuse.

- It requires that a physician examine a woman before providing drug-induced abortion. Further, the physician must follow "the standard of care" and the provider or his/her agent must also schedule a follow-up appointment for the woman.

- Mississippi funds abortions for women eligible for public assistance when necessary to preserve the woman's life, the pregnancy is the result of rape or incest, or in cases involving fetal abnormalities.

- No money in the Mississippi Children's Trust Fund, established to assist child abuse and neglect programs, may be used for abortion counseling.

- Mississippi restricts the use of state facilities for the performance of abortions.

- Public school nurses are prohibited from providing abortion counseling or referring any student to abortion counseling or an abortion clinic.

- Insurance companies participating in the state insurance Exchanges, established pursuant to the federal healthcare law, cannot offer policies that provide abortion coverage within the Exchanges, except in cases of life endangerment, rape, or incest.

- Health insurance funds for state employees may not be used for insurance coverage of abortion unless an abortion is necessary to preserve the life or physical health of the mother.

- Mississippi offers "Choose Life" and "We Love Life" specialty license plates, the proceeds of which benefit pregnancy resource centers and/or other organizations providing abortion alternatives.

LEGAL RECOGNITION AND PROTECTION OF THE UNBORN AND NEWLY BORN

- The killing of an unborn child at any stage of gestation is a form of homicide.

- Mississippi defines a nonfatal assault on an unborn child as a criminal offense.

- Further, Mississippi law also provides that an attack on a pregnant woman resulting in a stillbirth or miscarriage is a criminal assault.

- Mississippi authorizes a wrongful death (civil) action when an unborn child (after quickening) is killed through violence or negligence.

- It has created a specific affirmative duty of physicians to provide medical care and treatment to infants born alive at any stage of development.

- Mississippi law protects the anonymity of the parent relinquishing a newborn under the state's infant abandonment statute.

BIOETHICS LAWS

- Mississippi maintains no laws regarding human cloning, destructive embryo research, fetal experimentation, assisted reproductive technologies, or human egg harvesting.

- It promotes ethical forms of research through an umbilical cord blood banking program.

- In each of the last four years, Mississippi has enacted appropriations measures prohibiting state funds from being used in research in which a human embryo is killed or destroyed.

PATIENT PROTECTION LAWS

- In Mississippi, suicide by physician is a felony.

- Mississippi has created a Physicians Orders for Life-Sustaining Treatment (POLST) Paradigm program.

HEALTHCARE FREEDOM OF CONSCIENCE

PARTICIPATION IN ABORTION

- The Mississippi Healthcare Rights of Conscience Act, based on AUL model legislation, provides comprehensive freedom of conscience protection for healthcare providers, institutions, and insurance companies (including pharmacists and pharmacies) who conscientiously object to participating in any healthcare service including abortion.

PARTICIPATION IN RESEARCH HARMFUL TO HUMAN LIFE

- Mississippi protects the civil rights of all healthcare providers who conscientiously object to participating in any healthcare services, including destructive embryo research and human cloning.

DID YOU KNOW?

- In 2018, Mississippi passed a bill that prohibits abortions after 15 weeks of gestation. The law is enjoined and in ongoing litigation.

- Mississippi considered legislation that would have prohibited abortion based on a prenatal diagnosis of Down syndrome.

- Planned Parenthood has challenged the cumulative impact of the abortion regulations in the state. Litigation is ongoing.

WHAT HAPPENS AFTER *ROE* IS OVERTURNED?

- Mississippi has a law, conditioned on *Roe* being overturned, that makes abortion illegal, which may be enforceable. If not, abortion will be legal up to 20 weeks of pregnancy.

RECOMMENDATIONS
for Mississippi

WOMEN'S PROTECTION PROJECT PRIORITIES

- Enhanced penalties and enforcement mechanisms for the state's abortion-related laws
- Drug-Induced Abortion Information and Reporting Act
- Parental Involvement Enhancement Act
- Component of the Child Protection Act providing remedies for third-party interference with parental rights

INFANTS' PROTECTION PROJECT PRIORITIES

- Unborn Infants Dignity Act
- Prenatal Nondiscrimination Act
- Unborn Wrongful Death Act (for a pre-viable child)

PATIENT PROTECTION ACT PRIORITIES

- Joint Resolution Opposing Suicide by Physician
- Charlie Gard Act (formerly the Life Sustaining Care Act)
- Pain Medicine Education Act

ADDITIONAL PRIORITIES

ABORTION

- State Constitutional Amendment (providing that there is no state constitutional right to abortion)
- Prenatal Nondiscrimination Act

LEGAL RECOGNITION AND PROTECTION FOR THE UNBORN

- Pregnant Woman's Protection Act

BIOETHICS

- Human Cloning Prohibition Act
- Destructive Embryo Research Act
- Prohibition on Public Funding of Human Cloning and Destructive Embryo Research Act

Missouri | RANKING: 11

Missouri has been a leader in protecting women and their children from the harms inherent in abortion. It maintains comprehensive informed consent and parental involvement require-ments, regulates the provision of drug-induced abortion, and has some of the most stringent limits on abortion funding in the nation. However, the state provides little protection to human embryos outside the womb, having amended its state constitution to allow cloning for biomedical research.

ABORTION

- The Missouri Legislature has found that the life of each human being begins at conception.

- As applied to its abortion-related laws, Missouri maintains a narrow definition of "medical emergency." A medical emergency is found to exist only in situations where a woman's life or a "major bodily function" is at risk.

- Missouri prohibits partial-birth abortion.

- Missouri has a post-viability abortion ban that allows an abortion only when the life of the mother is endangered by a physical disorder, physical illness, or physical injury, including a life-endangering physical condition caused by or arising from the pregnancy itself, or when continuation of the pregnancy will create a serious risk of substantial and irreversible physical impairment of a major bodily function of the pregnant woman. The law also requires a determination of gestational age according to specified standards, includes specific reporting requirements, and requires a second physician to concur that an abortion is "medically necessary."

- At least 72 hours prior to abortion, a woman must be advised of the risks of abortion, given informa-tion about the development of her unborn child, and provided information on resources available to assist her in bringing her child to term. The law also requires that she be informed that abortion ends the "life of a separate, unique, living human being." This law is in ongoing litigation.

- Women seeking abortions at or after 22 weeks gestation must be counseled on fetal pain.

- Abortion providers must offer an ultrasound to every woman seeking an abortion.

- An abortion facility must provide a woman with confidential access to a telephone and a list of protective resources if she indicates that she is being coerced by a third party into seeking an abortion.

- A physician may not perform an abortion on an unemancipated minor under the age of 18 without the informed, written consent of one parent or a court order. Further, only a parent or guardian can transport a minor across state lines for an abortion.

- Missouri requires abortion facilities to meet the same health and safety standards as facilities performing other surgeries in an ambulatory setting, including regulations prescribing the physical design and layout for facilities that perform surgical abortions and a requirement that abortion providers at ambulatory surgical centers have privileges to perform surgical procedures at a licensed hospital in the community. These two regulations are in ongoing litigation.

- Missouri requires annual, on-site and unannounced inspections of abortion clinics.

- Only physicians licensed by the state, practicing in Missouri, and having surgical privileges at a hospital within a 30-mile radius of the facility where the abortion is performed and that offers obstetrical or gynecological care may perform abortions. The Eighth Circuit has upheld this requirement.

- Missouri law provides that no person shall perform or induce a "medical abortion" unless such person has proof of medical malpractice insurance with coverage amounts of at least $500,000.

- Missouri has an enforceable abortion reporting law but does not require the reporting of information to the Centers for Disease Control and Prevention (CDC). The measure applies to both surgical and nonsurgical abortions and requires abortion providers to report short-term complications.

- Missouri requires that the initial dose in an abortion-inducing drug regimen be administered in the presence of a physician. The physician or an agent of the physician must also make all reasonable efforts to ensure that the woman comes back for a follow-up appointment. This case is in ongoing litigation.

- Missouri follows the federal standard for Medicaid funding for abortions, permitting the use of federal or state matching Medicaid funds for abortions necessary to preserve the life of the woman or when the pregnancy is the result of rape or incest.

- Missouri law provides that it is unlawful for any public funds to be expended for the purpose of performing or assisting an abortion not necessary to save the life of the mother or for the purpose of encouraging or counseling a woman to have an abortion not necessary to save her life.

- It has an extensive list of additional limitations on abortion funding including the following: public facilities may not be used for performing, assisting in, or counseling a woman on abortion unless it is necessary to preserve her life; a state employee may not participate in an abortion; no school district or charter school or personnel or agents of these schools may provide abortion services or permit instruction by providers of abortion services; family planning services may not include abortions unless it is certified by a physician that the life of the mother is in danger; Missouri Alternatives to Abortions Services Program funding may not be granted to organizations or affiliates of organizations that perform or induce, assist in the performance or induction of, or refer for abortions; research grants may not be used in research projects that involve abortion services, human cloning, or prohibited human research and cannot share costs with another prohibited study; and no money from the legal expense fund may be used to defend abortion.

- Insurance companies participating in the state insurance Exchanges established pursuant to the federal healthcare law cannot offer policies that provide abortion coverage, except in cases of life endangerment.

- Private health insurance policies are prohibited from including coverage for abortion unless an abortion is necessary to preserve the life of the woman or an optional rider is purchased. Missouri also prohibits abortion coverage for state employees except in cases of life endangerment. Further, Missouri protects individual and group insurance consumers from paying for insurance coverage that violates their moral or religious beliefs.

- State health insurance for uninsured children cannot be used to encourage, counsel, or refer for abortions, with exceptions for life endangerment or in cases of rape or incest.

- Missouri provides direct taxpayer funding to pregnancy resource centers and prohibits organizations that receive this funding from using those funds to provide abortion counseling or to make referrals for abortion.

- Missouri also provides tax credits for donations to pregnancy resource centers that do not perform or refer women for abortions.

- Missouri has appropriated federal and state funds for women "at or below 200 percent of the Federal Poverty Level" to be used to encourage women to carry their pregnancies to term, to pay for adoption expenses, and/or to assist with caring for dependent children.

LEGAL RECOGNITION AND PROTECTION OF THE UNBORN AND NEWLY BORN

- Under Missouri law, the killing of an unborn child at any stage of development is defined as a form of homicide.

- Missouri has enacted AUL's Pregnant Woman's Protection Act, which provides an affirmative defense to women who use force to protect their unborn children from criminal assaults.

- It allows a wrongful death (civil) action when an unborn child at any stage of development is killed through a negligent or criminal act.

- Missouri has created a specific affirmative duty of physicians to provide medical care and treatment to infants born alive at any stage of development.

- Missouri has a "Baby Moses" law, establishing a safe haven for mothers to legally leave their infants at designated places and ensuring that the infants receive appropriate care and protection.

- It funds drug treatment programs for pregnant women and newborns.

BIOETHICS LAWS

- In November 2006, Missouri voters approved a ballot initiative amending the state constitution to allow cloning for biomedical research (while banning cloning to produce children) and destructive embryo research. This constitutional amendment may mean that the state's ban on public funding relates only to cloning-to-produce-children, making it a "clone-and-kill" state.

- Missouri's prohibition on fetal experimentation applies only to a fetus aborted alive.

- Missouri has created a program funding the establishment of umbilical cord blood banks. The state Department of Health and Senior Services is required to post resources regarding umbilical cord blood on its website including information on the potential value and uses of cord blood. State law authorizes a licensed physician giving care to a pregnant woman to provide information about this website.

- Missouri maintains no laws regarding assisted reproductive technologies or human egg harvesting.

PATIENT PROTECTION LAWS

- In Missouri, suicide by physician constitutes manslaughter.

- Missouri has established a Missouri Palliative Care and Quality of Life Interdisciplinary Council, in order to improve quality and delivery of patient-centered and family-focused care. Missouri also established a "Palliative Care Consumer and Professional Information and Education Program" with a stated purpose of maximizing the effectiveness of palliative care and ensuring that comprehensive and accurate information about palliative care is available to the public, healthcare providers, and healthcare facilities.

HEALTHCARE FREEDOM OF CONSCIENCE

PARTICIPATION IN ABORTION

- A physician, nurse, midwife, or hospital is not required to admit or treat a woman for the purpose of abortion if such admission or treatment is contrary to religious, moral, or ethical beliefs or established policy. Protection is also provided to medical and nursing students.

- A law requiring insurance coverage for obstetrical and gynecological care provides: "Nothing in this chapter shall be construed to require a health carrier to perform, induce, pay for, reimburse, guarantee, arrange, provide any resources for, or refer a patient for an abortion."

PARTICIPATION IN RESEARCH HARMFUL TO HUMAN LIFE

- Missouri currently provides no protection for the rights of healthcare providers who conscientiously object to participation in human cloning, destructive embryo research, or other forms of medical research that violate a provider's moral or religious beliefs.

DID YOU KNOW?

- Missouri passed legislation requiring, among other provisions, annual inspections of abortion clinics, informed consent provisions for women considering abortion, and mandating that abortion clinics have emergency measures in place to handle complications from abortion procedures. Portions of the law have been challenged in litigation.

- In 2018, Missouri considered various legislation that would have prohibited abortions based on the sex, race, or diagnosis of genetic abnormality of the unborn child, prohibited a person from transporting a minor across state lines to obtain an abortion with appropriate consent required by law, and prohibited abortions at or after 5 months (i.e., 20 weeks) on the basis of the pain experienced by unborn children.

WHAT HAPPENS AFTER *ROE* IS OVERTURNED?

- Abortion will be legal up to viability.

RECOMMENDATIONS
for Missouri

WOMEN'S PROTECTION PROJECT PRIORITIES

- Enhanced penalties and enforcement mechanisms for the state's abortion-related laws
- Drug-Induced Abortion Information and Reporting Act
- Component of the Child Protection Act mandating evidence retention

INFANTS' PROTECTION ACT PRIORITIES

- Unborn Infants Dignity Act
- Prenatal Nondiscrimination Act
- Perinatal Hospice Information Act

PATIENT PROTECTION ACT PRIORITIES

- Joint Resolution Opposing Suicide by Physician
- Charlie Gard Act (formerly the Life Sustaining Care Act)
- Pain Medicine Education Act

ADDITIONAL PRIORITIES

ABORTION

- Defunding the Abortion Industry and Advancing Women's Health Act

LEGAL RECOGNITION AND PROTECTION FOR THE UNBORN

- Law criminalizing nonfatal assaults on the unborn

BIOETHICS

- Assisted Reproductive Technologies Disclosure and Risk Reduction Act

HEALTHCARE FREEDOM OF CONSCIENCE

- Healthcare Freedom of Conscience Act

Montana | RANKING: 40

Montana state courts have held that the state constitution provides a broader "right" to abortion than that interpreted in the federal constitution, making it difficult for the state to enact comprehensive, commonsense regulations that protect maternal health.

ABORTION

- State courts have held that the Montana Constitution provides a broader right to abortion than that interpreted in the U.S. Constitution. Under the auspices of these decisions, several state laws have been declared unconstitutional, including laws limiting taxpayer funding for abortions, requiring parental notice prior to a minor undergoing an abortion, requiring a 24-hour reflection period prior to an abortion, mandating that state-prepared informed consent information be offered to a woman prior to an abortion, and requiring that only a licensed physician perform an abortion.

- Montana prohibits partial-birth abortion performed after viability.

- Montana requires one parent be notified 48 hours in advance if the minor seeking the abortion is under 16. In 2013, the state passed a law requiring notarized written consent of a parent or legal guardian as well as proof of identification and relationship. The written consent requirement is permanently enjoined.

- A Montana law requires that licensed physicians or physician assistants perform abortions. It is one of a small minority of states that do not limit the performance of abortions to only licensed physicians. The law is enjoined and in ongoing litigation.

- Montana has an enforceable abortion reporting law but does not require the reporting of information to the Centers for Disease Control and Prevention (CDC). The measure applies to both surgical and nonsurgical abortions.

- Montana taxpayers are required by court order to fund "medically necessary" abortions for women eligible for public assistance. This requirement essentially equates to funding abortion-on-demand in light of the U.S. Supreme Court's broad definition of "health" in the context of abortion.

- Montana offers "Choose Life" license plates, the proceeds of which benefit pregnancy resource centers and/or other organizations providing abortion alternatives.

- Montana maintains a Freedom of Clinic Access (FACE) law, making it a crime to block access to an abortion facility and restricting how close sidewalk counselors and demonstrators can be to the facility.

LEGAL RECOGNITION AND PROTECTION OF THE UNBORN AND NEWLY BORN

- Montana permits the prosecution of a third party who intentionally kills an unborn child who has reached at least eight weeks development.

- Under Montana law, a person commits an offense if he "purposefully, knowingly, or negligently causes the death of a premature infant born alive, if such infant is viable."

- Montana allows a wrongful death (civil) action when a viable unborn child is killed through a negligent or criminal act.

- It has created a specific affirmative duty of physicians to provide medical care and treatment to infants born alive at any stage of development.

- Montana has a "Baby Moses" law, establishing a safe haven for mothers to legally leave their infants at designated places and ensuring the infants receive appropriate care and protection.

- Specific professionals are required to report any infant affected by drug exposure.

- Montana maintains a measure allowing a woman who loses a child after 20 weeks gestation to obtain a Certificate of Birth Resulting in Stillbirth.

BIOETHICS LAWS

- Montana only prohibits cloning to produce children, making it a "clone-and-kill" state since it does not prohibit cloning-for-research.

- Montana does not prohibit destructive embryo research, and its prohibition on fetal experimentation applies only to children born alive (i.e., it does not apply to aborted fetuses).

- Montana does not promote ethical forms of research.

- It maintains no meaningful regulation of assisted reproductive technologies or human egg harvesting.

PATIENT PROTECTION LAWS

- The Montana Supreme Court has stated that it finds nothing in Montana Supreme Court precedent or state statutes indicating that suicide by physician is against public policy—thus potentially paving the way for suicide by physician in the state.

HEALTHCARE FREEDOM OF CONSCIENCE

PARTICIPATION IN ABORTION AND CONTRACEPTION

- On the basis of religious or moral beliefs, an individual, partnership, association, or corporation may refuse to participate in an abortion or to provide advice concerning abortion.

- A private hospital or healthcare facility is not required, contrary to religious or moral tenets, stated religious beliefs, or moral convictions, to admit a woman for an abortion or to permit the use of its facilities for an abortion.

- Montana has a "contraceptive equity" requirement, meaning that health insurance coverage must include coverage for contraception. There is no conscience exemption for employers or insurers with a religious or moral objection to contraception.

PARTICIPATION IN RESEARCH HARMFUL TO HUMAN LIFE

- Montana currently provides no protection for the rights of healthcare providers who conscientiously object to participation in human cloning, destructive embryo research, or other forms of medical research that violate a provider's moral or religious beliefs.

DID YOU KNOW?

- In 2017, the Montana legislature passed a bill that would prohibit abortions at or after 5 months (i.e., 20 weeks) on the basis of the pain experienced by unborn children. However, this was vetoed by the Governor.

- Additionally, Montana passed a bill that included a requirement abortion providers document information such as the gestational age and vital signs of the fetus after the abortion procedure. However, this was also vetoed by the Governor.

WHAT HAPPENS AFTER *ROE* IS OVERTURNED?

- Abortion will be legal up to at least viability due to a state court decision.

RECOMMENDATIONS
for Montana

WOMEN'S PROTECTION PROJECT PRIORITIES

- Enhanced penalties and enforcement mechanisms for the state's abortion-related laws
- Women's Right to Know Act with reflection period
- Coercive Abuse Against Mothers Prevention Act
- Women's Health Protection Act (abortion clinic regulations)
- Drug-Induced Abortion Information and Reporting Act
- Parental Involvement Enhancement Act
- Child Protection Act

INFANTS' PROTECTION PROJECT PRIORITIES

- Unborn Infants Dignity Act
- Prenatal Nondiscrimination Act
- Perinatal Hospice Information Act
- Unborn Wrongful Death Act

PATIENT PROTECTION ACT PRIORITIES

- Suicide by Physician Ban Act
- Joint Resolution Opposing Suicide by Physician
- Charlie Gard Act (formerly the Life Sustaining Care Act)
- Pain Medicine Education Act

ADDITIONAL PRIORITIES

ABORTION

- State constitutional amendment (providing that there is no state constitutional right to abortion)
- Defunding the Abortion Industry and Advancing Women's Health Act
- Federal Abortion-Mandate Opt-Out Act

LEGAL RECOGNITION AND PROTECTION FOR THE UNBORN

- Crimes Against the Unborn Child Act (to protect a child from conception)
- Pregnant Woman's Protection Act

BIOETHICS

- Human Cloning Prohibition Act
- Destructive Embryo Research Act
- Prohibition on Public Funding of Human Cloning and Destructive Embryo Research Act

PATIENT PROTECTION

- Suicide by Physician Ban Act

HEALTHCARE FREEDOM OF CONSCIENCE

- Healthcare Freedom of Conscience Act

Nebraska | RANKING: 10

Nebraska maintains a number of laws and regulations protecting women and unborn children, including a limitation on abortion at 5 months (i.e., 20 weeks) development, a prohibition on "webcam abortions," and a law defining the killing of an unborn child at any stage of gestation as homicide.

ABORTION

- Nebraska prohibits abortions at or after 5 months (i.e., 20 weeks) on the basis of the pain experienced by unborn children.

- Under Nebraska law, a physician may not perform an abortion on a woman until at least 24 hours after counseling the woman on the risks of abortion, the risks of continued pregnancy, and the probable gestational age of the unborn child. Nebraska also provides materials describing the development of the unborn child, the medical and psychological risks of abortion, available state benefits, and public and private agencies offering alternatives to abortion.

- The provision of informed consent and state-prepared materials must include information on perinatal hospice. In 2017, Nebraska passed the Perinatal Hospice Information Act, based on AUL model legislation, which requires that provision of informed consent and state-prepared materials include information on perinatal hospice.

- An abortion provider who conducts an ultrasound prior to performing an abortion must display the ultrasound image of the unborn child so that the woman may see it.

- Nebraska prohibits coercing a woman to have an abortion and provides that such coercion is a Class III misdemeanor.

- A physician may not perform an abortion on an unemancipated minor under the age of 18 without the written, notarized consent of one parent, unless there is a medical emergency or the minor obtains a court order. If the minor is a victim of rape, incest, or abuse by a parent, she may obtain the consent of a grandparent.

- Nebraska mandates minimum health and safety standards for abortion facilities which, at any point during a calendar year, perform ten or more abortions during a single calendar week. The regulations prescribe medically appropriate standards for the building or facility, staffing, and medical testing of clinic employees.

- Only physicians licensed by the State of Nebraska may perform abortions.

- Nebraska has an enforceable abortion reporting law but does not require the reporting of information to the Centers for Disease Control and Prevention (CDC). The measure applies to both surgical and nonsurgical abortions and requires abortion providers to report short-term complications.

- Nebraska prohibits so-called "webcam abortions" by requiring that a physician be present in the same room with a patient when he/she performs, induces, or attempts to perform or induce an abortion.

- Nebraska follows the federal standard for Medicaid funding for abortions, permitting the use of federal or state matching Medicaid funds for abortions necessary to preserve the life of the woman or when the pregnancy is the result of rape or incest.

- State-funded prenatal services may not be used for abortion counseling, referral for abortion, or funding for abortion.

- No funds appropriated or distributed under the Nebraska Health Care Funding Act may be used for abortions, abortion counseling, or referrals for abortions.

- No funding from the Woman's Health Initiative Fund may be used to pay for abortions.

- Nebraska prohibits organizations that receive public funds from using those funds to provide abortions, abortion counseling, or to make referrals for abortions.

- It prohibits insurance companies from offering abortion coverage within state insurance Exchanges established pursuant to the federal healthcare law, except in cases of life endangerment.

- Nebraska prohibits private insurance companies from covering abortion, except in cases of life endangerment. Further, group health insurance contracts or health maintenance agreements paid for with public funds may not include abortion coverage unless an abortion is necessary to preserve the life of a woman.

- Nebraska prohibits Federal Title X money to fund programs "where abortion is a method of family planning." Programs cannot assist, provide counseling, or refer for abortion.

LEGAL RECOGNITION AND PROTECTION OF THE UNBORN AND NEWLY BORN

- Under Nebraska law, the killing of an unborn child at any stage of gestation is defined as a form of homicide. Nebraska law also provides penalties for the vehicular homicide of an unborn child.

- Nebraska criminalizes nonfatal assaults on an unborn child.

- State law maintains that any person who commits certain enumerated criminal offenses against a pregnant woman shall be punished by the imposition of the next higher penalty classification.

- Nebraska allows a wrongful death (civil) action when an unborn child at any stage of development is killed through a negligent or criminal act.

- Nebraska law requires that "all reasonable steps, in accordance with the sound medical judgment of the attending physician, shall be employed to preserve the life of a child" who is born alive following an attempted abortion at any stage of development.

- Nebraska has a "Baby Moses" law, prohibiting the criminal prosecution of someone who relinquishes a child to an on-duty hospital employee.

- It funds drug treatment programs for pregnant women and newborns.

BIOETHICS LAWS

- Nebraska does not prohibit human cloning or destructive embryo research, but it prohibits state facilities or funds from being used for human cloning or destructive embryo research.

- Nebraska prohibits experimentation only on infants aborted alive but does not prohibit experimentation on dead fetuses.

- Funds appropriated or distributed under the Nebraska Health Care Funding Act may not be used for research or activity using fetal tissue obtained from induced abortion or human embryonic stem cells or for the purpose of obtaining other funding for such use.

- Nebraska provides funding for ethical forms of stem-cell research.

- Nebraska does not regulate assisted reproductive technologies or human egg harvesting.

PATIENT PROTECTION LAWS

- In Nebraska, assisting a suicide is a felony.

HEALTHCARE FREEDOM OF CONSCIENCE

PARTICIPATION IN ABORTION

- A person is not required to participate in an abortion.

- A hospital, institution, or other facility is not required to admit a woman for an abortion or to allow the performance of an abortion within its facility.

PARTICIPATION IN RESEARCH HARMFUL TO HUMAN LIFE

- Nebraska currently provides no protection for the rights of healthcare providers who conscientiously object to participation in human cloning, destructive embryo research, and other forms of medical research that violate a provider's moral or religious beliefs.

DID YOU KNOW?

- In 2018, Nebraska passed a budget bill including language that prevented abortion providers, like Planned Parenthood, from being eligible to receive Title X funding.

WHAT HAPPENS AFTER *ROE* IS OVERTURNED?

- Abortion will be legal up to 20 weeks of pregnancy.

RECOMMENDATIONS
for Nebraska

WOMEN'S PROTECTION PROJECT PRIORITIES

- Enhanced penalties and enforcement mechanisms for the state's abortion-related laws
- Drug-Induced Abortion Information and Reporting Act
- Parental Involvement Enhancement Act
- Child Protection Act

INFANTS' PROTECTION PROJECT PRIORITIES

- Unborn Infants Dignity Act
- Prenatal Nondiscrimination Act

PATIENT PROTECTION ACT PRIORITIES

- Joint Resolution Opposing Suicide by Physician
- Charlie Gard Act (formerly the Life Sustaining Care Act)
- Pain Medicine Education Act

ADDITIONAL PRIORITIES

ABORTION

- Defunding the Abortion Industry and Advancing Women's Health Act

LEGAL RECOGNITION AND PROTECTION FOR THE UNBORN

- Prohibition on wrongful birth and wrongful life lawsuits
- Pregnant Woman's Protection Act

BIOETHICS

- Human Cloning Prohibition Act
- Destructive Embryo Research Act
- Prohibition on Public Funding of Human Cloning and Destructive Embryo Research Act

HEALTHCARE FREEDOM OF CONSCIENCE

- Healthcare Freedom of Conscience Act

Nevada | RANKING: 44 |

Nevada enacted a Freedom of Choice Act in 1990, providing for a legal right to abortion in the state even if Roe v. Wade is eventually overturned. As a result, it has continuously failed to enact commonsense, protective laws designed to protect women and unborn children from the harms inherent in abortion. Further, emerging and unethical biotechnologies are completely unregulated in Nevada.

ABORTION

- Nevada maintains a Freedom of Choice Act. It mandates a legal right to abortion even if *Roe v. Wade* is eventually overturned, specifically providing that abortions may be performed within 24 weeks after the commencement of a pregnancy. Because Nevada voters approved a ballot initiative providing this state "right" to abortion, the statute will remain in effect and cannot be amended, repealed, or otherwise changed except by a direct vote of the people.

- A physician may not perform an abortion on a woman until after the physician or other qualified person informs her of the probable gestational age of her unborn child, describes the abortion procedure to be used and its risks, and explains the physical and emotional consequences of abortion.

- Nevada's parental notification law prohibits a physician from performing an abortion on an unemancipated minor under the age of 18 until notice had been given to one parent or a court order had been secured. The law was declared unconstitutional.

- Only physicians licensed by the State of Nevada or employed by the United States and using accepted medical practices and procedures may perform abortions. Chiropractic physicians and osteopathic medical professionals are explicitly prohibited from performing abortions.

- Nevada has an enforceable abortion reporting law but does not require the reporting of information to the Centers for Disease Control (CDC).

- Nevada follows the federal standard for Medicaid funding for abortions, permitting the use of federal or state matching Medicaid funds for abortions necessary to preserve the life of the woman or when or state matching Medicaid funds for abortions necessary to preserve the life of the woman or when the pregnancy is the result of rape or incest.

LEGAL RECOGNITION AND PROTECTION OF THE UNBORN AND NEWLY BORN

- Nevada criminal law defines the killing of an unborn child after "quickening" (discernible movement in the womb) as a form of homicide.

- It allows a wrongful death (civil) action when a viable unborn child is killed through a negligent or criminal act.

- Under Nevada law, all reasonable steps must be taken to preserve the life and health of an infant "whenever an abortion results in the birth of an infant capable of sustained survival by natural or artificial supportive systems."

- Nevada defines substance abuse during pregnancy as "child abuse" under civil child welfare statutes.

BIOETHICS LAWS

- Nevada does not ban human cloning, destructive embryo research, or fetal experimentation, nor does it promote ethical forms of research.

- It does not regulate assisted reproductive technologies or human egg harvesting.

- In 2013, Nevada enacted a measure permitting gestational surrogacy.

PATIENT PROTECTION LAWS

- The legal status of suicide by physician in Nevada is undetermined. It has not enacted a specific statute prohibiting suicide by physician, and it does not recognize common law crimes (including suicide by physician). Further, there is no judicial decision stating whether suicide by physician is a form of homicide under Nevada's general homicide laws.

- Nevada maintains a Physician Orders for Life-Sustaining Treatment (POLST) Paradigm Program.

HEALTHCARE FREEDOM OF CONSCIENCE

PARTICIPATION IN ABORTION AND CONTRACEPTION

- Except in a medical emergency, an employer may not require a nurse, nursing assistant, or other employee to participate directly in the performance of an abortion if that person has previously signed and provided a written statement indicating a religious, moral, or ethical basis for conscientiously objecting to participation in abortions.

- Except in a medical emergency, a private hospital or licensed medical facility is not required to permit the use of its facilities for the performance of an abortion.

- Health plans providing prescription coverage must provide coverage for contraception. A conscience exemption applies to certain insurers affiliated with religious organizations.

PARTICIPATION IN RESEARCH HARMFUL TO HUMAN LIFE

- Nevada currently provides no protection for the rights of healthcare providers who conscientiously object to participation in human cloning, destructive embryo research, and other forms of medical research that violate a provider's moral or religious beliefs.

DID YOU KNOW?

- In 2017, Nevada considered a bill that would have legalized suicide by physician.

- Nevada also considered legislation that would have required parental notification for minors seeking an abortion.

WHAT HAPPENS AFTER *ROE* IS OVERTURNED?

- Abortion will be legal throughout pregnancy.

RECOMMENDATIONS
for Nevada

WOMEN'S PROTECTION PROJECT PRIORITIES

- Enhanced penalties and enforcement mechanisms for the state's abortion-related laws
- Reflection period before abortion
- Coercive Abuse Against Mothers Prevention Act
- Women's Health Protection Act (abortion clinic regulations)
- Drug-Induced Abortion Information and Reporting Act
- Parental Notification for Abortion Act
- Child Protection Act

INFANTS' PROTECTION PROJECT PRIORITIES

- Unborn Infants Dignity Act
- Prenatal Nondiscrimination Act
- Perinatal Hospice Information Act
- Unborn Wrongful Death Act (for a pre-viable child)

PATIENT PROTECTION ACT PRIORITIES

- Suicide by Physician Ban Act
- Joint Resolution Opposing Suicide by Physician
- Charlie Gard Act (formerly the Life Sustaining Care Act)
- Pain Medicine Education Act

ADDITIONAL PRIORITIES

ABORTION

- Repeal State FOCA
- Defunding the Abortion Industry and Advancing Women's Health Act
- Federal Abortion-Mandate Opt-Out Act

LEGAL RECOGNITION AND PROTECTION FOR THE UNBORN

- Crimes Against the Unborn Child Act (protecting an unborn child from conception)
- Pregnant Woman's Protection Act

BIOETHICS

- Human Cloning Prohibition Act
- Destructive Embryo Research Act
- Prohibition on Public Funding of Human Cloning and Destructive Embryo Research Act

PATIENT PROTECTION

- Suicide by Physician Ban Act

HEALTHCARE FREEDOM OF CONSCIENCE

- Healthcare Freedom of Conscience Act

New Hampshire | RANKING: 33

Pro-life legislators in New Hampshire had some success in enacting measures to protect women and their unborn children, but much work remains to be done. New Hampshire allows abortion after viability, even in cases where the mother's life or health is not in danger, and it does not maintain any informed consent requirements. Moreover, it does not criminalize the killing of an unborn child outside the context of abortion, and it is one of only three states that do not protect the conscience rights of healthcare professionals.

ABORTION

- New Hampshire prohibits partial-birth abortion.

- New Hampshire law allows abortions after viability, even in cases where the mother's life or health is not endangered.

- A physician may not perform an abortion on an unemancipated minor under the age of 18 until at least 48 hours after written notice has been delivered to one parent, except when there is a medical emergency or when the minor obtains a court order.

- The state Department of Health is required to collect, compile, and maintain abortion statistics and to prepare and submit an annual report to the general court.

- New Hampshire follows the federal standard for Medicaid funding for abortions, permitting the use of federal or state matching Medicaid funds for abortions necessary to preserve the life of the woman or when the pregnancy is the result of rape or incest.

- New Hampshire enacted a measure creating a "buffer zone" around abortion clinics, hampering the First Amendment speech rights of sidewalk counselors seeking to offer assistance to women entering or leaving abortion facilities. However, following litigation, the law is not being enforced.

LEGAL RECOGNITION AND PROTECTION OF THE UNBORN AND NEWLY BORN

- New Hampshire criminalizes the killing of an unborn child outside the context of abortion, when the child has attained 20 weeks or more gestation. It also provides that an attack on a pregnant woman which results in a stillbirth or miscarriage is a criminal assault.

- It allows a wrongful death (civil) action when a viable unborn child is killed through a negligent or criminal act.

- New Hampshire has a "Baby Moses" law, establishing a safe haven for mothers to legally leave their infants at designated places and ensuring the infants receive appropriate care and protection.

- New Hampshire has approved stillbirth certificates.

BIOETHICS LAWS

- New Hampshire does not ban human cloning, destructive embryo research, or fetal experimentation.

- It does not promote ethical forms of research.

- New Hampshire has enacted regulations applicable to practitioners and participants in assisted reproductive technologies.

PATIENT PROTECTION LAWS

- In New Hampshire, assisting suicide is a felony.

HEALTHCARE FREEDOM OF CONSCIENCE

PARTICIPATION IN ABORTION AND CONTRACEPTION

- New Hampshire currently provides no protection for the freedom of conscience of healthcare providers.

- New Hampshire law requires group or blanket health insurance policies issued or renewed by insurers, health service corporations, and health maintenance organizations to provide coverage for contraceptives if they otherwise provide coverage for outpatient services or other prescription drugs. The law contains no conscience exemptions for religious or other employers with ethical or moral objections to contraception.

PARTICIPATION IN RESEARCH HARMFUL TO HUMAN LIFE

- New Hampshire currently provides no protection for the rights of healthcare providers who conscientiously object to participation in human cloning, destructive embryo research, and other forms of medical research that violate a provider's moral or religious beliefs.

DID YOU KNOW?

- In 2017, the New Hampshire legislature passed a fetal homicide bill that criminalizes the killing of an unborn child outside the context of abortion, when the child has attained 20 weeks or more gestation. The governor vetoed the bill, however. In 2018, the legislature again introduced a fetal homicide bill.

- New Hampshire also considered legislation that would prohibit abortions after viability.

WHAT HAPPENS AFTER *ROE* IS OVERTURNED?

- Abortion will be legal throughout pregnancy.

RECOMMENDATIONS
for New Hampshire

WOMEN'S PROTECTION PROJECT PRIORITIES

- Enhanced penalties and enforcement mechanisms for the state's abortion-related laws
- Women's Right to Know Act with reflection period
- Coercive Abuse Against Mothers Prevention Act
- Women's Health Protection Act (abortion clinic regulations)
- Drug-Induced Abortion Information and Reporting Act
- Parental Consent for Abortion Act
- Parental Involvement Enhancement Act
- Child Protection Act

INFANTS' PROTECTION PROJECT PRIORITIES

- Unborn Infants Dignity Act
- Prenatal Nondiscrimination Act
- Perinatal Hospice Information Act
- Born-Alive Infant Protection Act
- Unborn Wrongful Death Act (for a pre-viable child)

PATIENT PROTECTION ACT PRIORITIES

- Joint Resolution Opposing Suicide by Physician
- Charlie Gard Act (formerly the Life Sustaining Care Act)
- Pain Medicine Education Act

ADDITIONAL PRIORITIES

ABORTION

- Defunding the Abortion Industry and Advancing Women's Health Act
- Federal Abortion-Mandate Opt-Out Act

LEGAL RECOGNITION AND PROTECTION FOR THE UNBORN

- Crimes Against the Unborn Child Act
- Pregnant Woman's Protection Act

BIOETHICS

- Human Cloning Prohibition Act
- Destructive Embryo Research Act
- Prohibition on Public Funding of Human Cloning and Destructive Embryo Research Act

HEALTHCARE FREEDOM OF CONSCIENCE

- Healthcare Freedom of Conscience Act

New Jersey | RANKING: 47

New Jersey is one of the most dangerous states for women and their unborn children. It provides no meaningful protection for women considering abortion or for unborn victims of violence. Further, it directly supports the destruction of human life by permitting destructive embryo research, cloning for biomedical research, and funding for unethical forms of research.

ABORTION

- The New Jersey Supreme Court has ruled that the state constitution provides a broader right to abortion than that interpreted in the U.S. Constitution. Pursuant to this ruling, the New Jersey Supreme Court has struck down the state's parental notification requirement and restrictions on the use of taxpayer funds to pay for abortions.

- New Jersey does not have an informed consent law or an enforceable parental involvement law for abortion.

- New Jersey requires that abortions after the first trimester be performed in licensed ambulatory care facilities or hospitals.

- Only physicians licensed to practice medicine and surgery in New Jersey may perform abortions.

- New Jersey provides court-ordered coverage for all "medically necessary" abortions for women eligible for public assistance. This requirement essentially equates to funding abortion-on-demand in light of the U.S. Supreme Court's broad definition of "health" in the context of abortion.

- Under the State Health Benefits plan, any contracts entered into by the State Health Benefits Commission must include coverage of abortion.

LEGAL RECOGNITION AND PROTECTION OF THE UNBORN AND NEWLY BORN

- New Jersey law does not recognize an unborn child as a potential victim of homicide or assault.

- It allows a wrongful death (civil) action only when an unborn child is born alive following a negligent or criminal act and dies thereafter.

- New Jersey does not require infants who survive abortions to be given appropriate, potentially life-saving medical care.

- New Jersey has a "Baby Moses" law, establishing a safe haven for mothers to legally leave their infants at designated places and ensuring that the infants receive appropriate care and protection.

BIOETHICS LAWS

- New Jersey prohibits cloning to produce children, but not cloning for biomedical research, making it a "clone-and-kill" state.

- It allows and funds destructive embryo research and does not prohibit fetal experimentation.

- General hospitals are to advise every pregnant patient of the option to donate umbilical cord blood or placental tissue. Healthcare professionals are to provide pregnant women with state-prepared materials on umbilical cord blood donation and storage "as early as practicable" and preferably in the first trimester of pregnancy.

- State funding earmarked for "stem cell research" may be available for adult stem-cell research.

- While New Jersey does not maintain any meaningful regulation of assisted reproductive technologies, state law requires that informed consent materials include information on embryo donation.

PATIENT PROTECTION LAWS

- In New Jersey, assisting a suicide is a felony.

- It has enacted a "bill of rights" for patients/residents of healthcare facilities including the right for competent patients/residents to refuse treatment.

HEALTHCARE FREEDOM OF CONSCIENCE

PARTICIPATION IN ABORTION AND CONTRACEPTION

- A person is not required to perform or assist in the performance of an abortion.

- A hospital or healthcare facility is not required to provide abortions. The New Jersey Supreme Court has determined that the law is unconstitutional as applied to nonsectarian or nonprofit hospitals.

- New Jersey requires individual, group, and small-employer health insurance policies, medical or hospital service agreements, health maintenance organizations, and prepaid prescription service organizations to provide coverage for contraceptives if they also provide coverage for other prescription drugs. The provision includes a conscience exemption so narrow it precludes the ability of most employers and insurers with moral or religious objections from exercising it.

PARTICIPATION IN RESEARCH HARMFUL TO HUMAN LIFE

- New Jersey currently provides no protection for the rights of healthcare providers who conscientiously object to participation in human cloning, destructive embryo research, and other forms of medical research that violate a provider's moral or religious beliefs.

DID YOU KNOW?

- In 2018, New Jersey considered legislation that would have prohibited abortion at 5 months (i.e., 20 weeks) gestation.

- New Jersey also considered a constitutional amendment regarding parental notification for medical or surgical abortion procedures performed on minors.

WHAT HAPPENS AFTER *ROE* IS OVERTURNED?

- Abortion will be legal throughout pregnancy due to a state court decision.

RECOMMENDATIONS
for New Jersey

WOMEN'S PROTECTION PROJECT PRIORITIES

- Enhanced penalties and enforcement mechanisms for the state's abortion-related laws
- Women's Right to Know Act with reflection period
- Coercive Abuse Against Mothers Prevention Act
- Women's Health Protection Act (abortion clinic regulations)
- Drug-Induced Abortion Information and Reporting Act
- Parental Notification for Abortion Act
- Components of the Child Protection Act related to evidence retention and remedies for third-party interference with parental rights

INFANTS' PROTECTION PROJECT PRIORITIES

- Unborn Infants Dignity Act
- Prenatal Nondiscrimination Act
- Perinatal Hospice Information Act
- Born-Alive Infant Protection Act
- Unborn Wrongful Death Act

PATIENT PROTECTION ACT PRIORITIES

- Joint Resolution Opposing Suicide by Physician
- Charlie Gard Act (formerly the Life Sustaining Care Act)
- Pain Medicine Education Act

ADDITIONAL PRIORITIES

ABORTION

- State Constitutional Amendment (providing that there is no state constitutional right to abortion)
- Defunding the Abortion Industry and Advancing Women's Health Act
- Federal Abortion-Mandate Opt-Out Act

LEGAL RECOGNITION AND PROTECTION FOR THE UNBORN

- Crimes Against the Unborn Child Act
- Pregnant Woman's Protection Act

BIOETHICS

- Human Cloning Prohibition Act
- Destructive Embryo Research Act
- Prohibition on Public Funding of Human Cloning and Destructive Embryo Research Act

HEALTHCARE FREEDOM OF CONSCIENCE

- Healthcare Freedom of Conscience Act

New Mexico | RANKING: 39

New Mexico does not adequately protect the health and safety of women seeking abortions. It lacks an informed consent law, an enforceable parental involvement law, and comprehensive health and safety regulations for facilities performing abortions.

ABORTION

- The New Mexico Supreme Court has held that the Equal Rights Amendment to the state constitution provides a broader right to abortion than that interpreted in the U.S. Constitution. Under this ruling, the court has struck down restrictions on the use of taxpayer funding to pay for abortions.

- New Mexico prohibits partial-birth abortion performed after viability.

- New Mexico does not have an informed consent law.

- The state Attorney General has issued an opinion that New Mexico's parental notice law does not provide the constitutionally required judicial bypass procedure and is unenforceable.

- New Mexico maintains no regulations mandating that abortion facilities meet minimum patient care standards.

- Only physicians licensed in New Mexico may perform abortions.

- New Mexico has an enforceable abortion reporting law but does not require the reporting of information to the Centers for Disease Control and Prevention (CDC). The measure applies to both surgical and nonsurgical abortions.

- New Mexico provides court-ordered coverage for all "medically necessary" abortions for women eligible for public assistance. This requirement essentially equates to funding abortion-on-demand in light of the U.S. Supreme Court's broad definition of "health" in the context of abortion.

LEGAL RECOGNITION AND PROTECTION OF THE UNBORN AND NEWLY BORN

- New Mexico law does not recognize an unborn child as a potential victim of homicide or assault.

- New Mexico defines criminal assaults on a pregnant woman that result in miscarriage, stillbirth, or "damage to pregnancy" as enhanced offenses for sentencing purposes.

- It allows a wrongful death (civil) action when a viable unborn child is killed through a negligent or criminal act.

- New Mexico does not require that an infant who survives an abortion be given appropriate medical care.

- New Mexico has a "Baby Moses" law, establishing a safe haven for mothers to legally leave their infants at designated places and ensuring that the infants receive appropriate care and protection.

- It provides for both reports of "spontaneous fetal death" (for an unborn child who has reached at least 20 weeks gestation) and for certificates of stillbirth.

BIOETHICS LAWS

- New Mexico does not prohibit human cloning or destructive embryo research.

- Its prohibition on fetal experimentation applies only to experimentation that might be harmful to a live child (i.e., it does not apply to aborted children).

- All healthcare providers are required to advise pregnant patients of the option to donate umbilical cord blood following delivery.

- New Mexico maintains no meaningful regulation of assisted reproductive technologies or human egg harvesting, but its Uniform Parentage Act includes "donation of embryos" in its definition of "assisted reproduction."

PATIENT PROTECTION LAWS

- In New Mexico, assisting a suicide is a felony.

HEALTHCARE FREEDOM OF CONSCIENCE

PARTICIPATION IN ABORTION AND CONTRACEPTION

- A person associated with, employed by, or on the staff of a hospital who objects on religious or moral grounds is not required to participate in an abortion.

- A hospital is not required to admit a woman for the purpose of performing an abortion.

- Health insurance plans that provide prescription coverage must also provide coverage for contraception. There is a conscience exemption for religious employers.

PARTICIPATION IN RESEARCH HARMFUL TO HUMAN LIFE

- New Mexico currently provides no protection for the rights of healthcare providers who conscientiously object to participation in human cloning, destructive embryo research, and other forms of medical research that violate a provider's moral or religious beliefs.

DID YOU KNOW?

- In 2017, the House Select Investigative Panel on Infant Lives referred abortion clinic Southwestern Women's Options, to the New Mexico Attorney General's Office, for potential criminal violations associated with its fetal tissue program.

- In 2018, New Mexico considered legislation that would enact parental notification for abortion, protections for pain-capable unborn children, and require medical care for infants who are born alive.

WHAT HAPPENS AFTER *ROE* IS OVERTURNED?

- Abortion will be legal up to at least viability and likely throughout pregnancy based on existing law with broad exceptions enacted before *Roe*.

RECOMMENDATIONS
for New Mexico

WOMEN'S PROTECTION PROJECT PRIORITIES

- Enhanced penalties and enforcement mechanisms for the state's abortion-related laws
- Women's Right to Know Act with reflection period
- Coercive Abuse Against Mothers Prevention Act
- Women's Health Protection Act (abortion clinic regulations)
- Drug-Induced Abortion Information and Reporting Act
- Parental Notification for Abortion Act
- Child Protection Act

INFANTS' PROTECTION PROJECT PRIORITIES

- Unborn Infants Dignity Act
- Prenatal Nondiscrimination Act
- Perinatal Hospice Information Act
- Born-Alive Infant Protection Act
- Unborn Wrongful Death Act (for a pre-viable child)

PATIENT PROTECTION ACT PRIORITIES

- Joint Resolution Opposing Suicide by Physician
- Charlie Gard Act (formerly the Life Sustaining Care Act)
- Pain Medicine Education Act

ADDITIONAL PRIORITIES

ABORTION

- State Constitutional Amendment (providing that there is no state constitutional right to abortion)
- Defunding the Abortion Industry and Advancing Women's Health Act
- Federal Abortion-Mandate Opt-Out Act

LEGAL RECOGNITION AND PROTECTION FOR THE UNBORN

- Crimes Against the Unborn Child Act
- Pregnant Woman's Protection Act

BIOETHICS

- Human Cloning Prohibition Act
- Destructive Embryo Research Act
- Prohibition on Public Funding of Human Cloning and Destructive Embryo Research Act

HEALTHCARE FREEDOM OF CONSCIENCE

- Healthcare Freedom of Conscience Act

New York | RANKING: 43

New York lags far behind the majority of states in protecting maternal health or its taxpayers. For example, it does not have either an informed consent or parental involvement law, and it does not provide effective limits on public funding for abortion. It also fails to limit or effectively regulate destructive embryo research and similar technologies.

ABORTION

- In *Hope v. Perales*, the due process provision of the New York Constitution was interpreted as protecting a woman's right to an abortion.

- New York does not have an informed consent law for abortion and does not protect the right of parents to be involved in the abortion decisions of their minor daughters.

- Under current legal precedent, New York's requirement that abortions after the first trimester be performed in hospitals is unenforceable.

- New York limits the performance of abortions to licensed physicians.

- It has an enforceable abortion reporting law but does not require the reporting of information to the Centers for Disease Control and Prevention (CDC). The measure applies to both surgical and nonsurgical abortions.

- New York taxpayers are required by statute to fund "medically necessary" abortions for women receiving public assistance. This essentially equates to funding abortion-on-demand in light of the U.S. Supreme Court's broad definition of "health" in the context of abortion.

- New York provides funding to pregnancy resource centers and other abortion alternatives.

- New York maintains the crime of "aggravated interference with health care services" in the first and second degrees. The statute provides, in pertinent part, that "a person is guilty of the crime of aggravated interference with health care services... when he or she... causes physical injury to such other person who was obtaining or providing, or was assisting another person to obtain or provide reproductive health services."

LEGAL RECOGNITION AND PROTECTION OF THE UNBORN AND NEWLY BORN

- Under New York law, the killing of an unborn child after the 24th week of pregnancy is defined as a homicide.

- It allows a wrongful death (civil) action only when an unborn child is born alive following a negligent or criminal act and dies thereafter.

- New York law states that the "opportunity to obtain medical treatment of an infant prematurely born alive in the course of an abortion shall be the same as the rights of an infant born spontaneously." Thus, it has created a specific affirmative duty of physicians to provide medical care and treatment to infants born alive at any stage of development.

- New York has a "Baby Moses" law, establishing a safe haven for mothers to legally leave their infants at designated places and ensuring the infants receive appropriate care and protection.

- It funds drug treatment programs for pregnant women and newborns.

BIOETHICS LAWS

- New York does not prohibit human cloning, destructive embryo research, or fetal experimentation.

- New York maintains a state board that disburses state monies for destructive embryo research. The monies may not fund cloning to produce children.

- New York does not regulate assisted reproductive technologies.

- New York is the first state to fund the dangerous procedure of human egg harvesting.

PATIENT PROTECTION LAWS

- New York expressly prohibits suicide by physician, which is defined as a form of manslaughter. This prohibition has been upheld by the U.S. Supreme Court and the state's highest appeals court.

HEALTHCARE FREEDOM OF CONSCIENCE

PARTICIPATION IN ABORTION AND CONTRACEPTION

- A person who objects in writing and on the basis of religious beliefs or conscience is not required to perform or assist in an abortion.

- Staff members of the state Department of Social Services may refuse to provide family planning services if it conflicts with their cultural values, conscience, or religious convictions.

- Health plans that provide prescription coverage must provide coverage for contraception. The provision includes a conscience exemption so narrow it precludes the ability of most employers and insurers with moral or religious objections from exercising it.

PARTICIPATION IN RESEARCH HARMFUL TO HUMAN LIFE

- New York currently provides no protection for the rights of healthcare providers who conscientiously object to participation in human cloning, destructive embryo research, and other forms of medical research that violate a provider's moral or religious beliefs.

DID YOU KNOW?

- In 2017, the New York Supreme Court unanimously ruled that there is no constitutional right to suicide by physician in the New York Constitution. However, New York continues to consider legislation legalizing suicide by physician.

- In 2018, New York considered legislation that would force pregnancy centers to (disclosure by crisis pregnancy centers).

WHAT HAPPENS AFTER *ROE* IS OVERTURNED?

- Abortion will be legal up to at least 24 weeks of pregnancy due to a state court decision.

RECOMMENDATIONS
for New York

WOMEN'S PROTECTION PROJECT PRIORITIES

- Enhanced penalties and enforcement mechanisms for the state's abortion-related laws
- Women's Right to Know Act with reflection period
- Coercive Abuse Against Mothers Prevention Act
- Women's Health Protection Act (abortion clinic regulations)
- Drug-Induced Abortion Information and Reporting Act
- Parental Notification for Abortion Act
- Child Protection Act

INFANTS' PROTECTION PROJECT PRIORITIES

- Unborn Infants Dignity Act
- Prenatal Nondiscrimination Act
- Perinatal Hospice Information Act
- Unborn Wrongful Death Act

PATIENT PROTECTION ACT PRIORITIES

- Joint Resolution Opposing Suicide by Physician
- Charlie Gard Act (formerly the Life Sustaining Care Act)
- Pain Medicine Education Act

ADDITIONAL PRIORITIES

ABORTION

- State Constitutional Amendment (providing that there is no state constitutional right to abortion)
- Defunding the Abortion Industry and Advancing Women's Health Act
- Federal Abortion-Mandate Opt-Out Act

LEGAL RECOGNITION AND PROTECTION FOR THE UNBORN

- Unborn Infants Dignity Act
- Crimes Against the Unborn Child Act
- Unborn Wrongful Death Act
- Pregnant Woman's Protection Act

BIOETHICS

- Human Cloning Prohibition Act
- Destructive Embryo Research Act
- Prohibition on Public Funding of Human Cloning and Destructive Embryo Research Act

HEALTHCARE FREEDOM OF CONSCIENCE

- Healthcare Freedom of Conscience Act

North Carolina | RANKING: 23

North Carolina has taken steps to protect the health and welfare of women and unborn children including the enactment of a prohibition on sex-selection abortions and an informed consent law. It protects unborn victims of violence from conception until birth. However, North Carolina maintains no laws regarding human cloning or destructive embryo research.

ABORTION

- North Carolina prohibits abortions at 5 months (i.e., 20 weeks) gestation. The law is in ongoing litigation.

- In 2012, North Carolina enacted a law defunding abortion providers. A similar 2011 law was enjoined.

- A physician may not perform an abortion on a woman until at least 72 hours after the woman has been informed of particular medical risks associated with the proposed abortion procedure to be employed (including psychological risks), the probable gestational age of her unborn child, medical risks associated with carrying her child to term, whether the physician who is to perform the abortion has liability insurance for malpractice, the location of the hospital that offers obstetrical or gynecological care located within 30 miles of the location where the abortion is performed or induced and at which the physician performing or inducing the abortion has clinical privileges, and if the physician performing the abortion does not have local hospital admitting privileges. Additional information about medical assistance benefits, alternatives to abortion, and the father's liability for child support must also be provided.

- An abortion provider must perform an ultrasound at least four hours before a woman has an abortion. Portions of the law requiring the display and explanation of the ultrasound image were challenged and invalidated, but the provision mandating the ultrasound itself has not been challenged.

- A physician may not perform an abortion on an unemancipated minor under the age of 18 without the written consent of one parent or a grandparent with whom the minor has lived for at least six months, unless there is a medical emergency or the minor obtains a court order.

- North Carolina prohibits sex-selection abortions.

- North Carolina has enacted comprehensive regulations establishing minimum health and safety standards for abortion clinics. Among the areas regulated are clinic administration, staffing, patient medical evaluations, and post-operative care.

- In 2013, the state Department of Health was given discretion to apply ambulatory surgical center standards to abortion facilities.

- Only physicians licensed to practice medicine in North Carolina may perform abortions. The physician must be present during the performance of the entire (surgical) abortion procedure.

- North Carolina has an enforceable abortion reporting law but does not require the reporting of information to the Centers for Disease Control and Prevention (CDC). The measure applies to both surgical and nonsurgical abortions.

- A physician must be present during the administration of the first drug in an abortion-inducing drug regimen.

- North Carolina follows the federal standard for Medicaid funding for abortions, permitting the use of federal or state matching Medicaid funds for abortions necessary to preserve the life of the woman or when the pregnancy is the result of rape or incest.

- North Carolina prohibits abortion coverage for public employees except in cases of life endangerment, rape, or incest.

- It has limited funding for abortion through the health insurance plans offered through the health insurance Exchanges required by the federal healthcare law or offered through local governments.

- North Carolina offers "Choose Life" license plates, the proceeds of which benefit entities providing abortion alternatives.

LEGAL RECOGNITION AND PROTECTION OF THE UNBORN AND NEWLY BORN

- North Carolina protects unborn victims of violence from conception until birth. Lily's Law provides that the crime of homicide also includes situations where a child is born and dies from injuries received in utero.

- North Carolina defines a criminal assault on a pregnant woman that results in miscarriage, stillbirth, or "damage to pregnancy" as an enhanced offense for sentencing purposes.

- It allows for a wrongful death (civil) action when a viable unborn child is killed through a negligent or criminal act.

- North Carolina has a "Baby Moses" law, establishing a safe haven for mothers to legally leave their infants at designated places and ensuring the infants receive appropriate care and protection.

- It funds drug treatment programs for pregnant women and newborns.

- North Carolina prohibits the sale of the remains of an unborn child resulting from an abortion or miscarriage. The law defines "sell" to mean the transfer of any consideration, but does not include payment for incineration, burial, or cremation services.

- North Carolina requires the mother's informed written consent for the donation of the remains of an unborn child after a spontaneous abortion or miscarriage. Her consent must be obtained prior to the donation and must be separate from any other prior consent.

BIOETHICS LAWS

- North Carolina maintains no laws regarding human cloning, destructive embryo research, fetal experimentation, assisted reproductive technologies, or human egg harvesting.

- North Carolina requires the state Department of Health and Human Services to make publicly available publications on umbilical cord stem cells and umbilical cord-blood banking. The Department also encourages healthcare professionals to provide the publications to their pregnant patients.

PATIENT PROTECTION LAWS

- North Carolina's treatment of suicide by physician is unclear. While the state has statutorily adopted the common law of crimes, it has also abolished the common law crime of suicide. Suicide by physician may still be a common law crime.

HEALTHCARE FREEDOM OF CONSCIENCE

PARTICIPATION IN ABORTION AND CONTRACEPTION

- An individual healthcare provider who objects on religious, moral, or ethical grounds is not required to participate in abortions.

- A hospital or other healthcare institution is not required to provide abortions.

- North Carolina provides some protection for the conscience rights of pharmacists and pharmacies.

- Health insurance plans that provide prescription coverage must also provide coverage for contraception. The provision includes a conscience exemption so narrow that it precludes the ability of most employers and insurers with moral or religious objections from exercising it.

PARTICIPATION IN RESEARCH HARMFUL TO HUMAN LIFE

- North Carolina currently provides no protection for the rights of healthcare providers who conscientiously object to participation in human cloning, destructive embryo research, or other forms of medical research that violate a provider's moral or religious beliefs.

DID YOU KNOW?

- In 2017, North Carolina considered legislation that would have required physicians give information about "the possibility of reversing the effects of a drug-induced abortion."

WHAT HAPPENS AFTER *ROE* IS OVERTURNED?

- Abortion will be legal up to 20 weeks of pregnancy.

RECOMMENDATIONS
for North Carolina

WOMEN'S PROTECTION PROJECT PRIORITIES

- Enhanced penalties and enforcement mechanisms for the state's abortion-related laws
- Drug-Induced Abortion Information and Reporting Act
- Parental Involvement Enhancement Act
- Components of the Child Protection Act related to evidence retention and remedies for third-party interference with parental rights

INFANTS' PROTECTION PROJECT PRIORITIES

- Unborn Infants Dignity Act
- Prenatal Nondiscrimination Act
- Perinatal Hospice Information Act
- Born-Alive Infant Protection Act
- Unborn Wrongful Death Act (for a pre-viable child)

PATIENT PROTECTION ACT PRIORITIES

- Suicide by Physician Ban Act
- Joint Resolution Opposing Suicide by Physician
- Charlie Gard Act (formerly the Life Sustaining Care Act)
- Pain Medicine Education Act

ADDITIONAL PRIORITIES

ABORTION

- Federal Abortion-Mandate Opt-Out Act

LEGAL RECOGNITION AND PROTECTION FOR THE UNBORN

- Pregnant Woman's Protection Act

BIOETHICS

- Human Cloning Prohibition Act
- Destructive Embryo Research Act
- Prohibition on Public Funding of Human Cloning and Destructive Embryo Research Act

PATIENT PROTECTION

- Suicide by Physician Ban Act

HEALTHCARE FREEDOM OF CONSCIENCE

- Healthcare Freedom of Conscience Act

North Dakota | RANKING: 16

North Dakota maintains strong legal protections for women considering abortion including a prohibition on abortions at or after 5 months (i.e., 20 weeks) development, comprehensive informed consent requirements, an admitting privileges requirement for abortion providers, and funding for organizations that promote abortion alternatives. In addition, North Dakota is one of only a handful of states that effectively prohibits human cloning for all purposes.

ABORTION

- North Dakota prohibits abortion at 5 months (i.e., 20 weeks) gestation.

- North Dakota passed a law prohibiting an abortion when the unborn child has a detectable heartbeat, as early as 6 weeks gestation. The law is permanently enjoined.

- North Dakota prohibits partial-birth abortion.

- North Dakota prohibits abortions sought solely on account of a child's sex or because the child has been diagnosed with a genetic abnormality.

- North Dakota has enacted a measure banning abortion should *Roe v. Wade* be overturned.

- A physician may not perform an abortion on a woman until at least 24 hours after the woman has been informed of the medical risks associated with abortion, the medical risks of carrying the pregnancy to term, the probable gestational age of the unborn child, state assistance benefits, the father's legal obligations, the availability of state-prepared information on the development of the unborn child, and a list of agencies that offer alternatives to abortion. A woman must also be informed that "the abortion will terminate the life of a whole, separate, unique, living human being" and be provided information about the abortion-breast cancer link.

- Abortion providers must offer a woman the opportunity to view an ultrasound image of her unborn child.

- North Dakota prohibits anyone from coercing a woman into an abortion. Further, abortion facilities must post a notice stating that no one can force a woman to have an abortion. In addition, North Dakota has enhanced the penalties for sex traffickers who coerce or force their victims to undergo abortions.

- A physician may not perform an abortion on an unmarried minor under the age of 18 without the written consent of both parents (or the surviving parent, custodial parent, or guardian), unless there is a medical emergency or the minor obtains a court order.

- Only physicians licensed to practice medicine or osteopathy in North Dakota or employed by the United States may perform abortions.

- North Dakota also requires abortion providers to have admitting privileges at a local hospital and to be board certified in obstetrics/gynecology, and abortion facilities must also obtain and maintain a transfer agreement with a local hospital to assist in the treatment of abortion-related complications. Further, clinics must have at least one staff member trained in cardiopulmonary resuscitation.

- North Dakota has an enforceable abortion reporting law but does not require the reporting of information to the Centers for Disease Control and Prevention (CDC). The measure applies to both surgical and nonsurgical abortions.

- A physician performing an abortion must report the post-fertilization age of the aborted child.

- In a law substantially based on AUL's Drug-Induced Abortion Information and Reporting Act, North Dakota regulates the provision of drug-induced abortion by requiring that the administration satisfy protocols approved by the U.S. Food & Drug Administration (FDA) and that the drugs be administered by or in the same room and in the physical presence of the physician who prescribed, dispensed, or otherwise provided the drug or chemical to the patient (thereby prohibiting "webcam abortions"). An abortion provider's challenge to the law failed in the North Dakota Supreme Court.

- North Dakota follows the federal standard for Medicaid funding for abortions, permitting the use of federal or state matching Medicaid funds for abortions necessary to preserve the life of the woman or when the pregnancy is the result of rape or incest.

- North Dakota law also provides that no state funds or funds from any agency, county, municipality, or any other subdivision thereof and no federal funds passing through the state treasury or a state agency may be used to pay for the performance of an abortion or for promoting the performance of an abortion unless it is necessary to prevent the death of the woman.

- State and federal funds for treatment and support services for victims of human trafficking may be used to refer for or counsel for family planning services, but may not be used to perform, refer for, or encourage abortion.

- No funds, grants, gifts, or services of an organization receiving funds distributed by the Children's Services Coordinating Committee may be used for the purposes of direct provision of contraception services, abortion, or abortion referrals to minors.

- An abortion may not be performed in a hospital owned or operated by the state, unless the abortion is necessary to preserve the life of the woman.

- State health insurance contracts, policies, and plans must exclude coverage for abortion unless the abortion is necessary to preserve the woman's life.

- Private insurance companies are also prohibited from covering abortions except in cases of life endangerment.

- North Dakota funds organizations that promote abortion alternatives.

LEGAL RECOGNITION AND PROTECTION OF THE UNBORN AND NEWLY BORN

- Under North Dakota criminal law, the killing of an unborn child at any stage of gestation is defined as homicide.

- North Dakota defines a nonfatal assault on an unborn child as a criminal offense.

- It allows a wrongful death (civil) action when a viable unborn child is killed through a negligent or criminal act.

- North Dakota has created a specific affirmative duty of physicians to provide medical care and treatment to infants born alive after viability.

- North Dakota requires healthcare professionals to report suspected prenatal drug exposure. In addition, healthcare professionals must test newborns for drug exposure when there is adequate suspicion of prenatal use by the mother.

BIOETHICS LAWS

- North Dakota prohibits both human cloning and fetal experimentation; however, it does not prohibit destructive embryo research.

- North Dakota allows healthcare professionals to inform pregnant patients of options relating to umbilical cord blood, and hospitals are to allow pregnant patients to arrange for such donations.

- The Uniform Parentage Act includes "donation of embryos" in its definition of "assisted reproduction." However, North Dakota does not maintain meaningful regulations of assisted reproductive technologies or human egg harvesting.

PATIENT PROTECTION LAWS

- In North Dakota, assisting a suicide is a felony.

HEALTHCARE FREEDOM OF CONSCIENCE

PARTICIPATION IN ABORTION

- A hospital, physician, nurse, hospital employee, or any other person is not under a legal duty or contractual obligation to participate in abortion.

PARTICIPATION IN RESEARCH HARMFUL TO HUMAN LIFE

- North Dakota currently provides no protection for the rights of healthcare providers who conscientiously object to participation in human cloning, destructive embryo research, and other forms of medical research that violate a provider's moral or religious beliefs.

DID YOU KNOW?

- There is currently only one clinic in North Dakota that performs abortions.

WHAT HAPPENS AFTER *ROE* IS OVERTURNED?

- North Dakota has a law, conditioned on *Roe* being overturned, that makes abortion illegal, which may be enforceable.

RECOMMENDATIONS
for North Dakota

WOMEN'S PROTECTION PROJECT PRIORITIES

- Enhanced penalties and enforcement mechanisms for the state's abortion-related laws
- Drug-Induced Abortion Information and Reporting Act
- Parental Involvement Enhancement Act
- Child Protection Act

INFANTS' PROTECTION PROJECT PRIORITIES

- Unborn Infants Dignity Act
- Perinatal Hospice Information Act
- Born-Alive Infant Protection Act (for a pre-viable child)
- Unborn Wrongful Death Act

PATIENT PROTECTION ACT PRIORITIES

- Joint Resolution Opposing Suicide by Physician
- Charlie Gard Act (formerly the Life Sustaining Care Act)
- Pain Medicine Education Act

ADDITIONAL PRIORITIES

ABORTION

- Defunding the Abortion Industry and Advancing Women's Health Act
- Federal Abortion-Mandate Opt-Out Act

LEGAL RECOGNITION AND PROTECTION FOR THE UNBORN

- Pregnant Woman's Protection Act

BIOETHICS

- Promotion of ethical forms of medical research

HEALTHCARE FREEDOM OF CONSCIENCE

- Healthcare Freedom of Conscience Act

Ohio | RANKING: 17

Ohio maintains fairly comprehensive protections for women considering abortions and their unborn children, and it was the first state to regulate the provision of drug-induced abortion. However, it does not adequately protect vulnerable patients at the Patient Protection, fails to prohibit suicide by physician, and maintains no protective laws regarding human cloning or destructive embryo research.

ABORTION

- Ohio prohibits abortion at 5 months (i.e., 20 weeks) gestation.

- Ohio prohibits partial-birth abortion.

- Ohio prohibits the performance of an abortion if the woman is seeking it because the child is diagnosed with or may have Down syndrome. The law is enjoined and in ongoing litigation.

- A post-viability abortion is only permitted when necessary to avoid the death of the pregnant woman or there is a serious risk of substantial and irreversible impairment of a major bodily function of the pregnant woman. Two physicians must verify the medical necessity.

- A physician may not perform an abortion on a woman until at least 24 hours after the physician informs her of the nature of the proposed abortion procedure and its risks, the probable gestational age of the unborn child, and the medical risks of carrying the pregnancy to term. The physician must also provide state-prepared materials describing the development of the unborn child, public and private agencies providing assistance, state medical assistance benefits, and the father's legal obligations.

- Ohio requires an abortion provider to offer a woman the opportunity to view an ultrasound and to obtain a copy of the image when an ultrasound is performed as part of the preparation for an abortion.

- Ohio has a fetal heartbeat law, requiring an abortion provider to attempt to find a fetal heartbeat. If a heartbeat is detected, the abortion provider must wait 24 hours to perform the abortion and inform the woman in writing about the existence of the heartbeat and the statistical probability of bring the baby to term based on the child's developmental stage.

- Abortion facilities must post signs informing a woman that no one can force her to have an abortion. The law increases the penalty for domestic violence if the offender knew the woman was pregnant, while also permitting the recovery of compensatory and exemplary damages when mandatory reporters fail to report suspected coercive abuse.

- A physician may not perform an abortion on an unemancipated minor under the age of 18 until receiving the consent of one parent or guardian, unless there is a medical emergency or the minor obtains a court order.

- Ohio licenses and regulates abortion facilities as a subset of ambulatory surgical centers.

- Ohio limits the performance of abortions to licensed physicians.

- Ohio has an enforceable abortion reporting law but does not require the reporting of information to the Centers for Disease Control and Prevention (CDC). The measure applies to both surgical and nonsurgical abortions and requires abortion providers to report short-term complications.

- Ohio has a law regulating the provision of RU-486 and creating criminal penalties for those providing the drug without following Food & Drug Administration's (FDA) guidelines. The law also requires abortion providers to inform the state medical board whenever RU-486 leads to "serious complications."

- Ohio follows the federal standard for Medicaid funding for abortions, permitting the use of federal or state matching Medicaid funds for abortions necessary to preserve the life of the woman or when the pregnancy is the result of rape or incest.

- Ohio maintains a "tiering system" for the allocation of family planning funding including funding for which abortion providers might be eligible. Under the system, first priority for funding is given to public entities that are operated by state or local government entities. Most abortion providers fall into the lowest priority category of this system.

- Ohio law also provides that state or local public funds shall not be used to subsidize abortions, except in cases of life endangerment, rape, or incest.

- Several state funding sources include abortion-related limitations. For example, women's health services grants may not be used to provide abortion services and may not be used for counseling or referrals for abortions, except in cases of medical emergency. Services using these grants must be physically and financially separate from abortion-providing and abortion-promoting activities. In addition, generic services funds may not be used to counsel or refer for abortions, except in cases of medical emergency, and the Breast Cancer Fund of Ohio may not use money for abortion information, counseling, or services, or for any abortion-related activities.

- State employee health insurance may not provide coverage for abortion unless the abortion is necessary to preserve the woman's life, the pregnancy is the result of rape or incest, or an additional premium is paid for an optional rider.

- Ohio offers "Choose Life" license plates, and the proceeds benefit non-profit groups that encourage adoption.

LEGAL RECOGNITION AND PROTECTION OF THE UNBORN AND NEWLY BORN

- Under Ohio criminal law, the killing of an unborn child at any stage of gestation is homicide, and it defines a nonfatal assault on an unborn child as a crime.

- Ohio allows a wrongful death (civil) action when a viable unborn child is killed through a negligent or criminal act.

- Ohio has a "Baby Moses" law, establishing a safe haven for mothers to legally leave their infants at designated places and ensuring the infants receive appropriate care and protection.

- It funds drug treatment programs for pregnant women and newborns.

- Under the Grieving Parents Act, the state permits a fetal death certificate and burial after the death of an unborn child.

BIOETHICS LAWS

- Ohio maintains no laws regarding human cloning or destructive embryo research; however, it prohibits fetal experimentation.

- The Ohio Department of Health has been directed to place printable information about umbilical cord blood banking and donation on its website. It also encourages healthcare professionals to provide this information to pregnant women.

- Ohio maintains no comprehensive regulations of assisted reproductive technologies or human egg harvesting, but has enacted laws regarding the parentage of donated embryos.

PATIENT PROTECTION LAWS

- Ohio has declared that suicide by physician is against public policy; however, state law does not criminalize the practice. Under existing Ohio law, an injunction may be issued to prevent a health-care professional from participating in a suicide, and assisting a suicide is grounds for professional discipline.

HEALTHCARE FREEDOM OF CONSCIENCE

PARTICIPATION IN ABORTION

- No person is required to participate in medical procedures that result in an abortion.

- A hospital is not required to permit its facilities to be used for abortions.

PARTICIPATION IN RESEARCH HARMFUL TO HUMAN LIFE

- Ohio currently provides no protection for the rights of healthcare providers who conscientiously object to participation in human cloning, destructive embryo research, or other forms of medical research that violate a provider's moral or religious beliefs.

DID YOU KNOW?

- In 2018, Ohio passed legislation similar to AUL's Prenatal Down Syndrome Abortion Ban.

- Ohio considered legislation that would have prohibited the dismemberment abortion procedure as well as legislation that would have created an instructional program aimed at educating the public on the humanity of the unborn child.

WHAT HAPPENS AFTER *ROE* IS OVERTURNED?

- Abortion will be legal up to 20 weeks of pregnancy.

RECOMMENDATIONS
for Ohio

WOMEN'S PROTECTION PROJECT PRIORITIES

- Enhanced penalties and enforcement mechanisms for the state's abortion-related laws
- Drug-Induced Abortion Information and Reporting Act
- Parental Involvement Enhancement Act
- Child Protection Act

INFANTS' PROTECTION PROJECT PRIORITIES

- Prenatal Nondiscrimination Act
- Perinatal Hospice Information Act
- Unborn Wrongful Death Act (for a pre-viable child)

PATIENT PROTECTION ACT PRIORITIES

- Suicide by Physician Ban Act
- Joint Resolution Opposing Suicide by Physician
- Charlie Gard Act (formerly the Life Sustaining Care Act)
- Pain Medicine Education Act

ADDITIONAL PRIORITIES

ABORTION

- Defunding the Abortion Industry and Advancing Women's Health Act
- Federal Abortion-Mandate Opt-Out Act

LEGAL RECOGNITION AND PROTECTION FOR THE UNBORN

- Pregnant Woman's Protection Act

BIOETHICS

- Human Cloning Prohibition Act
- Destructive Embryo Research Act
- Prohibition on Public Funding of Human Cloning and Destructive Embryo Research Act

PATIENT PROTECTION

- Suicide by Physician Ban Act

HEALTHCARE FREEDOM OF CONSCIENCE

- Healthcare Freedom of Conscience Act

Oklahoma | RANKING: 4

Protecting women and their unborn children remains a primary focus of Oklahoma legislators. Even in the face of threatened litigation by abortion advocates, Oklahoma continues to enact comprehensive and protective laws and regulations, counting it more important to protect women from a predatory abortion industry that values profits over women's lives and health.

ABORTION

- Oklahoma prohibits abortions at or after 5 months of pregnancy (i.e., 20 weeks) on the basis of the pain experienced by unborn children.

- Oklahoma prohibits partial-birth abortion.

- Oklahoma prohibits sex-selection abortions.

- It also prohibits the dismemberment abortion procedure. The law is enjoined and in ongoing litigation.

- Oklahoma possesses an enforceable abortion prohibition should the U.S. Constitution be amended or certain U.S. Supreme Court decisions be reversed or modified.

- Oklahoma has amended its definition of "abortion" to include the use of drug-induced abortion. It has also amended the definition of "medical emergency" as applied to all of its abortion laws, narrowing the exception to exclude "mental health" and applying it only to cases where a physical condition could cause the major impairment of a bodily function or death.

- Oklahoma requires that, 72 hours before an abortion, a woman receive counseling on the medical risks of abortion and pregnancy, the name of the physician performing the abortion, and the gestational age of the unborn child. The woman must also receive information on anatomical and physiological characteristics of fetuses at different stages of development and her right to receive state-prepared materials on potential government benefits, child support, and a list of support agencies and their services. A woman must also be informed that "[a]bortion shall terminate the life of a whole, separate, unique, living human being."

- Oklahoma has supplemented its informed consent requirements, mandating that women seeking abortions at 5 months gestation or later receive information about fetal pain.

- A woman at 6 weeks of gestation or later must be given an opportunity to hear the heartbeat of her unborn child.

- Oklahoma requires an ultrasound evaluation 72 hours prior to abortion for all patients who elect to have abortions.

- A woman considering abortion after a life-limiting diagnosis for her unborn child must receive information on perinatal hospice services at least 72 hours prior to the performance of the abortion.

- Abortion facilities must post signs indicating that a woman cannot be coerced into an abortion.

- A physician may not perform an abortion on an unemancipated minor without the written, notarized consent of a parent or guardian. A parent or guardian must provide government-issued proof of identification, and the abortion provider must also sign a document attesting to the quality of the identification provided. Judicial bypass proceedings must be initiated in the county where the minor resides, and judges must consider certain enumerated factors in assessing the maturity of the minor and the specific circumstances of the case. In a medical emergency, abortion providers must notify a parent or guardian of the minor's abortion no less than 24 hours after the procedure, unless the minor obtains a judicial waiver. Oklahoma provides a civil cause of action for a minor (or her parent/guardian) if an abortion provider fails to comply.

- Oklahoma maintains a separate parental notice provision that does not include a judicial bypass procedure.

- Oklahoma law mandates that abortion facilities comply with comprehensive health and safety standards, based in substantial part on AUL's Women's Health Defense Act. An additional requirement that abortions after the first trimester be performed in a hospital has been ruled unconstitutional.

- Only physicians licensed to practice medicine in Oklahoma may perform abortions. Abortion providers must have admitting privileges at a general medicine surgical hospital within 30 miles of the abortion facility and must remain on the premises in order to facilitate the transfer of emergency cases until all abortion patients are stable and ready to leave the recovery room. Abortion providers have challenged the requirement in state court.

- Abortion providers must report specific and detailed information about each abortion and abortion patient including aggregate information on the number of women receiving state abortion counseling materials and the number of abortions exempted from the counseling requirement because of a "medical emergency." In addition, abortion providers must report specific and detailed information regarding minors' abortions, including whether they obtained the mandatory parental consent, whether the minors sought judicial bypass of the consent requirement, and whether or not such bypass was granted. The requirements apply to both surgical and nonsurgical abortions, but do not require that any of this information be reported to the Centers for Disease Control and Prevention (CDC).

- In 2013, Oklahoma amended its abortion reporting statute to require the provision of additional information including a screenshot of the ultrasound image. In 2014, it added a requirement that any incidents of injury or death must be reported to the state Board of Health.

- Oklahoma comprehensively regulates drug-induced abortions, which includes a requirement that physicians physically examine a woman before administering the drugs, as well as a requirement that the drugs be administered as restricted by the U.S. Food & Drug Administration (FDA). Abortion providers have challenged the law in state court. An additional 2012 law explicitly prohibits the use of telemedicine to initiate a drug-induced abortion.

- Oklahoma enacted a law permitting a woman (or parent or legal guardian of a minor) to commence a civil action if an abortion provider violates the state's informed consent law, ultrasound requirement, fetal pain counseling requirement, parental involvement law, or any other law regulating a minor's abortion.

- Oklahoma follows the federal standard for Medicaid funding for abortions, permitting the use of federal or state matching Medicaid funds for abortions necessary to preserve the life of the woman or when the pregnancy is the result of rape or incest.

- Under Oklahoma law, no public funds can be used to encourage a woman to have an abortion (except to the extent required by federal Medicaid rules).

- Oklahoma prohibits taxpayer funding of any entity associated with another entity that provides, counsels, or refers for abortion.

- The state prohibits the use of research grants provided through the Oklahoma Health Research Act for abortion.

- Oklahoma law restricts the use of state facilities for the performance of abortions and provides that no state actor may perform an abortion except in cases of life endangerment, incest, or rape. Healthcare providers who are state employees may not provide abortions, abortion referrals, or abortion counseling.

- It prohibits insurance companies from offering abortion coverage within state insurance Exchanges established pursuant to the federal healthcare law, except in cases of life endangerment.

- Oklahoma also prohibits private health insurance coverage for abortions, except in cases of life endangerment.

- Oklahoma has directed the state Department of Health to "facilitate funding to nongovernmental entities that provide alternatives to abortion services." It has also allocated direct taxpayer funding to abortion alternatives.

- Oklahoma offers "Choose Life" license plates, the proceeds of which benefit pregnancy resource centers and/or other organizations providing abortion alternatives.

LEGAL RECOGNITION AND PROTECTION OF THE UNBORN AND NEWLY BORN

- Oklahoma criminalizes the unlawful killing of an unborn child from "the moment of conception."

- Oklahoma also criminalizes a nonfatal assault on an unborn child.

- The Pregnant Woman's Protection Act provides an affirmative defense to a woman who uses force to protect her unborn child from a criminal assault.

- Oklahoma allows a wrongful death (civil) action when an unborn child at any stage of development is killed through a negligent or criminal act.

- It prohibits civil causes of action for both "wrongful birth" and "wrongful life."

- Under Oklahoma law, "the rights to medical treatment of an infant prematurely born alive in the course of an abortion shall be the same as the rights of an infant of similar medical status prematurely born." Thus, Oklahoma has created a specific affirmative duty of physicians to provide medical care and treatment to infants born alive at any stage of development.

- Oklahoma has a "Baby Moses" law, establishing a safe haven for mothers to legally leave their infants at designated places and ensuring that the infants receive appropriate care and protection.

- Oklahoma requires healthcare professionals to report suspected prenatal drug exposure and mandates that the state Department of Human Services investigate when a newborn tests positive for controlled substances.

- Oklahoma created The Humanity of the Unborn Child Act and Fund, requiring the state Department of Health to develop, update, and maintain information on agencies and services available to assist a woman through pregnancy, upon childbirth, and while the child is in development (including adoption agencies). The comprehensive list of public and private agencies must include a description of services offered and information on how to contact each listed agency. In addition to promoting alternatives to abortion, the law also requires the Department of Health to develop and make available materials on fetal development.

BIOETHICS LAWS

- Oklahoma prohibits human cloning, destructive embryo research, and fetal experimentation.

- The state Department of Health has been directed to establish, operate, and maintain a public umbilical cord blood bank or cord blood collection operation. The Department has also been directed to establish a related education program, and each physician is to inform pregnant patients of the opportunity to donate to the bank following delivery.

- Oklahoma regulates the donation and transfer of human embryos used in assisted reproductive technologies and has recognized that donors of embryos relinquish all parental rights with respect to any resulting children.

- Oklahoma regulates assisted reproductive technologies.

PATIENT PROTECTION LAWS

- In Oklahoma, assisting a suicide is a felony.

- Oklahoma has a Physician Orders for Life-Sustaining Treatment (POLST) Act.

HEALTHCARE FREEDOM OF CONSCIENCE

PARTICIPATION IN ABORTION

- Oklahoma's Freedom of Conscience Act provides broad conscience protections for individuals and institutions.

- No person is required to participate in medical procedures that result in or are in preparation for an abortion except when necessary to preserve a woman's life.

- A private hospital is not required to permit abortions within its facilities.

PARTICIPATION IN RESEARCH HARMFUL TO HUMAN LIFE

- The Freedom of Conscience Act provides broad conscience protections for individuals and institutions.

DID YOU KNOW?

- In 2018, Oklahoma passed a resolution stating, among other things, that "human life is sacred from the point of conception" and "embryonic stem-cell research leads to the destruction of embryonic human beings."

- Oklahoma also considered legislation that would have prohibited abortion based on genetic abnormality as well as legislation that would have allowed suicide by physician.

WHAT HAPPENS AFTER *ROE* IS OVERTURNED?

- Abortion will be illegal, except to save the life of the mother, based on existing law enacted before *Roe*.

RECOMMENDATIONS
for Oklahoma

WOMEN'S PROTECTION PROJECT PRIORITIES

- Components of the Child Protection Act related to evidence retention and remedies for third-party interference with parental rights

INFANTS' PROTECTION PROJECT PRIORITIES

- Unborn Infants Dignity Act
- Prenatal Nondiscrimination Act
- Perinatal Hospice Information Act
- Unborn Wrongful Death Act (for a pre-viable child)

PATIENT PROTECTION ACT PRIORITIES

- Joint Resolution Opposing Suicide by Physician
- Charlie Gard Act (formerly the Life Sustaining Care Act)
- Pain Medicine Education Act

ADDITIONAL PRIORITIES

ABORTION

- Defunding the Abortion Industry and Advancing Women's Health Act

BIOETHICS

- Egg Provider Protection Act
- Assisted Reproductive Technologies Disclosure and Risk Reduction Act

Oregon | RANKING: 45

Oregon has an abysmal record on life, failing to protect women, the unborn, the sick, and the dying. Not only was Oregon the first state in the nation to legalize suicide by physician, but it does not mandate informed consent or parental involvement before abortion, does not recognize an unborn child as a potential victim of homicide or assault, and does not limit destructive embryo research or human cloning.

ABORTION

- Oregon does not provide even rudimentary protection for a woman considering an abortion. It does not have an informed consent law, an ultrasound requirement, a parental involvement law for minors seeking abortion, abortion facility regulations, or a prohibition on anyone other than a licensed physician performing an abortion.

- The state has an enforceable abortion reporting law but does not require the reporting of information to the Centers for Disease Control and Prevention (CDC). The measure applies to both surgical and nonsurgical abortions and requires abortion providers to report short-term complications.

- Oregon taxpayers fund "medically necessary" abortions for women eligible for state medical assistance for general care. This requirement essentially equates to funding abortion-on-demand in light of the U.S. Supreme Court's broad definition of "health" in the context of abortion.

LEGAL RECOGNITION AND PROTECTION OF THE UNBORN AND NEWLY BORN

- Oregon law does not recognize an unborn child as a potential victim of homicide or assault.

- It allows a wrongful death (civil) action when a viable unborn child is killed through a negligent or criminal act.

- Oregon does not require that an infant who survives an abortion be given appropriate, potentially life-saving medical care.

- Oregon has a "Baby Moses" law, establishing a safe haven for mothers to legally leave their infants at designated places and ensuring that the infants receive appropriate care and protection.

- It funds drug treatment programs for pregnant women and newborns.

BIOETHICS LAWS

- Oregon maintains no laws regarding human cloning, destructive embryo research, or fetal experimentation; nor does it promote ethical forms of research.

- Further, it does not regulate assisted reproductive technologies or human egg harvesting.

PATIENT PROTECTION LAWS

- Oregon permits suicide by physician under statutorily specified circumstances, but prohibits the sale of "suicide kits."

HEALTHCARE FREEDOM OF CONSCIENCE

PARTICIPATION IN ABORTION AND CONTRACEPTION

- A physician is not required to participate in or give advice about abortion if he or she discloses this election to the patient.

- A hospital employee or medical staff member is not required to participate in abortions if he or she has notified the hospital of this election.

- A private hospital is not required to admit a woman for an abortion.

- A state Department of Human Services employee who objects in writing may refuse to offer family planning and birth control services.

- Health plans that provide prescription coverage must also cover prescription contraceptives. Religious employers may refuse coverage if their primary purpose is the inculcation of religious values, if they primarily employ and serve people with the same values, and if they are nonprofit entities under federal law.

PARTICIPATION IN RESEARCH HARMFUL TO HUMAN LIFE

- Oregon currently provides no protection for the rights of healthcare providers who conscientiously object to participation in human cloning, destructive embryo research, or other forms of medical research that violate a provider's moral or religious beliefs.

DID YOU KNOW?

- In 2018, Oregon considered a constitutional amendment that would prohibit public funding for abortion.

- Also in 2018, Oregon again considered legislation that would prohibit late-term sex-selective abortions.

- Oregon also considered legislation that would have prohibited abortion at 20 weeks except in medical emergencies and would have required an annual publication of abortion statistics from the state.

WHAT HAPPENS AFTER *ROE* IS OVERTURNED?

- Abortion will be legal throughout pregnancy.

RECOMMENDATIONS
for Oregon

WOMEN'S PROTECTION PROJECT PRIORITIES

- Enhanced penalties and enforcement mechanisms for the state's abortion-related laws
- Women's Right to Know Act with reflection period
- Coercive Abuse Against Mothers Prevention Act
- Women's Health Protection Act (abortion clinic regulations)
- Drug-Induced Abortion Information and Reporting Act
- Parental Notification for Abortion Act
- Child Protection Act

INFANTS' PROTECTION PROJECT PRIORITIES

- Unborn Infants Dignity Act
- Prenatal Nondiscrimination Act
- Perinatal Hospice Information Act
- Born-Alive Infant Protection Act
- Unborn Wrongful Death Act (for a pre-viable child)

PATIENT PROTECTION ACT PRIORITIES

- Suicide by Physician Ban Act
- Joint Resolution Opposing Suicide by Physician
- Charlie Gard Act (formerly the Life Sustaining Care Act)
- Pain Medicine Education Act

ADDITIONAL PRIORITIES

ABORTION

- Defunding the Abortion Industry and Advancing Women's Health Act
- Federal Abortion-Mandate Opt-Out Act

LEGAL RECOGNITION AND PROTECTION FOR THE UNBORN

- Crimes Against the Unborn Child Act
- Pregnant Woman's Protection Act

BIOETHICS

- Human Cloning Prohibition Act
- Destructive Embryo Research Act
- Prohibition on Public Funding of Human Cloning and Destructive Embryo Research Act

PATIENT PROTECTION

- Repeal of law permitting suicide by physician

HEALTHCARE FREEDOM OF CONSCIENCE

- Healthcare Freedom of Conscience Act

Pennsylvania | RANKING: 12

Pennsylvania's efforts to protect women and unborn children from the negative consequences of abortion have been ground-breaking, as memorialized in the landmark case *Planned Parenthood v. Casey*. Pennsylvania has led the way for other states by enacting such measures as informed consent, parental consent, and state funding of abortion alternatives. Moreover, Pennsylvania is also one of a small number of states that prohibits destructive embryo research.

ABORTION

- In the landmark case *Planned Parenthood v. Casey*, Pennsylvania's informed consent requirements, mandated 24-hour reflection period prior to an abortion, and parental consent requirement for a minor seeking an abortion were upheld by the U.S. Supreme Court.

- Pennsylvania requires abortion providers to state in their printed materials that it is illegal for anyone to coerce a woman into having an abortion.

- The state's parental consent law requires one-parent consent unless there is a medical emergency or a minor obtains a court order. The law permits substitute consent by any adult standing in loco parentis if neither parent is available.

- Pennsylvania requires that abortion facilities meet the same patient care standards as facilities performing other outpatient surgeries. Despite the not-forgotten Kermit Gosnell scandal and following the Supreme Court's decision in *Whole Woman's Health v. Hellerstedt*, Planned Parenthood challenged Pennsylvania's health and safety requirements for abortion facilities.

- Only physicians or doctors of osteopathy licensed to practice medicine in Pennsylvania may perform abortions. Abortion providers must also maintain transfer agreements with local hospitals to facilitate the treatment of abortion-related complications.

- Pennsylvania has an enforceable abortion reporting law but does not require the reporting of information to the Centers for Disease Control and Prevention (CDC). The measure applies to both surgical and nonsurgical abortions and requires abortion providers to report short-term complications.

- Pennsylvania follows the federal standard for Medicaid funding for abortions, permitting the use of federal or state matching Medicaid funds for abortions necessary to preserve the life of the woman or when the pregnancy is the result of rape or incest.

- Pennsylvania does not provide public funding or public facilities for an abortion unless the abortion is necessary to preserve the woman's life or the pregnancy is the result of rape or incest.

- No public funds for legal services or IOLTA (Interest on Lawyer Trust Account) funds may be used to advocate for or oppose abortion.

- Programs receiving funds through the state Department of Public Welfare Women's Services programs may not be used to promote, refer for, or perform abortions, or engage in any counseling to encourage abortion. Physical and financial separation of recipients of these funding programs from entities providing abortion services is required.

- Pennsylvania prohibits the use of family planning funds for abortion-related activities and requires family planning services providers and subcontractors to keep a state-funded family planning project physically and financially separate from abortion-related activities, with exceptions for abortions in cases of life endangerment, rape, or incest.

- Pennsylvania prohibits abortion coverage in its state health insurance Exchanges required under the federal healthcare law.

- Health plans funded by the state may not include coverage for abortion unless the abortion is necessary to preserve a woman's life or the pregnancy is the result of rape or incest.

- Pennsylvania also requires any insurance providers offering healthcare or disability insurance within the state to offer policies that do not cover abortion except when necessary to preserve a woman's life or when the pregnancy is the result of rape or incest.

- Pennsylvania has allocated millions of dollars to pregnancy resource centers and other abortion alternative programs. Entities receiving the funds cannot perform abortions or provide abortion counseling.

- Pennsylvania offers "Choose Life" license plates, the proceeds of which are used to fund adoption and abortion alternatives services.

LEGAL RECOGNITION AND PROTECTION OF THE UNBORN AND NEWLY BORN

- Under Pennsylvania law, the killing of an unborn child at any stage of gestation is defined as homicide.

- Pennsylvania defines a nonfatal assault on an unborn child as a criminal offense.

- It allows a wrongful death (civil) action when a viable unborn child is killed through a negligent or criminal act.

- Pennsylvania has created a specific affirmative duty for physicians to provide medical care and treatment to infants born alive at any stage of development.

- Pennsylvania funds drug treatment programs for pregnant women and newborns. It also ensures adequate care for babies determined to have been prenatally exposed to alcohol or illegal substances.

- Pennsylvania law provides for "fetal death registrations."

BIOETHICS LAWS

- Pennsylvania does not prohibit human cloning, but it does prohibit destructive embryo research.

- Pennsylvania prohibits experimentation on a live human fetus, but allows experimentation on a dead fetus with the consent of the mother.

- A healthcare professional providing services to a pregnant woman must advise her of the option to donate umbilical cord blood following delivery, and all healthcare facilities and providers must permit the woman to arrange for an umbilical cord donation.

- Pennsylvania requires quarterly reports of assisted reproductive technologies data, including the number of women implanted and the number of eggs fertilized, destroyed, or discarded.

PATIENT PROTECTION LAWS

- In Pennsylvania, assisting a suicide is a felony.

HEALTHCARE FREEDOM OF CONSCIENCE

PARTICIPATION IN ABORTION

- If an objection is made in writing and is based on religious, moral, or professional grounds, a physician, nurse, staff member, or other employee of a hospital or healthcare facility is not required to participate in abortions and cannot be held liable for refusing to participate. Medical and nursing students are also protected.

- Except for facilities that perform abortions exclusively, each facility that performs abortions must prominently post a notice of the right not to participate in abortions.

- A private hospital or other healthcare facility is not required to perform abortions and may not be held liable for this refusal.

- Pennsylvania also specifically protects healthcare providers who object to providing drug-induced abortion.

PARTICIPATION IN RESEARCH HARMFUL TO HUMAN LIFE

- Pennsylvania currently provides no protection for the rights of healthcare providers who conscientiously object to participation in human cloning, destructive embryo research, or other forms of medical research that violate a provider's moral or religious beliefs.

DID YOU KNOW?

- In 2017, Pennsylvania passed legislation that included a prohibition on abortions after 5 months and the dismemberment abortion procedure. It was vetoed by Governor Tom Wolf.

- Pennsylvania considered a bill that would prohibit abortions based on the unborn child's diagnosis of Down syndrome.

WHAT HAPPENS AFTER *ROE* IS OVERTURNED?

- Abortion will be legal up to at least 24 weeks of pregnancy.

RECOMMENDATIONS
for Pennsylvania

WOMEN'S PROTECTION PROJECT PRIORITIES

- Enhanced penalties and enforcement mechanisms for the state's abortion-related laws
- Drug-Induced Abortion Information and Reporting Act
- Parental Involvement Enhancement Act
- Child Protection Act

INFANTS' PROTECTION PROJECT PRIORITIES

- Unborn Infants Dignity Act
- Prenatal Nondiscrimination Act
- Perinatal Hospice Information Act

PATIENT PROTECTION ACT PRIORITIES

- Joint Resolution Opposing Suicide by Physician
- Charlie Gard Act (formerly the Life Sustaining Care Act)
- Pain Medicine Education Act

ADDITIONAL PRIORITIES

ABORTION

- Defunding the Abortion Industry and Advancing Women's Health Act

BIOETHICS

- Human Cloning Prohibition Act
- Prohibition on Public Funding of Human Cloning and Destructive Embryo Research Act

HEALTHCARE FREEDOM OF CONSCIENCE

- Healthcare Freedom of Conscience Act

Rhode Island | RANKING: 28

Rhode Island provides some basic protections for women and girls considering abortion; however, it has failed to respond appropriately to the growing use of drug-induced abortion, increasing evidence of substandard abortion facilities, and increasing evidence of abortion's harm to women. It also fails to provide adequate legal protections for unborn children in contexts outside of abortion.

ABORTION

- Rhode Island possesses an enforceable abortion prohibition should the U.S. Constitution be amended or certain U.S. Supreme Court decisions be reversed or modified.

- A physician may not perform an abortion until the physician or the physician's agent has informed her of the probable gestational age of her unborn child and the nature and risks of the proposed abortion procedure. The woman must also sign a statement indicating she was informed that, if she decides to carry her child to term, she may be able to place the child with either a relative or with another family through foster care or adoption.

- A physician may not perform an abortion on an unemancipated minor under the age of 18 without the consent of one parent unless there is a medical emergency or the minor obtains a court order.

- Rhode Island has a complex system of abortion clinic regulations under which different standards apply at different stages of pregnancy and different facilities may be used to perform abortions at different stages of gestation.

- "Termination procedures" (non-surgical abortion procedures) must be performed by a licensed physician or "other licensed healthcare practitioner acting within his/her scope of practice."

- Rhode Island has an enforceable abortion reporting law but does not require the reporting of information to the Centers for Disease Control and Prevention (CDC). The measure applies to both surgical and nonsurgical abortions.

- Rhode Island follows the federal standard for Medicaid funding for abortions, permitting the use of federal or state matching Medicaid funds for abortions necessary to preserve the life of the woman or when the pregnancy is the result of rape or incest.

- Rhode Island prohibits abortion coverage for public employees (explicitly including city and town employees) except when a woman's life or health is endangered or in cases of rape or incest.

LEGAL RECOGNITION AND PROTECTION OF THE UNBORN AND NEWLY BORN

- Under Rhode Island law, the killing of an unborn child after "quickening" (discernible movement in the womb) is homicide.

- It allows a wrongful death (civil) action when a viable unborn child is killed through a negligent or criminal act.

- Any physician, nurse, or other licensed medical provider who knowingly and intentionally fails to provide reasonable medical care and treatment to an infant born alive in the course of an abortion, and as a result the infant dies, is guilty of the crime of manslaughter. Thus, Rhode Island has created a specific affirmative duty to provide medical care and treatment to infants born alive at any stage of development.

- Rhode Island defines substance abuse during pregnancy as "child abuse" under civil child-welfare statutes. It also requires healthcare professionals to report suspected prenatal drug exposure.

- Rhode Island maintains a measure allowing a woman who loses a child after 20 weeks of pregnancy to obtain a Certificate of Birth Resulting in Still Birth.

BIOETHICS LAWS

- Rhode Island allows cloning to produce children, as well as for biomedical research, making it a "clone-and-kill" state.

- Rhode Island prohibits harmful experimentation on a live human fetus but allows experimentation on a dead fetus if consent of the mother is obtained.

- Every obstetrical professional or facility is to inform a pregnant woman of the options relating to stem cells that are contained in the umbilical cord blood, and each hospital or other obstetrical facility must cooperate with the collection staff of a cord blood bank designated by the woman and facilitate the donation of the cord blood.

- Rhode Island maintains no meaningful regulation of assisted reproductive technologies or human egg harvesting.

PATIENT PROTECTION LAWS

- Under Rhode Island law, assisting a suicide is a felony.

- The state maintains a Physician Orders for Life-Sustaining Treatment (POLST) Paradigm Program.

HEALTHCARE FREEDOM OF CONSCIENCE

PARTICIPATION IN ABORTION AND CONTRACEPTION

- A physician or other person associated with, employed by, or on the staff of a healthcare facility who objects in writing and on religious and/or moral grounds is not required to participate in abortions.

- Health insurance plans that provide prescription coverage are also required to provide coverage for contraception. The provision includes a conscience exemption so narrow it precludes the ability of most employers and insurers with moral or religious objections from exercising it.

PARTICIPATION IN RESEARCH HARMFUL TO HUMAN LIFE

- Rhode Island provides no protection for the rights of healthcare providers who conscientiously object to participation in human cloning, destructive embryo research, and other forms of medical research that violate a provider's moral or religious beliefs.

DID YOU KNOW?

- In 2017, the Rhode Island legislature allowed a sunset clause to expire on a provision that previously banned cloning to produce children.

- In 2018, Rhode Island passed an honorary resolution honoring Kristen Dart and "wishing her much success as a political Director for Planned Parenthood Empire State."

WHAT HAPPENS AFTER *ROE* IS OVERTURNED?

- Abortion will not be legal based on existing law enacted after *Roe*.

RECOMMENDATIONS
for Rhode Island

WOMEN'S PROTECTION PROJECT PRIORITIES

- Enhanced penalties and enforcement mechanisms for the state's abortion-related laws
- Reflection period for abortion
- Coercive Abuse Against Mothers Prevention Act
- Women's Health Protection Act (abortion clinic regulations)
- Drug-Induced Abortion Information and Reporting Act
- Parental Involvement Enhancement Act
- Child Protection Act

INFANTS' PROTECTION PROJECT PRIORITIES

- Unborn Infants Dignity Act
- Prenatal Nondiscrimination Act
- Perinatal Hospice Information Act
- Unborn Wrongful Death Act

PATIENT PROTECTION ACT PRIORITIES

- Joint Resolution Opposing Suicide by Physician
- Charlie Gard Act (formerly the Life Sustaining Care Act)
- Pain Medicine Education Act

ADDITIONAL PRIORITIES

ABORTION

- Defunding the Abortion Industry and Advancing Women's Health Act
- Federal Abortion-Mandate Opt-Out Act

LEGAL RECOGNITION AND PROTECTION FOR THE UNBORN

- Crimes Against the Unborn Child Act (providing protection from conception)
- Pregnant Woman's Protection Act

BIOETHICS

- Human Cloning Prohibition Act
- Destructive Embryo Research Act
- Prohibition on Public Funding of Human Cloning and Destructive Embryo Research Act

HEALTHCARE FREEDOM OF CONSCIENCE

- Healthcare Freedom of Conscience Act

South Carolina | RANKING: 22

South Carolina maintains a number of life-affirming laws protecting women and the unborn from the harms inherent in abortion. These laws include comprehensive informed consent requirements and health and safety standards for abortion facilities. However, like many other states, South Carolina does not effectively regulate emerging biotechnologies, failing to prohibit human cloning, destructive embryo research, or fetal experimentation.

ABORTION

- South Carolina prohibits partial-birth abortion.

- In 2016, South Carolina enacted a prohibition on abortions when the probable post-fertilization age of the unborn child is 20 or more weeks. Prior existing law further prohibits abortions after 24 weeks gestation unless the attending physician and another independent physician certify in writing that the abortion is necessary to preserve the woman's life or health. If both physicians certify the abortion is necessary to preserve the woman's mental health, an independent psychiatrist must also certify that the abortion is necessary.

- A physician may not perform an abortion on a woman until 24 hours after she is informed of the probable gestational age of her unborn child, the abortion procedure to be used, and the availability of state-prepared written materials describing fetal development, listing agencies offering alternatives to abortion, and describing available medical assistance benefits.

- South Carolina requires that a woman be offered an ultrasound and the opportunity to view the image prior to an abortion.

- A physician may not perform an abortion on an unemancipated minor under the age of 17 without the informed written consent of one parent, a grandparent, or any other person who has standing *in loco parentis*, unless there is a medical emergency, the minor is a victim of incest, or the minor obtains a court order.

- South Carolina has enacted comprehensive health and safety regulations for abortion facilities. These regulations are based on national abortion industry standards and cover such areas as clinic administration, physical plant, sanitation standards, patient care, post-operative recovery, and proper maintenance of patient records.

- Only a physician licensed to practice medicine in South Carolina may perform an abortion.

- South Carolina has an enforceable abortion reporting law but does not require the reporting of information to the Centers for Disease Control and Prevention (CDC). The law applies to both surgical and nonsurgical abortions. In 2014, South Carolina added reporting requirements mandating that abortion providers report whether they have hospital admitting privileges and report abortion complications.

- South Carolina follows the federal standard for Medicaid funding for abortions, permitting the use of federal or state matching Medicaid funds for abortions necessary to preserve the life of the woman or when the pregnancy is the result of rape or incest. In 2018, the governor of South Carolina signed an executive order terminating abortion providers as qualified providers under its state Medicaid program. The order is enjoined and in ongoing litigation.

- State law provides that no state funds may be expended to perform abortions, except those authorized by Medicaid under federal law. Further, South Carolina maintains the following funding restrictions: money appropriated to the Adolescent Pregnancy Prevention Initiative may not be used for transportation to or from abortion services; state funds appropriated for family planning may not be used to pay for an abortion; the South Carolina Department of Health and Environmental Control and its employees may not provide referral services or counseling for abortion; and funds appropriated under the South Carolina Birth Defects Program may not be used to counsel or refer women for abortions.

- South Carolina prohibits health plans offered through the state's health insurance Exchanges required under the federal healthcare law from including abortion coverage.

- State taxpayer funds appropriated to the State Health Insurance Plan may not be used to pay for an abortion except in cases of rape or incest, or to preserve a woman's life. In addition, $100 must be used to create printed materials that let the reader know an unborn child at twenty weeks or more is capable of feeling pain.

LEGAL RECOGNITION AND PROTECTION OF THE UNBORN AND NEWLY BORN

- The Unborn Victims of Violence Act provides that the killing of an unborn child at any stage of gestation may be prosecuted as homicide. It also criminalizes a nonfatal assault on an unborn child.

- South Carolina allows a wrongful death (civil) action when a viable unborn child is killed through a negligent or criminal act.

- South Carolina law protects infants who survive abortions.

- South Carolina has a "Baby Moses" law, establishing a safe haven for mothers to legally leave their infants at designated places and ensuring that the infants receive appropriate care and protection.

- It defines substance abuse during pregnancy as "child abuse" under civil child-welfare statutes.

BIOETHICS LAWS

- South Carolina does not prohibit human cloning, destructive embryo research, or fetal experimentation, nor does it promote ethical forms of research.

- South Carolina does not regulate the provision of assisted reproductive technologies or human egg harvesting.

PATIENT PROTECTION LAWS

- Under South Carolina law, suicide by physician is a felony.

HEALTHCARE FREEDOM OF CONSCIENCE

PARTICIPATION IN ABORTION

- A physician, nurse, technician, or other employee of a hospital, clinic, or physician who objects in writing is not required to recommend, perform, or assist in the performance of an abortion.

- A healthcare provider's conscientious objection to performing or assisting in abortions may not be the basis for liability or discrimination. A person discriminated against in employment may bring a civil action for damages and reinstatement.

- Except in an emergency, a private or nongovernmental hospital or clinic is not required to permit the use of its facilities for the performance of an abortion or to admit a woman for an abortion.

- A hospital's refusal to perform or to permit the performance of abortions within its facility may not be the basis for civil liability.

PARTICIPATION IN RESEARCH HARMFUL TO HUMAN LIFE

- South Carolina currently provides no protection for the rights of healthcare providers who conscientiously object to participation in human cloning, destructive embryo research, and other forms of medical research that violate a provider's moral or religious beliefs.

DID YOU KNOW?

- In 2018, South Carolina lawmakers considered a prohibition on the dismemberment abortion procedure.

- In 2018, South Carolina's Governor, Henry McMaster, signed an executive order stating "the preservation of life is the ultimate right to be protected and necessarily includes the life of unborn children" and declaring abortion clinics and affiliated physicians as "unqualified to provide family planning services."

WHAT HAPPENS AFTER *ROE* IS OVERTURNED?

- Abortion will be legal up to 20 weeks of pregnancy.

RECOMMENDATIONS
for South Carolina

WOMEN'S PROTECTION PROJECT PRIORITIES

- Enhanced penalties and enforcement mechanisms for the state's abortion-related laws
- Coercive Abuse Against Mothers Prevention Act
- Drug-Induced Abortion Information and Reporting Act
- Parental Involvement Enhancement Act
- Child Protection Act

INFANTS' PROTECTION PROJECT PRIORITIES

- Unborn Infants Dignity Act
- Prenatal Nondiscrimination Act
- Perinatal Hospice Information Act
- Born-Alive Infant Protection Act
- Unborn Wrongful Death Act (for a pre-viable child)

PATIENT PROTECTION ACT PRIORITIES

- Joint Resolution Opposing Suicide by Physician
- Charlie Gard Act (formerly the Life Sustaining Care Act)
- Pain Medicine Education Act

ADDITIONAL PRIORITIES

ABORTION

- Defunding the Abortion Industry and Advancing Women's Health Act

LEGAL RECOGNITION AND PROTECTION FOR THE UNBORN

- Pregnant Woman's Protection Act

BIOETHICS

- Human Cloning Prohibition Act
- Destructive Embryo Research Act
- Prohibition on Public Funding of Human Cloning and Destructive Embryo Research Act

HEALTHCARE FREEDOM OF CONSCIENCE

- Healthcare Freedom of Conscience Act

South Dakota | RANKING: 6

South Dakota maintains some of the most comprehensive and protective abortion-related laws in the nation, protecting women and the unborn through health and safety standards and comprehensive informed consent requirements. Moreover, South Dakota is one of only a small number of states that prohibits destructive embryo research, human cloning, and fetal experimentation.

ABORTION

- South Dakota prohibits partial-birth abortion.

- It also prohibits sex-selection abortions.

- South Dakota provides that it is a misdemeanor to intentionally perform an abortion of an unborn child capable of feeling pain (defined as occurring at 20 weeks after fertilization), unless the abortion is necessary to prevent a serious health risk to the mother. In 2017, South Dakota increased the penalties on abortion providers who violate this prohibition.

- South Dakota maintains a law that would "on the date that the states are given the exclusive authority to regulate abortion" ban abortion throughout pregnancy except if necessary to preserve a woman's life. It specifically applies both to surgical and chemical abortions and applies at all stages of pregnancy.

- A physician may not perform an abortion on a woman until at least 72 hours (excluding weekends and holidays) after she has been informed of the probable gestational age of her unborn child, the medical risks of abortion, the medical risks of carrying the pregnancy to term, and the name of the physician who will perform the abortion. She must also be informed about available medical assistance benefits, the father's legal responsibilities, and her right to review additional information prepared by state health department officials.

- South Dakota requires that women be informed that "the abortion will terminate the life of a whole, separate, unique, living human being;" that the woman "has an existing relationship with the unborn human being and that the relationship enjoys protection under the United States Constitution and under the laws of South Dakota;" and that "by having an abortion her existing relationship and her existing constitutional rights with regards to that relationship will be terminated."

- South Dakota requires that a woman be informed of the risk of suicide and suicide ideation following abortion.

- South Dakota requires that a woman be offered an ultrasound and the opportunity to view the image prior to undergoing an abortion. The law also requires that abortion providers report the number of women who undergo abortions after choosing to view ultrasounds.

- South Dakota requires informed consent to include information on the possibility of discontinuing drug-induced abortion and requiring the Department of Health to include such information on its website.

- A physician must perform an assessment of a woman's medical and personal circumstances prior to an abortion. Moreover, a woman exhibiting certain risk factors must receive counseling about mental health risks associated with abortion.

- South Dakota requires a woman consult with a state-registered pregnancy help center before undergoing an abortion. Registered pregnancy help centers are required to have licensed medical and mental health professionals on staff or available through a collaborative agreement. This law is in ongoing litigation.

- Abortion providers must also screen women for coercion, and give them information regarding help to escape sex trafficking. Providers must also inform them that they cannot be forced to have an abortion because of the child's gender, and must post signs informing a woman that she cannot be coerced into undergoing a sex-selection abortion. State-prepared, written informed consent materials must include information that sex-selection abortions are illegal.

- A physician may not perform an abortion on an unemancipated minor under the age of 18 until at least 48 hours after providing written notice to one parent or after obtaining a court order. South Dakota also requires parental notification within 24 hours after the performance of an "emergency abortion" on a minor; however, an exception to the requirement is permitted if a minor indicates that she will seek a judicial bypass.

- South Dakota requires that all abortion facilities meet minimum health and safety standards. Further, beginning at the 12th week of pregnancy and through the 22nd week of pregnancy, abortions must be performed in a hospital, or if one is not available, "in a licensed physician's medical clinic or office of practice subject to the requirements of §34-23A-6 [blood supply requirements]." Further, an abortion after 22 weeks of pregnancy may only be performed by a physician, in a hospital, and only in the case of a medical emergency.

- The state Department of Health includes information on an abortion clinic's inspection on its public website, including the date of the inspection, the results, and details of any required corrective action.

- Only a physician licensed by the state or a physician practicing medicine or osteopathy and employed by the state or the United States may perform an abortion. The state medical board prohibits physician assistants and nurses from entering into practice agreements under which they may perform abortions.

- No surgical or chemical abortion may be scheduled except by a licensed physician and only after the physician physically and personally meets with the pregnant woman, consults with her, and performs an assessment of her medical and personal circumstances.

- For each abortion performed, an abortion provider must complete a reporting form mandated and provided by the South Dakota Department of Health. The required information includes: (1) the method of abortion; (2) the approximate gestational age of the fetus; (3) the specific reason for the abortion; (4) the entity, if any, that paid for the abortion; (5) a description of any complications from the abortion; (6) the method used to dispose of fetal tissue; (7) the specialty area of the attending physician; (8) whether the attending physician has been subject to license revocation, suspension, or other professional sanction; (9) the number of previous abortions the woman has had; (10) the number of previous live births she has had; (11) whether she received the RH test and tested positive for the RH-negative factor; and (12) her marital and educational status and race. The provision applies to both surgical and nonsurgical abortions, but does not require that any information be reported to the Centers for Disease Control and Prevention (CDC). This requirement was amended to mandate details on the gender of the unborn child.

- South Dakota prohibits public funding for abortion unless the procedure is necessary to preserve the woman's life (in contravention of federal law).

- South Dakota prohibits health plans offered through the state's health insurance Exchanges required under the federal healthcare law from including abortion coverage.

- Abortion providers are required to disseminate information on how to fight sex trafficking.

- It offers "Choose Life" license plates, the proceeds of which benefit pregnancy resource centers and/or other organizations providing abortion alternatives.

- The state Department of Health must maintain a registry of state "pregnancy help centers." A center seeking to be listed on the registry must certify that it has a licensed medical director and that the center does not perform abortions, has no affiliation with any organization or physician that performs abortion, and that it does not refer women for abortions. The law excludes agencies that place children for adoption from the registry.

LEGAL RECOGNITION AND PROTECTION OF THE UNBORN AND NEWLY BORN

- Under South Dakota law, the killing of an unborn child at any stage of gestation is defined as a form of homicide.

- South Dakota defines a nonfatal assault on an unborn child as a crime.

- It allows a wrongful death (civil) action when an unborn child at any stage of development is killed through a negligent or criminal act.

- South Dakota has created a specific affirmative duty for physicians to provide medical care and treatment to an infant born alive at any stage of development.

- It defines substance abuse during pregnancy as "child abuse" under civil child-welfare statutes.

- South Dakota maintains a measure allowing a woman who loses a child after 20 weeks gestation to obtain a Certificate of Birth Resulting in a Stillbirth.

- South Dakota prohibits the sale of fetal body parts.

BIOETHICS LAWS

- South Dakota prohibits human cloning for any purpose, destructive embryo research, and fetal experimentation.

- However, it does not promote ethical forms of research.

- South Dakota maintains no meaningful regulation of assisted reproductive technologies or human egg harvesting.

PATIENT PROTECTION LAWS

- Suicide by physician is a felony in South Dakota.

HEALTHCARE FREEDOM OF CONSCIENCE

PARTICIPATION IN ABORTION

- South Dakota law protects the rights of physicians, nurses, counselors, social workers, and other persons to refuse to perform, assist in, provide referrals for, or counsel for abortions.

- A healthcare provider's conscientious objection to performing or assisting in an abortion may not be a basis for liability, dismissal, or other prejudicial actions by a hospital or medical facility with which the person is affiliated or employed.

- A counselor, social worker, or other person in a position to address "the abortion question . . . as part of [the] workday routine" who objects to providing abortion advice or assistance may not be held liable to any person or subject to retaliation by an institution with which the person is affiliated or employed.

- No hospital is required to admit a woman for the purpose of abortion. The refusal of a hospital to participate in abortions may not be a basis for liability.

- A pharmacist is not required to dispense medication if there is reason to believe the medication would be used to cause an abortion.

PARTICIPATION IN RESEARCH HARMFUL TO HUMAN LIFE

- South Dakota currently provides no specific protection for the rights of healthcare providers who conscientiously object to participation in human cloning, destructive embryo research, or other forms of medical research that violate a provider's moral or religious beliefs.

DID YOU KNOW?

- In its legislative findings in 2018, South Dakota found the Planned Parenthood located in Sioux Falls had "been providing pre-abortion counseling that [did] not comply with the mandatory disclosures required" and that this failure was "contrary to the interests of pregnant mothers and pregnant mothers' need to make informed and voluntary decisions."

WHAT HAPPENS AFTER *ROE* IS OVERTURNED?

- South Dakota has a law, conditioned on *Roe* being overturned, that makes abortion illegal, which may be enforceable.

RECOMMENDATIONS
for South Dakota

WOMEN'S PROTECTION PROJECT PRIORITIES

- Enhanced penalties and enforcement mechanisms for the state's abortion-related laws
- Coercive Abuse Against Mothers Prevention Act
- Drug-Induced Abortion Information and Reporting Act
- Parental Consent for Abortion Act
- Parental Involvement Enhancement Act
- Child Protection Act

INFANTS' PROTECTION PROJECT PRIORITIES

- Unborn Infants Dignity Act
- Prenatal Nondiscrimination Act
- Perinatal Hospice Information Act

PATIENT PROTECTION ACT PRIORITIES

- Joint Resolution Opposing Suicide by Physician
- Charlie Gard Act (formerly the Life Sustaining Care Act)
- Pain Medicine Education Act

ADDITIONAL PRIORITIES

ABORTION

- Defunding the Abortion Industry and Advancing Women's Health Act

BIOETHICS

- Assisted Reproductive Technologies Disclosure and Risk Reduction Act

HEALTHCARE FREEDOM OF CONSCIENCE

- Healthcare Freedom of Conscience Act

Tennessee | RANKING: 18

In response to a state Supreme Court decision that manufactured a state constitutional right to abortion in the Tennessee constitution, Tennesseans passed a constitutional amendment in November 2014, declaring "[n]othing in this Constitution secures or protects a right to abortion or requires the funding of an abortion." The amendment enabled legislators to immediately consider and enact legislation that would have been invalidated under the former Supreme Court decision.

ABORTION

- The Tennessee Constitution has been amended to include the following: "Nothing in this Constitution secures or protects a right to abortion or requires the funding of an abortion. The people retain the right through their elected state representatives and state senators to enact, amend, or repeal statutes regarding abortion, including, but not limited to, circumstances of pregnancy resulting from rape or incest or when necessary to save the life of the mother." The enactment was in response to a Tennessee Supreme Court decision that read a constitutional right to abortion into the state constitution. This amendment is in ongoing litigation.

- Tennessee prohibits partial-birth abortion.

- No abortion may be performed after viability except in a medical emergency.

- Tennessee's informed consent law prohibits a physician from performing an abortion on a woman until at least 48 hours after the woman receives oral, in-person counseling on: (a) the probable gestational age of her unborn child at the time the abortion is to be performed, (b) that her unborn child may be viable if she is 24 weeks or more pregnant, (c) the risks and medical benefits of abortion, and (d) the particular risks associated with her pregnancy and continuing the pregnancy to term. The law was rewritten after a former version was permanently enjoined by the Tennessee Supreme Court. The new law is in ongoing litigation.

- Abortion facilities must post signs notifying a woman that it is against the law for anyone to coerce her into having an abortion.

- A physician may not perform an abortion on an unemancipated minor under the age of 18 without the written consent of one parent unless there is a medical emergency, the minor is the victim of incest, or the minor obtains a court order.

- A federal district court has declared Tennessee's abortion clinic regulations unconstitutional (as applied to the particular abortion provider who challenged the law). A 2015 provision defining "ambulatory surgical treatment centers" to include facilities where 50 or more surgical abortions are performed in a calendar year is no longer enforced. The state permanently stopped enforcing the law "in light of the Supreme Court's current case law and to avoid the expense and utilization of resources on continued litigation."

- Only a physician licensed or certified by the state may perform an abortion. Tennessee law provides that a nurse practitioner or physician's assistant may not write or sign a prescription, dispense any drug or medication, or perform any procedure involving a drug or medication whose sole purpose is to cause an abortion.

- Tennessee also requires abortion providers to have admitting privileges at a hospital located in the same county as the abortion facility or in an adjacent county. The law year is no longer enforced. The state permanently stopped enforcement "in light of the Supreme Court's current case law and to avoid the expense and utilization of resources on continued litigation."

- It has an enforceable abortion reporting law but does not require the reporting of information to the Centers for Disease Control and Prevention (CDC). The annual report issued by the state Department of Health must report whether the ultrasound performed prior to the abortion detected a heartbeat, what abortion method was used—differentiating between medical and surgical abortions—and, if a surgical abortion was performed, what procedure was used.

- No licensed physician may perform or attempt to perform any abortion, including a chemical abortion, or prescribe any drug or device intended to cause a chemical abortion, except in the physical presence of the pregnant woman. This requirement effectively prohibits "webcam abortions."

- Tennessee follows the federal standard for Medicaid funding for abortions, permitting the use of federal or state matching Medicaid funds for abortions necessary to preserve the life of the woman or when the pregnancy is the result of rape or incest.

- Tennessee prohibits the use of funds for abortion or abortion research within the state Genetic Testing Program.

- Tennessee law provides that all federal money provided to the state for family planning services will be used fully by government-run health agencies, and none will be paid to third-party providers or private organizations or entities. This law prevents abortion providers from receiving family planning funds.

- A 2018 law declared it is "the policy of the state to favor childbirth" so that "family planning services that do not include elective abortions" or promote elective abortions are favored when distributing state funds. In accordance with this, the law required that Tennessee seek a Medicaid waiver to exclude elective abortion providers from the TennCare program.

- It prohibits insurance companies from offering abortion coverage within state insurance Exchanges established pursuant to the federal healthcare law.

- Tennessee offers "Choose Life" license plates, the proceeds of which provide funding to pregnancy resource centers.

- Tennessee implemented a "tiering system" for the allocation of family planning funding including funding for which abortion providers might be eligible. Under the system, first priority for funding is given to public entities that are operated by state or local government entities. Most abortion providers fall into the lowest priority category of this system.

- Tennessee's ultrasound law requires that If an ultrasound is performed prior to the abortion procedure, it must be reported whether or not the person performing the ultrasound detected a heartbeat, and that the woman shall be offered "the opportunity to learn the results of the ultrasound."

LEGAL RECOGNITION AND PROTECTION OF THE UNBORN AND NEWLY BORN

- Tennessee law includes an unborn child at any point in gestation as a potential victim of homicide.

- Tennessee law provides for enhanced penalties for murdering a pregnant woman.

- It allows a wrongful death (civil) action only when an unborn child is born alive following a negligent or criminal act and dies thereafter.

- Tennessee has created a specific affirmative duty for physicians to provide medical care and treatment to an infant born alive at any stage of development.

- Tennessee has a "Baby Moses" law, establishing a safe haven for mothers to legally leave their infants at designated places and ensuring that the infants receive appropriate care and protection.

- Tennessee law provides for the prosecution of women for alcohol or drug abuse while pregnant.

- Tennessee requires publicly funded substance abuse facilities to give preference to pregnant women and requires any facility capable of accommodating a pregnant woman to provide such treatment. The law also prohibits state officials from filing for protective services for the child if the mother is less than 5 months (i.e., 20 weeks) into her pregnancy and seeks substance abuse treatment as part of her prenatal care.

- Tennessee law provides for a Certificate of Birth Resulting in Stillbirth.

- Tennessee requires that physicians report on the final disposition of aborted children (with exceptions for those aborted through the use of drug-induced abortion and where the expulsion of the aborted baby does not occur at the clinic). The law also prohibits the transfer of the remains for anything of value including "any reimbursements" for incurred costs.

- Tennessee requires written consent of the mother for any medical experiments on, research on, or photography of an aborted fetus. The law includes an exception for the purpose of capturing images that are reasonably believed to depict evidence of a violation of state or federal law.

BIOETHICS LAWS

- Tennessee does not prohibit human cloning or destructive embryo research. Further, it allows fetal experimentation with the consent of the mother.

- The state Department of Health encourages healthcare professionals to provide pregnant women with a publication containing information on cord blood banking.

- Tennessee maintains no meaningful regulation of assisted reproductive technologies or human egg harvesting.

- However, it provides for the relinquishment of rights to an embryo (i.e., embryo adoption).

PATIENT PROTECTION LAWS

- Suicide by physician is a felony in Tennessee.

- Tennessee maintains a Physician Orders for Life-Sustaining Treatment (POLST) Paradigm Program.

HEALTHCARE FREEDOM OF CONSCIENCE

PARTICIPATION IN ABORTION

- A physician is not required to perform an abortion, and no person may be required to participate in the performance of an abortion.

- A hospital is not required to permit the performance of an abortion within its facilities.

PARTICIPATION IN RESEARCH HARMFUL TO HUMAN LIFE

- Tennessee currently provides no protection for the rights of healthcare providers who conscientiously object to participation in human cloning, destructive embryo research, or other forms of medical research that violate a provider's moral or religious beliefs.

DID YOU KNOW?

- In 2018, Tennessee enacted legislation that requires an ultrasound be performed prior to the abortion procedure.

- Tennessee also created a Monument to Unborn Children Fund which will develop a plan for the state to commission a monument in memory of the victims of abortion.

WHAT HAPPENS AFTER *ROE* IS OVERTURNED?

- Abortion will be legal up to viability.

RECOMMENDATIONS
for Tennessee

WOMEN'S PROTECTION PROJECT PRIORITIES

- Enhanced penalties and enforcement mechanisms for the state's abortion-related laws
- Drug-Induced Abortion Information and Reporting Act
- Parental Involvement Enhancement Act
- Components of the Child Protection Act related to mandatory reporting of suspected child abuse and providing remedies for interference with parental rights

INFANTS' PROTECTION PROJECT PRIORITIES

- Unborn Infant Dignity Act
- Prenatal Nondiscrimination Act
- Perinatal Hospice Information Act
- Unborn Wrongful Death Act

PATIENT PROTECTION ACT PRIORITIES

- Joint Resolution Opposing Suicide by Physician
- Charlie Gard Act (formerly the Life Sustaining Care Act)
- Pain Medicine Education Act

ADDITIONAL PRIORITIES

LEGAL RECOGNITION AND PROTECTION FOR THE UNBORN

- Pregnant Woman's Protection Act

BIOETHICS

- Human Cloning Prohibition Act
- Destructive Embryo Research Act
- Prohibition on Public Funding of Human Cloning and Destructive Embryo Research Act

HEALTHCARE FREEDOM OF CONSCIENCE

- Healthcare Freedom of Conscience Act

Texas | RANKING: 13

As a result of aggressive life-affirming legislative action in recent years, Texas has become one of the most protective states in the nation – and a prominent target of abortion activists. However, in its June 2016 decision in *Whole Woman's Health v. Hellerstedt*, the Supreme Court reversed the Fifth Circuit Court of Appeals and struck down Texas' requirement that abortion facilities meet the same health and safety standards as other outpatient facilities performing invasive surgical procedures, as well as a requirement that abortion providers maintain hospital admitting privileges to facilitate the treatment of medical emergencies and abortion complications.

ABORTION

- Texas possesses an enforceable abortion prohibition should the U.S. Constitution be amended or certain U.S. Supreme Court decisions be reversed or modified.

- Texas prohibits abortion at 5 months (i.e., 20 weeks) based on medical evidence that an unborn child at that stage of development can feel pain.

- Texas prohibits the dismemberment abortion procedure. The law is enjoined and in ongoing litigation.

- Texas prohibits partial-birth abortion.

- Another law provides that a third-trimester abortion may not be performed on a viable fetus unless necessary to preserve the woman's life or prevent a "substantial risk of serious impairment" to her physical or mental health or when the fetus has a severe and irreversible abnormality. An additional law provides that a third-trimester abortion may not be performed on a viable fetus unless necessary to prevent "severe, irreversible brain damage" to the woman, paralysis, or if the fetus has a severe and irreversible "brain impairment."

- A physician may not perform an abortion on a woman until at least 24 hours after obtaining her informed consent and after informing her of the nature and risks of the proposed abortion procedure, including the gestational development of the unborn child and available assistance from both public and private agencies. The counseling must be in-person if a woman lives within 100 miles of the abortion facility.

- Texas also explicitly requires a physician to inform a woman seeking abortion of the abortion-breast cancer link.

- Texas requires the performance of an ultrasound before an abortion. The abortion provider must display the ultrasound image, make audible the heart auscultation, and provide a medical description of the images depicted in the ultrasound image.

- Texas prohibits insurance companies from coercing a woman's abortion decision through force or by threatening adverse alteration to an insurance plan.

- A physician may not perform an abortion on an unemancipated minor under the age of 18 without the written, notarized consent of one parent or a guardian, unless there is a medical emergency or the minor obtains a court order. Further, Texas has created a presumption that an abortion patient is a minor unless valid government identification is shown. Texas also limits the venue options for requesting a judicial bypass order, stipulates that a minor must be present in court for the required hearing, requires the judge to find by "clear and convincing evidence" that the minor should be granted the court order, and prescribes the factors the judge will consider in making his/her determination.

- A Texas law requiring that abortion facilities meet the same health and safety standards as other facilities performing outpatient surgeries was struck down by the U.S. Supreme Court in *Whole Woman's Health v. Hellerstedt*.

- Texas' requirement that abortion providers maintain hospital admitting privileges was also struck down in *Whole Woman's Health v. Hellerstedt*.

- Texas has an enforceable abortion reporting law but does not require the reporting of information to the Centers for Disease Control and Prevention (CDC). The measure applies to both surgical and nonsurgical abortions and requires abortion providers to report deaths that occur in their facilities, as well as short-term complications.

- Texas requires that physicians providing "medical abortions" be able to do the following: accurately date a pregnancy, determine that the pregnancy is not ectopic, and provide surgical intervention or provide for the patient to receive a surgical abortion. The patient must be examined by a physician and informed of the risks and benefits of the procedure and the possibility that a surgical abortion may be required. A 2013 law requiring a physician to examine a woman before dispensing drug-induced abortion and requiring a physician to follow a certain protocol has been upheld by the Fifth Circuit.

- Texas follows the federal standard for Medicaid funding for abortions, permitting the use of federal or state matching Medicaid funds for abortions necessary to preserve the life of the woman or when the pregnancy is the result of rape or incest.

- The Texas Supreme Court has upheld a law limiting taxpayer assistance for abortion to cases where the abortion is necessary to preserve a woman's life or when the pregnancy is the result of rape or incest.

- Funds administered under the Maternal and Infant Health Improvement Program for Women and Children cannot be used for abortions, except in cases of life endangerment.

- State agencies may not contract with entities that perform or promote elective abortions or are affiliates of entities that perform or promote elective abortions under a Women's Health Care Services project (family planning funding).

- Texas has enacted laws prohibiting state contracts with entities that perform elective abortions. The restrictions have been challenged in state court, but remain in force while the lawsuit proceeds.

- Texas continues to allocate millions of dollars to the mission of pregnancy resource centers and other entities providing abortion alternatives.

- It offers "Choose Life" license plates, the proceeds of which benefit abortion alternatives.

LEGAL RECOGNITION AND PROTECTION OF THE UNBORN AND NEWLY BORN

- Under Texas law, the killing of an unborn child at any stage of gestation is defined as a form of homicide.

- Texas defines a nonfatal assault on an unborn child as a criminal offense.

- Texas allows parents and other relatives to bring a wrongful death (civil) lawsuit when an unborn child at any stage of development is killed through the negligence or criminal act of another.

- Under Texas law, a "living human child born alive after an abortion or premature birth is entitled to the same rights, powers and privileges as are granted by the laws of [Texas] to any other child born alive after the normal gestational period." Texas has thus created a specific affirmative duty of physicians to provide medical care and treatment to infants born alive at any stage of development.

- Texas defines substance abuse during pregnancy as "child abuse" under civil child-welfare statutes. It has also created a task force charged, in part, with advising on potential criminal liability for a woman who exposes her unborn child to controlled substances.

- It also requires that health care facilities must properly bury or cremate fetal and embryonic remains. This law is in ongoing litigation.

BIOETHICS LAWS

- Texas does not prohibit human cloning or destructive embryo research. Further, it does not prohibit fetal experimentation outright, but includes "fetal tissue" in its ban on the sale or transfer of "human organs."

- However, it specifically allows the use of adult stem cells in hospitals under certain circumstances, and it has created a funding mechanism for funding of adult stem-cell research projects.

- The state Department of State Health Services publishes a brochure related to umbilical cord-blood donation, and physicians are to provide the brochure to their pregnant patients.

- Texas law provides that blood obtained by a blood bank may be used for the collection of adult stem cells if the donor consents.

- Texas maintains no meaningful regulation of assisted reproductive technologies or human egg harvesting, but the Uniform Parentage Act includes the "donation of embryos" in its definition of "assisted reproduction."

PATIENT PROTECTION LAWS

- Suicide by physician is a felony in Texas.

HEALTHCARE FREEDOM OF CONSCIENCE

PARTICIPATION IN ABORTION

- A physician, nurse, staff member, or employee of a hospital who objects to participating directly or indirectly in an abortion may not be required to participate in an abortion.

- A healthcare provider's conscientious objection to participating in abortions may not be a basis for discrimination in employment or education. A person whose rights are violated may bring an action for relief, including back pay and reinstatement.

- A private hospital or healthcare facility is not required to make its facilities available for the performance of an abortion unless a physician determines that the woman's life is immediately endangered.

PARTICIPATION IN RESEARCH HARMFUL TO HUMAN LIFE

- Texas currently provides no protection for the rights of healthcare providers who conscientiously object to participation in human cloning, destructive embryo research, or other forms of medical research that violate a provider's moral or religious beliefs.

DID YOU KNOW?

- In 2017, Texas passed legislation prohibiting the partial-birth abortion procedure.

- Planned Parenthood has challenged the cumulative impact of the abortion regulations in the state. Litigation is ongoing.

WHAT HAPPENS AFTER *ROE* IS OVERTURNED?

- Abortion will not be legal, except to save the life of the mother, based on existing law enacted before *Roe*.

RECOMMENDATIONS
for Texas

WOMEN'S PROTECTION PROJECT PRIORITIES

- Enhanced penalties and enforcement mechanisms for the state's abortion-related laws
- Components of the Child Protection Act related to evidence retention and remedies for third-party interference with parental rights

INFANTS' PROTECTION PROJECT PRIORITIES

- Unborn Infants Dignity Act
- Prenatal Nondiscrimination Act
- Perinatal Hospice Information Act

PATIENT PROTECTION ACT PRIORITIES

- Joint Resolution Opposing Suicide by Physician
- Charlie Gard Act (formerly the Life Sustaining Care Act)
- Pain Medicine Education Act

ADDITIONAL PRIORITIES

ABORTION

- Federal Abortion-Mandate Opt-Out Act

LEGAL RECOGNITION AND PROTECTION FOR THE UNBORN

- Unborn Infant Dignity Act

BIOETHICS

- Human Cloning Prohibition Act
- Destructive Embryo Research Act
- Prohibition on Public Funding of Human Cloning and Destructive Embryo Research Act

HEALTHCARE FREEDOM OF CONSCIENCE

- Healthcare Freedom of Conscience Act

Utah | RANKING: 25

In recent years, Utah has enacted several commonsense measures designed to protect women and the unborn from the harms inherent in abortion, fulfilling the public policy of the state "to encourage all persons to respect the right to life." Much work remains to be done, however, in the field of biotechnologies. Utah does not prohibit human cloning, destructive embryo research, or fetal experimentation, nor does it promote ethical alternatives to destructive research.

ABORTION

- The Utah legislature has resolved that "it is the finding and policy of the Legislature…that unborn children have inherent and inalienable rights that are entitled to protection by the state of Utah pursuant to the provisions of the Utah Constitution… The state of Utah has a compelling interest in the protection of the lives of unborn children… It is the intent of the Legislature to protect and guarantee to unborn children their inherent and inalienable right to life…."

- Moreover, the legislature has found and declared that "it is the public policy of this state to encourage all persons to respect the right to life of all other persons, regardless of age, development, condition or dependency, including all…unborn persons."

- Utah prohibits partial-birth abortion. While modeled after the federal ban, Utah's law provides harsher penalties.

- Utah prohibits post-viability abortions except in cases of life endangerment, "serious risk of substantial and irreversible impairment of a major bodily function," severe fetal abnormality as certified by two physicians, or rape or incest reported to the police.

- A physician may not perform an abortion on a woman until at least 72 hours after first presenting her with an information module. The module will present information such as the state "prefers childbirth over abortion;" adoption is "a preferred and positive choice and alternative to abortion;" services are available to assist during pregnancy and after birth, such as medical assistance benefits for prenatal care, childbirth, and neonatal care; and medical evidence showing unborn children 20 weeks gestational age and older "may be capable of experiencing pain during an abortion procedure."

- The physician must also inform her, in a face-to-face consultation, of the probable gestational age of her unborn child; fetal development; the nature of, risks of, and alternatives to the proposed abortion procedure; how the abortion procedure will affect the fetus; and the medical risks of carrying the pregnancy to term.

- Informed consent provisions are waived if there is a medical emergency or if two physicians who practice maternal-fetal medicine concur, in writing in the patient's medical record, that the unborn child has a defect that is uniformly diagnosable and lethal.

- Utah also requires that women seeking abortions be informed of the unique risks associated with chemical abortions, and that it may be possible to reverse the chemical abortion process.

- If an ultrasound is performed before an abortion, the abortion provider must offer to show it to the woman. The ultrasound provision is waived if there is a medical emergency or if two physicians who practice maternal-fetal medicine concur, in writing in the patient's medical record, that the unborn child has a defect that is uniformly diagnosable and lethal.

- Utah requires that an anesthetic or analgesic be administered to an unborn child in an abortion performed after 20 weeks gestation.

- Utah prohibits and criminalizes acts intended to coerce a woman into undergoing an abortion. It also requires abortion providers to affirmatively state in printed materials that it is illegal for someone to coerce a woman into having an abortion.

- A physician may not perform an abortion on a minor until the physician obtains the consent of one parent or guardian, unless there is a medical emergency or a minor obtains a court order.

- Utah mandates comprehensive health and safety regulations and an annual licensing requirement for facilities that provide abortions during the first and second trimesters of pregnancy.

- Only a physician or osteopathic physician licensed by the state may perform an abortion. Further, abortion providers must maintain hospital admitting privileges or a transfer agreement with a third-party physician who maintains such privileges.

- Abortions can only be performed in an abortion clinic or hospital unless there is a medical emergency.

- Utah has an enforceable abortion reporting law but does not require the reporting of information to the Centers for Disease Control (CDC). The measure applies to both surgical and nonsurgical abortions.

- Utah funds abortions for women eligible for public assistance when necessary to preserve the woman's life, the woman's physical health is threatened by a continued pregnancy, or the pregnancy is the result of rape or incest.

- No agency of the state or its political subdivisions may approve any application for state funds to directly or indirectly support any organization or healthcare provider that provides abortion services to unmarried minors without written consent of a minor's parent or guardian.

- Utah prohibits insurance companies from offering abortion coverage within state insurance Exchanges established pursuant to the federal healthcare law, except in cases of life endangerment, serious risk of substantial and irreversible impairment of major bodily function, lethal defect of the unborn baby, rape, or incest.

- Utah also prohibits private insurance companies from covering abortion, except in cases of life endangerment, serious risk of substantial and irreversible impairment of major bodily function, lethal defect of the unborn baby, rape, or incest.

- Utah offers "Choose Life" license plates, the proceeds of which benefit abortion alternatives.

LEGAL RECOGNITION AND PROTECTION OF THE UNBORN AND NEWLY BORN

- Under Utah law, the killing of an unborn child at any stage of gestation is defined as a form of homicide.

- Utah allows a wrongful death (civil) action only when an unborn child is born alive following a negligent or criminal action and dies thereafter.

- Utah has a "Baby Moses" law, establishing a safe haven for mothers to legally leave their infants at designated places and ensuring the infants receive appropriate care and protection.

- Utah requires substance abuse treatment programs receiving public funds to give priority admission to pregnant women and teenagers. It also requires healthcare professionals to report suspected prenatal drug exposure.

- Utah regulations include exposure to alcohol or other "harmful" substances in utero in the state's definitions of "abuse," "neglect," and "dependency."

- Utah has removed prohibitions (in certain cases) on the prosecution of a woman for killing her unborn child.

BIOETHICS LAWS

- Utah does not prohibit human cloning, destructive embryo research, or fetal experimentation.

- It does not promote ethical alternatives to destructive embryo research.

- Utah does not provide any meaningful regulation of assisted reproductive technologies or human egg harvesting. Further, state law authorizes gestational agreements.

- The Uniform Parentage Act includes "donation of embryos" in its definition of "assisted reproduction."

PATIENT PROTECTION LAWS

- Utah does not have a specific statute criminalizing suicide by physician, and the legal status of suicide by physician in the state is currently indeterminable.

HEALTHCARE FREEDOM OF CONSCIENCE

PARTICIPATION IN ABORTION

- A healthcare provider who objects on religious or moral grounds is not required to participate in abortions.

- A healthcare facility is not required to admit a woman for the performance of an abortion.

- A healthcare provider or healthcare facility's conscientious objection to participating in abortion may not be a basis for civil liability or other recriminatory action.

- Moral or religious objections to abortion may not be a basis for discrimination including dismissal, demotion, suspension, discipline, harassment, retaliation, adverse change in status, termination of, adverse alteration of, or refusal to renew an association or agreement; or refusal to provide a benefit, privilege, raise, promotion, tenure, or increased status that the healthcare provider would have otherwise received. Importantly, Utah provides a private right of action for discrimination, providing equitable relief including reinstatement and damages.

PARTICIPATION IN RESEARCH HARMFUL TO HUMAN LIFE

- Utah currently provides no protection for the rights of healthcare providers who conscientiously object to participation in human cloning, destructive embryo research, or other forms of medical research that violate a provider's moral or religious beliefs.

DID YOU KNOW?

- In 2018, Utah considered legislation that would have prohibited abortion based on the unborn child's diagnosis of Down syndrome.

WHAT HAPPENS AFTER *ROE* IS OVERTURNED?

- Abortion will be legal up to 20 weeks of pregnancy.

RECOMMENDATIONS
for Utah

WOMEN'S PROTECTION PROJECT PRIORITIES

- Enhanced penalties and enforcement mechanisms for the state's abortion-related laws
- Drug-Induced Abortion Information and Reporting Act (add reporting requirements)
- Parental Involvement Enhancement Act
- Child Protection Act

INFANTS' PROTECTION PROJECT PRIORITIES

- Unborn Infants Dignity Act
- Prenatal Nondiscrimination Act
- Perinatal Hospice Information Act
- Born-Alive Infant Protection Act
- Unborn Wrongful Death Act

PATIENT PROTECTION ACT PRIORITIES

- Suicide by Physician Ban Act
- Joint Resolution Opposing Suicide by Physician
- Charlie Gard Act (formerly the Life Sustaining Care Act)
- Pain Medicine Education Act

ADDITIONAL PRIORITIES

ABORTION

- Defunding the Abortion Industry and Advancing Women's Health Act

BIOETHICS

- Human Cloning Prohibition Act
- Destructive Embryo Research Act
- Prohibition on Public Funding of Human Cloning and Destructive Embryo Research Act

PATIENT PROTECTION

- Suicide by Physician Ban Act

HEALTHCARE FREEDOM OF CONSCIENCE

- Healthcare Freedom of Conscience Act

Vermont | RANKING: 48

Vermont has a dismal record on life, lacking the most basic legal protections for women considering abortion and for unborn victims of criminal violence, and the state provides no regulation of emerging biotechnologies. Further, Vermont has legalized suicide by physician and is one of only a few states that does not protect healthcare freedom of conscience.

ABORTION

- The Vermont Constitution has been construed to provide a broader right to abortion than interpreted in the U.S. Constitution.

- Further, the Vermont legislature has resolved that "it is critical for the... personal health and happiness of American women, that the right of women... to make their own personal medical decisions about reproductive and gynecological issues be vigilantly preserved and protected... This legislative body reaffirms the right of every Vermont woman to privacy, autonomy, and safety in making personal decisions regarding reproduction and family planning..."

- Vermont allows abortions after viability, even in cases where the mother's life or health is not endangered.

- Vermont does not provide even rudimentary protection for women or minors considering abortions. It does not have an informed consent law, ultrasound requirement, parental involvement law for minors seeking abortions, abortion provider regulations, or a prohibition on anyone other than a licensed physician performing an abortion.

- It has an enforceable abortion reporting law but does not require the reporting of information to the Centers for Disease Control and Prevention (CDC). The requirement applies to both surgical and nonsurgical abortions.

- Vermont taxpayers fund "medically necessary" abortions for women receiving public assistance. This requirement essentially equates to funding abortion-on-demand in light of the U.S. Supreme Court's broad definition of "health" in the context of abortion.

LEGAL RECOGNITION AND PROTECTION OF THE UNBORN AND NEWLY BORN

- Vermont law does not recognize an unborn child as a potential homicide or assault victim.

- It allows a wrongful death (civil) action when a viable unborn child is killed through a negligent or criminal act.

- Vermont does not require infants who survive abortions to be given appropriate, potentially life-saving medical care.

- Vermont's Baby Safe Haven Law allows mothers to legally leave their infants at designated places and ensures the infants receive appropriate care and protection. It permits a person or facility receiving an infant to not reveal the identity of the person relinquishing the child unless there is suspected abuse.

BIOETHICS LAWS

- Vermont does not prohibit or limit human cloning, destructive embryo research, or fetal experimentation.

- It does not promote ethical alternatives to destructive embryo research.

- Vermont does not regulate assisted reproductive technologies or human egg harvesting.

PATIENT PROTECTION LAWS

- Suicide by physician is legal in Vermont. Importantly, the law fails to include some of the most basic legal protections for those considering suicide by physician. A physician who has only examined a patient once is permitted to prescribe life-ending drugs to the patient. The physician is not required to refer the patient for an evaluation by a psychiatrist to determine if the patient is depressed or being coerced to end his/her life. Further, the law does not require witnesses to be present when the patient takes a life-ending medication, increasing the possibility that persons who may wish to hasten a patient's death might be with the patient and pressure the patient to end his/her life or even administer the lethal drugs instead of the patient.

- Vermont requires the state Department of Health to provide an annual report on end-of-life care and pain management. It also has a Patient's Bill of Rights for Palliative Care and Pain Management, ensuring that healthcare providers inform patients of all of their treatment options. A lawsuit alleging that this provision violates the rights of conscientious providers resulted in a representation by the state that the Patient's Bill of Rights would not be interpreted to infringe conscience rights.

- Vermont maintains a Physician Orders for Life-Sustaining Treatment (POLST) Paradigm Program.

HEALTHCARE FREEDOM OF CONSCIENCE

PARTICIPATION IN ABORTION

- Vermont currently provides no protection for the rights of conscience of healthcare providers who conscientiously object to participating or assisting in abortions or any other healthcare procedure.

PARTICIPATION IN RESEARCH HARMFUL TO HUMAN LIFE

- Vermont currently provides no protection for the rights of healthcare providers who conscientiously object to participation in human cloning, destructive embryo research, or other forms of medical research that violate a provider's moral or religious beliefs.

DID YOU KNOW?

- In 2018, Vermont considered legislation that would have created a right to have an abortion, as well as legislation that would have created a special fund to support Planned Parenthood from a tax on certain drugs.

WHAT HAPPENS AFTER *ROE* IS OVERTURNED?

- Abortion will be legal throughout pregnancy.

RECOMMENDATIONS
for Vermont

WOMEN'S PROTECTION PROJECT PRIORITIES

- Enhanced penalties and enforcement mechanisms for the state's abortion-related laws
- Women's Right to Know Act with reflection period
- Coercive Abuse Against Mothers Prevention Act
- Women's Health Protection Act (abortion clinic regulations)
- Drug-Induced Abortion Information and Reporting Act
- Parental Notification for Abortion Act
- Child Protection Act

INFANTS' PROTECTION PROJECT

- Unborn Infants Dignity Act
- Prenatal Nondiscrimination Act
- Perinatal Hospice Information Act
- Born-Alive Infant Protection Act
- Unborn Wrongful Death Act

PATIENT PROTECTION ACT PRIORITIES

- Suicide by Physician Ban Act
- Joint Resolution Opposing Suicide by Physician
- Charlie Gard Act (formerly the Life Sustaining Care Act)
- Pain Medicine Education Act

ADDITIONAL PRIORITIES

ABORTION

- State Constitutional Amendment (providing that there is no state constitutional right to abortion)
- Defunding the Abortion Industry and Advancing Women's Health Act
- Federal Abortion-Mandate Opt-Out Act

LEGAL RECOGNITION AND PROTECTION FOR THE UNBORN

- Crimes Against the Unborn Child Act
- Pregnant Woman's Protection Act

BIOETHICS

- Human Cloning Prohibition Act
- Destructive Embryo Research Act
- Prohibition on Public Funding of Human Cloning and Destructive Embryo Research Act

PATIENT PROTECTION

- Repeal Suicide by physician Law and Enact Suicide by Physician Ban Act

HEALTHCARE FREEDOM OF CONSCIENCE

- Healthcare Freedom of Conscience Act

Virginia | RANKING: 20

Virginia provides fairly comprehensive legal protections for women, the unborn, and newly born children. It is also one of only a small number of states that has enacted meaningful, protective regulations for emerging biotechnologies. In recent years, pro-abortion forces have launched multiple efforts to repeal or undermine the state's life-affirming regulations, but those efforts have thus far failed.

ABORTION

- Virginia prohibits "partial-birth infanticide" (i.e., partial-birth abortion).

- A third-trimester abortion may not be performed unless the attending physician and two other physicians certify in writing that continuation of the pregnancy is likely to result in the woman's death or would "substantially and irremediably impair" the woman's physical or mental health. Further, measures for life support for the unborn child "must be available and utilized if there is any clearly visible evidence of viability."

- A physician may not perform an abortion on a woman until at least 24 hours after the woman is provided with in-person counseling, including "a full, reasonable, and comprehensible medical explanation of the nature, benefits, risks of and alternatives to abortion;" the probable gestational age of her unborn child; and descriptions of available assistance and benefits, agencies and organizations providing alternatives to abortion, and the father's legal responsibilities.

- Virginia requires that a woman undergo an ultrasound and have the opportunity to view the images prior to an abortion.

- A physician may not perform an abortion on an unemancipated minor under the age of 18 until he or she secures written consent from one parent or "authorized person" who has care and control of the minor, unless the minor is the victim of rape, incest, or child abuse, there is a medical emergency, or the minor secures a court order.

- Virginia law regulates any facility in which five or more first trimester abortions per month are performed as a category of "hospital." Under the law, the Virginia Board of Health also promulgated specific health and safety regulations, which are under Executive Review.

- Virginia also requires that second-trimester abortions be performed in a hospital or ambulatory surgical center. The U.S. Supreme Court has upheld the constitutionality of this requirement.

- Only a physician licensed by the state to practice medicine and surgery may perform an abortion. Abortion providers must also maintain a transfer agreement with a local hospital to facilitate the treatment of abortion complications.

- Virginia has an enforceable abortion reporting law but does not require the reporting of information to the Centers for Disease Control and Prevention (CDC). The measure applies to both surgical and nonsurgical abortions.

- It provides abortion funding for women eligible for public assistance only in cases of rape, incest, fetal abnormality, or when the life of the mother is in jeopardy.

- No abortion-related expenditures from general or non-general fund sources may be made out of any appropriations by the General Assembly, except as otherwise required by federal law or state statute.

- No post-partum family planning funds provided to women under the state's Medicaid program may be used to make direct referrals for abortion.

- Virginia prohibits insurance companies from offering abortion coverage within state insurance Exchanges established pursuant to the federal healthcare law, except in cases of life endangerment, rape, or incest.

- Benefits provided to state employees through the Commonwealth of Virginia Health Benefits Plan may not provide coverage for abortion unless the procedure is necessary to preserve the woman's life or health, the pregnancy is the result of rape or incest that has been reported to a law enforcement or public health agency, or a physician certifies that the fetus is believed to have an incapacitating physical deformity or mental deficiency.

- Virginia offers "Choose Life" license plates, the proceeds of which benefit abortion alternatives. Unfortunately, it also offers a pro-abortion license plate, "Trust Women/Respect Choice." However, while Planned Parenthood and other abortion providers are eligible to receive the proceeds from the plates, they are specifically prohibited from using the earned revenue for "abortion services."

LEGAL RECOGNITION AND PROTECTION OF THE UNBORN AND NEWLY BORN

- Under Virginia law, the killing of an unborn child at any stage of gestation is defined as a form of homicide.

- For purposes of "homicide" and "child abuse," a "human infant who has been born alive and is fully brought forth from the mother has achieved an independent and separate existence, regardless of whether the umbilical cord has been cut or the placenta detached."

- Virginia permits recovery for the death of an unborn child at any stage of development in a wrongful death (civil) action.

- Virginia protects infants born alive at any stage of development from "deliberate acts" undertaken by a physician that result in the death of the infant.

- Virginia has enacted a "Baby Moses" law, establishing a safe haven for mothers to legally leave their infants at designated places and ensuring the infants receive appropriate care and protection.

- Virginia requires emergency personnel to report child abuse including cases of in utero exposure to controlled substances, and healthcare providers are required to report to the state Department of Social Services any diagnosis of fetal alcohol spectrum disorders or other medical condition caused by exposure to controlled substances during pregnancy.

- It also funds drug treatment programs for pregnant women and newborns.

BIOETHICS LAWS

- Virginia prohibits human cloning for any purpose, but it does not prohibit destructive embryo research or fetal experimentation.

- Virginia prohibits tax credits for research on human cells, on tissue derived from induced abortions, and on stem cells obtained from human embryos. This prohibition is an annual rider.

- Virginia maintains the Virginia Cord Blood Bank Initiative as a public resource for advancing basic and clinical research and for the treatment of patients with life-threatening diseases or debilitating conditions. All women admitted to a hospital or birthing facility may be offered the opportunity to donate umbilical cord blood to the initiative. Likewise, every licensed practitioner who renders prenatal care is to provide information to pregnant patients regarding the option of umbilical cord blood banking.

- It has also created a special fund in the state treasury entitled the Christopher Reeve Stem Cell Research Fund. No monies from the fund may be provided to entities that conduct research with stem cells obtained from human embryos.

- Virginia maintains some regulation of assisted reproductive technologies but does not regulate human egg harvesting.

PATIENT PROTECTION LAWS

- Virginia does not have a specific statute criminalizing suicide by physician. However, Virginia has adopted the common law of crimes, which includes the crime of suicide by physician.

- In 2018, Virginia passed legislation that requires hospitals to develop a process for the patient to obtain a second opinion regarding the medical and ethical appropriateness of proposed medical care, review by an interdisciplinary medical review committee, and a written explanation of the decision.

HEALTHCARE FREEDOM OF CONSCIENCE

PARTICIPATION IN ABORTION

- Any person who objects in writing and on personal, ethical, moral, and/or religious grounds is not required to participate in abortions.

- A physician, hospital, or medical facility is not required to admit a woman for the purposes of performing an abortion.

- The conscientious objection of an individual healthcare provider, hospital, or medical facility to participating in an abortion may not be a basis for a claim for damages, denial of employment, disciplinary action, or any other recriminatory action.

- Virginia currently provides no protection for the rights of healthcare providers who conscientiously object to participation in human cloning, destructive embryo research, or other forms of medical research that violate a provider's moral or religious beliefs.

DID YOU KNOW?

- In 2017, Virginia's Governor vetoed legislation prohibiting the use of taxpayer funds to pay for abortions, and establishing a "tiering system" for the allocation of family planning funding that would prioritize healthcare providers that do not perform abortions.

- Virginia considered legislation that states "any person who, as a result of driving under the influence, causes the death of the fetus of another Is guilty of involuntary manslaughter."

- Planned Parenthood has challenged the cumulative impact of the abortion regulations in the state. Litigation is ongoing.

WHAT HAPPENS AFTER *ROE* IS OVERTURNED?

- Abortion will be legal throughout pregnancy.

RECOMMENDATIONS
for Virginia

WOMEN'S PROTECTION PROJECT PRIORITIES

- Enhanced penalties and enforcement mechanisms for the state's abortion-related laws
- Coercive Abuse Against Mothers Prevention Act
- Drug-Induced Abortion Information and Reporting Act
- Parental Involvement Enhancement Act
- Child Protection Act

INFANTS' PROTECTION PROJECT PRIORITIES

- Unborn Infants Dignity Act
- Prenatal Nondiscrimination Act
- Perinatal Hospice Information Act

PATIENT PROTECTION ACT PRIORITIES

- Suicide by Physician Ban Act
- Joint Resolution Opposing Suicide by Physician
- Charlie Gard Act (formerly the Life Sustaining Care Act)
- Pain Medicine Education Act

ADDITIONAL PRIORITIES

ABORTION

- Defunding the Abortion Industry and Advancing Women's Health Act

LEGAL RECOGNITION AND PROTECTION FOR THE UNBORN

- Pregnant Woman's Protection Act

BIOETHICS

- Destructive Embryo Research Act

PATIENT PROTECTION

- Suicide by Physician Ban Act

HEALTHCARE FREEDOM OF CONSCIENCE

- Healthcare Freedom of Conscience Act

Washington | RANKING: 50

Washington does not adequately protect women from the negative consequences of abortion, nor does it protect unborn children from criminal violence. Washington has failed to enact commonsense, publicly supported laws pertaining to informed consent, parental involvement, abortion provider regulations, or fetal homicide, and it does not regulate emerging biotechnologies. Moreover, Washington explicitly permits suicide by physician.

ABORTION

- Washington maintains a Freedom of Choice Act. The Act mandates a right to abortion even if *Roe v. Wade* is eventually overturned, specifically providing: "The sovereign people hereby declare that every individual possesses a fundamental right of privacy with respect to personal reproductive decisions. Accordingly, it is the public policy of the [S]tate of Washington that: (1) Every individual has the fundamental right to choose or refuse birth control; (2) Every woman has the fundamental right to choose or refuse to have an abortion...; (3) ... the state shall not deny or interfere with a woman's fundamental right to choose or refuse to have an abortion; and (4) the state shall not discriminate against the exercise of these rights in the regulation or provision of benefits, facilities, services, or information."

- A state voter initiative declared: "The state may not deny or interfere with a woman's right to choose to have an abortion prior to viability of the fetus, or to protect her life or health."

- No abortion may be performed after viability unless necessary to protect the woman's life or health.

- Washington does not have an informed consent law for abortion, parental involvement law for minors seeking abortion, or abortion facility regulations.

- Only a physician licensed in Washington may perform an abortion.

- Washington has an enforceable abortion reporting law but does not require the reporting of information to the Centers for Disease Control and Prevention (CDC). The measure applies to both surgical and nonsurgical abortions and requires abortion providers to report short-term complications.

- Washington taxpayers are required by statute to fund "medically necessary" abortions for women receiving state public assistance, requiring funding of abortion-on-demand in light of the U.S. Supreme Court's broad definition of "health" in the context of abortion. It must also provide benefits, services, or information to permit women to obtain abortions if it provides comparable maternity care benefits, services, or information.

- Washington protects physical access to abortion clinics and curtails the First Amendment rights of pro-life sidewalk counselors and demonstrators.

- Health plans issued or renewed starting in 2019 must cover voluntary sterilization and, if the plan covers maternity care, it must provide "substantially equivalent coverage" for abortion procedures.

LEGAL RECOGNITION AND PROTECTION OF THE UNBORN AND NEWLY BORN

- Under Washington criminal law, the killing of an unborn child after "quickening" is defined as a form of homicide.

- It allows a wrongful death (civil) action when a viable unborn child is killed through negligence or a criminal act.

- Under Washington law, "the right of medical treatment of an infant born alive in the course of an abortion procedure shall be the same as the right of an infant born prematurely of equal gestational age." Thus, Washington has created a specific affirmative duty of physicians to provide medical care and treatment to infants born alive at any stage of development.

- Washington has enacted a "Baby Moses" law, establishing a safe haven for mothers to legally leave their infants at designated places and ensuring the infants receive appropriate care and protection.

- It funds drug treatment programs for pregnant women and newborns.

BIOETHICS LAWS

- Washington law does not prohibit human cloning, destructive embryo research, or fetal experimentation.

- All persons licensed to provide prenatal care or practice medicine must provide information to all pregnant women regarding the differences between public and private umbilical cord blood banking and the opportunity to donate the blood and tissue extracted from the placenta and umbilical cord following delivery.

- Washington maintains no meaningful regulation of assisted reproductive technologies or human egg harvesting.

- The Uniform Parentage Act includes "donation of embryos" in its definition of "assisted reproduction."

PATIENT PROTECTION LAWS

- Washington has legalized suicide by physician by voter initiative. The law creates financial incentives for healthcare insurance companies to deny coverage for life-saving treatment and to pressure vulnerable patients to choose suicide—a practice already occurring in Oregon. Moreover, the law does not provide safeguards for those suffering from mental illness or depression and requires physicians participating in patient suicides to falsify death certificates.

- The initiative superseded a prior law which made suicide by physician a felony. That law had been upheld in the landmark case of *Washington v. Glucksberg*, in which the U.S. Supreme Court refused to recognize a federal constitutional right to suicide by physician.

HEALTHCARE FREEDOM OF CONSCIENCE

PARTICIPATION IN ABORTION AND CONTRACEPTION

- An individual healthcare worker or private medical facility cannot be required by law or contract to participate in the performance of abortions.

- No person may be discriminated against in employment or professional privileges because of participating or refusing to participate in abortions.

- Washington protects individual healthcare providers, as well as private hospitals and medical facilities, who conscientiously object to participating in any healthcare procedure. However, this protection does not extend to public hospitals and medical facilities.

- Washington has a "contraceptive equity" law, requiring health insurance coverage for contraception. No exemption is provided for employers or insurers with a moral or religious objection to contraception.

PARTICIPATION IN RESEARCH HARMFUL TO HUMAN LIFE

- Washington currently provides no protection for the rights of healthcare providers who conscientiously object to participation in human cloning, destructive embryo research, or other forms of medical research that violate a provider's moral or religious beliefs.

DID YOU KNOW?

- In 2018, Washington passed a law requiring health plans to cover contraception and voluntary sterilization, and if the plan covers maternity care, it must provide "substantially equivalent coverage" for abortion procedures.

- Washington considered legislation requiring parental notification for minors seeking an abortion as well as legislation stating life begins from conception.

WHAT HAPPENS AFTER *ROE* IS OVERTURNED?

- Abortion will be legal throughout pregnancy.

RECOMMENDATIONS
for Washington

WOMEN'S PROTECTION PROJECT PRIORITIES

- Enhanced penalties and enforcement mechanisms for the state's abortion-related laws
- Women's Right to Know Act with reflection period
- Coercive Abuse Against Mothers Prevention Act
- Women's Health Protection Act (abortion clinic regulations)
- Drug-Induced Abortion Information and Reporting Act
- Parental Notification for Abortion Act
- Child Protection Act

INFANTS' PROTECTION PROJECT PRIORITIES

- Unborn Infants Dignity Act
- Prenatal Nondiscrimination Act
- Perinatal Hospice Information Act
- Unborn Wrongful Death Act (for a pre-viable child)

PATIENT PROTECTION ACT PRIORITIES

- Suicide by Physician Ban Act
- Joint Resolution Opposing Suicide by Physician
- Charlie Gard Act (formerly the Life Sustaining Care Act)
- Pain Medicine Education Act

ADDITIONAL PRIORITIES

ABORTION

- Repeal of State FOCA
- Defunding the Abortion Industry and Advancing Women's Health Act
- Federal Abortion-Mandate Opt-Out Act

LEGAL RECOGNITION AND PROTECTION FOR THE UNBORN

- Crimes Against the Unborn Child Act (protecting a child from conception)
- Pregnant Woman's Protection Act

BIOETHICS

- Human Cloning Prohibition Act
- Destructive Embryo Research Act
- Prohibition on Public Funding of Human Cloning and Destructive Embryo Research Act

PATIENT PROTECTION

- Limits on the provision of suicide by physician such as family member notification and mental health evaluations

HEALTHCARE FREEDOM OF CONSCIENCE

- Healthcare Freedom of Conscience Act

West Virginia | RANKING: 27 |

Although the state Supreme Court has ruled that the state constitution provides for a broader right to abortion than that interpreted in the U.S. Constitution, West Virginia maintains some basic protections for women considering abortion. For example, written materials required under an informed consent law include information about the abortion-breast cancer link, and the risky process of prescribing drug-induced abortions online is prohibited.

ABORTION

- The West Virginia Supreme Court has ruled that the state constitution provides for a broader right to abortion than that interpreted in the U.S. Constitution.

- West Virginia prohibits abortions at or after 5 months (i.e., 20 weeks) on the basis of the pain experienced by unborn children.

- West Virginia prohibits dismemberment abortions.

- A physician may not perform an abortion on a woman until at least 24 hours after obtaining her informed consent and after informing her of the nature and risks of the proposed abortion procedure, the risks of carrying the pregnancy to term, and the probable gestational age of her unborn child.

- At least 24 hours prior to an abortion, a woman must also receive information about medical assistance benefits that may be available for prenatal care, childbirth, and neonatal care; the father's liability for child support; and her right to review state-prepared materials describing the development of her unborn child, outlining common methods of abortion, discussing the medical risks of abortion, and listing agencies that offer alternatives to abortion. She may review this information either in print or on the state's website.

- West Virginia prohibits the dangerous practice of using telemedicine to administer abortion-inducing drugs.

- West Virginia includes information about the abortion-breast cancer link in the educational materials that a woman must receive prior to abortion.

- If an ultrasound is performed before an abortion, the abortion provider must offer to show it to the woman. The woman must also be given the opportunity of having the image explained to her.

- A physician may not perform an abortion on an unemancipated minor under the age of 18 until at least 48 hours after actual notice has been provided to one parent, unless there is a medical emergency or the minor secures a court order. The law also allows an abortion to be performed without parental notice if a physician who is not performing the abortion determines that the minor is "mature enough to make the abortion decision independently or that parental notice is not in the minor's best interest."

- West Virginia has an enforceable abortion reporting law but does not require the reporting of information to the Centers for Disease Control and Prevention (CDC). The measure applies to both surgical and nonsurgical abortions.

- West Virginia taxpayers are required to fund "medically necessary" abortions for women receiving state medical assistance. This requirement essentially equates to funding abortion-on-demand in light of the U.S. Supreme Court's broad definition of "health" in the context of abortion.

LEGAL RECOGNITION AND PROTECTION OF THE UNBORN AND NEWLY BORN

- West Virginia law recognizes an unborn child at any stage of gestation as a potential victim of homicide.

- It also criminalizes nonfatal assaults on the unborn.

- West Virginia allows a wrongful death (civil) action when an unborn child at any stage of development is killed through a negligent or criminal act.

- West Virginia does not require physicians or hospitals to provide appropriate and potentially life-saving care to infants who survive attempted abortions.

- West Virginia has enacted a "Baby Moses" law, establishing a safe haven for mothers to legally leave their infants at designated places and ensuring that the infants receive appropriate care and protection.

BIOETHICS LAWS

- West Virginia does not prohibit human cloning, destructive embryonic research, or fetal experimentation.

- It does not promote ethical alternatives to destructive embryo research.

- West Virginia does not regulate assisted reproductive technologies or human egg harvesting.

PATIENT PROTECTION LAWS

- West Virginia does not have a specific statute criminalizing suicide by physician. However, suicide by physician remains a common law crime.

- West Virginia has enacted "right to try" legislation, providing terminally ill patients with expanded opportunities to try investigational medications that have not yet received Food & Drug Administration (FDA) approval.

HEALTHCARE FREEDOM OF CONSCIENCE

PARTICIPATION IN ABORTION AND CONTRACEPTION

- West Virginia protects the civil rights of healthcare providers, including individuals, hospitals, and other medical facilities possessing conscientious objections to participating in abortions.

- West Virginia has a "contraceptive equity" law, requiring health insurance coverage for contraception. The law provides an exemption to employers or insurers with a conscientious objection to contraceptives.

PARTICIPATION IN RESEARCH HARMFUL TO HUMAN LIFE

- West Virginia currently provides no protection for the rights of healthcare providers who conscientiously object to participation in human cloning, destructive embryo research, or other forms of medical research that violate a provider's moral or religious beliefs.

DID YOU KNOW?

- West Virginia considered an amendment to the state constitution "clarifying that nothing in the constitution secures or protects a right to abortion, and nothing in the constitution requires the funding of an abortion."

- West Virginia's legislature considered various legislation that would strengthen its protection of life, including a requirement the abortion be performed by a licensed physician and a requirement that parental consent be given in writing at the facility where the abortion is to be performed. It also considered legislation that would prohibit the state funding of abortion.

WHAT HAPPENS AFTER *ROE* IS OVERTURNED?

- Abortion will be illegal, except to save the life of the mother, based on existing law enacted before *Roe*.

RECOMMENDATIONS
for West Virginia

WOMEN'S PROTECTION PROJECT PRIORITIES

- Enhanced penalties and enforcement mechanisms for the state's abortion-related laws
- Coercive Abuse Against Mothers Prevention Act
- Women's Health Protection Act (abortion clinic regulations)
- Drug-Induced Abortion Information and Reporting Act
- Parental Consent for Abortion Act
- Parental Involvement Enhancement Act
- Child Protection Act

INFANTS' PROTECTION PROJECT PRIORITIES

- Unborn Infants Dignity Act
- Prenatal Nondiscrimination Act
- Perinatal Hospice Information Act
- Born-Alive Infant Protection Act

PATIENT PROTECTION ACT PRIORITIES

- Suicide by Physician Ban Act
- Joint Resolution Opposing Suicide by Physician
- Charlie Gard Act (formerly the Life Sustaining Care Act)
- Pain Medicine Education Act

ADDITIONAL PRIORITIES

ABORTION

- State Constitutional Amendment (providing that there is no state constitutional right to abortion)
- Defunding Abortion Providers and Advancing Women's Health Act
- Federal Abortion-Mandate Opt-Out Act

LEGAL RECOGNITION AND PROTECTION FOR THE UNBORN

- Pregnant Woman's Protection Act

BIOETHICS

- Human Cloning Prohibition Act
- Destructive Embryo Research Act
- Prohibition on Public Funding of Human Cloning and Destructive Embryo Research Act

PATIENT PROTECTION

- Suicide by Physician Ban Act

HEALTHCARE FREEDOM OF CONSCIENCE

- Healthcare Freedom of Conscience Act

Wisconsin | RANKING: 24

Wisconsin has continued to prioritize maternal health over abortion industry influence and profits, prohibiting late-term abortions and requiring comprehensive informed consent for abortions. Wisconsin is also one of a small number of states that maintains a broad, enforceable abortion prohibition should the U.S. Constitution be amended to protect unborn life or the U.S. Supreme Court overturn *Roe v. Wade*.

ABORTION

- Wisconsin prohibits partial-birth abortion but the state's Attorney General issued a statement declaring the law unenforceable and finding it possibly restrictive of other abortion procedures.

- Wisconsin prohibits abortions at or after 5 months (i.e., 20 weeks) on the basis of the pain experienced by unborn children.

- No abortion may be performed after viability unless necessary to preserve the woman's life or health. Moreover, a physician must use the abortion method most likely to preserve the life and health of the unborn child unless that method would increase the risk to the woman.

- Wisconsin possesses an enforceable abortion prohibition should the U.S. Constitution be amended or certain U.S. Supreme Court decisions be reversed or modified.

- A physician may not perform an abortion on a woman until at least 24 hours after the woman is informed of the probable gestational age of her unborn child, the details of the proposed abortion procedure and its inherent risks, the particular medical risks of her pregnancy, her right to view an ultrasound prior to an abortion, available medical assistance benefits, the father's legal responsibilities, and alternatives to abortion. Women must also be provided information on the post-fertilization age of the unborn child.

- Wisconsin requires the performance of an ultrasound before an abortion.

- The provision of informed consent and state-prepared materials must include information on perinatal hospice.

- Wisconsin requires abortion providers to state in their printed materials that it is illegal for anyone to coerce a woman into having an abortion.

- A physician may not perform an abortion on an unemancipated minor without the informed, written consent of one parent, grandparent, aunt, uncle, or sibling who is at least 25 years of age, unless the minor is the victim of rape, incest, or child abuse; there is a medical emergency; or the minor obtains a court order. Further, the law gives discretion to a psychiatrist or psychologist to waive consent based on a belief that the minor will commit suicide rather than obtain consent or seek a court order.

- Wisconsin imposes minimal health and safety requirements on abortion facilities. Further, physicians may only perform first-trimester abortions within 30 minutes of a hospital.

- Only a licensed physician may perform an abortion. A law requiring that individual abortion providers maintain hospital admitting privileges was invalidated by the Seventh Circuit Court of Appeals.

- Wisconsin has an enforceable abortion reporting law but does not require the reporting of information to the Centers for Disease Control and Prevention (CDC). The measure applies to both surgical and nonsurgical abortions and requires abortion providers to report short-term complications.

- Wisconsin prohibits the use of telemedicine to administer drug-induced abortion and requires that such drugs be provided only by physicians, but the law has been challenged in state court.

- Wisconsin provides state funding for abortions for women eligible for public assistance that are directly and medically necessary to preserve the woman's life, to prevent grave, long-lasting physical health damage to the woman, or when the pregnancy is the result of sexual assault or incest reported to law enforcement authorities.

- Generally, no state, local, or federal funds passing through the state's pregnancy programs, projects, or services may be used to perform, promote, refer for, or counsel for abortion. However, referrals may be made if the abortion is necessary to preserve the woman's life. Further, the law only applies to the extent it does not compromise federal funding.

- Wisconsin's Private Employer Health Care Purchasing Alliance, a voluntary program for private employers, may not include coverage for abortion unless the abortion is needed to preserve the woman's life. Further, coverage for abortions that are "medically necessary" may be obtained only by an optional rider or supplemental coverage provision that is offered and provided on an individual basis and for which an additional premium is paid. Under no circumstances is an employer required to provide coverage for abortion.

- Wisconsin prohibits abortion coverage in the state health insurance Exchange required under the federal healthcare law except in cases of life endangerment, rape, incest, or possible "grave, long-lasting physical health damage."

LEGAL RECOGNITION AND PROTECTION OF THE UNBORN AND NEWLY BORN

- Under Wisconsin law, the killing of an unborn child at any stage of gestation is defined as a form of homicide.

- Wisconsin defines a nonfatal assault on an unborn child as a crime.

- It allows wrongful death (civil) actions when a viable unborn child is killed through a negligent or criminal act.

- Wisconsin has created a specific affirmative duty of physicians to provide medical care and treatment to infants born alive at any stage of development.

- Wisconsin has enacted a "Baby Moses" law, establishing a safe haven for mothers to legally leave their infants at designated places and ensuring the infants receive appropriate care and protection.

- It defines substance abuse during pregnancy as "child abuse" under civil child-welfare statutes.

BIOETHICS LAWS

- Wisconsin does not ban human cloning, destructive embryo research, or fetal experimentation.

- Wisconsin provides funding for destructive embryo research.

- It requires that healthcare providers offer pregnant women information on options to donate umbilical cord blood following delivery.

- Wisconsin maintains no comprehensive measures regulating assisted reproductive technologies or human egg harvesting.

PATIENT PROTECTION LAWS

- Under Wisconsin law, assisting in a suicide is a felony.

HEALTHCARE FREEDOM OF CONSCIENCE

PARTICIPATION IN ABORTION AND CONTRACEPTION

- A physician or other person associated with, employed by, or on staff with a hospital who objects in writing and on moral or religious grounds is not required to participate in abortions.

- A healthcare provider's conscientious objection to participating in abortion may not be a basis for damages, discrimination in employment or education, disciplinary action, or other recriminatory action.

- An individual or entity is not required, because of the receipt of any grant, contract, or loan under state or federal law, to participate in or make its facilities available for the performance of an abortion if such action is contrary to stated religious or moral beliefs.

- A hospital's conscientious, moral, or religious objection to permitting or performing an abortion may not be a basis for civil damages.

- Wisconsin has a "contraceptive equity" requirement, meaning health insurance coverage must include coverage for contraception. No exemption is provided for employers or insurers with moral or religious objections to contraception.

PARTICIPATION IN RESEARCH HARMFUL TO HUMAN LIFE

- Wisconsin currently provides no protection for the rights of healthcare providers who conscientiously object to participation in human cloning, destructive embryo research, or other forms of medical research that violate a provider's moral or religious beliefs.

DID YOU KNOW?

- In 2018, Wisconsin considered legislation prohibiting various governmental agencies from covering abortion in their taxpayer funded employee insurance plans.

- Wisconsin also considered legislation that would have legalized suicide by physician.

WHAT HAPPENS AFTER *ROE* IS OVERTURNED?

- Abortion will be illegal, except to save the life of the mother, based on existing law enacted before *Roe*.

RECOMMENDATIONS
for Wisconsin

WOMEN'S PROTECTION PROJECT PRIORITIES

- Enhanced penalties and enforcement mechanisms for the state's abortion-related laws
- Women's Health Protection Act (abortion facility regulations)
- Drug-Induced Abortion Information and Reporting Act
- Parental Involvement Enhancement Act
- Child Protection Act

INFANTS' PROTECTION PROJECT PRIORITIES

- Unborn Infants Dignity Act
- Prenatal Nondiscrimination Act
- Perinatal Hospice Information Act
- Unborn Wrongful Death Act (for a pre-viable child)

PATIENT PROTECTION ACT PRIORITIES

- Joint Resolution Opposing Suicide by Physician
- Charlie Gard Act (formerly the Life Sustaining Care Act)
- Pain Medicine Education Act

ADDITIONAL PRIORITIES

ABORTION

- Defunding the Abortion Industry and Advancing Women's Health Act

LEGAL RECOGNITION AND PROTECTION FOR THE UNBORN

- Pregnant Woman's Protection Act

BIOETHICS

- Human Cloning Prohibition Act
- Destructive Embryo Research Act
- Prohibition on Public Funding of Human Cloning and Destructive Embryo Research Act

HEALTHCARE FREEDOM OF CONSCIENCE

- Healthcare Freedom of Conscience Act

Wyoming | RANKING: 35

Wyoming lacks many basic legal protections for life. For example, Wyoming does not require informed consent for abortion, mandate minimum health and safety standards for abortion facilities, or protect unborn victims of violence. It also fails to regulate or proscribe emerging biotechnologies, and it does not statutorily prohibit suicide by physician.

ABORTION

- A physician may not perform an abortion on an unemancipated minor under the age of 18 who is not in active military service or who has not lived independently and apart from her parents for more than six months without receiving the consent of one parent, unless there is a medical emergency or the minor obtains a court order.

- Wyoming does not have an informed consent law for abortion, but does require that women seeking abortions be informed at least 24 hours prior to an abortion of their right to view an ultrasound of their unborn child and to hear their child's heartbeat.

- No abortion may be performed after viability unless necessary to protect the woman from "imminent peril that substantially endangers her life or health."

- Only a physician licensed to practice medicine in the state and using accepted medical procedures may perform an abortion.

- Wyoming has an enforceable abortion reporting law but does not require the reporting of information to the Centers for Disease Control and Prevention (CDC). The measure applies to both surgical and nonsurgical abortions and requires abortion providers to report short-term complications.

- Wyoming follows the federal standard for Medicaid funding for abortions, permitting the use of federal or state matching Medicaid funds for abortions necessary to preserve the life of the woman or when the pregnancy is the result of rape or incest.

LEGAL RECOGNITION AND PROTECTION OF THE UNBORN AND NEWLY BORN

- Wyoming law does not recognize an unborn child as a potential victim of homicide or assault.

- Wyoming law defines an attack on a pregnant woman resulting in a miscarriage or stillbirth as a criminal assault. It also provides enhanced penalties for murdering a pregnant woman.

- Wyoming allows a wrongful death (civil) action only when an unborn child is born alive following a negligent or criminal act and dies thereafter.

- Wyoming law requires that the "commonly accepted means of care shall be employed in the treatment of any viable infant aborted alive with any chance of survival."

- Wyoming has a "Baby Moses" law, establishing a safe haven for mothers to legally leave their infants at designated places and ensuring the infants receive appropriate care and protection.

BIOETHICS LAWS

- Wyoming has not banned human cloning or destructive embryo research.

- It does not promote ethical alternatives to destructive embryo research.

- Wyoming maintains no comprehensive measures regulating assisted reproductive technologies or human egg harvesting, but it includes "donation of embryos" in the definition of "assisted reproduction."

- Wyoming enacted legislation prohibiting the sale of fetal tissue.

PATIENT PROTECTION LAWS

- Wyoming has not enacted a statutory prohibition against suicide by physician. Moreover, since it does not recognize common law crimes (including assisting in suicide), the legal status of suicide by physician in Wyoming is unclear.

- It maintains a Physician Orders for Life-Sustaining Treatment (POLST) Paradigm Program.

HEALTHCARE FREEDOM OF CONSCIENCE

PARTICIPATION IN ABORTION AND HEALTHCARE SYSTEMS

- A person is not required to participate in an abortion or in any act that assists in the performance of an abortion.

- A healthcare provider's conscientious objection to participation in an abortion may not be the basis for civil liability, discrimination in employment, or the imposition of other sanctions by a hospital, person, firm, association, or group. Moreover, a healthcare provider injured because of a violation of his/her right of conscience may bring a civil action for damages or injunctive relief.

- A private hospital, institution, or facility is not required to perform or to admit a woman for the purposes of performing an abortion.

- A private hospital, institution, or facility's conscientious objection to permitting an abortion within its facility or admitting a patient for an abortion may not be a basis for civil liability.

- Wyoming voters approved a state constitutional amendment providing that no one can be compelled to participate in any healthcare system. By doing so, they voted to protect the freedom of conscience of individuals, employers, and healthcare providers who object to providing or paying for certain services, such as abortion and drugs with life-ending mechanisms of action.

PARTICIPATION IN RESEARCH HARMFUL TO HUMAN LIFE

- Wyoming currently provides no protection for the rights of healthcare providers who conscientiously object to participation in human cloning, destructive embryo research, or other forms of medical research that violate a provider's moral or religious beliefs.

DID YOU KNOW?

- In 2017, Wyoming passed legislation requiring that women seeking abortions be informed at least 24 hours prior to an abortion of their right to view an ultrasound of their unborn child and to hear their child's heartbeat.

- Wyoming also considered legislation that would require a public report providing statistics on abortions performed in the previous year.

WHAT HAPPENS AFTER *ROE* IS OVERTURNED?

- Abortion will be legal up to viability and possibly throughout pregnancy.

RECOMMENDATIONS
for Wyoming

WOMEN'S PROTECTION PROJECT PRIORITIES

- Enhanced penalties and enforcement mechanisms for the state's abortion-related laws
- Women's Right to Know Act
- Coercive Abuse Against Mothers Prevention Act
- Women's Health Protection Act (abortion clinic regulations)
- Drug-Induced Abortion Information and Reporting Act
- Parental Involvement Enhancement Act
- Components of the Child Protection Act related to evidence retention and remedies for third-party interference with parental rights

INFANTS' PROTECTION PROJECT PRIORITIES

- Unborn Infants Dignity Act
- Prenatal Nondiscrimination Act
- Perinatal Hospice Information Act
- Unborn Wrongful Death Act

PATIENT PROTECTION ACT PRIORITIES

- Suicide by Physician Ban Act
- Joint Resolution Opposing Suicide by Physician
- Charlie Gard Act (formerly the Life Sustaining Care Act)
- Pain Medicine Education Act

ADDITIONAL PRIORITIES

ABORTION

- Defunding the Abortion Industry and Advancing Women's Health Act
- Federal Abortion-Mandate Opt-Out Act

LEGAL RECOGNITION AND PROTECTION FOR THE UNBORN

- Crimes Against the Unborn Child Act
- Pregnant Woman's Protection Act

BIOETHICS

- Human Cloning Prohibition Act
- Destructive Embryo Research Act
- Prohibition on Public Funding of Human Cloning and Destructive Embryo Research Act

PATIENT PROTECTION

- Suicide by Physician Ban Act

HEALTHCARE FREEDOM OF CONSCIENCE

- Healthcare Freedom of Conscience Act

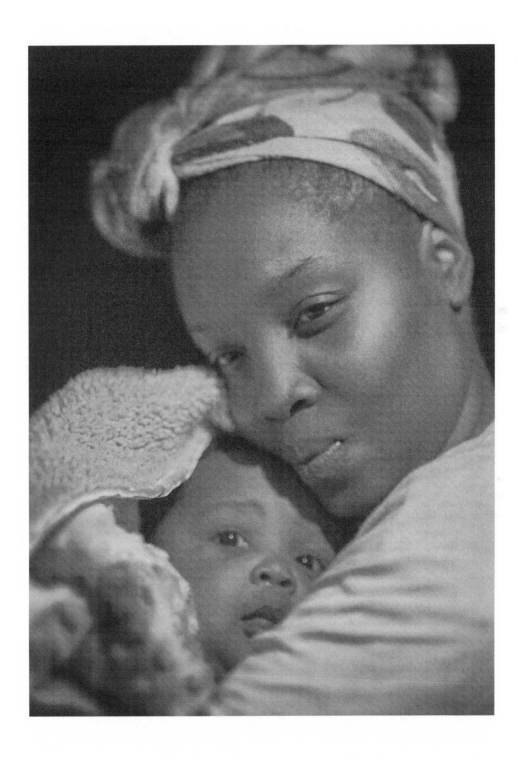

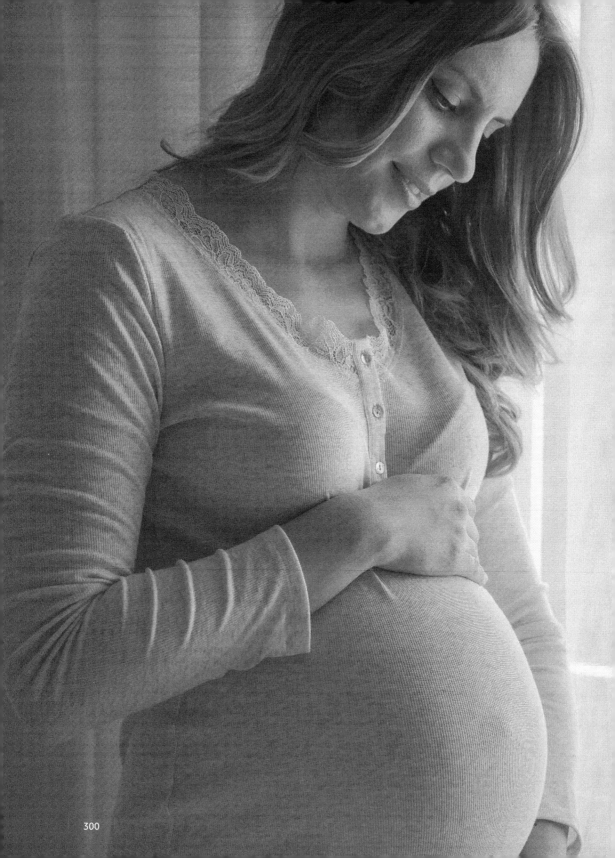

Infants' Protection Project

Affirming All Life

Abortion is a story that is often told without discussing who is involved. Pro-abortion feminists talk about "empowerment" or "choice." Abortion industry lobbyists seek to compel taxpayer funding for a Supreme Court-conferred "right." Carefully crafted language is routinely used to obscure the reality that a human life hangs in the balance.

Acknowledging the humanity and promise of every child, including those yet unborn, Americans United for Life launched the *Infants' Protection Project* in December 2015.

A complement to AUL's hugely successful *Women's Protection Project*, the *Infants' Protection Project* showcases AUL's uniquely effective "mother-child strategy" and exposes the lie propagated by the abortion industry that a woman's interests are often at odds with those of her unborn child.

The *Infants' Protection Project* is also a natural extension of AUL's decades-long leadership in advocating for the legal protection of unborn children both within and outside the context of abortion. Such protection is possible, even in the face of the Supreme Court's evolving abortion jurisprudence. For example, writing on the constitutionality of laws limiting abortion, former Supreme Court Justice Anthony Kennedy acknowledged "that medical procedures must be governed by moral principles having their foundation in the intrinsic value of human life, including life of the unborn."

Model legislation featured in the *Infants' Protection Project* provides legal recognition and protection to unborn children and affirms their humanity:

- The **"Missouri Preamble"** provides that each life begins at conception; that unborn children have protectable interests in life, health, and well-being; and that parents have protectable interests in the life, health, and well-being of their unborn children. The Act further provides that all state laws shall be interpreted to extend every protection to unborn children consistent with the U.S. Constitution and Supreme Court jurisprudence. It is based on a 1986 Missouri law that was upheld by the Supreme Court.

- The **Unborn Infants Dignity Act** ensures that every mother of a deceased unborn infant is given the opportunity to ensure that her child is treated with dignity and respect and that the bodies of aborted infants are not exploited for scientific or pecuniary gain.

  Deceased unborn infants deserve the same respect as other human beings. Tragically, many states do not ensure that miscarried, stillborn, or aborted infants are treated with dignity such as receiving proper burials. Many states also fail to require fetal death reporting and the issuance of fetal death certificates for unborn infants lost early in pregnancy, and do not offer grieving parents "Certificates of Birth Resulting in Stillbirth" or similar legal documents. The *Unborn Infants Dignity Act* remedies these deficiencies.

- The **Prenatal Nondiscrimination Act** bans abortions performed solely for reasons of sex-selection or genetic abnormalities such as Down syndrome.

- The **Partial-Birth Abortion Ban Act** bans the unnecessary and barbaric partial-birth abortion procedure and is modeled after the federal *Partial-Birth Abortion Ban Act*, which was upheld by the Supreme Court in *Gonzales v. Carhart*.

- The **Born-Alive Infant Protection Act** protects all infants born alive during abortions or attempted abortions and includes appropriate enforcement mechanisms and penalties.

- The **Unborn Wrongful Death Act** permits a wrongful death claim for the death of an unborn child, at any stage of development or gestation, remedying both the lack of wrongful death laws in some states and the lack of comprehensive protection provided by most existing state laws.

- The **Perinatal Hospice Information Act** ensures that every woman considering an abortion after receiving a life-limiting fetal diagnosis is aware of the availability of perinatal hospice.

Decades ago, AUL's legal experts laid the intellectual groundwork necessary to implement fetal homicide laws nationwide. At the time of the *Roe* decision in 1973, only three states maintained these protective laws. Today, 39 states have enacted fetal homicide laws, and 30 of these states protect the unborn child beginning at conception. The *Infants' Protection Project* continues this formidable legacy.

THE "MISSOURI PREAMBLE": A FRAMEWORK FOR DEFINING AND PROTECTING PERSONHOOD

HOUSE/SENATE BILL NO. _____

By Representatives/Senators _____

SECTION 1. TEXT OF PREAMBLE.

The [*Legislature*] of the State of [*Insert name of State*] finds that:

(a) The life of each human being begins at conception;

(b) Unborn children have protectable interests in life, health, and well-being; and

(c) The natural parents of unborn children have protectable interests in the life, health, and well-being of their unborn children.

SECTION 2. EFFECTIVE DATE, INTERPRETATION, AND APPLICATION.

Effective [*Insert date*], the laws of the State of [*Insert name of State*] shall be interpreted and construed to acknowledge on behalf of the unborn child at every stage of development all the rights, privileges, and immunities available to other persons, citizens, and residents of the State of [*Insert name of State*], subject only to the Constitution of the United States [*, and*] decisional interpretations thereof by the United States Supreme Court [*, and specific provisions to the contrary in the statutes and constitution of the State of* [*Insert name of State*]].

SECTION 3. DEFINITIONS.

As used in this [*Section, Title, or other appropriate term*], the terms "unborn child" or "unborn children" mean the offspring of human beings from conception until birth.

SECTION 4. EXCLUSIONS.

Nothing in this [*Section, Title, or other appropriate term*] shall be interpreted as creating a cause of action against a woman for indirectly harming her unborn child by failing to properly care for herself or by failing to follow any particular program of prenatal care.

UNBORN INFANTS DIGNITY ACT

HOUSE/SENATE BILL NO. _____

By Representatives/Senators _____

[Drafter's Note: Provisions in this model legislation may be enacted individually or collectively, depending on the needs of an individual state. Further, AUL will work with legislators to ensure that the appropriate legislative findings and purposes in Section 2 and definitions in Section 3 are included in any proposed legislation.]

SECTION 1. TITLE.

This Act may be known and cited as the *"Unborn Infants Dignity Act."*

SECTION 2. LEGISLATIVE FINDINGS AND PURPOSE.

(a) The *[Legislature]* of the State of *[Insert name of State]* finds that:

  (1) Deceased unborn infants deserve the same respect and dignity as other human beings.

  (2) The laws of the State of *[Insert name of State]* do not ensure that a miscarried, stillborn, or aborted infant receives a proper burial or other respectful final disposition.

  (3) *[Insert name of State]* also fails to require fetal death reporting and the issuance of fetal death certificates *[except [Insert short description of circumstances when, under existing state law(s), the reporting of fetal deaths is required and/or a fetal death certificate is available]]*.

  (4) Further, while the loss of an unborn infant at any stage of development is often devastating to parents, *[Insert name of State]* only offers *[Certificates of Birth Resulting in Stillbirth]* to parents for fetal deaths that occur *[Insert short description of circumstances when, under existing state law(s), a certificate of stillbirth or similar document is available]*.

  (5) *[Insert name of State]* does not explicitly prohibit the sale, transfer, distribution, or donation of the bodily remains of aborted unborn infants for experimentation.

  (6) It is the public policy of the State of *[Insert name of State]* to promote childbirth over abortion. Permitting the sale, transfer, distribution, or donation of the bodily remains of aborted unborn infants, particularly for pecuniary gain, and the use of the bodies of aborted infants for experimentation violates *[Insert name of State]*'s public policy.

(b) Based on the findings in subsection (a), the purposes of this Act are to:

(1) Ensure that the mother of a deceased unborn infant is given the opportunity to bury or dispose of the bodily remains of her infant with dignity and respect;

(2) Require institutions where deceased unborn infants are delivered or where unborn infants are aborted to provide a dignified final disposition of the bodily remains of these infants;

(3) Require fetal death reports for all fetal deaths as defined in this Act;

(4) Ensure that parents of all stillborn infants are offered the opportunity to obtain a [*Certificate of Birth Resulting in Stillbirth*];

(5) Prohibit the sale, transfer, distribution, or other unlawful disposition of an infant born alive in the course of an abortion, a deceased unborn infant, or bodily remains of an aborted infant; [*and*]

(6) Prohibit the use of the bodily remains of an aborted infant for experimentation[; *and*]

[(7) *Ensure that the bodily remains of an unborn infant resulting from an occurrence other than an abortion are not sold, transferred, or distributed for experimentation without the mother's informed, written consent.*]

SECTION 3. DEFINITIONS.

[*Drafter's Note: These are recommended definitions, but some may not be compatible with a state's existing laws. Care should be taken to select only those definitions that are compatible with existing state law or with the intent of the proposed legislation (i.e., to modify or deviate from definitions in existing state law).*]

As used in this Act only:

(a) **"Abortion"** means the act of using or prescribing any instrument, medicine, drug, or any other substance, device, or means with the intent to terminate the clinically diagnosable pregnancy of a woman with the knowledge that the termination by those means will with reasonable likelihood cause the death of the unborn infant. Such use, prescription, or means is not an abortion if done with the intent to:

(1) Save the life or preserve the health of the unborn infant;

(2) Remove a dead unborn infant caused by spontaneous abortion; or

(3) Remove an ectopic pregnancy.

(b) **"Authorized representative"** has the same meaning as [*Insert appropriate reference(s) and/or citation(s) to state law(s)*].

(c) **"Bodily remains"** means the physical remains, corpse, or body parts of a dead unborn infant who has been expelled or extracted from his or her mother and who has reached a stage of development so that there are cartilaginous structures and/or fetal or skeletal parts, whether or not the remains have been obtained by induced, spontaneous, or accidental means. The death is indicated by the fact that, after such expulsion or extraction, the unborn infant does not breathe or show any other evidence of life such as beating of the heart, pulsation of the umbilical cord, or definite movement of voluntary muscles.

(d) **"Born alive"** or **"live birth"** means the complete expulsion or extraction of an infant from his or her mother, regardless of the state of gestational development, who, after expulsion or extraction, whether or not the umbilical cord has been cut or the placenta is attached, and regardless of whether the expulsion or extraction occurs as a result of natural or induced labor, cesarean section, or induced abortion, shows any evidence of life including, but not limited to, one or more of the following:

   (1) Breathing;
   (2) A heartbeat;
   (3) Umbilical cord pulsation; or
   (4) Definite movement of voluntary muscles.

(e) **"Cremation"** means [*Insert definition from state law(s); or "the process by which the following three steps are taken: (1) The reduction of the body of a deceased human to its essential elements by incineration; (2) the repositioning or moving of the body or remains during incineration to facilitate the process; and (3) the processing of the remains after removal from the cremation chamber."*]

(f) **"Experiment"** or **"experimentation"** means the use of an infant, unborn infant, or bodily remains of a dead unborn infant in any trial, test, procedure, or observation carried out with the goal of verifying, refuting, or establishing the validity of a hypothesis, but does not include pathological study or any treatment, medication, diagnostic or remedial tests, procedures, or observations which have the purpose of determining the life or health of the infant or unborn infant or preserving the life or health of the infant, unborn infant, or the infant's mother.

(g) **"Fetal death"** means death prior to expulsion or extraction from his or her mother of an unborn infant who has reached a stage of development so that there are cartilaginous structures and/or fetal or skeletal parts. The death is indicated by the fact that, after such expulsion or extraction, the unborn infant does not breathe or show any other evidence of life such as beating of the heart, pulsation of the umbilical cord, or definite movement of voluntary muscles.

(h) **"Fetus"** or **"human fetus"** means the offspring of human beings from conception until birth.

(i) **"Final disposition"** means the burial, [*interment*], cremation, or other legal disposition of a dead unborn infant.

(j) **"Infant"** means a child of the species *homo sapiens* who has been completely expulsed or extracted from his or her mother, regardless of the stage of gestational development, until the age of thirty (30) days post birth.

(k) **"Institution"** means any public or private organization, corporation, partnership, sole proprietorship, association, agency, or other entity that is involved in providing healthcare services including but not limited to hospitals, clinics, medical centers, ambulatory surgical centers, private physician's offices, university medical schools, and medical training facilities.

(l) **"Medical waste"** means discarded biologic product such as blood, tissue, or body parts removed from medical facilities, as well as bedding, bandages, syringes, and similar materials that have been used in treating patients. The term excludes **"bodily remains"** as defined in this Act.

(m) **"Miscarriage"** means the spontaneous or accidental death of an unborn infant before he or she is able to survive independently that does not result in the birth of a live infant. The death is indicated by the fact that, after the expulsion of the unborn infant, he or she does not breathe or show any other evidence of life such as beating of the heart, pulsation of the umbilical cord, or definite movement of voluntary muscles.

(n) **"Pathological study"** means the examination of body tissue for diagnostic or forensic purposes and any related activities necessary to perform such study. The term includes any study or test, genetic or otherwise, to determine paternity or the cause of death.

(o) **"Physician"** means any person licensed to practice medicine in this State. The term includes medical doctors and doctors of osteopathy.

(p) **"Pregnant"** or **"pregnancy"** means that female reproductive condition of having an unborn infant in the woman's uterus.

(q) **"Stillbirth"** means the birth of a human being who has died in the uterus. The death is indicated by the fact that, after the expulsion of the unborn infant, he or she does not breathe or show any other evidence of life such as beating of the heart, pulsation of the umbilical cord, or definite movement of voluntary muscles.

(r) **"Therapeutic"** means intended to treat or cure a disease or disorder by remedial agents or methods.

(s) **"Unauthorized incineration"** means the combined burning of bodily remains with medical waste as both **"bodily remains"** and **"medical waste"** are defined in this Act.

(t) **"Unborn infant"** means the offspring of human beings from conception until birth.

[(*u*) **"Valuable consideration"** *means anything that will confer benefit upon any person who performed or assisted with the performance of an abortion or an institution where the bodily remains of an aborted infant were expelled or extracted including but not limited to money, work, performance, assets, or a promise.*]

SECTION 4. RELEASE OF DEAD UNBORN INFANT TO MOTHER FOR FINAL DISPOSITION.

(a) In every instance of fetal death, irrespective of the duration of pregnancy, the individual in charge of the institution where the bodily remains were expelled or extracted, upon request of the mother, shall release to the mother or the mother's authorized representative the bodily remains for final disposition:

   (1) By burial, [*interment,*] or cremation as those terms are defined in [*Insert appropriate reference(s) to state law(s) or this Act*], or

   (2) When the bodily remains are the result of a miscarriage or stillbirth, in compliance with [*Insert appropriate reference(s) to the state's Anatomical Gift Act*].

(b) Such request may be made by the mother or her authorized representative prior to or shortly after the expulsion or extraction of the bodily remains.

SECTION 5. AUTHORIZATION FOR FINAL DISPOSITION OF DEAD UNBORN INFANT.

(a) In every instance of fetal death, irrespective of the duration of pregnancy, where a mother does not request the release of her dead unborn infant, the funeral director or other person assuming responsibility for the final disposition of the bodily remains shall obtain from the mother or her authorized representative a written authorization for final disposition on a form prescribed and furnished or approved by the [*Insert name of appropriate state department or agency*]. The authorization may allow final disposition to be by a funeral director or the individual in charge of the institution where the bodily remains were expelled or extracted.

(b) The mother or her authorized representative may direct the final disposition of the bodily remains to be:

(1) Burial, [*interment,*] or cremation as those terms are defined in [*Insert appropriate reference(s) to state law(s) or this Act*]; or

(2) When the bodily remains are the result of a miscarriage or stillbirth, in compliance with [*Insert appropriate reference(s) to the state's Anatomical Gift Act*].

After final disposition, the funeral director, the individual in charge of the institution, or other person making the final disposition shall retain the authorization for not less than seven (7) years.

(c) Irrespective of the duration of pregnancy, the individual in charge of the institution where the bodily remains were expelled or extracted must ensure that the final disposition of the bodily remains is:

(1) By burial, [*interment,*] or cremation as those terms are defined in [*Insert appropriate reference(s) to state law(s) or this Act*]; or

(2) When the bodily remains are the result of a miscarriage or stillbirth, in compliance with [*Insert appropriate reference(s) to the state's Anatomical Gift Act*].

Final disposition of bodily remains may not be by unauthorized incineration.

(d) If final disposition of the bodily remains is by cremation, the medical examiner of the county in which fetal death occurred shall sign the authorization for final disposition.

(e) Bodily remains may be moved from the place of death to be prepared for final disposition with the consent of the physician or county medical examiner who certifies the cause of death.

(f) A permit for final disposition issued under the laws of another state that accompanies bodily remains brought into [*Insert name of State*] is authorization for final disposition of the bodily remains in this State.

SECTION 6. FETAL DEATH CERTIFICATES.

(a) A fetal death certificate for each fetal death which occurs in this State shall be filed with the [*State Registrar*], within three (3) days after delivery, miscarriage, or an abortion.

(b) The funeral director or person assuming responsibility for the final disposition of the bodily remains shall file the fetal death certificate. In the absence of such a person, the physician in attendance at or after the expulsion or extraction of bodily remains shall file the certificate of fetal death. The physician shall obtain the personal data from the next of kin or the best qualified person or source available, complete the certificate as to personal data, and deliver the certificate to the person responsible for completing the medical certification of the cause of death within twenty-four (24) hours after the expulsion or extraction of the bodily remains.

(c)   The medical certification shall be completed and signed within forty-eight (48) hours after delivery by the physician in attendance at or after the expulsion or extraction, except when inquiry into the cause of death is required by [*Insert appropriate reference(s) to state law(s)*]. This certification shall record the sex of the infant when it can be determined.

SECTION 7. CERTIFICATE OF BIRTH FOR STILLBORN INFANT.

The [*Insert name of appropriate state department or agency*] shall establish a [*Certificate of Birth Resulting in Stillbirth*] to be offered to the parent(s) of a stillborn infant. The medical staff treating the stillbirth shall notify the parent(s) or their authorized representative of the ability to request the certificate. The certificate shall be available to any parent of a stillborn infant upon proper application. This certificate shall not be used as evidence of live birth or for identification purposes.

SECTION 8. PROHIBITIONS ON BUYING, SELLING, AND EXPERIMENTATION ON UNBORN INFANTS OR BODILY REMAINS RESULTING FROM ABORTION.

(a)   A person may only transfer, distribute, give away, accept, use, or attempt to use an infant born alive in the course of any abortion procedure, a deceased unborn infant, or the bodily remains of an aborted infant in accordance with the provisions of Sections 4 and 5 of this Act.

(b)   Except as provided in subsection (a) of this Section, no person shall [*intentionally or knowingly*] sell, transfer, distribute, give away, accept, use, or attempt to use an infant born alive in the course of an abortion procedure, a deceased unborn infant, or the bodily remains of an aborted infant.

(c)   Except as provided in subsection (a) of this Section, no person shall aid or abet any such sale, transfer, distribution, other unlawful disposition, acceptance, use, or attempted use of an infant born alive in the course of an abortion procedure, a deceased unborn infant, or bodily remains of an aborted infant.

(d)   No person shall use an infant born alive in the course of an abortion procedure, a deceased unborn infant, or the bodily remains of an aborted infant in any animal or human research, experimentation, or study or for transplantation, except:

(1) For diagnostic or remedial tests, procedures, or observations which have the purpose of determining the life or health of the infant or unborn infant or preserving the life or health of the infant, unborn infant, or the infant's mother; [*or*]

(2) For pathological study; [*or*]

[(3) *When the deceased unborn infant or bodily remains of an unborn infant result from an occurrence other than an abortion, with the mother's informed, written consent as provided for in [the state's Anatomical Gift Act or other relevant statute].*]

(e) No person shall experiment upon an unborn infant who is intended to be aborted unless the experimentation is therapeutic to the unborn infant.

(f) No person shall perform or offer to perform an abortion where part or all of the justification or reason for the abortion is that the bodily remains may be used for animal or human research, experimentation, or transplantation.

[*Drafter's Note: Only when a state cannot or refuses to enact Section 8, prohibiting experimentation on aborted unborn infants, should Section 9, ensuring informed consent from the mother of the aborted infant and prohibiting pecuniary gain for experimentation on aborted infants, be enacted.*]

SECTION 9. *INFORMED CONSENT REQUIRED FOR FETAL EXPERIMENTATION OR TRANSPLANTATION.*

Under circumstances in which the State of [Insert name of State] permits the use of bodily remains of aborted infants for animal or human research, experimentation, or study or for transplantation pursuant to [Insert specific reference(s) to state laws, regulations, or other authority permitting the use of bodily remains of aborted infants for animal or human research, experimentation, or study or for transplantation]:

(a) *That use shall only occur when the mother makes a signed, written statement declaring that:*

(1) *The mother donates the specific bodily remains for animal or human research, experimentation, or study or for transplantation;*

(2) *The donation is made without any restriction regarding the identity of individuals who may be the recipients of transplantations of any bodily remains;*

(3) *The mother has not been informed of the identity of any individuals who may be recipients of transplantations of bodily remains;*

(4) *The mother has been informed of any known medical risks to her or risks to her privacy that might be associated with the donation of the bodily remains;*

(5) The mother understands her right to obtain the bodily remains for final disposition in accordance with [Insert name of State] law; and

(6) The consent of the mother for the abortion was obtained prior to requesting or obtaining consent for a donation of the bodily remains for use in such research, experimentation, or study or for transplantation.

(b) The attending physician makes a signed, written, separate, but concurrent statement that:

(1) The bodily remains have been donated by the mother in accordance with this Act;

(2) The attending physician has disclosed to the mother the attending physician's interest and the interest of the attending physician's employer, if any, in the research, experimentation, study, or transplantation to be conducted with the specific bodily remains.

(3) No alteration(s) to the timing, method, or procedure(s) used to terminate the pregnancy will be [was] made solely for the purpose of obtaining the bodily remains; and

(4) The abortion was performed in accordance with applicable state law.

(c) No person shall [intentionally or knowingly] sell, transfer, distribute, give away, or accept bodily remains of an aborted infant for valuable consideration.

(d) No person shall make alteration(s) to the timing, method, or procedure(s) used to terminate the pregnancy solely for the purpose of obtaining the bodily remains.

(e) No person shall solicit or [intentionally or knowingly] acquire, receive, or accept a donation of the bodily remains of an aborted infant for the purpose of the transplantation of such bodily remains into another person or persons if:

(1) The donation will be or is made pursuant to a promise to the donating person that the donated bodily remains will be transplanted into a recipient or recipients specified by such person;

(2) The donated bodily remains will be transplanted into a relative or relatives of the donating person; or

(3) The person who solicits or knowingly acquires, receives, or accepts the donation has provided valuable consideration for the costs associated with the abortion.

(f) No person shall:

(1) Solicit or [intentionally or knowingly] acquire, receive, or accept a donation of the bodily remains of an aborted infant knowing that a human pregnancy was deliberately initiated to provide such bodily

remains; or

(2) [*Intentionally or knowingly*] *acquire, receive, or accept bodily remains obtained from a human fetus that was gestated in the uterus of a nonhuman animal or in an artificial uterus or womb.*

SECTION 10. CRIMINAL PENALTIES.

(a) An individual in charge of an institution where bodily remains were expelled or extracted who violates Section 4 shall be guilty of a [*Insert appropriate penalty/offense classification*] for each violation.

(b) The person assuming responsibility for the final disposition of bodily remains or an individual in charge of an institution where bodily remains were expelled or extracted who violates Section 5 shall be guilty of a [*Insert appropriate penalty/offense classification*] for each violation.

(c) Any person who [*intentionally or knowingly*] sells, transfers, distributes, gives away, accepts, uses, or attempts to use an infant born alive in the course of an abortion procedure, an unborn infant, or the bodily remains of an aborted infant in violation of this Act or who aids or abets any such sale, transfer, distribution, other unlawful disposition, acceptance, use, or attempted use of an infant, an unborn infant, or bodily remains of an aborted infant in violation of Section 8 shall be guilty of a [*Insert appropriate penalty/offense classification*] for each violation.

(d) Any person who experiments upon an infant born alive in the course of an abortion procedure, a deceased unborn infant, or the bodily remains of an aborted infant; experiments upon an unborn infant who is intended to be aborted; or performs or offers to perform an abortion where part or all of the justification or reason for the abortion is that the bodily remains may be used for animal or human research, experimentation, or study or for transplantation, in violation of Section 8, shall be guilty of a [*Insert appropriate penalty/offense classification*] for each violation.

[(e) *Any person who violates the requirements and restrictions in Section 9 shall be guilty of a* [*Insert appropriate penalty/offense classification for each violation*].]

SECTION 11. CIVIL AND ADMINISTRATIVE ACTIONS.

In addition to whatever remedies are available under the statutory [*or common*] law of this State, failure to comply with the requirements of this Act shall:

(a) Provide a basis for recovery for the parent(s) of the infant or unborn infant or the parent(s) or guardian(s) of the mother, if the mother is a minor, for the unlawful disposition of or experimentation upon an infant, unborn infant, or bodily remains. Such relief shall include:

    (1)   Money damages for all psychological injuries occasioned by the violation(s) of this Act; and

    (2)   Statutory damages equal to [*Insert number*] times the cost of the mother's delivery or abortion.

(b) Provide a basis for professional disciplinary action under [*Insert appropriate reference(s) to state statute(s) and/or administrative rule(s) concerning the state Medical Board or other appropriate state regulatory or licensing bodies' oversight and review authority*] for the suspension or revocation of any license for physicians, licensed vocational and registered nurses, or other licensed or regulated healthcare providers.

(c) Any conviction of any physician, licensed vocational or registered nurse, or other licensed or regulated healthcare provider for any failure to comply with the requirements of this Act shall result in the automatic suspension of his or her license for a period of at least one (1) year [*or other appropriate penalty*] and said license shall be reinstated after that time only under such conditions as the [*Insert reference(s) to appropriate state regulatory or licensing bodies*] shall require to ensure compliance with this Act.

SECTION 12. CONSTRUCTION.

(a) Nothing in this Act shall be construed to affect existing federal or state law regarding abortion.

(b) Nothing in this Act shall be construed as creating or recognizing a right to abortion.

(c) Nothing in this Act shall be construed to alter generally accepted medical standards.

SECTION 13. SEVERABILITY.

Any provision of this Act held to be invalid or unenforceable by its terms, or as applied to any person or circumstance, shall be construed so as to give it the maximum effect permitted by law, unless such holding shall be one of utter invalidity or unenforceability, in which event such provision shall be deemed severable herefrom and shall not affect the remainder hereof or the application of such provision to other persons not similarly situated or to other dissimilar circumstances.

SECTION 14. RIGHT OF INTERVENTION.

The [*Legislature*], by joint resolution, may appoint one or more of its members who sponsored or cosponsored this Act in his or her official capacity to intervene as a matter of right in any case in which the constitutionality of this Act is challenged.

SECTION 15. EFFECTIVE DATE.

This Act takes effect on [*Insert date*].

PRENATAL NONDISCRIMINATION ACT OF [*INSERT YEAR*]

HOUSE/SENATE BILL NO. _____

By Representatives/Senators _____

SECTION 1. TITLE.

This Act may be cited as the "Prenatal Nondiscrimination Act of [*Insert appropriate year*]."

SECTION 2. LEGISLATIVE FINDINGS.

The [*Legislature*] of the State of [*Insert name of State*] finds that:

(a) With regard to sex-selection abortion:

    (1) Women are a vital part of our society and culture and possess the same fundamental human rights as men.

    (2) In spite of this, sex-selection abortion, which is abortion done to prevent the birth of a child of an undesired sex, has been documented to exist, outside the U.S. and, increasingly, inside it, and the victims of sex-selection abortion are overwhelmingly female.

    (3) The United States, along with other countries, has petitioned the United Nations General Assembly to declare sex-selection abortion a crime against women.

    (4) Countries such as India, Great Britain, and China have taken steps to end sex-selection abortion. For example, China and India do not allow doctors to reveal the sex of an unborn child.

    (5) The United States prohibits discrimination on the basis of sex in various areas including employment, education, athletics, and health insurance.

    (6) It is undesirable to have a sex imbalance within a society, particularly when there is a shortage of women. Countries with high rates of male-preference have experienced ill effects as a result of an increasing number of young, unmarried men.

    (7) A large population of young, unmarried men can be a cause of increased violence and militancy within a society.

(b) With regard to abortion and Down syndrome:

   (1) Persons with Down syndrome possess the same fundamental human rights as all other human beings.

   (2) In spite of this, various studies have found that a high degree – in excess of seventy (70) percent - of unborn children diagnosed with Down syndrome are aborted.

   (3) Recent years have seen an increase in the use of amniocentesis and other prenatal testing to diagnose potential health problems in unborn children.

   (4) Amniocentesis and other prenatal testing often give correct results, but also give many false-positive results.

   (5) Roughly one (1) in every seven hundred (700) to one thousand (1,000) children is born with Down syndrome.

   (6) Down syndrome is not considered a severe disability.

   (7) In various circumstances, the United States prohibits discrimination against persons with Down syndrome.

   (8) In many situations, such as education, the United States requires that accomodations be made for the benefit of persons with Down syndrome.

   (9) Persons with Down syndrome contribute to American culture and are a valuable part of our society.

  (10) Many persons with Down syndrome are able to maintain employment, obtain an education, and live with varying degrees of independence.

  (11) As technology advances and as medical treatments and educational methods improve, persons with Down syndrome will increasingly be self-dependent and productive citizens.

(c) With regard to abortion and genetic abnormalities:

   (1) Persons with physical or mental deformities or handicaps possess the same fundamental human rights as all other human beings.

   (2) The United States prohibits discrimination against persons with physical or mental deformities or handicaps in various circumstances including housing and employment.

   (3) In many situations, the United States requires that accommodations be made for the benefit of persons with physical or mental deformities or handicaps.

   (4) In spite of this, studies have revealed that a high percentage of unborn children who are diagnosed with genetic abnormalities or a potential for genetic abnormalities are aborted.

   (5) Recent years have seen an increase in the use of amniocentesis and other prenatal testing to diagnose potential health problems in unborn children.

   (6) Amniocentesis and other prenatal testing often give correct results, but also give false-positive results.

(7) There are approximately four thousand (4,000) known genetic abnormalities.

(8) Persons with physical or mental deformities or handicaps contribute to American culture and are a valuable part of our society.

(9) Many persons with physical or mental deformities or handicaps are able to support themselves financially, obtain an education, and live independently.

(10) As technology advances and as medical treatments and educational methods improve, persons with physical or mental deformities or handicaps will increasingly be self-dependent and productive citizens.

(d) With regard to maternal health:

(1) It is undisputed that abortion's risks to maternal health increases as gestation increases.

(2) The risk of death at eight (8) weeks' gestation is one death per one (1) million abortions; at sixteen (16) to twenty (20) weeks, that risk rises to one death per twenty-nine thousand (29,000) abortions; and at twenty one (21) weeks' gestation or later, the risk of death is one per every eleven thousand (11,000) abortions.

(3) This means that a woman seeking an abortion at twenty (20) weeks is thirty five (35) times more likely to die from the abortion than she was in the first trimester. At twenty one (21) weeks or more, she is ninety one (91) times more likely to die from an abortion than she was in the first trimester.

(4) Because abortions performed solely based on a child's sex or genetic diagnosis are generally performed later in pregnancy, women undergoing these abortions are unnecessarily exposed to increased health risks including a exponentially higher risk of death.

(e) Based on the findings in subsections (a) through (d), the purposes of this Act are to:

(1) Ban abortions performed solely for reasons of sex-selection or diagnosed or feared genetic abnormalities; and

(2) To protect women from the risks inherent in later-term abortions.

SECTION 3. DEFINITIONS.

As used in this Act only:

(a) **"Abortion"** means the act of using or prescribing any instrument, medicine, drug, or any other substance, device, or means with the intent to terminate the clinically diagnosable pregnancy of a woman with knowledge that the termination by those means will with reasonable likelihood cause the death of the unborn child. Such use, prescription, or means is not an abortion if done with the intent to:

(1)   Save the life or preserve the health of the unborn child;

(2)   Remove a dead unborn child caused by spontaneous abortion; or

(3)   Remove an ectopic pregnancy.

(b)   **"Down syndrome"** refers to a chromosome disorder associated either with an extra chromosome twenty one (21) (in whole or in part) or an effective trisomy for chromosome twenty one (21). Down syndrome is sometimes referred to as "trisomy 21 syndrome."

(c)   **"Genetic abnormality"** means any defect, disease, or disorder that is inherited genetically. The term genetic abnormality includes, but is not limited to: any physical disability, any mental disability or retardation, any physical disfigurement, scoliosis, dwarfism, Down syndrome, albinism, Amelia, or any other type of physical or mental abnormality or disease.

(d)   **"Incompetent"** means any person who has been adjudged a disabled person and has had a guardian appointed for him/her under the [*Insert state Probate Act or other appropriate state law*].

(e)   **"Minor"** means any person under the age of eighteen (18) who is not and has not been married and has not been legally emancipated.

(f)   **"Physician"** means any person licensed to practice medicine in this State. The term includes medical doctors and doctors of osteopathy.

(g)   **"Pregnant woman"** means any female, including those who have not reached the age of eighteen (18) [*or minors*], who is in the reproductive condition of having an unborn child in her uterus.

(h)   **"Sex-selection abortion"** means an abortion performed because of the sex of the unborn child.

(i)   **"Unborn child"** means the offspring of human beings from conception until birth.

(j)   **"Viability"** means the state of fetal development when, in the judgment of the physician based on the particular facts of the case before him or her and in light of the most advanced medical technology and information available to him or her, there is a reasonable likelihood of sustained survival of the unborn child outside the body of his or her mother, with or without artificial support.

SECTION 4. PROHIBITION ON SEX-SELECTION ABORTION.

(a) No person may intentionally perform or attempt to perform an abortion with the knowledge that the pregnant woman is seeking the abortion because of the sex of the unborn child.

(b) Nothing in this Section shall be construed to proscribe the performance of an abortion because the unborn child has a genetic abnormality or disorder that is linked to the unborn child's sex.

[Drafter's Note: If a particular state is also seeking to ban abortions performed because of genetic abnormalities, this subsection (b) may need to be removed or modified.]

(c) If this Section is held invalid as applied to the period of pregnancy prior to viability, then it shall remain applicable to the period of pregnancy subsequent to viability.

SECTION 5. PROHIBITION ON ABORTION FOR DOWN SYNDROME.

(a) No person may intentionally perform or attempt to perform an abortion with knowledge that the pregnant woman is seeking the abortion because the unborn child has been diagnosed with either Down syndrome or a potential for Down syndrome.

(b) If this Section is held invalid as applied to the period of pregnancy prior to viability, then it shall remain applicable to the period of pregnancy subsequent to viability.

SECTION 6. PROHIBITION ON ABORTION FOR A GENETIC ABNORMALITY.

(a) No person may intentionally perform or attempt to perform an abortion with knowledge that the pregnant woman is seeking the abortion because the unborn child has been diagnosed with either a genetic abnormality or a potential for a genetic abnormality.

(b) If this Section is held invalid as applied to the period of pregnancy prior to viability, then it shall remain applicable to the period of pregnancy subsequent to viability.

SECTION 7. CRIMINAL PENALTIES.

Any physician or other person who intentionally or knowingly performs or attempts to perform an abortion prohibited by this Act shall be guilty of a [*Insert appropriate offense/penalty classification*], and shall be fined not less than [*Insert appropriate amount or possible range of fine*] or be imprisoned [*at hard labor*] not less than [*Insert appropriate time period or range*], or both.

SECTION 8. CIVIL PENALTIES AND PROFESSIONAL SANCTIONS.

(a) Any physician or person who intentionally or knowingly violates this Act shall be liable for damages and shall, if applicable, have his or her medical license suspended or revoked. He or she may also be enjoined from future acts prohibited by Sections 4, 5 and 6 of this Act.

(b) **Civil Damages.** A pregnant woman upon whom an abortion has been performed in violation of this Act, the parent or legal guardian of the woman if she is an unemancipated minor as defined in [*Insert citation(s) or other reference(s) to appropriate state statute(s)*], or the legal guardian [*or conservator*] of the woman if she has been adjudged incompetent under [*Insert citation(s) or other reference(s) to state statute(s) relating to petition and hearing, independent evaluation, etc.*] may commence a civil action for any knowing, intentional, or reckless violation of the Act and may seek both actual and punitive damages. Such damages shall include, but are not limited to:

   (1) Money damages for all psychological and physical injuries occasioned by the violation(s) of this Act; and

   (2) Statutory damages equal to [*Insert number*] times the cost of the abortion performed in violation of this Act.

(c) **Action Against a Medical License.** Any physician who performs an abortion in violation of this Act shall be considered to have engaged in unprofessional conduct for which his or her [*certificate or*] license to provide healthcare services in the State of [*Insert name of State*] shall be suspended or revoked by the [*Insert name of state Medical Board or other appropriate entity*].

(d) **Injunctive Relief.** A cause of action for injunctive relief against any physician or other person who has knowingly violated this Act may be maintained by the woman upon whom the abortion was performed or attempted to be performed in violation of this Act; any person who is the spouse, parent, guardian, [*conservator*], or a current or former licensed healthcare provider of the woman upon whom an abortion has been performed or attempted to be performed in violation of this Act; by the Office of the Attorney General of [*Insert name of State*]; or by a [*criminal District*] Attorney with appropriate jurisdiction. The injunction shall prevent the physician or person from performing further abortions in violation of this Act.

(e) **Contempt Proceedings.** Any physician or other person who knowingly violates the terms of an injunction issued in accordance with this Act shall be subject to [*civil and/or criminal*] contempt and shall be fined not less than [*Insert appropriate amount or possible range of fine*], or be imprisoned [*at hard labor*] not less than [*Insert appropriate time period or range*], or both.

[*Drafter's Note: If only civil contempt is selected as the appropriate remedy for failure to comply with a validly issued injunction, then any reference(s) to imprisonment or other criminal penalties should be removed from subparagraph 8(e).*]

SECTION 9. EXCLUSION OF LIABILITY FOR WOMAN WHO UNDERGOES ABORTION PROHIBITED UNDER THIS ACT.

(a) No woman upon whom an abortion in violation of this Act is performed or attempted may be prosecuted under the provisions of this Act or otherwise held criminally or civilly liable for any violation.

(b) In any criminal proceeding or action brought under this Act, any woman upon whom an abortion in violation of this Act is performed or attempted is entitled to all rights, protections, and notifications afforded to crime victims under [*Insert citation(s) or other reference(s) to state law(s) or administrative policies associated with the state's Victim-Witness Protection or similar program*].

(c) In every civil proceeding or action brought under this Act, the anonymity of the woman upon whom an abortion is performed or attempted shall be preserved from public disclosure unless she gives her consent to such disclosure. A court of competent jurisdiction, upon motion or sua sponte, shall issue orders to the parties, witnesses, and counsel and shall direct the sealing of the record and exclusion of individuals from courtrooms or hearing rooms, to the extent necessary to safeguard her identity from public disclosure. In the absence of written consent of the woman upon whom an abortion has been performed or attempted, anyone who initiates a proceeding or action under Section 8(b) or Section 8(d) of this Act shall do so under a pseudonym.

SECTION 10. CONSTRUCTION.

(a) Nothing in this Act shall be construed as creating or recognizing a right to abortion.

(b) It is not the intention of this Act to make lawful an abortion that is currently unlawful.

SECTION 11. SEVERABILITY.

Any provision of this Act held to be invalid or unenforceable by its terms, or as applied to any person or circumstance, shall be construed so as to give it the maximum effect permitted by law, unless such holding shall be one of utter invalidity or unenforceability, in which event such provision shall be deemed severable herefrom and shall not affect the remainder hereof or the application of such provision to other persons not similarly situated or to other, dissimilar circumstances.

SECTION 12. RIGHT OF INTERVENTION

The [*Legislature*], by joint resolution, may appoint one or more of its members who sponsored or cosponsored this Act in his or her official capacity to intervene as a matter of right in any case in which the constitutionality of this law is challenged.

SECTION 13. EFFECTIVE DATE.

This Act takes effect on [*Insert date*].

PARTIAL-BIRTH ABORTION BAN ACT

HOUSE/SENATE BILL NO. _____

By Representatives/Senators _____

SECTION 1. TITLE.

This Act may be known and cited as the "Partial-Birth Abortion Ban Act."

SECTION 2. LEGISLATIVE FINDINGS AND PURPOSES.

(a)   The [*Legislature*] of the State of [*Insert name of State*] finds that:

(1)   Partial-birth abortion is a gruesome and inhumane procedure that is never medically necessary and, as such, should be prohibited.

(2)   In 2003, the 108th United States Congress passed the *Partial-Birth Abortion Ban Act of 2003* (18 U.S.C. §1531), and President George W. Bush signed it into law.

(3)   Later, on April 18, 2007, the U.S. Supreme Court upheld the *Partial-Birth Abortion Ban Act of 2003* ("the federal ban") in *Gonzales v. Carhart*, 550 U.S. 124 (2007), specifically ruling that a ban on partial-birth abortion need not include a maternal "health" exception to be constitutional.

(4)   This Act's language stems from and uses as its primary influence the language of the federal ban as upheld in *Gonzales v. Carhart*.

(5)   This Act – a state ban on partial-birth abortion – is needed to supplement the federal ban. Importantly, the federal ban was narrowly tailored to reach only those partial-birth abortion procedures that implicate Congress' power to regulate interstate or foreign commerce. U.S. CONST. art. 1, § 8, cl. 3. Without this Act, partial-birth abortions performed, but not affecting these categories of commerce, are not prohibited under the federal ban.

(6)   Partial-birth abortions pose serious risks to women's long-term health.

(7)   There is a substantial evidentiary record upon which the [*Legislature*] of the State of [*Insert name of State*] has based its conclusion that a maternal "health" exception is not constitutionality required in a state ban on partial-birth abortion.

(8)   Moreover, the medical evidence clearly supports the informed judgment of the State of [*Insert name of State*] that a partial-birth abortion is never medically necessary to preserve a woman's health and instead poses serious health risks to the woman.

(9) Specifically, partial-birth abortion poses serious risks including, but not limited to: an increased risk of cervical incompetence as a result of cervical dilation that makes it difficult or impossible for a woman to successfully carry a subsequent pregnancy to term; an increased risk of uterine rupture, abruption, amniotic fluid embolus, and trauma to the uterus as a result of converting the child to a footling breech position – a procedure which, according to a leading obstetrics text-book, "there are very few, if any, indications for other than for delivery of a second twin;" and a risk of lacerations and secondary hemorrhaging as a result of the physician blindly forcing a sharp instrument into the base of the unborn child's skull while he or she is lodged in the birth canal – an act which could result in severe bleeding and subsequent shock.

(10) There is no credible medical evidence that partial-birth abortions are safer than other abortion procedures. No controlled studies of partial-birth abortion have been conducted nor have any comparative studies been conducted to demonstrate its safety and efficacy compared to other abortion methods. Furthermore, there have been no articles published in peer-reviewed jour-nals that establish that partial-birth abortions are superior in any way to established abortion procedures.

(11) In light of this overwhelming evidence, the State of [*Insert name of State*] has a compelling interest in prohibiting partial-birth abortion. Both *Roe v. Wade*, 410 U.S. 113 (1973), and *Planned Parenthood v. Casey*, 505 U.S. 833 (1992), recognized a governmental interest in protecting the life of a child during the birth [*or delivery*] process. This interest is specifically implicated during a partial-birth abortion because labor is induced and the birth process is begun before an abortion is attempted or the child is actually aborted [*or killed*].

(12) In fact, partial-birth abortion kills a child who is mere inches away from birth and being considered a "person" under *Roe*. Thus, the State of [*Insert name of State*] clearly has a heightened interest in protecting the life of the partially-born child.

(13) The public's perception of the appropriate role of a physician during a child's birth is undermined by aborting a child in the manner that purposefully seeks to kill the child inches from birth.

(14) Partial-birth abortion is disturbingly similar to the killing of a newborn infant and blurs the legal and moral lines between infanticide and abortion. This Act reinforces that line at birth – just as the Supreme Court established in *Roe v. Wade* – while also preserving the integrity of the medical profession and promoting respect for human life.

(15) The vast majority of infants killed during partial-birth abortions are alive until the very end of the procedure. Medical science has established that an unborn child can feel pain when subjected to painful stimuli like that inflicted during a partial-birth abortion procedure. Moreover, fetal pain experts believe that an unborn child's perception of pain can be even more intense than that of newborn infants and older children subjected to the same stimuli.

(b) Based on the findings in subsection (a) of this Act, the [*Legislature*]'s purposes are to:

(1) Conclusively establish that partial-birth abortion is never medically indicated to preserve the health of the mother and instead poses significant maternal health risks;

(2) Clearly define the line between abortion and infanticide; and

(3) Safeguard the role of a physician during childbirth.

SECTION 3. DEFINITIONS.

As used in this Act only:

(a) **"Medical facility"** means any public or private hospital, clinic, center, medical school, medical training institution, healthcare facility, physician's office, infirmary, dispensary, ambulatory surgical treatment center, or other institution or location wherein medical care is provided to any person.

(b) **"Partial-birth abortion"** means an abortion in which the person performing the abortion:

(1) Deliberately and intentionally vaginally delivers a living fetus until, in the case of a head-first presentation, the entire fetal head is outside the body of the mother, or, in the case of breech presentation, any part of the fetal trunk past the navel is outside the body of the mother, for the purpose of performing an overt act that the person knows will kill the partially delivered living fetus; and

(2) Performs the overt act, other than completion of delivery, which kills the partially delivered living fetus.

(c) **"Physician"** means a doctor of medicine or osteopathy legally authorized to practice medicine and surgery by the State in which the doctor performs such activity, or any other person legally authorized by the State to perform abortions; provided, however, that any person who is not a physician or not otherwise legally authorized by the State to perform abortions, but who nevertheless directly performs a partial-birth abortion, shall be subject to the provisions of this Act.

SECTION 4. PROHIBITION.

A person shall not knowingly perform or attempt to perform a partial-birth abortion.

SECTION 5. LIMITATIONS.

No person shall perform or induce a partial-birth abortion on a viable fetus unless such person is a physician and has a documented referral from another physician not legally or financially affiliated with the physician performing or inducing the abortion and both physicians determine that the life of the mother is endangered by a physical disorder, physical illness, or physical injury, including a life-endangering physical condition caused by or arising from the pregnancy itself.

SECTION 6. REPORTING.

(a) If a physician determines in accordance with the provisions of Section 5 that a partial-birth abortion is necessary and performs a partial-birth abortion on the woman, the physician shall report such determination and the reasons for such determination in writing to the medical facility in which the abortion is performed for inclusion in the report of the medical facility to the [*Insert appropriate state department, department head, or regulatory body*]; or if the abortion is not performed in a medical facility, the physician shall report the reasons for such determination in writing to the [*Insert appropriate state department, department head, or regulatory body*] as part of the written report made by the physician to [*Insert appropriate state department, department head, or regulatory body*]. The physician shall retain a copy of the written reports required under this Section for not less than five (5) years.

(b) Failure to report under this Section does not subject the physician to criminal or civil penalties.

(c) Subsection (b) does not preclude sanctions, disciplinary action, or any other appropriate action by the [*Insert appropriate citation or reference to state Medical Board or other appropriate agency*].

SECTION 7. CRIMINAL PENALTIES.

(a) Any person who intentionally or knowingly violates this Act is guilty of a [*Insert appropriate offense/penalty classification*].

(b) Any physician who intentionally or knowingly performs a partial-birth abortion and thereby kills a human fetus shall be fined not less than ten thousand dollars ($10,000) nor more than one-hundred thousand dollars ($100,000) under this Act, or be imprisoned [*at hard labor*] not less than one (1) year nor more than ten (10) years, or both.

SECTION 8. CIVIL PENALTIES.

(a)   The father, if married to the mother at the time she receives a partial-birth abortion procedure, and, if the mother has not attained the age of eighteen (18) years at the time of the abortion, the maternal grandparents of the fetus may in a civil action obtain appropriate relief.

(b)   Such relief shall include:

(1)   Money damages for all injuries, psychological and physical, occasioned by the violation of this Act; and

(2)   Statutory damages equal to [*Insert number*] times the cost of the partial-birth abortion.

SECTION 9. REVIEW BY STATE MEDICAL BOARD [OF LICENSURE AND SUPERVISION].

(a)   A physician-defendant accused of an offense under this Act may seek a hearing before the State Medical Board [*or other appropriate state agency*] as to whether the physician's conduct was necessary to save the life of the mother whose life was endangered by a physical disorder, physical illness, or physical injury, including a life-endangering physical condition caused by or arising from the pregnancy itself.

(b)   The findings on this issue shall be admissible at the civil or criminal trial of the physician-defendant. Upon a motion of the physician-defendant, the court shall delay the beginning of the trial for not more than thirty (30) days to permit such a hearing to take place.

SECTION 10. PENALTIES FOR AMBULATORY HEALTH CARE FACILITIES.

(a)   An ambulatory healthcare [*or surgical*] facility licensed pursuant to [*Insert reference(s) to appropriate state statute(s) or administrative regulation(s)*] in which the partial-birth abortion is performed in violation of this Act shall be subject to immediate revocation of its license by the [*Insert name of appropriate state department or agency*].

(b)   An ambulatory healthcare [*or surgical*] facility licensed pursuant to [*Insert references to appropriate state statute(s) or administrative regulation(s)*] in which the partial-birth abortion is performed in violation of this Act shall lose all state funding for [*Insert number*] years and will be required to reimburse the state for funds from the calendar [*or fiscal*] year in which the partial-birth abortion was performed.

SECTION 11. PROSECUTORIAL EXCLUSION.

A woman upon whom a partial-birth abortion is performed may not be prosecuted under the provisions of this Act.

SECTION 12. CONSTRUCTION.

(a) Nothing in this Act shall be construed as creating or recognizing a right to abortion.

(b) It is not the intention of this Act to make lawful an abortion that is currently unlawful.

SECTION 13. SEVERABILITY.

Any provision of this Act held to be invalid or unenforceable by its terms, or as applied to any person or circumstance, shall be construed so as to give it the maximum effect permitted by law, unless such holding shall be one of utter invalidity or unenforceability, in which event such provision shall be deemed severable herefrom and shall not affect the remainder hereof or the application of such provision to other persons not similarly situated or to other, dissimilar circumstances.

SECTION 14. RIGHT OF INTERVENTION.

The [Legislature], by joint resolution, may appoint one or more of its members who sponsored or cosponsored this Act in his or her official capacity to intervene as a matter of right in any case in which the constitutionality of this law is challenged.

SECTION 15. EFFECTIVE DATE.

This Act shall take effect on [Insert date].

BORN-ALIVE INFANT PROTECTION ACT

HOUSE/SENATE BILL NO. _____

By Representatives/Senators _____

SECTION 1. TITLE.

This Act may be known and cited as the "Born-Alive Infant Protection Act."

SECTION 2. LEGISLATIVE FINDINGS AND PURPOSE.

(a) The [*Legislature*] of the State of [*Insert name of State*] finds that:

  (1) The State of [*Insert name of State*] has a paramount interest in protecting all human life.
  (2) If an [*attempted*] abortion results in the live birth of an infant, the infant is a legal person for all purposes under the laws of this State.
  (3) It is not an infringement on a woman's right to terminate her pregnancy for this State to assert its interest in protecting an infant whose live birth occurred as the result of an [*attempted*] abortion.
  (4) Without proper legal protection, newly born infants who have survived [*attempted*] abortions have been denied appropriate life-saving or life-sustaining medical care and treatment and have been left to die.

(b) Based on the findings in subsection (a), the purposes of this Act are to:

  (1) Ensure the protection and promotion of the health and well-being of all infants born alive in this State; and
  (2) Mandate that healthcare providers give medically appropriate and reasonable life-saving and life-sustaining medical care and treatment to all born-alive infants.

SECTION 3. DEFINITIONS.

For the purposes of this Act only:

(a) **"Abortion"** means the act of using or prescribing any instrument, medicine, drug, or any other substance, device, or means with the intent to terminate the clinically diagnosable pregnancy of a woman with knowledge that the termination by those means will with reasonable likelihood cause the death of the unborn child. Such use, prescription, or means is not an abortion if done with the intent to:

(1) Save the life or preserve the health of the unborn child;
(2) Remove a dead unborn child caused by spontaneous abortion; or
(3) Remove an ectopic pregnancy.

(b) **"Born alive"** or **"live birth"** means the complete expulsion or extraction of an infant from his or her mother, regardless of the state of gestational development, who, after expulsion or extraction, whether or not the umbilical cord has been cut or the placenta is attached, and regardless of whether the expulsion or extraction occurs as a result of natural or induced labor, cesarean section, or induced abortion, shows any evidence of life including, but not limited to, one or more of the following:

(5) Breathing;
(6) A heartbeat;
(7) Umbilical cord pulsation; or
(8) Definite movement of voluntary muscles.

(c) **"Consent"** means the voluntary agreement or acquiescence by a person of age and with the requisite mental capacity who is not under duress or coercion and who has knowledge or understanding of the act or action to which he or she has agreed or acquiesced.

(d) **"Facility"** or **"medical facility"** means any public or private hospital, clinic, center, medical school, medical training institution, healthcare facility, physician's office, infirmary, dispensary, ambulatory surgical treatment center, or other institution or location wherein medical care is provided to any person.

(e) **"Healthcare provider"** means any individual who may be asked to participate in any way in a healthcare service, including, but not limited to, the following: a physician; physician's assistant; nurse; nurses' aide; medical assistant; hospital employee; clinic employee; nursing home employee; pharmacist; pharmacy employee; researcher; medical or nursing school faculty, student, or employee; counselor; social worker; or any professional, paraprofessional, or any other person who furnishes or assists in the furnishing of healthcare services.

(f) **"Infant"** means a child of the species homo sapiens who has been completely expulsed or extracted from his or her mother, regardless of the stage of gestational development, until the age of thirty (30) days post birth.

(g) **"Nurse"** means a person who has undergone training, passed an examination, and obtained a license from the State of [*Insert name of State*] conferring authorization to provide care for patients. The term includes registered nurses, licensed practical nurses, [*and*] licensed vocational nurses[, *and* [*Insert other appropriate terms*]].

(h) **"Physician"** means a person licensed to practice medicine in the State of [*Insert name of State*]. This term includes medical doctors and doctors of osteopathy.

(i) **"Premature"** or **"preterm"** means occurring prior to the thirty-seventh (37th) week of gestation.

SECTION 4. REQUIREMENTS AND RESPONSIBILITIES.

(a) A person shall not deny or deprive an infant of nourishment with the intent to cause or allow the death of the infant for any reason including, but not limited to:

(1) The infant was born with a handicap;
(2) The infant is not wanted by the parent(s) or guardian(s); or
(3) The infant is born alive by natural or artificial means.

(b) A person shall not deprive an infant of medically appropriate and reasonable medical care, medical treatment, or surgical care.

(c) The requirements of this Section shall not be construed to prevent an infant's parent(s) or guardian(s) from refusing to give consent to medical treatment or surgical care which is not medically necessary or reasonable including care or treatment which:

(1) Is not necessary to save the life of the infant;
(2) Has a potential risk to the infant's life or health that outweighs the potential benefit to the infant of the treatment or care; or
(3) Is treatment that will do no more than temporarily prolong the act of dying when death is imminent.

(d) A physician performing an abortion must take all medically appropriate and reasonable steps to preserve the life and health of a born-alive infant. If an abortion performed in a hospital results in a live birth, the physician attending the abortion shall provide immediate medical care to the infant, inform the mother of the live birth, and request transfer of the infant to an on-duty resident or emergency care physician who shall provide medically appropriate and reasonable medical care and treatment to the infant.

If an abortion performed in a facility other than a hospital results in a live birth, the physician attending the abortion shall provide immediate medical care to the infant and call 9-1-1 for an emergency transfer of the infant to a hospital that shall provide medically appropriate and reasonable care and treatment to the infant.

(e) If the physician described in subsection (d) of this Section is unable to perform the duties in that paragraph because he is assisting the woman on whom the abortion was performed, then an attending physician's assistant, nurse, or other healthcare provider must assume the duties outlined in subsection (d) of this Section.

(f) Any born-alive infant including one born in the course of an abortion procedure shall be treated as a legal person under the laws of this State, with the same rights to medically appropriate and reasonable care and treatment, and birth and death (if death occurs) certificates shall be issued accordingly.

(g) If, before the abortion, the mother [, *and if married, her husband,*] has [*or have*] stated in writing that she does [*or they do*] not wish to keep the infant in the event that the abortion results in a live birth, and this writing is not retracted before the [*attempted*] abortion, the infant, if born alive, shall immediately upon birth become a ward of [*Insert name of appropriate state child welfare department or agency*].

(h) No person may use any born-alive infant for any type of scientific research or other kind of experimentation except as necessary to protect or preserve the life and health of the born-alive infant.

[OPTIONAL: SECTION 5. INFANTICIDE. [CONSIDER THIS SECTION IF THE STATE'S CRIMINAL CODE DOES NOT INCLUDE THE CRIME OF INFANTICIDE, OR IF THE STATE DOES NOT WISH TO ADD ANOTHER DEFINITION TO THE EXISTING CRIME OF INFANTICIDE.]

(a) **"Infanticide"** *means any deliberate act that:*

(1) *Is intended to kill an infant who has been born alive; and*
(2) *That does kill such infant.*

(b) *Any physician, nurse, or other healthcare provider who deliberately fails to provide medically appropriate and reasonable care and treatment to a born-alive infant and, as a result of that failure the infant dies, shall be guilty of the crime of infanticide.*]

SECTION [6]. EXCEPTIONS.

The parent(s) or guardian(s) of a born-alive infant will not be held criminally or civilly liable for the actions of a physician, nurse, or other healthcare provider that are in violation of this Act and to which the parent(s) or guardian(s) did not give consent.

SECTION [7]. CRIMINAL PENALTIES.

(a) Any physician, nurse, or other healthcare provider who intentionally, knowingly, or negligently fails to provide medically appropriate and reasonable care and treatment to a born-alive infant in the course of an [*attempted*] abortion shall be guilty of a [*Insert appropriate classification*] felony and upon conviction shall be fined an amount not exceeding [*Insert appropriate amount*], imprisoned not less than [*Insert appropriate term*] years and not exceeding [*Insert appropriate term*] years, or both [*or "will be punished according to the sentencing guidelines found in the [Criminal/Penal Code] of [Insert name of State]"*].

[OPTIONAL *(if Act includes Section on "Infanticide")*: (b) *Any person found guilty of the crime of infanticide shall be fined an amount not exceeding [Insert appropriate amount], or imprisoned not less than [Insert appropriate term] years and not exceeding [Insert appropriate term] years, or both [or "will be punished according to the sentencing guidelines found in the [Criminal/Penal Code] of [Insert name of State]."]]*

[(c)] Any violation of Section 4, subsection (h) of this Act [*concerning the research use of a born-alive infant*] is a [*Insert appropriate classification*] felony and upon conviction shall be fined an amount not exceeding [*Insert appropriate amount*], or imprisoned not less than [*Insert appropriate term*] years and not exceeding [*Insert appropriate term*] years, or both [*or "will be punished according to the sentencing guidelines found in the [Criminal/Penal Code] of [Insert name of State]"*].

SECTION [8]. CIVIL AND ADMINISTRATIVE ACTION.

In addition to whatever remedies are available under the statutory [*or common*] law of this State, failure to comply with the requirements of this Act shall

(a) Provide a basis for a civil action for compensatory and punitive damages. Any conviction under this Act shall be admissible in a civil suit as prima facie evidence of a failure to provide medically appropriate and reasonable care and treatment to a born-alive infant. Any civil action may be based on a claim that the death of or injury to the born-alive infant was a result of simple negligence, gross negligence, wantonness, willfulness, intentional conduct, or another violation of the legal standard of care.

(b) Provide a basis for professional disciplinary action under [*Insert appropriate reference(s) to state statute(s) and/or administrative rule(s) concerning the state medical board's oversight and review authority*] for the suspension or revocation of any license for physicians, licensed and registered nurses, or other licensed or regulated persons. Any conviction of any person for any failure to comply with the requirements of this Act shall result in the automatic suspension of his or her license for a period of at least one (1) year [*or other appropriate penalty*] and said license shall be reinstated after that time only under such conditions as the [*Insert reference(s) to appropriate regulatory or licensing body*] shall require to ensure compliance with this Act.

(c) Provide a basis for recovery for the parent(s) of the infant or the parent(s) or guardian(s) of the mother if the mother is a minor for the wrongful death of the infant under [*Insert reference(s) to state's wrongful death statute(s)*], whether or not the infant was viable at the time the [*attempted*] abortion was performed.

SECTION [9]. CONSTRUCTION.

(a) Nothing in this Act shall be construed to affirm, deny, expand, or contract any legal status or legal right applicable to any member of the species homo sapiens at any point prior to being born alive (as defined in this Act).

(b) Nothing in this Act shall be construed to affect existing federal or state law regarding abortion.

(c) Nothing in this Act shall be construed as creating or recognizing a right to abortion.

(d) Nothing in this Act shall be construed to alter generally accepted medical standards.

SECTION [10]. SEVERABILITY.

Any provision of this Act held to be invalid or unenforceable by its terms, or as applied to any person or circumstance, shall be construed so as to give it the maximum effect permitted by law, unless such holding shall be one of utter invalidity or unenforceability, in which event such provision shall be deemed severable herefrom and shall not affect the remainder hereof or the application of such provision to other persons not similarly situated or to other dissimilar circumstances.

SECTION [11]. RIGHT OF INTERVENTION.

The [*Legislature*], by joint resolution, may appoint one or more of its members who sponsored or cosponsored this Act in his or her official capacity to intervene as a matter of right in any case in which the constitutionality of this law is challenged.

SECTION [12]. EFFECTIVE DATE.

This Act takes effect on [*Insert date*].

STATE OF THE STATES:
WHERE ARE WE NOW?

BORN-ALIVE INFANT PROTECTION (BAIPA)

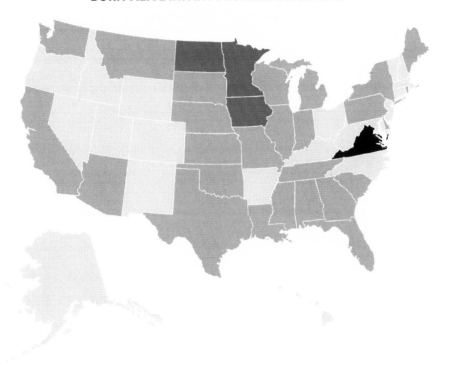

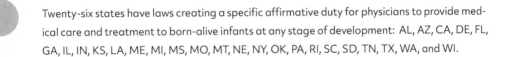

Twenty-six states have laws creating a specific affirmative duty for physicians to provide medical care and treatment to born-alive infants at any stage of development: AL, AZ, CA, DE, FL, GA, IL, IN, KS, LA, ME, MI, MS, MO, MT, NE, NY, OK, PA, RI, SC, SD, TN, TX, WA, and WI.

Three states have laws creating a specific affirmative duty for physicians to provide medical care and treatment to born-alive infants after viability: IA, MN, and ND.

One state protects born-alive infants at any stage of development from "deliberate acts" undertaken by a physician that result in the death of the infant: VA.

UNBORN INFANTS WRONGFUL DEATH ACT

HOUSE/SENATE BILL NO. _____

By Representatives/Senators _____

SECTION 1. TITLE.

This Act may be known and cited as the "Unborn Infants Wrongful Death Act."

SECTION 2. LEGISLATIVE FINDINGS AND PURPOSES.

(a)   The [*Legislature*] of the State of [*Insert name of State*] finds that:

   (1)   This State has statutorily recognized a wrongful death civil cause of action [*Insert appropriate statutory or other reference(s)*] since [*Insert date*].

   (2)   A wrongful death cause of action is intended to correct a flaw in the common law where no cause of action survived a victim's death. Thus, a tortfeasor (wrongdoer) could escape liability merely because he or she inflicted injuries so severe that they resulted in the death of the victim.

   (3)   The wrongful death cause of action provides for damages to be paid by a wrongdoer to his or her victim's survivors, thus deterring tortious and harmful behavior and providing for restitution to a victim's estate.

   (4)   This State has an interest in protecting every human being including unborn children from tortious and harmful acts.

   (5)   Parents of unborn children have protectable interests in the life, health, and well-being of their children.

   (6)   Tortious behavior which results in the death of an unborn child carries the same social and emotional cost as that which results in the death of a born and living human being including bereavement, a loss of society, and the lawlessness and disregard for life which characterizes negligent, harmful, or wrongful behavior.

(b)   For these reasons, the [*Legislature*] finds that the exclusion of unborn children from coverage under the State's wrongful death cause of action is at cross purposes with the justifications for the statute[*s*], and that a cause of action for the wrongful death of an unborn child at any stage of gestation or development should be permitted under the laws of this State.

SECTION 3. DEFINITIONS.

As used in this Act only:

(a) **"Abortion"** means the act of using or prescribing any instrument, medicine, drug, or any other substance, device, or means with the intent to terminate the clinically diagnosable pregnancy of a woman with knowledge that the termination by those means will with reasonable likelihood cause the death of the unborn child. Such use, prescription, or means is not an abortion if done with the intent to:

   (1)   Save the life or preserve the health of the unborn child;

   (2)   Remove a dead unborn child caused by spontaneous abortion; or

   (3)   Remove an ectopic pregnancy.

(b) **"Born alive"** means the substantial expulsion or extraction of an infant from its mother, regardless of the duration of the pregnancy, who, after expulsion or extraction, whether or not the umbilical cord has been cut or the placenta is attached, and regardless of whether the expulsion or extraction occurs as a result of natural or induced labor, cesarean section, or induced abortion, shows any evidence of life including, but not limited to, one or more of the following:

   (1) Breathing;

   (2) A heartbeat;

   (3) Umbilical cord pulsation; or

   (4) Definite movement of voluntary muscles.

(c) **"Conception"** means the fusion of a human spermatozoon with a human ovum.

(d) **"Healthcare provider"** means any individual who may be asked to participate in any way in a healthcare service including, but not limited to, the following: a physician's assistant; nurse; nurses' aide; medical assistant; hospital employee; clinic employee; nursing home employee; pharmacist; pharmacy employee; researcher; medical or nursing school faculty, student, or employee; counselor; social worker; or any professional, paraprofessional, or any other person who furnishes or assists in the furnishing of healthcare services.

(e) **"Physician"** means a doctor legally authorized to practice medicine or surgery in this State [*or any other individual legally authorized by this State to perform abortions; provided, however, that any individual who is not a physician and not otherwise legally authorized by this State to perform abortions, but who nevertheless performs an abortion shall be subject to the provisions of this Act*].

(f) **"Unborn child"** means the offspring of human beings from conception until birth.

SECTION 4. CAUSE OF ACTION.

The state or location of gestation or development of an unborn child when an injury is caused, when an injury takes effect, or at death shall not foreclose maintenance of a cause of action under the law of this State arising from the death of the unborn child caused by a wrongful act, neglect, carelessness, lack of skill, or default.

SECTION 5. EXCEPTIONS.

(a) There shall be no cause of action against a physician or a medical institution for the wrongful death of an unborn child caused by an abortion where the abortion was permitted by law and the requisite consent was lawfully given. However, a cause of action is not prohibited where an abortion is performed in violation of state law or where the child is born alive and subsequently dies.

(b) There shall be no cause of action against a physician, another healthcare provider, or a medical institution for the wrongful death of an unborn child in utero based on the alleged misconduct of the physician or medical institution where the defendant did not know and, under standard medical practice in the community, had no medical reason to know of the pregnancy of the woman or the existence of the unborn child.

SECTION 6. CONSTRUCTION.

(a) This Act does not create, recognize, endorse, or condone a right to an abortion.

(b) It is not the intention of this Act to make lawful an abortion that is currently unlawful.

SECTION 7. SEVERABILITY.

Any provision of this Act held to be invalid or unenforceable by its terms, or as applied to any person or circumstance, shall be construed so as give it the maximum effect permitted by law, unless such holding shall be one of utter invalidity or unenforceability, in which event such provision shall be deemed severable herefrom and shall not affect the remainder hereof or the application of such provision to other persons not similarly situated or to other, dissimilar circumstances.

SECTION 8. RIGHT OF INTERVENTION.

The [*Legislature*], by joint resolution, may appoint one or more of its members who sponsored or cosponsored this Act in his or her official capacity, to intervene as a matter of right to defend this law in any case in which its constitutionality is challenged.

SECTION 9. EFFECTIVE DATE.

This Act takes effect on [*Insert date*].

STATE OF THE STATES:
WHERE ARE WE NOW?

WRONGFUL DEATH (CIVIL ACTION)

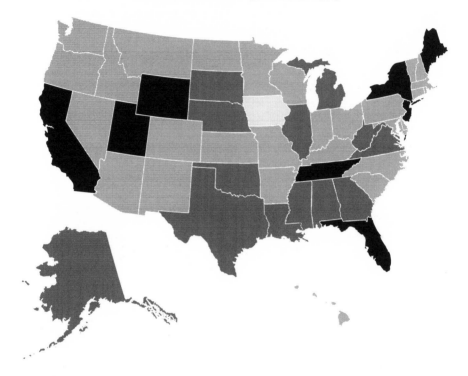

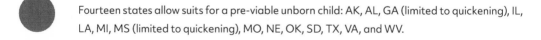
Twenty-seven states and the District of Columbia permit a wrongful death action if an unborn child was viable at the time of his/her death: AZ, AR, CO, CT, DE, DC, HI, ID, IN, KS, KY, MD, MA, MN, MT, NV, NH, NM, NC, ND, OH, OR, PA, RI, SC, VT, WA, and WI.

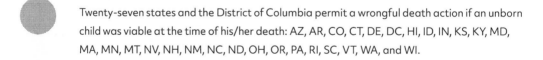
Fourteen states allow suits for a pre-viable unborn child: AK, AL, GA (limited to quickening), IL, LA, MI, MS (limited to quickening), MO, NE, OK, SD, TX, VA, and WV.

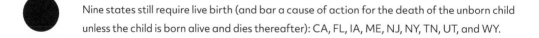
Nine states still require live birth (and bar a cause of action for the death of the unborn child unless the child is born alive and dies thereafter): CA, FL, IA, ME, NJ, NY, TN, UT, and WY.

PERINATAL HOSPICE INFORMATION ACT

HOUSE/SENATE BILL NO. _____

By Representatives/Senators _____

SECTION 1. TITLE.

This Act may be known as the "Perinatal Hospice Information Act."

SECTION 2. LEGISLATIVE FINDINGS AND PURPOSES.

(a) The [*Legislature*] of the State of [*Insert name of State*] finds that:

    (1) As prenatal diagnosis improves, increasingly more lethal fetal anomalies are diagnosed earlier in pregnancy.

    (2) Currently, parents are often given minimal options: terminating the pregnancy or simply waiting for their child to die. The majority of parents choose to terminate their pregnancies, while only [*twenty (20)*] percent of parents decide to continue their pregnancies.

    (3) Studies indicate that choosing to terminate the pregnancy can pose severe long-term psychological risks for a woman including the risk of posttraumatic stress, depression, and anxiety. On the other hand, a family that chooses to continue a pregnancy under the supportive, compassionate care of a perinatal hospice team report being emotionally and spiritually prepared for the death of their child.

    (4) Studies reveal that, when given the option, [*at least eighty (80) to eighty-seven (87) percent of parents*] choose to continue their pregnancies in the supportive environment of perinatal hospice care.

(b) Based on the findings in subsection (a), it is the purpose of this Act to:

    (1) Guarantee that a woman considering an abortion after a diagnosis of a lethal fetal anomaly is presented with information on the option of perinatal hospice care; and

    (2) Ensure that any abortion choice that a woman makes has been fully informed.

SECTION 3. DEFINITIONS.

As used in this Act only:

(a) **"Abortion"** means the act of using or prescribing any instrument, medicine, drug, or any other substance, device, or means with the intent to terminate the clinically diagnosable pregnancy of a woman with knowledge that the termination by those means will with reasonable likelihood cause the death of the unborn child. Such use, prescription, or means is not an abortion if done with the intent to:

    (1) Save the life or preserve the health of the unborn child;

    (2) Remove a dead unborn child caused by spontaneous abortion; or

    (3) Remove an ectopic pregnancy.

(b) **"Department"** means the Department of [*Insert appropriate title*] of the State of [*Insert name of State*].

(c) **"Lethal fetal anomaly"** means a fetal condition diagnosed before birth that will with reasonable certainty result in the death of the unborn child within three (3) months after birth.

(d) **"Medical emergency"** means that condition which, on the basis of the physician's good faith clinical judgment, so complicates the medical condition of a pregnant woman as to necessitate the immediate termination of her pregnancy to avert her death or for which a delay will create serious risk of substantial and irreversible impairment of a major bodily function.

(e) **"Perinatal hospice"** means comprehensive support to the pregnant woman and her family that includes support from the time of diagnosis, through the time of birth and the death of the infant, and through the postpartum period. Supportive care may include (but is not limited to) counseling and medical care by maternal-fetal medical specialists, obstetricians, neonatologists, anesthesia specialists, clergy, social workers, and specialty nurses focused on alleviating fear and ensuring that the woman and her family experience the life and death of their child in a comfortable and supportive environment.

(f) **"Physician"** means any person licensed to practice medicine in this State. The term includes medical doctors and doctors of osteopathy.

SECTION 4. INFORMED CONSENT FOR ABORTION TO INCLUDE INFORMATION ON PERINATAL HOSPICE.

(a) Except in the case of a medical emergency, in the case of a woman seeking an abortion of her unborn child diagnosed with a lethal fetal anomaly, consent to an abortion is voluntary and informed only if at least twenty-four (24) hours before the abortion:

   (1) The physician who is to perform the abortion [*or the referring physician*] has informed the woman, orally and in person, that perinatal hospice services are available and has offered this care as an alternative to abortion; and

   (2) The woman is given a list of perinatal hospice programs available both in her state and nationally, prepared by the Department and organized geographically by location.

(b) If perinatal hospice services are declined in favor of abortion, the woman must certify in writing both her decision to forgo such services and proceed with the abortion, and that she received the materials listed in subsection 4(a)(2) of this Section.

SECTION 5. PUBLICATION OF MATERIALS.

The Department shall cause to be published the printed materials described in Section 4(a)(2) in English and Spanish [*and/or other appropriate language(s)*] within [*Insert appropriate number*] days after this Act becomes law.

SECTION 6. PROFESSIONAL SANCTIONS.

(a) **Unprofessional Conduct.** Any violation of this Act shall constitute unprofessional conduct pursuant to [*Insert appropriate statutes for medical doctors and surgeons and osteopathic doctors*] and shall result in [*permanent or insert appropriate time period*] revocation of the violator's license to practice medicine.

(b) **Trade, Occupation, or Profession.** Any violation of this Act may be the basis for denying an application for, denying an application for the renewal of, or revoking any license, permit, certificate, or any other form of permission required to practice or engage in a trade, occupation, or profession.

SECTION 7. SEVERABILITY.

Any provision of this Act held to be invalid or unenforceable by its terms, or as applied to any person or circumstance, shall be construed so as to give it the maximum effect permitted by law, unless such holding shall be one of utter invalidity or unenforceability, in which event such provision shall be deemed severable herefrom and shall not affect the remainder hereof or the application of such provision to other persons not similarly situated or to other, dissimilar circumstances.

SECTION 8. RIGHT OF INTERVENTION.

The [*Legislature*], by joint resolution, may appoint one or more of its members who sponsored or co-sponsored this Act, as a matter of right and in his or her official capacity, to intervene to defend this law in any case in which its constitutionality is challenged or questioned.

SECTION 9. EFFECTIVE DATE.

This Act takes effect on [*Insert date*].

MODEL LEGISLATION

Women's Protection Project

Promoting Health & Safety

The pro-life movement will never abandon women to the whims of an under-regulated, predatory abortion industry. Even in the face of a controversial Supreme Court decision prioritizing abortion industry "access" over women's health and safety and ongoing efforts by abortion advocates to invalidate hundreds of life-affirming state laws, pro-life Americans remain committed to protecting women and their unborn children from abortion industry profiteers like Planned Parenthood and from the well-documented physical and psychological harms of abortion.

The Supreme Court's June 2016 decision in *Whole Woman's Health v. Hellerstedt* invalidated a Texas law mandating that abortion clinics meet the same patient care standards as other facilities performing invasive, outpatient surgeries and requiring that individual abortion providers maintain admitting privileges at local hospitals to facilitate emergency care and the treatment of post-abortion complications. In striking down the law, the five-justice majority placed a clear priority on "mere access" to abortion facilities, accepting at face value the self-serving claims of abortion advocates that enforcement of the Texas requirements would force abortion clinics to close.

The *Hellerstedt* majority, however, also suggests that states may still regulate abortion facilities to ensure some degree of patient safety and to address problems with substandard abortion providers. Importantly, the Court acknowledged that the "Kermit Gosnell scandal," involving a Philadelphia abortionist who operated a dangerous and unsanitary clinic for years before being investigated and prosecuted for homicide and more than 200 violations of state abortion laws, was

"terribly wrong" and involved "deplorable crimes." The Court also specifically acknowledged the importance of abortion facilities being "inspected at least annually" and the inclusion of appropriate enforcement mechanisms, such as civil and criminal penalties, in state abortion regulations.

Whether it involves regulating abortion providers or establishing the medical standard of care under which abortions must be done, laws predicated on the state's interest in safeguarding maternal health still maintain the strongest potential both to protect women and withstand potential judicial review. Recognizing this, the *Women's Protection Project* is composed of:

- **The Women's Late-Term Pregnancy Health Act**, which prohibits abortions at or after 20 weeks based on concerns for women's health and the pain experienced by unborn children.

- **The Women's Health Protection Act**, which requires abortion facilities to meet medically appropriate health and safety standards designed specifically for such facilities and based on the abortion industry's own treatment protocols.

- **The Enforcement Module**, which provides options for the criminal, civil, and administrative enforcement of all abortion-related statutes and details enhanced inspection requirements for abortion facilities.

- **The Abortion Reporting Act**, which requires abortion providers to report demographic information about women undergoing abortions and mandates that any medical provider treating abortion-related complications report information about those complications to state officials.

- **The Women's Right to Know Act**, which provides a woman at least twenty-four (24) hours before an abortion with detailed information regarding her medical and psychological risks; her child's gestational age, development, and pain capability; and the abortion procedure itself.

- **The Drug-Induced Abortion Information and Reporting Act**, which requires abortion providers to inform women about the efficacy and dangers of drug-induced abortion and mandates that women be told that drug-induced abortions can be reversed. The Act also requires the reporting of complications related to drug-induced abortions.

- **The Coercive Abuse Against Mothers Prevention Act**, which prohibits coercing a woman to undergo an abortion and requires abortion facilities to post signs concerning coercion and to report suspected cases of coercive abuse.

- **The Child Protection Act**, which strengthens requirements that abortion facilities report all cases of suspected statutory rape and sexual abuse, mandates the collection of forensic evidence for certain abortions done on minors, and prohibits a third-party from aiding or abetting a minor in circumventing her state's parental involvement law.

- **The Parental Involvement Enhancement Act**, which strengthens state parental involvement laws with requirements for notarized consent forms and for identification and proof of relationship for a parent or guardian providing the requisite consent, as well as more stringent standards for judicial bypass proceedings.

AUL's *Women's Protection Project* is the legal blueprint for protecting women and their children from an increasingly under-regulated and rapacious abortion industry. American women deserve more than the abortion industry's false promises that "mere access" to abortion guarantees their health and well-being. After all, Gosnell's squalid clinic provided "mere access" to abortion, and many women paid the price for this "access" with their lives, with their fertility, and with their physical and mental health.

WOMEN'S LATE-TERM PREGNANCY HEALTH ACT

HOUSE/SENATE BILL NO. _____

By Representatives/Senators _____

SECTION 1. TITLE.

This Act may be known and cited as the "Women's Late-Term Pregnancy Health Act."

SECTION 2. LEGISLATIVE FINDINGS AND PURPOSES.

(a) The [*Legislature*] of the State of [*Insert name of State*] finds that:

    (1) Abortion can cause serious physical and psychological (both short- and long-term) complications for women, including but not limited to: uterine perforation, uterine scarring, cervical perforation or other injury, infection, bleeding, hemorrhage, blood clots, failure to actually terminate the pregnancy, incomplete abortion (retained tissue), pelvic inflammatory disease, endometritis, missed ectopic pregnancy, cardiac arrest, respiratory arrest, renal failure, metabolic disorder, shock, embolism, coma, placenta previa in subsequent pregnancies, preterm birth in subsequent pregnancies, free fluid in the abdomen, organ damage, adverse reactions to anesthesia and other drugs, psychological or emotional complications including depression, anxiety, sleeping disorders, an increased risk of breast cancer, and death.

    (2) Abortion has a higher medical risk when the procedure is performed later in pregnancy. Compared to an abortion at eight (8) weeks gestation or earlier, the relative risk increases exponentially at higher gestations. L. Bartlett et al., *Risk factors for legal induced abortion-related mortality in the United States*, OBSTETRICS & GYNECOLOGY 103(4):729 (2004).

    (3) In fact, the incidence of major complications is highest after twenty (20) weeks of gestation. J. Pregler & A. DeCherney, WOMEN'S HEALTH: PRINCIPLES AND CLINICAL PRACTICE 232 (2002).

    (4) According to the Alan Guttmacher Institute, the risk of death associated with abortion increases with the length of pregnancy, from one death for every one million abortions at or before eight weeks gestation to one per 29,000 abortions at 16 to 20 weeks gestation and one per 11,000 abortions at 21 or more weeks gestation (citing L. Bartlett et al., *Risk factors for legal induced abortion-related mortality in the United States*, OBSTETRICS & GYNECOLOGY 103(4):729–737 (2004)).

(5) After the first trimester, the risk of hemorrhage from an abortion, in particular, is greater, and the resultant complications may require a hysterectomy, other reparative surgery, or a blood transfusion.

(6) The State of [*Insert name of State*] has a legitimate concern for the public's health and safety. *Williamson v. Lee Optical*, 348 U.S. 483, 486 (1955).

(7) The State of [*Insert name of State*] "has legitimate interests from the outset of pregnancy in protecting the health of women." *Planned Parenthood of Southeastern Pennsylvania v. Casey*, 505 U.S. 833, 847 (1992). More specifically, the State of [*Insert name of State*] "has a legitimate concern with the health of women who undergo abortions." *Akron v. Akron Ctr. for Reproductive Health, Inc.*, 462 U.S. 416, 428-29 (1983).

(8) In addition, there is substantial and well-documented medical evidence that an unborn child by at least 20 weeks gestation has the capacity to feel pain during an abortion. K. Anand, *Pain and its effects in the human neonate and fetus*, N.E.J.M. 317:1321 (1987).

(b) Based on the findings in subsection (a), the [*Legislature*]'s purposes in promulgating this Act are to:

(1) Prohibit abortions at or after 20 weeks gestation, except in cases of a medical emergency [*based on the documented risks to women's health*].

(2) Prohibit abortions at or after 20 weeks gestation, in part, because of the pain felt by an unborn child upon being aborted.

(3) Define "medical emergency" to encompass "significant health risks," namely, only those circumstances in which a pregnant woman's life or a major bodily function is threatened. *Gonzales v. Carhart*, 550 U.S. 124, 161 (2007).

SECTION 3. DEFINITIONS.

For purposes of this Act only:

(a) **"Abortion"** means the act of using or prescribing any instrument, medicine, drug, or any other substance, device, or means with the intent to terminate the clinically diagnosable pregnancy of a woman with knowledge that the termination by those means will with reasonable likelihood cause the death of the unborn child. Such use, prescription, or means is not an abortion if done with the intent to:

(1) Save the life or preserve the health of the unborn child;

(2) Remove a dead unborn child caused by spontaneous abortion; or

(3) Remove an ectopic pregnancy.

(b) **"Attempt to perform"** means an act or omission of a statutorily required act that, under the circumstances as the actor believes them to be, constitutes a substantial step in a course of conduct planned to culminate in the performance or induction of an abortion.

(c) **"Conception"** means the fusion of a human spermatozoon with a human ovum.

(d) **"Gestational age"** means the time that has elapsed since the first day of the woman's last menstrual period.

(e) **"Major bodily function"** includes, but is not limited to, functions of the immune system, normal cell growth, and digestive, bowel, bladder, neurological, brain, respiratory, circulatory, endocrine, and reproductive functions.

(f) **"Medical facility"** means any public or private hospital, clinic, center, medical school, medical training institution, healthcare facility, physician's office, infirmary, dispensary, ambulatory surgical treatment center, or other institution or location wherein medical care is provided to any person.

(g) **"Physician"** means any person licensed to practice medicine in this State. The term includes medical doctors and doctors of osteopathy.

(h) **"Pregnant"** or **"pregnancy"** means that female reproductive condition of having an unborn child in the [*woman's*] uterus.

(i) **"Probable gestational age"** means what, in reasonable medical judgment, will with reasonable probability be the gestational age of the unborn child at the time the abortion is considered, performed, or attempted.

(j) **"Reasonable medical judgment"** means that medical judgment that would be made by a reasonably prudent physician [*in the community*], knowledgeable about the case and the treatment possibilities with respect to the medical condition(s) involved.

(k) **"Unborn child"** means the offspring of human beings from conception until birth.

SECTION 4. PROHIBITION.

(a) Except in the case of a medical emergency as specifically defined in Subsection 4(c) of this Act, no abortion shall be performed, induced, or attempted unless the physician [*or the referring physician*] has first made a determination of the probable gestational age of the unborn child. In making such a determination, the physician [*or referring physician*] shall make such inquiries of the pregnant woman and perform or cause to be performed all such medical examinations, imaging studies, and tests as a reasonably prudent physician [*in the community*], knowledgeable about the medical facts and conditions of both the woman and the unborn child involved, would consider necessary to perform and consider in making an accurate diagnosis with respect to gestational age.

(b) Except in a medical emergency as specifically defined in Subsection 4(c) of this Act, no physician or person shall knowingly perform, induce, or attempt to perform an abortion upon a pregnant woman when the probable gestational age of her unborn child has been determined to be at least twenty (20) weeks.

(c) **Medical Emergency Exception:** For the purposes of this Act only, **"medical emergency"** means a condition in which an abortion is necessary to preserve the life of the pregnant woman whose life is endangered by a physical disorder, physical illness, or physical injury, including a life-endangering physical condition caused by or arising from the pregnancy itself, or when continuation of the pregnancy will create a serious risk of substantial and irreversible impairment of a major bodily function (as specifically defined in subsection 3(e) of this Act) of the pregnant woman.

SECTION 5. REPORTING.

(a) Any physician who performs an abortion pursuant to subsection 4(c) of this Act shall report, in writing, to the medical facility in which the abortion is performed the reason(s) for the determination that a medical emergency existed. The physician's written report shall be included in a written report from the medical facility to the [*Insert appropriate state department, department head, or regulatory body*], made within a reasonable period of time as determined by the [*Insert appropriate state department, department head, or regulatory body*]. If the abortion is not performed in a medical facility, the physician shall report, in writing, the reason(s) for the determination that a medical emergency existed to the [*Insert appropriate state department, department head, or regulatory body*] as part of the written report made by the physician to the [*Insert appropriate state department, department head, or regulatory body*]. The physician and the medical facility shall retain a copy of the written reports required under this Section for not less than five (5) years.

(b) Failure to report under this Section does not subject the physician to criminal or civil penalties under Sections 6 and 7 of this Act.

(c) Subsection 4(b) does not preclude sanctions, disciplinary action, or any other appropriate action by the [*Insert appropriate citation or reference to state Medical Board or other appropriate agency*].

SECTION 6. CRIMINAL PENALTIES.

(a) Any person who intentionally or knowingly violates this Act is guilty of a [*Insert appropriate penalty/ offense classification*].

(b) Any physician who intentionally or knowingly performs or induces an abortion in violation of this Act and thereby kills an unborn child shall be fined not less than ten thousand (10,000) nor more than one-hundred thousand (100,000) dollars under this Act, or be imprisoned [*at hard labor*] not less than one (1) year nor more than ten (10) years, or both.

SECTION 7. CIVIL REMEDIES.

(a) The woman, the father of the unborn child if married to the mother at the time she receives an abortion in violation of this Act, and/or, if the mother has not attained the age of eighteen (18) years at the time of the abortion, the maternal grandparents of the unborn child may in a civil action obtain appropriate relief, unless the pregnancy resulted from the plaintiff's criminal conduct or, if brought by the maternal grandparents, the maternal grandparents consented to the abortion.

(b) Such relief shall include

   (1) Money damages for all psychological and physical injuries occasioned by the violation of this Act; and
   (2) Statutory damages equal to [*Insert number*] times the cost of the abortion performed in violation of this Act.

SECTION 8. REVIEW BY STATE MEDICAL BOARD [*OF MEDICAL LICENSURE AND SUPERVISION*].

(a) A physician-defendant accused of violating this Act may seek a hearing before the State Medical Board [*or other appropriate state agency*] as to whether the physician's conduct was necessary to save the life of the mother whose life was endangered by a physical disorder, physical illness, or physical injury, including a life-endangering physical condition caused by or arising from the pregnancy itself; and/or as to whether the continuation of the pregnancy would have created a serious risk of substantial and irreversible impairment of a major bodily function (as specifically defined in subsection 3(e) of this Act) of the pregnant woman.

(b) The findings on this issue shall be admissible at any criminal and civil trial of the physician-defendant. Upon a motion of the physician-defendant, the court shall delay the beginning of the trial(s) for not more than thirty (30) days to permit such a hearing to take place.

SECTION 9. PENALTIES FOR MEDICAL FACILITIES.

(a) A medical facility licensed pursuant to [*Insert reference(s) to appropriate statute(s) or regulation(s)*] in which an abortion is performed, induced or attempted in violation of this Act shall be subject to immediate revocation of its license by the [*Insert name of appropriate department or agency*].

(b) A medical facility licensed pursuant to [*Insert references to appropriate statute(s) or regulation(s)*] in which an abortion is performed, induced or attempted in violation of this Act shall be precluded from eligibility for any and all state funding for [*Insert number*] years and will be required to reimburse the State for funds from the calendar [*fiscal*] year in which the abortion in violation of this Act was performed.

SECTION 10. PROSECUTORIAL EXCLUSION.

A woman upon whom an abortion in violation of this Act is performed, induced or attempted may not be prosecuted under this Act.

SECTION 11. CONSTRUCTION.

(a) Nothing in this Act shall be construed as creating or recognizing a right to abortion.

(b) It is not the intention of this Act to make lawful an abortion that is currently unlawful.

SECTION 12. SEVERABILITY.

Any provision of this Act held to be invalid or unenforceable by its terms, or as applied to any person or circumstance, shall be construed so as to give it the maximum effect permitted by law, unless such holding shall be one of utter invalidity or unenforceability, in which event such provision shall be deemed severable herefrom and shall not affect the remainder hereof or the application of such provision to other persons not similarly situated or to other, dissimilar circumstances.

SECTION 13. RIGHT OF INTERVENTION.

The [*Legislature*], by joint resolution, may appoint one or more of its members, who sponsored or cosponsored this Act in his or her official capacity, to intervene as a matter of right in any case in which the constitutionality of this law is challenged.

SECTION 14. EFFECTIVE DATE.

This Act shall take effect on [*Insert date*].

WOMEN'S HEALTH PROTECTION ACT

HOUSE/SENATE BILL NO. _____

By Representatives/Senators _____

SECTION 1. TITLE.

This Act may be known and cited as the "Women's Health Protection Act."

SECTION 2. LEGISLATIVE FINDINGS AND PURPOSES.

(a) The Legislature of the State of [*Insert name of State*] finds that:

    (1) The vast majority of all abortions in this State are performed in clinics devoted primarily to providing abortions and family planning services. Most women who seek abortions at these facilities do not have any physician-patient relationship with the physician who performs the abortion either before or after the procedure. They ordinarily do not return to the facility for post-surgical care. In most instances, the woman's only actual contact with the abortion provider occurs simultaneously with the abortion procedure, with little opportunity to ask questions about the procedure, potential complications, and proper follow-up care.

    (2) "The medical, emotional, and psychological consequences of an abortion are serious and can be lasting ...." *H.L. v. Matheson*, 450 U.S. 398, 411 (1981).

    (3) Abortion can lead to both short-term and long-term medical complications. Potential complications from abortion include, among others, heavy and/or uncontrolled bleeding, hemorrhage, infection, uterine perforation, uterine scarring, blood clots, cervical tears, incomplete abortion (retained tissue), failure to actually terminate the pregnancy, free fluid in the abdomen, acute abdomen, organ damage, missed ectopic pregnancies, cardiac arrest, sepsis, respiratory arrest, reactions to anesthesia and other drugs, and even death.

    (4) The risks for second-trimester abortions are greater than for first-trimester abortions. The risk of hemorrhage, in particular, is greater, and the resultant complications may require a hysterectomy, other reparative surgery, or a blood transfusion.

    (5) The State of [*Insert name of State*] has a legitimate concern for the public's health and safety. *Williamson v. Lee Optical*, 348 U.S. 483, 486 (1985).

(6) The State of [*Insert name of State*] "has legitimate interests from the outset of pregnancy in protecting the health of women." *Planned Parenthood of Southeastern Pennsylvania v. Casey*, 505 U.S. 833, 847 (1992).

(7) More specifically, the State of [*Insert name of State*] "has a legitimate concern with the health of women who undergo abortions." *Akron v. Akron Ctr. for Reproductive Health, Inc.*, 462 U.S. 416, 428-29 (1983).

(8) The U.S. Supreme Court has specifically acknowledged that a State has "a legitimate interest in seeing to it that abortion, like any other medical procedure, is performed under circumstances that insure maximum safety for the patient. This interest obviously extends at least to the performing physician and his staff, to the facilities involved, to the availability of after-care, and to adequate provision for any complication or emergency that might arise." *Roe v. Wade*, 410 U.S. 113, 150 (1973).

(b) Based on the findings in subsection (a), the purposes of this Act are to:

(1) Regulate abortion clinics consistent with and to the extent permitted by the decisions of the U.S. Supreme Court and other courts; and

(2) Provide for the protection of public health through the development, establishment, and enforcement of medically appropriate standards of care and safety in abortion clinics.

SECTION 3. DEFINITIONS.

As used in this Act only:

(a) **"Abortion"** means the act of using or prescribing any instrument [*, medicine, drug, or any other substance, device, or means*] with the intent to terminate the clinically diagnosable pregnancy of a woman with knowledge that the termination by those means will with reasonable likelihood cause the death of the unborn child. Such use [*, prescription, or means*] is not an abortion if done with the intent to:

(1) Save the life or preserve the health of the unborn child;

(2) Remove a dead unborn child caused by spontaneous abortion; or

(3) Remove an ectopic pregnancy.

(b) **"Abortion clinic"** means a facility, other than an accredited hospital, in which five (5) or more first-trimester abortions in any month or any second- or third-trimester abortions are performed.

(c)   **"Born alive,"** with respect to a member of the species *homo sapiens*, means the complete expulsion or extraction from his or her mother of that member, at any stage of development, who after such expulsion or extraction breathes or has a beating heart, pulsation of the umbilical cord, or definite movement of voluntary muscles, regardless of whether the umbilical cord has been cut, and regardless of whether the expulsion or extraction occurs as a result of natural or induced labor, cesarean section, or induced abortion.

(d)   **"Conception"** and **"fertilization"** each means the fusion of the human spermatozoon with a human ovum.

(e)   **"Department"** means the [*Insert name of state health department or other appropriate agency*].

(f)   **"Director"** means the Director of the [*Insert name of state health department or other appropriate agency*].

(g)   **"Gestation"** means the time that has elapsed since the first day of the woman's last menstrual period.

(h)   **"Licensee"** means an individual, a partnership, an association, a limited liability company, or a corporation authorized by the [*Insert name of state health department or other appropriate agency*] to operate an abortion clinic.

(i)   **"Physician"** means a person licensed to practice medicine in the State of [*Insert name of State*]. This term includes medical doctors and doctors of osteopathy.

(j)   **"Unborn child"** means the offspring of human beings from conception until birth.

SECTION 4. LICENSURE REQUIREMENTS.

(a)   Beginning on [*Insert effective date*], all abortion clinics shall be licensed by the Department. Any existing abortion clinic, as defined by this Act, shall make application for licensure within ninety (90) days of the effective date of this Act.

(b)   An application for a license shall be made to the Department on forms provided by it and shall contain such information as the Department reasonably requires, which shall include affirmative evidence of ability to comply with such reasonable standards, rules, and regulations as are lawfully prescribed hereunder. Additional information required by the Department shall be supplied on supplemental forms as needed.

(c) Following receipt of an application for license and if the applicant and the facility meet the requirements established by this Act and the minimum standards, administrative rules, and regulations adopted in pursuance thereof, the Department shall issue a license which is valid for a period of one (1) year.

(d) A temporary or provisional license may be issued to an abortion clinic for a period of six (6) months in cases where sufficient compliance with minimum standards, rules, and regulations require an extension of time, if a disapproval has not been received from any other state or local agency otherwise authorized to inspect such facilities. The failure to comply must not be detrimental to the health and safety of the public.

(e) A license shall apply only to the location and licensee stated on the application and such license, once issued, is not be transferable from one place to another or from one licensee to another. If the location of the facility is changed, the license shall be automatically revoked. A new application form shall be completed prior to all license renewals.

(f) An application for a license or license renewal to operate an abortion clinic shall be accompanied by a fee of [*Insert appropriate amount*], which is hereby levied as the license fee for operation of an abortion clinic for a period of one (1) year. The fees herein levied and collected shall be paid into the [*general fund*].

(g) Each license issued hereunder shall be for a period of one (1) year from the date of issuance unless sooner revoked, shall be on a form prescribed by the Department, and may be renewed from year to year upon application and payment of the license fee as in the case of procurement of the original license.

(h) The Department may deny, suspend, revoke, or refuse to renew a license in any case in which it finds that there has been a substantial failure of the applicant or licensee to comply with the requirements of this Act or the minimum standards, administrative rules, and regulations adopted by the Department pursuant to this Act. In such case, the Department shall furnish the person, applicant, or licensee thirty (30) days' notice specifying the reason(s) for the action. However, if the Department finds that public health, safety, or welfare imperatively requires emergency action, and incorporates a finding to that effect in its order, summary suspension of a license may be ordered pending proceedings for revocation or other action. These proceedings shall be promptly instituted and determined.

(i) Any person, applicant, or licensee who feels aggrieved by the action of the Department in denying, suspending, revoking, or refusing to renew a license may appeal the Department's action in accordance with the delay, notice, and other procedures established [*Insert reference(s) to agency/administrative appeal procedure(s) within the Department*].

(j) Any person, applicant, or licensee who feels aggrieved by the action of the [*appellate board or other appropriate agency or body*] may, within thirty (30) days after notification of such action, appeal suspensively to the [*Insert name of court*], except in cases in which summary suspension has been imposed pursuant to Section 4(h) of this Act. A record of all proceedings before the [*appellate board or other appropriate agency or body*] shall be made and kept on file with the [*appellate board or other appropriate agency or body*]. The [*appellate board or other appropriate agency or body*] shall transmit a certified copy of the record to the [*Insert name of court*]. The [*Insert name of court*] shall try the appeal de novo.

SECTION 5. INSPECTIONS AND INVESTIGATIONS.

(a) The Department shall establish policies and procedures for conducting pre-licensure and re-licensure inspections of abortion clinics. Prior to issuing or reissuing a license, the Department shall conduct an on-site inspection to ensure compliance with this Act, with the [*minimum standards, applicable regulations, or administrative rules*] promulgated by the Department under this Act, and with [*Insert citation(s) or reference(s) to other standards, regulations, and administrative rules related to the provision of abortion*].

(b) The Department shall also establish policies and procedures for conducting inspections and investigations pursuant to complaints received by the Department and made against any abortion clinic, or pursuant to information that has come into the possession of the Department by whatever source. The Department shall receive, record, and dispose of complaints received by it or raised internally in accordance with established policies and procedures.

(c) If the Director determines that there is reasonable cause to believe a licensee, licensed abortion clinic, or abortion clinic that is required to be licensed pursuant to this Act is not adhering to the requirements of this Act, [*the minimum standards, regulations, or administrative rules*] promulgated by the Department under the authority of this Act, or with [*Insert citation(s) or reference(s) to other standards, regulations, and administrative rules related to the provision of abortion*], the Director and any duly-designated employee or agent of the Director, including [*county health representatives*] and county or municipal fire inspectors, consistent with standard medical practices, may enter on and into the premises of the licensee, licensed abortion clinic, or abortion clinic that is required to be licensed, during regular business hours of the licensee or abortion clinic to determine compliance with this Act, with the [*minimum standards, applicable regulations, or administrative rules*] promulgated by the Department under this Act, and with [*Insert citation(s) or reference(s) to other standards, regulations, and administrative rules related to the provision of abortion*]; local fire ordinances or rules; and [*Insert reference(s) to any other applicable requirements*].

(d) An application for a license pursuant to this Act and [*the minimum standards, regulations, or administrative rules*] promulgated by the Department under the authority of this Act constitutes permission for, and complete acquiescence in, an entry or inspection of the premises during the pendency of the application and, if licensed, during the term of the license.

(e) If an inspection or investigation conducted pursuant to this Section 5(a), 5(b), or 5(c) reveals that a licensee or licensed abortion clinic is not adhering to the requirements of this Act, with the [*minimum standards, applicable regulations, or administrative rules*] promulgated by the Department under this Act, and with [*Insert citation(s) or reference(s) to other standards, regulations, and administrative rules related to the provision of abortion*]; local fire ordinances or rules; and [*Insert reference(s) to any other applicable requirements*], the Director may take action to deny, suspend, revoke, or refuse to renew a license to operate an abortion clinic.

SECTION 6. [*MINIMUM STANDARDS, ADMINISTRATIVE RULES, OR REGULATIONS*] FOR ABORTION CLINICS.

The Department shall establish [*minimum standards, administrative rules, or regulations*] for the licensing and operation of abortion clinics. Such [*minimum standards, administrative rules, or regulations*] become effective upon approval by the Director.

SECTION 7. [*MINIMUM STANDARDS, ADMINISTRATIVE RULES, OR REGULATIONS*] FOR ABORTION CLINICS.

(a) The Director shall adopt [*rules*] for an abortion clinic's physical facilities. At a minimum these rules shall prescribe [*standards*] for:

   (1) Adequate private space that is specifically designated for interviewing, counseling, and performing medical evaluations.
   (2) Dressing rooms for staff and patients.
   (3) Appropriate lavatory areas.
   (4) Areas for pre-procedure hand washing.
   (5) Private procedure rooms.
   (6) Adequate lighting and ventilation for abortion procedures.
   (7) Surgical or gynecologic examination tables and other fixed equipment.
   (8) Post-procedure recovery rooms that are supervised, staffed, and equipped to meet the patients' needs.

(9) Emergency exits to accommodate a stretcher or gurney.

(10) Areas for cleaning and sterilizing instruments.

(11) Adequate areas for the secure storage of medical records and necessary equipment and supplies.

(12) The display in the abortion clinic, in a place that is conspicuous to all patients, of the clinic's current license issued by the Department.

(b) The Director shall adopt [*rules*] to prescribe abortion clinic supply and equipment [*standards*], including supplies and equipment that are required to be immediately available for use in an emergency. At a minimum these [*rules*] shall:

(1) Prescribe required equipment and supplies, including medications, required for the performance, in an appropriate fashion, of any abortion procedure that the medical staff of the abortion clinic anticipates performing and for monitoring the progress of each patient throughout the procedure and recovery period.

(2) Require that the number or amount of equipment and supplies at the abortion clinic is adequate at all times to assure sufficient quantities of clean and sterilized durable equipment and supplies to meet the needs of each patient.

(3) Prescribe required equipment, supplies, and medications that shall be available and ready for immediate use in an emergency and requirements for written protocols and procedures to be followed by staff in an emergency, such as the loss of electrical power.

(4) Prescribe the mandated equipment and supplies for required laboratory tests and the requirements for protocols to maintain laboratory equipment located in the abortion clinic or any equipment operated by clinic staff.

(5) Require ultrasound equipment in all abortion clinics.

(6) Require that all equipment is safe for patients and the staff, meets applicable federal standards, and is checked annually.

(c) The Director shall adopt [*rules*] relating to abortion clinic personnel. At a minimum these [*rules*] shall require that:

(1) The abortion clinic designate a medical director who is licensed to practice medicine [*and surgery*] in the State of [*Insert name of State*].

(2) Physicians performing abortions are licensed to practice medicine [*and surgery*] in the State of [*Insert name of State*], demonstrate competence in the procedure(s) involved, and are acceptable to the medical director of the abortion clinic.

(3) Surgical assistants [*or other appropriate classification(s) of healthcare provider(s)*] receive training in counseling, patient advocacy, and the specific responsibilities of the services the surgical assistants [*or other appropriate classification(s) of healthcare provider(s)*] provide at an abortion clinic.

(4) Volunteers, if any, receive training in the specific responsibilities of the services that volunteers provide at an abortion clinic, including but not limited to counseling and patient advocacy, and as provided in the administrative [*rules*] adopted by the Director for different types of volunteers based on their responsibilities.

(d) The Director shall adopt [*rules*] relating to the medical screening and evaluation of each abortion clinic patient. At a minimum these [*rules*] shall require:

(1) A medical history including the following:
   a. Reported allergies to medications, antiseptic solutions, or latex.
   b. Obstetric and gynecologic history.
   c. Past surgeries.
   d. Medication that the patient is currently taking.
(2) A physical examination including a bimanual examination estimating uterine size and palpation of the adnexa.
(3) The appropriate pre-procedure testing including:
   a. Urine or blood tests for pregnancy, if ordered by a physician.
   b. A test for anemia.
   c. Rh typing, unless reliable written documentation of blood type is available.
   d. Other tests as indicated from the physical examination.
(4) When medically appropriate, an ultrasound examination for abortion patients. The [*rules*] shall require that if a person who is not a physician performs an ultrasound examination, that person shall have documented evidence that he or she completed a course or other acceptable training in the operation of ultrasound equipment as prescribed in [*rule*]. A physician or other licensed health-care professional shall review, at the request of the patient, the ultrasound evaluation results with the patient before the abortion procedure is performed, including permitting the patient to view the active ultrasound image and learn the probable gestational age of the unborn child.
(5) That a physician is responsible for estimating the gestational age of the unborn child based on the ultrasound examination, if performed, and obstetric standards that are in accord with established standards of care regarding the estimation of gestational age as defined in [*rule*] and shall write the estimate in the patient's medical record. The physician shall keep original prints of each ultrasound examination of a patient, if performed, in the patient's medical record.

(e) The Director shall adopt [*rules*] relating to the abortion procedure. At a minimum these [*rules*] shall require that:

(1) Medical personnel are available to all patients throughout their abortion procedures.

(2) Standards for the safe performance of abortion procedures that conform to obstetric standards and are in accord with established standards of care, including those regarding the estimation of gestational age as defined in [*rule*].

(3) Appropriate use of local anesthesia, analgesia, and sedation if ordered by the physician.

(4) The use of appropriate precautions such as the establishment of intravenous access at least for patients undergoing second- or third-trimester abortions.

(5) The use of appropriate monitoring of the vital signs and other defined signs and markers of the patient's status throughout the abortion procedure and during the recovery period until the patient's condition is deemed to be stable in the recovery room.

(f) The Director shall adopt [*rules*] that prescribe minimum recovery room standards for the abortion clinic. At a minimum these [*rules*] shall require:

(1) The provision of immediate post-procedure care including observation in a supervised recovery room for as long as the patient's condition warrants.

(2) That the clinic arrange hospitalization if any complication beyond the management capability of the staff occurs or is suspected.

(3) A licensed healthcare professional, trained in the management of the recovery area and capable of providing basic cardiopulmonary resuscitation (CPR) and related emergency procedures, actively monitor patients in the recovery room.

(4) A physician shall sign the discharge order and be readily accessible and available until the last patient is discharged.

(5) That a physician discusses RhO(d) immune globulin with each patient for whom it is indicated and assures that it is offered to the patient in the immediate post-operative period or that it is be available to her within seventy-two (72) hours after completion of the abortion procedure. If the patient refuses, a refusal form approved by the Department shall be signed by the patient and a witness and included in the patient's medical record.

(6) Written instructions with regard to post-abortion coitus, signs of possible complications and problems, and general aftercare are given to each patient. Each patient shall have specific instructions regarding access to medical care for complications, including a telephone number to call for medical emergencies.

(7) There is a specified minimum length of time that a patient remains in the recovery room by type of abortion procedure and duration of gestation.

(8) The physician ensures that a licensed healthcare professional from the abortion clinic makes a good faith effort to contact the patient by telephone, with the patient's consent, within twenty-four (24) hours after surgery to assess the patient's recovery.

(9) Equipment and services are located in the recovery room to provide appropriate emergency resuscitative and life support procedures pending the transfer of the patient or a child born alive to the hospital.

(g) The Director shall adopt [*rules*] that prescribe standards for follow-up care for abortion patients. At a minimum these [*rules*] shall require that:

(1) A post-abortion medical visit is offered and, if requested, scheduled for two (2) to three (3) weeks after the abortion procedure. The post-abortion visit will include, at minimum, a medical examination and a review of the results of all laboratory tests.

(2) A urine [*or blood*] test for pregnancy is obtained at the time of the follow-up visit to rule out continuing pregnancy. If a continuing pregnancy is suspected, the patient shall be appropriately evaluated and a physician consulted.

(h) The Director shall adopt [*rules*] to prescribe minimum abortion clinic incident reporting. At a minimum these [*rules*] shall require that:

(1) The abortion clinic records each incident resulting in a patient's or a born alive child's [*serious*] injury occurring at an abortion clinic and shall report these incidents in writing to the Department within ten (10) days after the incident. For the purposes of this paragraph, "serious injury" means an injury that occurs at an abortion clinic and that creates a serious risk of substantial impairment of a major body organ or function.

(2) If a patient's death occurs, other than the death of an unborn child properly reported pursuant to law, the abortion clinic reports it to the Department not later than the next Department work day.

(3) Incident reports are filed with the Department and appropriate professional regulatory boards.

(i) The Department shall not release personally identifiable patient or physician information.

(j) The [*rules*] adopted by the Director pursuant to this Act will not limit the ability of a physician or other healthcare professional to advise a patient on any health issue.

(k) The provisions of this Act and [*the rules and regulations*] adopted pursuant hereto shall be in addition to any other laws, administrative or other rules, and regulations which are applicable to facilities defined as "abortion clinics" under this Act.

SECTION 8. CRIMINAL PENALTIES.

(a) Whoever operates an abortion clinic as defined in this Act without a valid license issued by the Department is guilty of [*Insert proper penalty/offense classification*].

(b) Any person who intentionally [*or knowingly*] violates this Act or any [*rules or regulations*] adopted pursuant hereto is guilty of [*Insert proper penalty/offense classification*].

SECTION 9. CIVIL PENALTIES AND FINES.

(a) Any violation of this Act or any [*rules or regulations*] adopted under this Act may be subject to a civil penalty or fine up to [*Insert appropriate amount*] imposed by the Department.

(b) Each day of violation constitutes a separate violation for purposes of assessing civil penalties or fines.

(c) In deciding whether and to what extent to impose fines, the Department shall consider the following factors:

  (1) Gravity of the violation including the probability that death or serious physical harm to a patient or individual will result or has resulted;
  (2) Size of the population at risk as a consequence of the violation;
  (3) Severity and scope of the actual or potential harm;
  (4) Extent to which the provisions of the applicable statute(s) and regulation(s) were violated;
  (5) Any indications of good faith exercised by the licensee;
  (6) The duration, frequency, and relevance of any previous violations committed by the licensee; and
  (7) Financial benefit to the licensee of committing or continuing the violation(s).

(d) Both the Office of the Attorney General and the Office of the District Attorney [*or other appropriate authority*] for the county in which the violation occurred may institute a legal action to enforce collection of civil penalties or fines.

SECTION 10. INJUNCTIVE REMEDIES.

In addition to any other penalty provided by law, whenever in the judgment of the Director, any person has engaged, or is about to engage, in any acts or practices which constitute, or will constitute, a violation of this Act, or any [*rule or regulation*] adopted under the provision of this Act, the Director shall make application to any court of competent jurisdiction for an order enjoining such acts and practices, and upon a showing by the Director that such person has engaged, or is about to engage, in any such acts or practices, an injunction, restraining order, or such other order as may be appropriate shall be granted by such court without bond.

SECTION 11. CONSTRUCTION.

(a)   Nothing in this Act shall be construed as creating or recognizing a right to abortion.

(b)   It is not the intention of this Act to make lawful an abortion that is currently unlawful.

SECTION 12. RIGHT OF INTERVENTION.

The [*Legislature*], by joint resolution, may appoint one or more of its members, who sponsored or cosponsored this Act in his or her official capacity to intervene as a matter of right in any case in which the constitutionality of this Act, any portion thereof or any [*rule or regulation*] adopted pursuant hereto is challenged.

SECTION 13. SEVERABILITY.

Any provision of this Act held to be invalid or unenforceable by its terms, or as applied to any person or circumstance, shall be construed so as to give it the maximum effect permitted by law, unless such holding shall be one of utter invalidity or unenforceability, in which event such provision shall be deemed severable herefrom and shall not affect the remainder hereof or the application of such provision to other persons not similarly situated or to other, dissimilar circumstances.

SECTION 14. EFFECTIVE DATE.

This Act takes effect on [*Insert date*].

ENFORCEMENT OPTIONS FOR STATE ABORTION LAWS

[Drafter's Note: AUL should be consulted for drafting assistance with regard to these enforcement options. For example, AUL can assist in the drafting of specific findings of fact that should be adopted in support of the enforcement options legislators propose. These model provisions may be enacted in whole or in part, as stand-alone legislation or as an amendment to existing abortion laws.]

GENERAL CRIMINAL LIABILITY

(a)   A *[person]* who intentionally, knowingly, or recklessly violates any provision of *[this [Act or Section] or any rules and regulations adopted under this [Act or Section]; OR insert specific reference(s) to state abortion-related statute(s), regulations(s), or rule(s)] is guilty of a [Insert appropriate penalty/offense classification].*

In this Section, **"intentionally"** is defined by *[Section] [Insert appropriate section number]* of the *[Criminal/ Penal Code].*

(b)   No criminal penalty may be assessed against the woman upon whom the abortion is performed for a violation of any provision of *[this [Act or Section] or any rules and regulations adopted under this [Act or Section]; OR insert specific reference(s) to state abortion-related statute(s), regulation(s), or rule(s)].*

GENERAL CIVIL LIABILITY

OPTION 1: CIVIL PENALTIES ADMINISTERED BY STATE AUTHORITIES

(a)   Any violation of *[this [Act or Section] or any rules and regulations adopted under this [Act or Section]; OR insert specific reference(s) to state abortion-related statute(s), regulation(s), or rule(s)] may be subject to a civil penalty or fine up to [Insert appropriate amount] imposed by [Insert name of appropriate state official(s), department(s), and/or agency/ agencies].*

(b)   No civil penalty may be assessed against the woman upon whom the abortion is performed for a violation of any provision of *[this [Act or Section] or any rules and regulations adopted under this [Act or Section]; OR insert specific reference(s) to state abortion-related statute(s), regulation(s), or rule(s)].*

(c) Each day of violation constitutes a separate violation for purposes of assessing civil penalties or fines.

(d) In deciding whether and to what extent to impose fines, the [*Insert name of appropriate state official(s), department(s), or agency/agencies*] shall consider the following factors:

(1) Gravity of the violation(s) including the probability that death or serious physical harm to a patient or individual will result or has resulted;

(2) Size of the population at risk as a consequence of the violation(s);

(3) Severity and scope of the actual or potential harm(s);

(4) Extent to which the provisions of the applicable statute(s) and regulation(s) were violated;

(5) Any indications of good faith exercised by [*abortion facility, physician, licensee, and/or other appropriate term*];

(6) Duration, frequency, and relevance of any previous violations committed by the [*abortion facility, physician, licensee, and/or other appropriate term*]; and

(7) Financial benefit to the [*abortion facility, physician, licensee, and or other appropriate term*] of committing or continuing the violation(s).

(e) Both the Office of the Attorney General and the Office of the District Attorney [*or other appropriate authority*] for the county in which the violation(s) occurred may institute a legal action to enforce collection of civil penalties or fines.

OPTION 2: STATUTORY CAUSE OF ACTION FOR HARMED PARTY

Any [*person*] who violates [*this* [*Act or Section*] *or any rules and regulations adopted under this* [*Act or Section*]; *OR insert specific reference(s) to state abortion-related statute(s), regulation(s), or rule(s)*] shall be civilly liable to the person or persons adversely affected by the violation(s). A court may award damages to the person or persons adversely affected by any violation(s) of [*this* [*Act or Section*] *or any rules and regulations adopted under this* [*Act or Section*]; *OR insert specific reference(s) to state abortion-related statute(s), regulation(s), or rule(s)*] including compensation for emotional, physical, and psychological harm; attorneys' fees, litigation costs, and punitive damages.

ADMINISTRATIVE ACTION AGAINST A FACILITY'S LICENSE

The [*Insert reference(s) to appropriate state official(s), department(s), and/or agency/agencies*] may deny, suspend, revoke, or refuse to renew [*a license*] in any case in which it finds that there has been a substantial failure by any [*person, physician, licensee, applicant, abortion facility, and/or other appropriate term(s)*] to comply with the requirements of [*this [Act or Section] or any rules and regulations adopted under this [Act or Section]; OR insert specific reference(s) to state abortion-related statute(s), regulation(s), or rule(s)*]. In such case, the [*Insert reference(s) to appropriate state official(s), department(s), and/or agency/agencies*] shall furnish the [*person, physician, licensee, applicant, abortion facility, and/or other appropriate term(s)*] thirty (30) days' notice specifying reasons for the action(s). However, If the [*Insert reference(s) to appropriate state official(s), department(s), and/or agency/agencies*] finds that public health, safety, or welfare imperatively requires emergency action, and incorporates a finding to that effect in its order, summary suspension of a license may be ordered pending proceedings for revocation or other action. These proceedings shall be promptly instituted and determined.

Any [*person, physician, licensee, applicant, abortion facility, and/or other appropriate term(s)*] who [*that*] feels aggrieved by the action of the [*Insert reference(s) to appropriate state official(s), department(s), and/or agency/agencies*] in denying, suspending, revoking, or refusing to renew a license may appeal the action in accordance with the [*delay, notice, and other*] procedures established [*Insert reference(s) to applicable agency or administrative appeal procedure(s)*].

INJUNCTIVE REMEDY

In addition to any other penalty provided by law, whenever in the judgment of the [*Insert reference(s) to appropriate state official(s), department(s), and/or agency/agencies*], any [*person, physician, licensee, abortion facility, and/or other appropriate term(s)*] has engaged, or is about to engage, in any acts or practices which constitute or will constitute a violation of [*this [Act or Section] or any rules and regulations adopted under this [Act or Section]; OR insert specific reference(s) to state abortion-related statute(s), regulation(s), or rule(s)*], the [*Insert reference(s) to appropriate state official(s), department(s), and/or agency/agencies*] shall make application to any court of competent jurisdiction for an order enjoining such acts and practices, and upon a showing by the [*Insert reference(s) to appropriate state official(s), department(s), and/or agency/agencies*] that such [*person, physician, licensee, abortion clinic, and/or other appropriate term(s)*] has engaged or is about to engage in any such acts or practices, an injunction, restraining order, or such other order as may be appropriate shall be granted by such court without bond.

PROFESSIONAL AND DISCIPLINARY REMEDIES

In addition to whatever remedies are available under the common or statutory law or regulations of this State, failure to comply with the requirements of [*this [Act or Section] or any rules and regulations adopted under this [Act or Section]*; OR *insert specific reference(s) to state abortion-related statute(s), regulation(s), or rule(s)*] shall:

(a)   Provide a basis for a civil malpractice action for actual and punitive damages.

(b)   Provide a basis for a professional disciplinary action under [*state Medical Malpractice Act or other appropriate statutory and/or administrative authority*].

INSPECTIONS AND INVESTIGATIONS OF LICENSED ABORTION FACILITIES

[*Drafter's Note: A critical element of ensuring the protection of maternal health and the adequate enforcement of laws, regulations, and administrative rules related to abortion is regular inspections of abortion providers and, when appropriate, administrative and criminal investigations. The model provisions provided below may be used to supplement existing state rules and protocols for the inspection and investigation of abortion providers.*]

(a)   The [*Department*] shall establish policies and procedures for conducting pre-licensure and re-licensure inspections of abortion clinics. Prior to issuing or reissuing a license, the [*Department*] shall conduct an on-site inspection to ensure compliance with this Act, with the [*minimum standards, applicable regulations, or administrative rules*] promulgated by the [*Department*] under this Act, and with [*Insert citation(s) or reference(s) to other standards, regulations, and administrative rules related to the provision of abortion*].

(b)   The [*Department*] shall also establish policies and procedures for conducting inspections and investigations pursuant to complaints received by the [*Department*] and made against any abortion clinic, or pursuant to information that has come into the possession of the [*Department*] by whatever source. The [*Department*] shall receive, record, and dispose of complaints received by it or raised internally in accordance with established policies and procedures.

(c)   If the [*Director*] determines that there is reasonable cause to believe a licensee, licensed abortion clinic, or abortion clinic that is required to be licensed pursuant to this Act is not adhering to the requirements of this Act, [*the minimum standards, regulations, or administrative rules*] promulgated by the [*Department*] under the authority of this Act, or with [*Insert citation(s) or reference(s) to other standards, regulations, and administrative rules related to the provision of abortion*], the [*Director*] and any duly-designated employee or agent of the [*Director*], including [*county health representatives*] and county or municipal fire inspectors, consistent with standard medical practices, may enter on and into the premises of the licensee, licensed abortion clinic, or abortion clinic that is required to be licensed, during regular business hours of the licensee or abortion clinic to determine compliance with this Act, with the [*minimum standards, applicable regulations, or administrative rules*] promulgated by the [*Department*] under this Act, and with [*Insert citation(s) or reference(s) to other standards, regulations, and administrative rules related to the provision of abortion*]; local fire ordinances or rules; and [*Insert reference(s) to any other applicable requirements*].

(d) An application for a license pursuant to this Act and [*the minimum standards, regulations, or administrative rules*] promulgated by the [*Department*] under the authority of this Act constitutes permission for, and complete acquiescence in, an entry or inspection of the premises during the pendency of the application and, if licensed, during the term of the license.

(e) If an inspection or investigation conducted pursuant to this Section 5(a), 5(b), or 5(c) reveals that a licensee or licensed abortion clinic is not adhering to the requirements of this Act, with the [*minimum standards, applicable regulations, or administrative rules*] promulgated by the [*Department*] under this Act, and with [*Insert citation(s) or reference(s) to other standards, regulations, and administrative rules related to the provision of abortion*]; local fire ordinances or rules; and [*Insert reference(s) to any other applicable requirements*], the [*Director*] may take action to deny, suspend, revoke, or refuse to renew a license to operate an abortion clinic.

SAMPLE COMPLAINT FORMS IN APPENDIX

Appendix A: Professional Complaint Form

Appendix B: Abortion Facility Complaint Form

Appendix C: Administrative Enforcement Complaint Form

APPENDIX A: PROFESSIONAL COMPLAINT FORM

[***Drafter's Note:*** *Many state medical boards and other professional licensing bodies have complaint forms that can be submitted online directly through the entities' websites. This form can be adapted for online submission or used as a downloadable mail-in form.*]

Sample Professional Complaint Form [1]

This form is to be used by anyone alleging a violation of [*Insert reference(s) to appropriate statutory or regulatory provision(s)*]. Please provide as much specific detail as possible, including full names of the clinic staff and/or other parties involved, date(s) of the incident(s), the type(s) of violation(s), and whether or not the incident was reported to clinic staff or another agency.

Please fill out this form completely and return to [*Insert name and address of state medical board or other professional licensing board*]

PERSONAL INFORMATION (OPTIONAL)

Last Name		First Name		Middle Initial
Address			City	
State		Zip	Telephone	
Email				

PHYSICIAN INFORMATION

Name			
Practice Address			City
State		Zip	Telephone
License Number			

ALLEGED VIOLATION(S)

Date of Incident(s):	Person(s) involved:

Nature of Incident: (mark all that apply)

- ☐ Quality of care
- ☐ Misdiagnosis of condition
- ☐ Patient abandonment/neglect
- ☐ Failure to release patient records
- ☐ Impairment/incompetence
- ☐ Sexual contact with patient
- ☐ Substance abuse
- ☐ Misfilled prescription
- ☐ Unlicensed provider or aiding/abetting unlicensed practice
- ☐ Insurance fraud
- ☐ Other

Description of Incident:

---

[1] Sample form is modeled after from Florida Health Care Facility Complaint Form, *available at* http://apps.ahca.myflorida.com/hcfc/ (last visited August 9, 2016); Florida Healthcare Practitioner Complaint Form, *available at* http://doh.state.fl.us/mqa/enforcement/frm_general-medUCF.pdf (last visited August 23, 2017); Oregon Medical Board Complaint Form, *available at* http://www.oregon.gov/omb/pdfforms/complaintform.pdf (last visited August 23, 2017); and Arizona Election Grievance Complaint Form, *available at* http://www.azsos.gov/election/grievance/Grievance_Form.pdf (last visited August 23, 2017).

APPENDIX B: ABORTION FACILITY COMPLAINT FORM

[**Drafter's Note:** *Many state agencies maintain complaint forms that can be submitted online directly through the agencies' websites. This form can be adapted for online submission or used as a downloadable mail-in form.*]

Sample Abortion Facility Complaint Form [2]

This form is to be used by anyone alleging a violation of [*Insert reference(s) to appropriate state statutory or regulatory provision(s)*]. Please provide as much specific detail as possible, including full names of the clinic staff and/or other parties involved, date(s) of the incident(s), the type(s) of violation(s), and whether or not the incident was reported to clinic staff or another agency.

Please fill out this form completely and return to [*Insert name and address of appropriate state department or agency*].

PERSONAL INFORMATION (OPTIONAL)

Last Name	First Name	Middle Initial
Address		City
State	Zip	Telephone
Email		

FACILITY INFORMATION

Name		
Address		City
State	Zip	Telephone

ALLEGED VIOLATION(S)

Date of Incident(s):	Person(s) involved:
Description of Incident:	

[2] Sample form is modeled after Florida Health Care Facility Complaint Form, *available at* http://apps.ahca.myflorida.com/hcfc/ (last visited August 23, 2017); and Arizona Election Grievance Complaint Form, *available at* http://www.azsos.gov/election/grievance/Grievance_Form.pdf (last visited August 23, 2017).

APPENDIX C: ADMINISTRATIVE ENFORCEMENT COMPLAINT FORM

[Drafter's Note: *Many state agencies maintain complaint forms that can be submitted online directly through the agencies' websites. This form can be adapted for online submission or used as a downloadable mail-in form and can be used for a variety of administrative violations.*]

Sample Administrative Enforcement Complaint Form [3]

This form is to be used by anyone alleging a violation of [*Insert reference(s) to appropriate state statutory and/or regulatory provision(s)*]. Please provide as much specific detail as possible, including full names of the clinic staff and/or other parties involved, date(s) of the incident(s), the type(s) of violation(s), and whether or not the incident was reported to clinic staff or another agency.

Please fill out this form completely and return to [*Insert name and address of appropriate state department or agency*].

PERSONAL INFORMATION (OPTIONAL)

Last Name	First Name	Middle Initial
Address		City
State	Zip	Telephone
Email		

FACILITY INFORMATION

Name		
Practice Address		City
State	Zip	Telephone

ALLEGED VIOLATION(S)

Date of Incident(s):	Person(s) involved:
Description of Incident:	

---

[3] Sample form is modeled after Florida Health Care Facility Complaint Form, *available at* http://apps.ahca.myflorida.com/hcfc/ (last visited August 23, 2017); Arizona Election Grievance Complaint Form, *available at* http://www.azsos.gov/election/grievance/Grievance_Form.pdf (last visited August 23, 2017); and New York Public Integrity Unit Complaint Form, *available at* http://www.ag.ny.gov/sites/default/files/pdfs/complaints/piu001_complaint_form.pdf (last visited August 23, 2017).

ABORTION REPORTING ACT

HOUSE/SENATE BILL NO. _____

By Representatives/Senators _____

SECTION 1. TITLE.

This Act may be known and cited as the "Abortion Reporting Act."

SECTION 2. LEGISLATIVE FINDINGS AND PURPOSES.

(a) The [*Legislature*] of the State of [*Insert name of State*] finds that:

   (1) [*Insert name of State*] "has legitimate interests from the outset of pregnancy in protecting the health of women." *Planned Parenthood of Southeastern Pennsylvania v. Casey*, 505 U.S. 833, 847 (1992).

   (2) Specifically, the State "has a legitimate concern with the health of women who undergo abortions." *Akron v. Akron Ctr. for Reproductive Health, Inc.* 462 U.S. 416, 428-29 (1983).

   (3) Abortion can cause short-term and long-term physical and psychological complications for women, including but not limited to: uterine perforation, cervical perforation, infection, heavy and/or uncontrolled bleeding, hemorrhage, blood clots, failure to actually terminate the pregnancy, incomplete abortion (retained tissue), pelvic inflammatory disease, endometritis, missed ectopic pregnancy, cardiac arrest, respiratory arrest, renal failure, metabolic disorder, shock, embolism, coma, placenta previa in subsequent pregnancies, preterm delivery in subsequent pregnancies, free fluid in the abdomen, adverse reactions to anesthesia and other drugs, an increased risk for developing breast cancer, psychological complications such as depression, suicidal ideation, anxiety, sleeping disorders, and death.

   (4) To facilitate reliable scientific studies and research on the safety and efficacy of abortion, it is essential that the medical and public health communities have access to accurate information both on the abortion procedure and on complications resulting from abortion.

   (5) Abortion "record keeping and reporting provisions that are reasonably directed to the preservation of maternal health and that properly respect a patient's confidentiality and privacy are permissible." *Planned Parenthood v. Danforth*, 428 U.S. 80 at 52, 79-81 (1976).

(6) Abortion and complication reporting provisions do not impose an "undue burden" on a woman's right to choose whether or not to terminate a pregnancy. Specifically, "[t]he collection of information with respect to actual patients is a vital element of medical research, and so it cannot be said that the requirements serve no purpose other than to make abortions more difficult." *Planned Parenthood of Southeastern Pennsylvania v. Casey*, 505 U.S. at 900-901.

(7) To promote its interest in maternal health and life, the State of [*Insert name of State*] maintains an interest in:

a. Collecting certain demographic information on all abortions performed in the State;

b. Collecting information on all complications from all abortions performed in the State; and

c. Compiling statistical reports based on abortion complication information collected pursuant to this Act for future scientific studies and public health research.

(b) Based on the findings in subsection (a), it is the purpose of this Act to promote the health and safety of women, by adding to the sum of medical and public health knowledge through the compilation of relevant data on all abortions performed in the State, as well as on all medical complications and maternal deaths resulting from these abortions.

SECTION 3. DEFINITIONS.

As used in this Act only:

(a) **"Abortion"** means the act of using or prescribing any instrument, medicine, drug, or any other substance, device, or means with the intent to terminate the clinically diagnosable pregnancy of a woman with knowledge that the termination by those means will with reasonable likelihood cause the death of the unborn child. Such use, prescription, or means is not an abortion if done with the intent to:

(1) Save the life or preserve the health of the unborn child;

(2) Remove a dead unborn child caused by spontaneous abortion; or

(3) Remove an ectopic pregnancy.

(b) **"Complication"** means any adverse physical or psychological condition arising from the induction or performance of an abortion, which includes but is not limited to uterine perforation, cervical perforation, infection, heavy and/or uncontrolled bleeding, hemorrhage, blood clots resulting in pulmonary embolism or deep vein thrombosis, failure to actually terminate the pregnancy, incomplete abortion (retained tissue), pelvic inflammatory disease, endometritis, missed ectopic pregnancy, cardiac arrest, respiratory arrest, renal failure, metabolic disorder, shock, embolism, coma, placenta previa in subsequent pregnancies, preterm delivery in subsequent pregnancies, free fluid in the abdomen, hemolytic reaction due to the administration of ABO-incompatible blood or blood products, hypoglycemia where onset occurs while patient is being cared for in the abortion facility, adverse reactions to anesthesia and other drugs, subsequent development of breast cancer, psychological complications such as depression, suicidal ideation, anxiety, and sleeping disorders, death, and any other "adverse event" as defined by the Food and Drug Administration (FDA) criteria provided in the Medwatch Reporting System.

(c) **"Department"** means the Department of [*Insert name of appropriate department or agency*] of the State of [*Insert name of State*].

(d) **"Facility"** means any public or private hospital, clinic, center, medical school, medical training institution, healthcare facility, physician's office, infirmary, dispensary, ambulatory surgical center, or other institution or location wherein medical care is provided to any person.

(e) **"Hospital"** means any institution licensed as a hospital pursuant to the laws of this State.

(f) **"Physician"** means any person licensed to practice medicine in this State. The term includes medical doctors and doctors of osteopathy.

(g) **"Pregnant"** or **"pregnancy"** means that female reproductive condition of having an unborn child in the [*woman's*] uterus.

SECTION 4. DEMOGRAPHIC REPORTING ON ABORTION.

(a) For the purpose of promoting maternal health and adding to the sum of medical and public health knowledge through the compilation of relevant data, a report of each abortion performed shall be made to the Department on forms prescribed by it. The reports shall be completed by the hospital or other [*licensed*] facility in which the abortion occurred, signed by the physician who performed the abortion, and transmitted to the Department within fifteen (15) days after each reporting month.

(b) Each report shall include, at minimum, the following information:

(1) Identification of the physician who performed the abortion, the facility where the abortion was performed, and the referring physician, agency, or service, if any;

(2) The county and state in which the woman resides;

(3) The woman's age and race;

(4) The number of the woman's previous pregnancies, number of live births, and number of previous abortions;

(5) The probable gestational age of the unborn child;

(6) The type of procedure performed or prescribed and the date of the abortion; and

(7) Preexisting medical condition(s) of the woman which would complicate her pregnancy, if any.

(c) Reports required under this subsection shall not contain:

(1) The name of the woman;

(2) Common identifiers such as her social security number or [*motor vehicle operator's license number*]; or

(3) Other information or identifiers that would make it possible to identify, in any manner or under any circumstances, a woman who has obtained or seeks to obtain an abortion.

(d) Every hospital or other [*licensed*] facility in which an abortion is performed within this State during any quarter year shall file with the Department a report showing the total number of abortions performed within the hospital or other [*licensed*] facility during that quarter year. This report shall also show the total abortions performed in each trimester of pregnancy. These reports shall be submitted on a form prescribed by the Department that will enable a hospital or other [*licensed*] facility to indicate whether or not it is receiving any state-appropriated funds. The reports shall be available for public inspection and copying only if the hospital or other [*licensed*] facility receives state-appropriated funds within the twelve (12)-calendar-month period immediately preceding the filing of the report. If the hospital or other [*licensed*] facility indicates on the form that it is not receiving state-appropriated funds, the Department shall regard that hospital or other [*licensed*] facility's report as confidential unless it receives other evidence that causes it to conclude that the hospital or facility receives state-appropriated funds.

(e) The Department shall prepare a comprehensive annual statistical report for the [*Legislature*] based upon the data gathered from reports under this subsection. The statistical report shall not lead to the disclosure of the identity of any physician or person filing a report under this subsection nor of any woman who is the subject of the report. The aggregated data shall also be made independently available to the public by the Department in a downloadable format.

(f) The Department shall summarize aggregate data from the reports required under this Act and submit the data to the U.S. Centers for Disease Control and Prevention (CDC) for the purpose of inclusion in the annual Vital Statistics Report. The aggregated data shall also be made independently available to the public by the Department in a downloadable format.

(g) Reports filed pursuant this subsection shall not be deemed public records and shall remain confidential, except that disclosure may be made to law enforcement officials upon an order of a court after application showing good cause. The court may condition disclosure of the information upon any appropriate safeguards it may impose.

(h) Absent a valid court order or judicial subpoena, neither the Department, any other state department, agency, or office nor any employees or contractor thereof shall compare data concerning abortions or abortion complications maintained in an electronic or other information system file with data in any other electronic or other information system, the comparison of which could result in identifying, in any manner or under any circumstances, a woman obtaining or seeking to obtain an abortion.

(i) Statistical information that may reveal the identity of a woman obtaining or seeking to obtain an abortion shall not be maintained by the Department, any other state department, agency, office, or any employee or contractor thereof.

(j) The Department or an employee or contractor of the Department shall not disclose to a person or entity outside the Department the reports or the contents of the reports required under this subsection, in a manner or fashion so as to permit the person or entity to whom the report is disclosed to identify, in any way or under any circumstances, the physician who performed the abortion and filed the report or the woman who is the subject of the report.

(k) Original copies of all reports filed under this subsection shall be available to the [*State Medical Board*] for use in the performance of its official duties.

(l) The Department shall communicate the reporting requirements in this subsection to all medical professional organizations, licensed physicians, hospitals, emergency rooms, abortion facilities [*or other appropriate term such as "reproductive health center"*], Department [*of Health*] clinics, ambulatory surgical facilities, and other healthcare facilities operating in the State.

SECTION 5. ABORTION COMPLICATION REPORTING.

(a) A hospital, [*licensed*] healthcare facility, or individual physician shall file a written report with the Department regarding each woman who comes under the hospital, [*licensed*] healthcare facility, or physician's care and reports any complication, requires medical treatment, or suffers death that the hospital staff, facility staff, or attending physician has reason to believe was caused by an abortion. The reports shall be completed by the hospital, [*licensed*] healthcare facility, or attending physician who treated the woman, signed by the attending physician, and transmitted to the Department within thirty (30) days of the discharge or death of the woman treated for the complication.

(b) Each report of a complication, medical treatment, or death following an abortion required under this subsection shall contain, at minimum, the following information:

(1) The age and race of the woman;

(2) The woman's state and county of residence;

(3) The number of previous pregnancies, number of live births, and number of previous abortions of the woman;

(4) The date the abortion was performed, as well as the reason for the abortion and the method used, if known;

(5) Identification of the physician who performed the abortion, the facility where the abortion was performed, and the referring physician, agency, or service, if any;

(6) The specific complication(s) that led to the treatment including; and

(7) The amount billed to cover the treatment of the specific complication(s), including whether the treatment was billed to Medicaid, insurance, private pay, or other method. This should include charges for any physician, hospital, emergency room, prescription or other drugs, laboratory tests, and other costs for the treatment rendered.

(c) Reports required under this subsection shall not contain:

(1) The name of the woman;

(2) Common identifiers such as her social security number or [*motor vehicle operator's license number*]; or

(3) Other information or identifiers that would make it possible to identify, in any manner or under any circumstances, a woman who has obtained an abortion and subsequently suffered an abortion-related complication.

(d) The Department shall prepare a comprehensive annual statistical report for the [*Legislature*] based upon the data gathered from reports under this subsection. The statistical report shall not lead to the disclosure of the identity of any physician or person filing a report under this subsection nor of a woman about whom a report is filed. The aggregated data shall also be made independently available to the public by the Department in a downloadable format.

(e) The Department shall summarize aggregate data from the reports required under this Act and submit the data to the U.S. Centers for Disease Control and Prevention (CDC) for the purpose of inclusion in the annual Vital Statistics Report. The aggregated data shall also be made independently available to the public by the Department in a downloadable format.

(f) Reports filed pursuant this subsection shall not be deemed public records and shall remain confidential, except that disclosure may be made to law enforcement officials upon an order of a court after application showing good cause. The court may condition disclosure of the information upon any appropriate safeguards it may impose.

(g) Absent a valid court order or judicial subpoena, neither the Department, any other state department, agency, or office, nor any employees or contractors thereof shall compare data concerning abortions or abortion complications maintained in an electronic or other information system file with data in any other electronic or other information system, a comparison of which could result in identifying, in any manner or under any circumstances, a woman obtaining or seeking to obtain an abortion.

(h) Statistical information that may reveal the identity of a woman obtaining or seeking to obtain an abortion shall not be maintained by the Department, any other state department, agency, office, or any employee or contractor thereof.

(i) The Department or an employee or contractor of the Department shall not disclose to a person or entity outside the Department the reports or the contents of the reports required under this subsection in a manner or fashion so as to permit the person or entity to whom the report is disclosed to identify, in any way or under any circumstances, the woman who is the subject of the report.

(j) Original copies of all reports filed under this subsection shall be available to the [*State Medical Board*] for use in the performance of its official duties.

(k) The Department shall communicate this reporting requirement to all medical professional organizations, licensed physicians, hospitals, emergency rooms, abortion facilities [*or other appropriate term such as "reproductive health center"*], Department [*of Health*] clinics, ambulatory surgical facilities, and other healthcare facilities operating in the State.

SECTION 6. REPORTING FORMS.

The Department shall create the forms required by this Act within sixty (60) days after the effective date of this Act. No provision of this Act requiring the reporting of information on forms published by the Department shall be applicable until ten (10) days after the requisite forms are first created or until the effective date of this Act, whichever is later.

SECTION 7. CRIMINAL PENALTIES AND PROFESSIONAL SANCTIONS.

(a) Any person who willfully delivers or discloses to the Department any report, record, or information required pursuant to this Act and known by him or her to be false is guilty of a [*Insert appropriate offense/penalty classification*].

(b) Any person who willfully discloses any information obtained from reports filed pursuant to this Act, other than the disclosure authorized by the Act or otherwise authorized by law, is guilty of a [*Insert appropriate offense/penalty classification*].

(c) Any person required under this Act to file a report, keep any records, or supply any information who willfully fails to file such report, keep such records, or supply such information at the time or times required by law or regulation, is guilty of unprofessional conduct, and his or her professional license shall be subject to suspension or revocation in accordance with procedures provided under the [*Insert reference(s) to the state Medical Practice Act or other appropriate statute(s) or administrative rule(s) or procedure(s)*].

(d) In addition to the above penalties, any facility that willfully violates any of the requirements of this Act shall upon conviction or affirmative finding that it has violated the provisions of this Act:

   (1) Have its license suspended for a period of six (6) months for the first violation.
   (2) Have its license suspended for a period of one (1) year for the second violation.
   (3) Have its license revoked upon a third or subsequent violation.

SECTION 8. CONSTRUCTION.

(a) Nothing in this Act shall be construed as creating or recognizing a right to abortion.

(b) It is not the intention of this Act to make lawful an abortion that is currently unlawful.

SECTION 9. RIGHT OF INTERVENTION.

The [*Legislature*], by joint resolution, may appoint one or more of its members who sponsored or cosponsored this Act in his or her official capacity to intervene as a matter of right in any case in which the constitutionality of this law is challenged.

SECTION 10. SEVERABILITY.

Any provision of this Act held to be invalid or unenforceable by its terms, or as applied to any person or circumstance, shall be construed so as to give it the maximum effect permitted by law, unless such holding shall be one of utter invalidity or unenforceability, in which event such provision shall be deemed severable herefrom and shall not affect the remainder hereof or the application of such provision to other persons not similarly situated or to other, dissimilar circumstances.

SECTION 11. EFFECTIVE DATE.

This Act takes effect on [*Insert date*].

STATE OF THE STATES:
WHERE ARE WE NOW?

DEMOGRAPHIC REPORTING

ABORTION COMPLICATION REPORTING

Forty states require reporting (to varying degrees) on both surgical and chemical abortions: AK, AZ, AR, CO, CT, DE, GA, ID, IN, IA, KS, KY, ME, MA, MI, MN, MS, MO, MT, NE, NH, NM, NY, NC, ND, OH, OK, OR, PA, RI, SC, SD, TX, UT, VT, VA, WA, WV, WI, and WY.

Twenty-five states require reporting (to varying degrees) on abortion complications: AL, AZ, AR, CT, FL, IL, IN, LA, MA, MI, MN, MS, MO, NE, OH, OK, OR, PA, SC, SD, TN, TX, WA, WI, and WY.

Seven states require reporting (to varying degrees) on surgical abortions only: AL, FL, HI, IL, LA, NV, and TN.

WOMEN'S RIGHT TO KNOW ACT

HOUSE/SENATE BILL NO. _____

By Representatives/Senators _____

SECTION 1. TITLE.

This Act may be known and cited as the "Women's Right to Know Act." [*Or, alternatively, as the "Women's Health Information Act" or the "Informed Consent for Abortion Act."*]

SECTION 2. LEGISLATIVE FINDINGS AND PURPOSES.

(a) The [*Legislature*] of the State of [*Insert name of State*] finds that:

    (1) It is essential to the psychological and physical well-being of a woman considering an abortion that she receives complete and accurate information on abortion and its alternatives.

    (2) The knowledgeable exercise of a woman's decision to have an abortion depends on the extent to which she receives sufficient information to make an informed choice between two alternatives: giving birth or having an abortion.

    (3) Adequate and legitimate informed consent includes information which "relat[es] to the consequences to the fetus." *Planned Parenthood v. Casey*, 505 U.S. 833, 882-883 (1992).

    (4) The vast majority of all abortions are performed in clinics devoted solely to providing abortions and family planning services. Most women who seek abortions at these facilities do not have any relationship with the physician who performs the abortion, before or after the procedure. They generally do not return to the facility for post-surgical care. In most instances, the woman's only actual contact with the physician occurs simultaneously with the abortion procedure, with little opportunity to receive counseling concerning her decision.

    (5) The decision to abort "is an important, and often a stressful one, and it is desirable and imperative that it be made with full knowledge of its nature and consequences." *Planned Parenthood v. Danforth*, 428 U.S. 52, 67 (1976).

    (6) "The medical, emotional, and psychological consequences of an abortion are serious and can be lasting. . . ." *H.L. v. Matheson*, 450 U.S. 398, 411 (1981).

    (7) Abortion facilities or providers often offer only limited or impersonal counseling opportunities.

    (8) Many abortion facilities or providers hire untrained and unprofessional "counselors" to provide pre-abortion counseling, but their primary goal is actually to "sell" or promote abortion services.

(b) Based on the findings in subsection (a), the purposes of this Act are to:

    (1) Ensure that every woman considering an abortion receives complete information on abortion and its alternatives, and that every woman submitting to an abortion does so only after giving her voluntary and fully-informed consent to the abortion procedure;

    (2) Protect an unborn child from a woman's uninformed decision to have an abortion;

    (3) Reduce "the risk that a woman may elect an abortion, only to discover later, with devastating psychological consequences, that her decision was not fully informed." *Planned Parenthood v. Casey*, 505 U.S. 833, 882 (1992); and

    (4) Adopt the construction of the term "medical emergency" accepted by the U.S. Supreme Court in *Planned Parenthood v. Casey*, 505 U.S. 833 (1992).

SECTION 3. DEFINITIONS.

As used in this Act only:

(a) **"Abortion"** means the act of using or prescribing any instrument, medicine, drug, or any other substance, device, or means with the intent to terminate the clinically diagnosable pregnancy of a woman with knowledge that the termination by those means will with reasonable likelihood cause the death of the unborn child. Such use, prescription, or means is not an abortion if done with the intent to:

    (1) Save the life or preserve the health of the unborn child;

    (2) Remove a dead unborn child caused by spontaneous abortion; or

    (3) Remove an ectopic pregnancy.

(b) **"Complication"** means any adverse physical or psychological condition arising from the performance of an abortion which includes, but is not limited to: uterine perforation, cervical perforation, infection, heavy and/or uncontrolled bleeding, hemorrhage, blood clots, failure to actually terminate the pregnancy, incomplete abortion (retained tissue), pelvic inflammatory disease, endometritis, missed ectopic pregnancy, cardiac arrest, respiratory arrest, renal failure, metabolic disorder, shock, embolism, coma, placenta previa in subsequent pregnancies, preterm birth in subsequent pregnancies, free fluid in the abdomen, adverse reactions to anesthesia and other drugs, psychological complications such as depression, anxiety, and sleeping disorders, and any other "adverse event" as defined by the federal Food and Drug Administration (FDA) criteria provided in the Medwatch Reporting System or similar reporting system recognized or cited by the federal Food and Drug Administration. The Department may further define "complication."

(c) **"Conception"** means the fusion of a human spermatozoon with a human ovum.

(d) **"Department"** means the Department of [*Insert appropriate title*] of the State of [*Insert name of State*].

(e) **"Facility"** or **"medical facility"** means any public or private hospital, clinic, center, medical school, medical training institution, healthcare facility, physician's office, infirmary, dispensary, ambulatory surgical treatment center, or other institution or location wherein medical care is provided to any person.

(f) **"First trimester"** means the first twelve (12) weeks of gestation.

(g) **"Gestation"** or **"gestational age"** means the time that has elapsed since the first day of the woman's last menstrual period.

(h) **"Hospital"** means an institution licensed pursuant to the provisions of the law of this State.

(i) **"Medical emergency"** means that condition which, on the basis of the physician's good faith clinical judgment, so complicates the medical condition of a pregnant woman as to necessitate the immediate termination of her pregnancy to avert her death or for which a delay will create serious risk of substantial and irreversible impairment of a major bodily function.

(j) **"Physician"** means any person licensed to practice medicine in this State. The term includes medical doctors and doctors of osteopathy.

(k) **"Pregnant"** or **"pregnancy"** means that female reproductive condition of having an unborn child in the [*woman's*] uterus.

(l) **"Qualified person"** means an agent of the physician who is a psychologist, licensed social worker, licensed professional counselor, registered nurse, or physician.

(m) **"Unborn child"** means the offspring of human beings from conception until birth.

(n) **"Viability"** means the state of fetal development when, in the judgment of the physician based on the particular facts of the case before him or her and in light of the most advanced medical technology and information available to him or her, there is a reasonable likelihood of sustained survival of the unborn child outside the body of his or her mother, with or without artificial support.

SECTION 4. INFORMED CONSENT REQUIREMENT.

No abortion shall be performed or induced without the voluntary and informed consent of the woman upon whom the abortion is to be performed or induced. Except in the case of a medical emergency, consent to an abortion is voluntary and informed if and only if:

(a) At least twenty-four (24) hours before the abortion, the physician who is to perform the abortion or the referring physician has informed the woman, orally and in person, of the following:

   (1) The name of the physician who will perform the abortion;

   (2) Medically accurate information that a reasonable patient would consider material to the decision of whether or not to undergo the abortion, including:

      a. A description of the proposed abortion method;

      b. The immediate and long-term medical risks associated with the proposed abortion method including, but not limited to, the risks of infection, hemorrhage, cervical or uterine perforation, danger to subsequent pregnancies, and increased risk of breast cancer; and

      c. Alternatives to the abortion;

   (3) The probable gestational age of the unborn child at the time the abortion is to be performed;

   (4) The probable anatomical and physiological characteristics of the unborn child at the time the abortion is to be performed;

   (5) The medical risks associated with carrying her child to term; and

   (6) Any need for anti-Rh immune globulin therapy if she is Rh negative, the likely consequences of refusing such therapy, and the cost of the therapy.

(b) At least twenty-four (24) hours before the abortion, the physician who is to perform the abortion, the referring physician, or a qualified person has informed the woman, orally and in person, that:

   (1) Medical assistance benefits may be available for prenatal care, childbirth, and neonatal care, and that more detailed information on the availability of such assistance is contained in the printed materials and informational DVD given to her and described in Section 5.

   (2) The printed materials and informational DVD in Section 5 describe the unborn child and list agencies that offer alternatives to abortion.

   (3) The father of the unborn child is liable to assist in the support of the child, even in instances where he has offered to pay for the abortion. In the case of rape or incest, this information may be omitted.

   (4) She is free to withhold or withdraw her consent to the abortion at any time without affecting her right to future care or treatment and without the loss of any state or federally funded benefits to which she might otherwise be entitled.

(5) The information contained in the printed materials and informational DVD given to her, as described in Section 5, are also available on a state-maintained website.

(c) The information required in subsections 4(a) and 4(b) is provided to the woman individually and in a private room to protect her privacy, to maintain the confidentiality of her decision, and to ensure that the information focuses on her individual circumstances and that she has an adequate opportunity to ask questions.

(d) At least twenty-four (24) hours before the abortion, the woman is given a copy of the printed materials and permitted to view or is given a copy of the informational DVD described in Section 5. If the woman is unable to read the materials, they shall be read to her. If the woman asks questions concerning any of the information or materials, answers shall be provided to her in a language she can understand.

[OPTIONAL: *Information on Fetal Pain: (e) At least twenty-four (24) hours prior to an abortion being performed or induced on an unborn child who is twenty (20) weeks' gestation or more, the physician performing the abortion on the pregnant woman, the referring physician, or a qualified person assisting the physician shall, orally and in person, offer information on fetal pain to the pregnant woman. This information and counseling shall include, but shall not be limited to, the following:*

    (1) *That, by twenty (20) weeks, the unborn child possesses all anatomical links in its nervous system (including spinal cord, nerve tracts, thalamus, and cortex) that are necessary in order to feel pain;*
    (2) *That an unborn child who is twenty (20) weeks' gestation or more is fully capable of experiencing pain;*
    (3) *A description of the actual steps in the abortion procedure to be performed or induced and at which steps in the abortion procedure the unborn child is capable of feeling pain;*
    (4) *That maternal anesthesia typically offers little pain prevention for the unborn child; and*
    (5) *That an anesthetic or analgesic is available in order to minimize and/or alleviate pain to the fetus.*]

[OPTIONAL: *Information on Chemical Abortion Reversal: (f) At least twenty-four (24) hours prior to an abortion being performed or induced utilizing drug-induced abortion, the physician performing the abortion on the pregnant woman, the referring physician, or a qualified person assisting the physician shall, orally and in person, inform the woman of the following:*

    (1) *That it may be possible to reverse the effects of the abortion should she change her mind, but that time is of the essence; and*
    (2) *That information on and assistance with reversing the effects of drug-induced abortion is available in the state-prepared materials.*

*For purposes of this Section, **"drug-induced abortion"** means a medicine, drug, or any other substance prescribed* *or dispensed with the intent of terminating the clinically diagnosable pregnancy of a woman, with knowledge that the termination will with reasonable likelihood cause the death of the unborn child. This includes off-label use of drugs known to have abortion-inducing properties, which are prescribed specifically with the intent of causing an abortion. This definition does not apply to drugs that may be known to cause an abortion, but which are prescribed for other medical indications (e.g., chemotherapeutic agents, diagnostic drugs, etc.).]*

[*(g)*]Prior to the abortion, the woman certifies in writing on a checklist form provided or approved by the Department that the information required to be provided under subsections 5(a), 5(b), 5(c), [*and*] 5(d)[*, 5(e), and 5(f)*] have been provided. All physicians who perform abortions shall report the total number of certifications received monthly to the Department. The Department shall make the number of certifications received available to the public on an annual basis.

[*(h)*]Except in the case of a medical emergency, the physician who is to perform the abortion shall receive and sign a copy of the written certification prescribed in subsection [*(g)*] of this Section prior to performing the abortion. The physician shall retain a copy of the checklist certification form in the woman's medical record.

[*(i)*] In the event of a medical emergency requiring an immediate termination of pregnancy, the physician who performed the abortion shall clearly certify in writing the nature of the medical emergency and the circumstances which necessitated the waiving of the informed consent requirements of this Act. This certification shall be signed by the physician who performed the emergency abortion and shall be permanently filed in both the records of the physician performing the abortion and the records of the facility where the abortion takes place.

[*(j)*] A physician shall not require or obtain payment for a service provided in relation to abortion from a patient who has inquired about an abortion or scheduled an abortion until the expiration of the twenty-four (24)-hour reflection period required in subsections 4(a), 4(b), [*and*] 4(d)[*, 4(e), and 4(f)*].

SECTION 5. PUBLICATION OF MATERIALS.

The Department shall cause to be published printed materials and an informational DVD in English [*and Spanish and other appropriate language(s)*] within [*Insert appropriate number*] days after this Act becomes law. The Department shall develop and maintain a secure internet website, which may be part of an existing website, to provide the information required by and described in this Section. No information regarding persons using the website shall be collected or maintained. The Department shall monitor the website on a weekly basis to prevent and correct tampering.

On an annual basis, the Department shall review and update, if necessary, the following easily comprehensible printed materials and informational DVD:

(a) Geographically indexed materials that inform the woman of public and private agencies and services available to assist a woman through pregnancy, upon childbirth, and while her child is dependent including, but not limited to, adoption agencies.

The materials shall include a comprehensive list of the agencies, a description of the services they offer, and the telephone numbers and addresses of the agencies and shall inform the woman about available medical assistance benefits for prenatal care, childbirth, and neonatal care.

The Department shall ensure that the materials described in this Section are comprehensive and do not directly or indirectly promote, exclude, or discourage the use of any agency or service described in this Section. The materials shall also contain a toll-free, twenty-four (24)-hour-a-day telephone number which may be called to obtain information about the agencies in the locality of the caller and of the services they offer.

The materials shall state that it is unlawful for any individual to coerce a woman to undergo an abortion [*Insert reference(s) to state's anti-coercion statute(s), if any*] and that if a minor is denied financial support by the minor's parents, guardian, or custodian because of the minor's refusal to have an abortion performed, the minor shall be deemed emancipated for the purposes of eligibility for public-assistance benefits, except that such benefits may not be used to obtain an abortion.

The materials shall also state that any physician who performs an abortion upon a woman without her informed consent may be liable to her for damages in a civil action at law and that the law permits adoptive parents to pay costs of prenatal care, childbirth, and neonatal care. The materials shall also include the following statement:

"There are many public and private agencies willing and able to help you to carry your child to term, and to assist you and your child after your child is born, whether you choose to keep your child or to place her or him for adoption. The State of [Insert name of State] strongly urges you to contact one or more of these agencies before making a final decision about abortion. The law requires that your physician or his or her agent give you the opportunity to call agencies like these before you undergo an abortion."

(b) Information on the support obligations of the father of a child who is born alive, including but not limited to the father's legal duty to support his child, which may include child support payments and health insurance, and the fact that paternity may be established by the father's signature on a birth certificate, by a statement of paternity, or by court action. The printed material shall also state that more information concerning establishment of paternity and child support services and enforcement may be obtained by calling state or county public assistance agencies.

(c) Materials that inform the pregnant woman of the probable anatomical and physiological characteristics of the unborn child at two (2) week gestational increments from fertilization to full term, including color photographs of the developing unborn child at two (2) week gestational increments. The descriptions shall include information about brain and heart functions, the presence of external members and internal organs during the applicable stages of development, and any relevant information on the possibility of the unborn child's survival. If a photograph is not available, a picture must contain the dimensions of the unborn child and must be realistic. The materials shall be objective, nonjudgmental, and designed to convey only accurate scientific information about the unborn child at the various gestational ages.

(d) Objective information describing the various surgical and drug-induced methods of abortion, as well as the immediate and long-term medical risks commonly associated with each abortion method including, but not limited to, uterine perforation, cervical perforation, infection, bleeding, hemorrhage, blood clots, failure to actually terminate the pregnancy, incomplete abortion (retained tissue), pelvic inflammatory disease, endometritis, missed ectopic pregnancy, cardiac arrest, respiratory arrest, renal failure, metabolic disorder, shock, embolism, coma, placenta previa in subsequent pregnancies, preterm birth in subsequent pregnancies, free fluid in the abdomen, adverse reactions to anesthesia and other drugs, any psychological or emotional complications such as depression, anxiety, and sleeping disorders, and any other "adverse event" as defined by the Food and Drug Administration (FDA) criteria provided in the Medwatch Reporting System, and the medical risks associated with carrying a child to term.

(e) A uniform resource locator (URL) for the state-maintained website where the materials described in Subsections 5(a), 5(b), 5(c), [and] 5(d)[,and 5(f)] can be found.

[OPTIONAL: *Information on Chemical Abortion Reversal: (f) Information on the potential ability of qualified medical professionals to reverse the effects of abortion obtained through the use of drug-induced abortion, such as mifepristone (brand name Mifeprex), commonly referred to as "RU-486," including information directing women to obtain further information at http://www.abortionpillreversal.com/ and by contacting (877) 558-0333 for assistance in locating a medical professional that can aide in the reversal of abortion.*]

[(g)] A checklist certification form to be used by the physician or a qualified person under subsection 4[(g)] of this Act, which will list all the items of information which are to be given to the woman by a physician or the agent under this Act.

[(h)]The materials shall be printed in a typeface large enough to be clearly legible.

[(*i*)] The Department shall produce a standardized DVD that may be used statewide, presenting the information described in Subsections 5(a), 5(b), 5(c), 5(d), [and] 5(e) [, and 5(f),] in accordance with the requirements of those subsections. In preparing the DVD, the Department may summarize and make reference to the printed, comprehensive list of geographically indexed names and services described in subsection 5(a). The DVD shall, in addition to the information described in subsections 5(a), 5(b), 5(c), 5(d), [and] 5(e) [, and 5(f)] show an ultrasound of the heartbeat of an unborn child at four (4) to five (5) weeks' gestational age, at six (6) to eight (8) weeks' gestational age, and each month thereafter until viability. That information shall be presented in an objective, unbiased manner designed to convey only accurate scientific information.

[(*j*)]The materials required under this Section and the DVD described in subsection 5([i]) shall be available at no cost from the Department upon request and in appropriate number to any person, facility, or hospital.

SECTION 6. MEDICAL EMERGENCIES.

When a medical emergency compels the performance of an abortion, the physician shall inform the woman, before the abortion if possible, of the medical indications supporting the physician's judgment that an immediate abortion is necessary to avert her death or that a twenty-four (24)-hour delay will cause substantial and irreversible impairment of a major bodily function.

SECTION 7. CRIMINAL PENALTIES.

Any person who intentionally, knowingly, or recklessly violates this Act is guilty of a [*Insert appropriate penalty/offense classification*].

SECTION 8. CIVIL REMEDIES AND PROFESSIONAL SANCTIONS.

(a) In addition to any and all remedies available under the common or statutory law of this State, failure to comply with the requirements of this Act shall:

   (1) Provide a basis for a civil malpractice action for actual and punitive damages.
   (2) Provide a basis for a professional disciplinary action under [*Medical Malpractice Act*].

(b) No civil liability may be assessed against the woman upon whom the abortion is performed.

(c) When requested, the court shall allow a woman to proceed using solely her initials or a pseudonym and may close any proceedings in the case and enter other protective orders to preserve the privacy of the woman upon whom the abortion was performed.

(d) If judgment is rendered in favor of the plaintiff, the court shall also render judgment for reasonable attorney's fees in favor of the plaintiff against the defendant.

(e) If judgment is rendered in favor of the defendant and the court finds that the plaintiff's suit was frivolous and brought in bad faith, the court may render judgment for reasonable attorney's fees in favor of the defendant against the plaintiff.

SECTION 9. CONSTRUCTION.

(a) Nothing in this Act shall be construed as creating or recognizing a right to abortion.

(b) It is not the intention of this law to make lawful an abortion that is currently unlawful.

SECTION 10. RIGHT OF INTERVENTION.

The [*Legislature*], by joint resolution, may appoint one or more of its members, who sponsored or cosponsored this Act in his or her official capacity, to intervene as a matter of right in any case in which the constitutionality of this law is challenged.

SECTION 11. SEVERABILITY.

Any provision of this Act held to be invalid or unenforceable by its terms, or as applied to any person or circumstance, shall be construed so as to give it the maximum effect permitted by law, unless such holding shall be one of utter invalidity or unenforceability, in which event such provision shall be deemed severable herefrom and shall not affect the remainder hereof or the application of such provision to other persons not similarly situated or to other, dissimilar circumstances.

SECTION 12. EFFECTIVE DATE.

This Act takes effect on [*Insert date*].

DRUG-INDUCED ABORTION INFORMATION AND REPORTING ACT

HOUSE/SENATE BILL NO. _____

By Representatives/Senators _____

SECTION 1. TITLE.

This Act may be known and cited as the "Drug-Induced Abortion Information and Reporting Act."

SECTION 2. LEGISLATIVE FINDINGS AND PURPOSES.

(a) The [*Legislature*] of the State of [*Insert name of State*] finds that:

   (1) In September 2000, the Food and Drug Administration (FDA) approved the distribution and use of RU-486, an abortion-inducing drug, under the rubric of 21 C.F.R. § 314.520, also referred to as "Subpart H," which is the only FDA approval process that allows for post-marketing restrictions. Specifically, the Code of Federal Regulations (CFR) provides for accelerated approval of certain drugs that are shown to be effective but "can be safely used only if distribution or use is restricted."

   (2) The FDA does not treat Subpart H drugs in the same manner as drugs that undergo the typical approval process.

   (3) In September 2000, the FDA prescribed a specific gestation, dosage, and administration protocol for RU-486.

   (4) The approved FDA protocol for RU-486 was modified in March 2016; however, the new FDA guidelines maintain that certain distribution restrictions are still necessary because of the drug's potential for serious complications.

   (5) As approved by the FDA, the new administration protocol consists of mifepristone, followed by misoprostol taken 24 to 48 hours later, through seventy (70) days LMP (a gestational measurement using the first day of the woman's "last menstrual period" as a marker). The patient is to return for a follow-up visit to confirm that a complete abortion has occurred.

   (6) The new FDA protocol also requires that the distribution and use of RU-486 be under the supervision of a qualified healthcare provider who has the ability to assess the duration of pregnancy, diagnose ectopic pregnancies, and provide surgical intervention (or has made plans to provide surgical intervention through another qualified physician).

(7) The use of RU-486 presents significant medical risks that increase with advancing gestational age, including, but not limited to, abdominal pain, cramping, vomiting, headache, fatigue, uterine hemorrhage, viral infections, and pelvic inflammatory disease.

(8) Studies document that increased rates of complications (including incomplete abortion) occur even within the FDA-approved gestational limit.

(9) In July 2011, the FDA reported 2,207 adverse events after women used RU-486 for abortions. Among these events were 14 deaths, 612 hospitalizations, 339 blood transfusions, and 256 infections (including 48 "severe infections").

(10) The Adverse Event Reports (AER) systems relied upon by the FDA have limitations and typically detect only a small proportion of events that actually occur.

(11) "Off-label" or so-called "evidence-based" use of RU-486 may be deadly. To date, 14 women have reportedly died after administration of RU-486, with eight deaths attributed to severe bacterial infections. All eight of those women administered RU-486 in an "off-label" or "evidence-based" manner then-advocated by abortion providers. The FDA has not been able to determine whether this off-label use led to the deaths.

(12) Medical evidence demonstrates that women who use drug-induced abortion risk more complications than those who undergo surgical abortions.

(13) The decision to abort "is an important, and often a stressful one, and it is desirable and imperative that it be made with full knowledge of its nature and consequences." *Planned Parenthood v. Danforth*, 428 U.S. 52, 67 (1976).

(14) The knowledgeable exercise of a woman's decision to have an abortion depends on the extent to which the woman receives information sufficient to make an informed choice.

(15) Some women come to regret their decision to abort shortly after ingesting mifepristone, the first drug in the RU-486 regimen.

(16) In recent years, physicians have developed a method to potentially reverse the effects of mifepristone. This abortion pill reversal process, which has been discussed in a peer-reviewed study, is based upon a well-established medical regimen that is used in other areas of healthcare—specifically, methotrexate and "leucovorin rescue."

(17) Methotrexate, a chemotherapy drug, kills rapidly dividing cells (cancer cells). It works by blocking the action of folic acid. Typically, physicians allow the methotrexate to work for a day or two, and then give the patient a high dose of folic acid (leucovorin) to compensate for what has been lost. This high dosage of folic acid, in essence, "kicks" the methotrexate off of the cells. This flooding of the patient's body with folic acid is called a "leucovorin rescue" and is a well-established medical procedure.

(18) Understanding the science behind the mechanism of action of mifepristone has allowed physicians to design a specific "rescue" for a woman who has used mifepristone to induce an abortion, but has not yet ingested the second drug in the RU-486 regimen. Since physicians know exactly how mifepristone works (i.e., by blocking progesterone), physicians know that treating a woman

with progesterone can "kick off" the mifepristone (i.e., displace mifepristone from the progesterone receptors). This allows the woman's body to respond naturally to the progesterone and to effectively fight the effects of the mifepristone-induced blockage.

(19) In short, mifepristone floods the progesterone receptors (thus, blocking progesterone). To block or "reverse" the effects of the mifepristone, a pregnant woman's body is flooded with progesterone.

(20) Progesterone itself has been used safely in pregnancies for decades. It is used in in vitro fertilization, infertility treatments, and high-risk pregnancies (such as those experiencing pre-term labor). Using progesterone to reverse the effects of mifepristone is a targeted response that is safe for the woman.

(21) As of October 2018, it had been reported that five hundred (500) babies had been born following this reversal process.

(22) To facilitate reliable scientific studies and research on the safety and efficacy of drug-induced abortion, it is essential that the medical and public health communities have access to accurate information both on the efficacy and use of drug-induced abortion, as well as on resulting complications.

(23) Abortion "record keeping and reporting provisions that are reasonably directed to the preservation of maternal health and that properly respect a patient's confidentiality and privacy are permissible." *Planned Parenthood v. Danforth*, 428 U.S. 80 at 52, 79-81 (1976).

(24) Abortion and complication reporting provisions do not impose an "undue burden" on a woman's right to choose whether or not to terminate a pregnancy. Specifically, "[t]he collection of information with respect to actual patients is a vital element of medical research, and so it cannot be said that the requirements serve no purpose other than to make abortions more difficult." *Planned Parenthood v. Casey*, 505 U.S. 833 at 900-901 (1992).

(25) To promote its interest in maternal health and life, the State of [Insert name of State] maintains an interest in:

    a. Collecting certain demographic information on all drug-induced abortions performed in the State;

    b. Collecting information on complications from all drug-induced abortions performed in the State; and

    c. Compiling statistical reports based on abortion complication information collected pursuant to this Act for future scientific studies and public health research.

(b) Based on the findings in subsection (a), it is the purpose of this Act to:

    (1) Protect the health and welfare of every woman considering a drug-induced abortion;

    (2) Ensure that a [*qualified healthcare provider*] examines a woman prior to dispensing an abortion-inducing drug in order to confirm the gestational age of the fetus prior to administering the abortion

inducing drug, the intrauterine location of the fetus, and that the fetus is alive since administration of mifepristone with miscarriage is unnecessary and exposes the woman to unnecessary risks associated with both mifepristone and misoprostol;

(3) Ensure that a [*qualified healthcare provider*] does not prescribe or dispense an abortion-inducing drug beyond the FDA-approved gestational limit;

(4) Reduce "the risk that a woman may elect an abortion, only to discover later, with devastating psychological consequences, that her decision was not fully informed." *Planned Parenthood v. Casey*, 505 U.S. 833, 882 (1992);

(5) Ensure that every woman considering a drug-induced abortion receives comprehensive information on drug-induced abortion, including the potential to reverse the effects of the drugs should she change her mind, and that every woman submitting to an abortion does so only after giving her voluntary and fully informed consent to the procedure; and

(6) Promote the health and safety of women, by adding to the sum of medical and public health knowledge through the compilation of relevant data on drug-induced abortions performed in the State, as well as on all medical complications and maternal deaths resulting from these abortions.

SECTION 3. DEFINITIONS.

As used in this Act only:

(a) **"Abortion"** means the act of using or prescribing any instrument, medicine, drug, or any other substance, device, or means with the intent to terminate the clinically diagnosable pregnancy of a woman, with knowledge that the termination by those means will with reasonable likelihood cause the death of the unborn child. Such use, prescription, or means is not an abortion if done with the intent to:

(1) Save the life or preserve the health of the unborn child;

(2) Remove a dead unborn child caused by spontaneous abortion;

(3) Remove an ectopic pregnancy; or

(4) Treat a maternal disease or illness for which the prescribed drug is indicated.

(b) **"Abortion-inducing drug"** means a medicine, drug, or any other substance prescribed or dispensed with the intent of terminating the clinically diagnosable pregnancy of a woman, with knowledge that the termination will with reasonable likelihood cause the death of the unborn child. This includes the off-label use of drugs known to have abortion-inducing properties, which are prescribed specifically with the intent of causing an abortion, such as misoprostol (Cytotec), and methotrexate. This definition does not apply to drugs that may be known to cause an abortion, but which are prescribed for other medical indications (e.g., chemotherapeutic agents, diagnostic drugs, etc.).

The use of such drugs to induce abortion is also known as **"chemical," "medical"** or **"drug-induced"** abortion.

(c) **"Department"** means the Department of [*Insert appropriate title*] of the State of [*Insert name of State*].

(d) **"Final printed labeling (FPL)"** means the FDA-approved informational document for an abortion-inducing drug which outlines the protocol authorized by the FDA and agreed upon by the drug company applying for FDA authorization of that drug.

(e) **"LMP"** or "gestational age" means the time that has elapsed since the first day of the woman's last menstrual period.

(f) **"Medical emergency"** means that condition which, on the basis of the qualified healthcare provider's good faith clinical judgment, so complicates the medical condition of a pregnant woman as to necessitate the immediate termination of her pregnancy to avert her death or for which a delay will create serious risk of substantial and irreversible impairment of a major bodily function.

(g) **"Mifeprex regimen"** means the abortion-inducing drug regimen that involves administration of mifepristone (brand name "Mifeprex") and misoprostol. It is the only abortion-inducing drug regimen approved by the FDA. It is also known as the "RU-486 regimen" or simply "RU-486."

(h) **"Mifepristone"** means the first drug used in the Mifeprex regimen.

(i) **"Misoprostol"** means the second drug used in the Mifeprex regimen.

(j) **"Physician"** means any person licensed to practice medicine in this State. The term includes medical doctors and doctors of osteopathy.

(k) **"Pregnant"** or **"pregnancy"** means that female reproductive condition of having an unborn child in the mother's [*woman's*] uterus.

(l) **"Qualified healthcare provider"** means a healthcare provider licensed in this State who has the ability to assess the duration of pregnancy, diagnose ectopic pregnancies, and provide surgical intervention or has made plans to provide surgical intervention through another qualified physician.

(m) **"Qualified person"** means an agent of the physician who is a psychologist, licensed social worker, licensed professional counselor, registered nurse, or physician.

(n) **"Unborn child"** means the offspring of human beings from conception until birth.

SECTION 4. UNLAWFUL DISTRIBUTION OF DRUG-INDUCED ABORTION.

(a) Because the failure and complication rates from a drug-induced abortion increase with advancing gestational age; because the physical symptoms of drug-induced abortion can be identical to the symptoms of ectopic pregnancy; and, because drug-induced abortion do not treat ectopic pregnancies but rather are contraindicated in ectopic pregnancies, the qualified healthcare provider giving, selling, dispensing, administering, or otherwise providing or prescribing an abortion-inducing drug must first examine the woman and document, in the woman's medical chart, the gestational age and intrauterine location of the pregnancy prior to giving, selling, dispensing, administering, or otherwise providing or prescribing an abortion-inducing drug.

(b) Every pregnant woman to whom a qualified healthcare provider gives, sells, dispenses, administers, or otherwise provides or prescribes any abortion-inducing drug shall be provided with a copy of the drug's final printing label (FPL).

(c) Every qualified healthcare provider, other than a physician, giving, selling, dispensing, administering, or otherwise providing or prescribing an abortion-inducing drug must have a signed contract with a physician who agrees to handle complications and be able to produce that signed contract on demand by the patient or by the Department. Every pregnant woman to whom a qualified healthcare provider gives, sells, dispenses, administers, or otherwise provides or prescribes any abortion-inducing drug shall receive the name and phone number of the contracted physician.

(d) The qualified healthcare provider giving, selling, dispensing, administering, or otherwise providing or prescribing any abortion-inducing drug or an agent of the qualified healthcare provider shall inform the patient that she may schedule an appointment to take each drug included in the regimen under the supervision of the qualified healthcare provider.

(e)   The qualified healthcare provider giving, selling, dispensing, administering, or otherwise providing or prescribing any abortion-inducing drug or an agent of the qualified healthcare provider shall schedule a follow-up visit for the woman at approximately seven (7) to fourteen (14) days after administration of the abortion-inducing drug to confirm that the pregnancy is completely terminated and to assess the degree of bleeding. The qualified healthcare provider or an agent of the qualified healthcare provider shall make all reasonable efforts to ensure that the woman returns for the scheduled appointment. A brief description of the efforts made to comply with this subsection, including the date, time, and identification by name of the person making such efforts, shall be included in the woman's medical record.

SECTION 5. INFORMED CONSENT REQUIREMENTS FOR DRUG-INDUCED ABORTION.

(a)   No abortion-inducing drug shall be given, sold, dispensed, administered, or otherwise provided or prescribed without the voluntary and informed consent of the woman to whom the abortion-inducing drug is given, sold, dispensed, administered, or otherwise provided or prescribed.

(b)   Except in the case of a medical emergency, consent to a drug-induced abortion must be obtained at least [*twenty-four (24) or insert existing state law requirement*] hours before the abortion-inducing drug is given to, sold to, dispensed to, administered to, or otherwise provided or prescribed to the woman.

(c)   A form created by the Department shall be used by a qualified healthcare provider to obtain the consent required prior to giving, selling, dispensing, administering, or otherwise providing or prescribing an abortion-inducing drug.

(d)   A consent form is not valid and consent is not sufficient, unless:

(1)   The patient initials each entry, list, description, or declaration required to be on the consent form (as detailed in subsections (e)(1) through (e)(6) of this Section);

(2)   The patient signs the "consent statement" described in subsection (e)(6) of this Section; and

(3)   The qualified healthcare provider signs the "qualified healthcare provider declaration" described in subsection (e)(7) of this Section.

(e)   The consent form shall include, but is not limited to, the following:

(1)   The probable gestational age of the unborn child as determined by both patient history and by ultrasound results used to confirm the gestational age;

(2)   A detailed description of the drug-induced abortion regimen or procedure;

(3) A detailed list of the risks related to the specific drug-induced abortion regimen or procedure to be used including, but not limited to hemorrhage (heavy bleeding); failure to remove all products of conception which may require an additional procedure; sepsis; sterility; and possible continuation of pregnancy;

(4) That the risks of complications from a drug-induced abortion, including incomplete abortion, increase with advancing gestational age;

(5) That it may be possible to reverse the effects of the drug-induced abortion should she change her mind, but that time is of the essence;

(6) That information on and assistance with reversing the effects of drug-induced abortion are available in the state-prepared materials; and

(7) A "consent statement" which must be signed by the patient. The consent statement must include, but is not limited to the following declarations, which must be individually initialed by the patient:

    a. That the patient understands that the abortion-inducing drug regimen or procedure will end her pregnancy and will result in the death of her unborn child;

    b. That the patient is not being forced to have an abortion, that she has the choice not to have the abortion, and that she may withdraw her consent to the abortion-inducing drug regimen or procedure;

    c. That the patient understands that the drug-induced abortion regimen or procedure to be used has specific risks and may result in specific complications;

    d. That she has been given a copy of the final printing label (FPL) of the chosen abortion-inducing drug regimen or procedure to be used.

    e. That the patient has been given the opportunity to ask questions about her pregnancy, the development of her unborn child, alternatives to abortion, the abortion regimen or procedure to be used, and the risks and complications inherent in the regimen or procedure to be used;

    f. That she was specifically given "[i]nformation on the potential ability of qualified medical professionals to reverse the effects of an abortion obtained through the use of drug-induced abortion, such as mifepristone (brand name "Mifeprex"), commonly referred to as "RU-486," including information directing women to obtain further information at http://www.abortionpillreversal.com/ and by contacting (877) 558-0333 for assistance in locating a medical professional that can aide in the reversal of an abortion."

    g. That she has been provided access to state-prepared, printed materials on informed consent for abortion [*and*] the state-prepared and maintained website on informed consent for abortion[*, and the state-prepared informational DVD on informed consent for abortion*].

    h. That she has been given the name and phone number of the contracted physician who has agreed to provide medical care and treatment in the event of complications associated with the abortion-inducing drug regimen or procedure;

    i. That she has been informed that she may schedule an appointment to take each drug included in the abortion-inducing regimen or procedure under the direct supervision of the qualified healthcare provider;

j. That the qualified healthcare provider or an agent of the qualified healthcare provider will schedule an in person follow-up visit for the woman at approximately seven (7) to fourteen (14) days after administration of the abortion-inducing drug regimen or procedure to confirm that the pregnancy is completely terminated and to assess the degree of bleeding and other complications; and

k. That the patient has received or been given sufficient information to give her informed consent to the abortion-inducing drug regimen or procedure.

(7) A "qualified healthcare provider declaration," which must be signed by the qualified healthcare provider, stating that the qualified healthcare provider or another qualified person has explained the abortion-inducing drug regimen or procedure to be used, has provided all of the information required in subsections (e)(1) through (e)(6) of this Section, and has answered all of the woman's questions.

SECTION 6. INFORMATION REQUIRED IN STATE-PREPARED MATERIALS.

(a) The Department shall cause to be published in the state-prepared, printed materials on informed consent for abortion [*and*] the state-prepared and maintained website on informed consent for abortion[, *and the state-prepared informational DVD*] required under [*Insert reference(s) to state statutes, administrative rules, or other authority related to informed consent for abortion*] the following statement:

"Information on the potential ability of qualified medical professionals to reverse the effects of an abortion obtained through the use of drug-induced abortion, such as mifepristone (brand name "Mifeprex"), commonly referred to as "RU-486," including information directing women to obtain further information at http://www.abortionpillreversal.com/ and by contacting (877) 558-0333 for assistance in locating a medical professional that can aide in the reversal of an abortion."

(b) On an annual basis, the Department shall review and update, if necessary, the statement required in subsection 5(a) of this Section.

SECTION 7. REPORTING ON DRUG-INDUCED ABORTIONS.

(a) For the purpose of promoting maternal health and adding to the sum of medical and public health knowledge through the compilation of relevant data, a report of each drug-induced abortion performed shall be made to the Department on forms prescribed by it. The reports shall be completed by the hospital or other [*licensed*] facility in which the abortion-inducing drug was given, sold, dispensed, administered, or otherwise provided or prescribed; signed by the qualified healthcare provider who gave, sold, dispensed, administered, or otherwise provided or prescribed the abortion-inducing drug; and transmitted to the Department within fifteen (15) days after each reporting month.

(b) Each report shall include, at minimum, the following information:

   (8) Identification of the qualified healthcare provider who gave, sold, dispensed, administered, or otherwise provided or prescribed the abortion-inducing drug;

   (9) Whether the abortion drug regimen or procedure was completed at the hospital or [*licensed*] facility in which the abortion-inducing drug was given, sold, dispensed, administered, or otherwise provided or prescribed or at an alternative location;

   (10) The referring physician, agency, or service, if any;

   (11) The county and state in which the woman resides;

   (12) The woman's age and race;

   (13) The number of the woman's previous pregnancies, number of live births, and number of previous abortions;

   (14) The probable gestational age of the unborn child as determined by both patient history and by ultrasound results used to confirm the gestational age. The report will include the date of the ultrasound and gestational age determined on that date;

   (15) The abortion-inducing drug used and the date it was given, sold, dispensed, administered, or otherwise provided or prescribed to the woman; and

   (16) Preexisting medical condition(s) of the woman which would complicate her pregnancy, if any; and

   (17) Whether the patient returned for a follow-up examination to determine completion of the abortion procedure and to assess bleeding and the date and results of any such follow-up examination.

(c) Reports required under this subsection shall not contain:

   (4) The name of the woman;

   (5) Common identifiers such as her social security number or [*motor vehicle operator's license number*]; or

   (6) Other information or identifiers that would make it possible to identify, in any manner or under any circumstances, a woman who has obtained or seeks to obtain a drug-induced abortion.

(d) If a qualified healthcare provider provides an abortion-inducing drug to another for the purpose of inducing an abortion as authorized in Sections 4 and 5 of this Act, and if the qualified healthcare provider knows that the woman who uses the abortion-inducing drug for the purpose of inducing an abortion experiences, during or after the use of the abortion-inducing drug, an adverse event, the qualified healthcare provider shall provide a written report of the adverse event within three (3) days of the event to the FDA via the Medwatch Reporting System [*and*] to the Department [*and to the State Medical Board*].

For the purposes of this Act, an **"adverse event"** shall be defined according to the FDA criteria given in the Medwatch Reporting System.

(e) The Department shall prepare a comprehensive annual statistical report for the [*Legislature*] based upon the data gathered from reports under this Section. The statistical report shall disclose the identity of any qualified healthcare provider, physician, or person filing a report under this Section nor of any woman who is the subject of the report. The aggregated data shall also be made independently available to the public by the Department in a downloadable format.

(f) The Department shall summarize aggregate data from the reports required under this Act and submit the data to the U.S. Centers for Disease Control and Prevention (CDC) for the purpose of inclusion in the annual Vital Statistics Report. The aggregated data shall also be made independently available to the public by the Department in a downloadable format.

(g) Reports filed pursuant to this Section shall not be deemed public records and shall remain confidential, except that disclosure may be made to law enforcement officials upon an order of a court after application showing good cause. The court may condition disclosure of the information upon any safeguards it deem appropriate.

(h) Absent a valid court order or judicial subpoena, neither the Department, any other state department, agency, or office nor any employees thereof shall compare data concerning abortions or abortion complications maintained in an electronic or other information system file with data in any other electronic or other information system, the comparison of which could result in identifying, in any manner or under any circumstances, a woman obtaining or seeking to obtain a drug-induced abortion.

(i) Statistical information that may reveal the identity of a woman obtaining or seeking to obtain a drug-induced abortion shall not be maintained by the Department, any other state department, agency, office, or any employee or contractor thereof.

(j)   Neither the Department nor any employee or contractor of the Department shall disclose to a person or entity outside the Department the reports or the contents of the reports required under this Section, in a manner or fashion so as to permit the person or entity to whom the report is disclosed to identify, in any way or under any circumstances, the qualified healthcare provider who prescribed the drug-induced abortion and filed the report or the woman who is the subject of the report.

(k)   Original copies of all reports filed under this Section shall be available to the Department [*and the State Medical Board*] for use in the performance of its official duties.

[(*l*)   *The Department [and the State Medical Board] shall compile and retain all reports it receives under this Section. All reports the Department [and the Board] receive[s] are public records open to inspection under [Insert citation(s) to or appropriate reference(s) to applicable state code section(s) regarding public records]. In no case shall the Department [or the State Medical Board] release to any person or entity the name or any other personal identifying information regarding a person who uses an abortion-inducing drug for the purpose of inducing an abortion and who is the subject of a report the Department [and the State Medical Board] receives under this provision.*]

(m)   The Department shall communicate the reporting requirements in this Section to all medical professional organizations, licensed physicians, hospitals, emergency rooms, abortion facilities [*or other appropriate term such as "reproductive health center"*], Department [*of Health*] clinics, ambulatory surgical facilities, and other healthcare facilities operating in the State.

SECTION 8. PRODUCTION OF REPORTING FORMS.

The Department shall create and distribute the forms required by this Act within sixty (60) days after the effective date of this Act. No provision of this Act requiring the reporting of information on forms published by the Department shall be applicable until ten (10) days after the requisite forms are first created and distributed or until the effective date of this Act, whichever is later.

SECTION 9. CRIMINAL PENALTIES.

(a)   A [*person*] who intentionally, knowingly, or recklessly violates any provision of this Act is guilty of a [*Insert appropriate penalty/offense classification*]. In this Section, "intentionally" is defined by Section [*Insert section number or other appropriate reference*] of the [*state penal/criminal code*].

(b) No criminal penalty may be assessed against the pregnant woman upon whom the drug-induced abortion is attempted, induced, or performed.

SECTION 10. CIVIL REMEDIES AND PROFESSIONAL SANCTIONS.

(a) In addition to whatever remedies are available under the common or statutory law of this State, failure to comply with the requirements of this Act shall:

   (1) Provide a basis for a civil malpractice action for actual and punitive damages;
   (2) Provide a basis for a professional disciplinary action under [*Medical Malpractice Act*]; and
   (3) Provide a basis for recovery for the woman's survivors for the wrongful death of the woman under the [*Wrongful Death Act*].

(b) No civil liability may be assessed against the pregnant woman upon whom the drug-induced abortion is attempted, induced, or performed.

(c) When requested, the court shall allow a woman to proceed using solely her initials or a pseudonym and may close any proceedings in the case and enter other protective orders to preserve the privacy of the woman upon whom the drug-induced abortion was attempted, induced, or performed.

(d) If judgment is rendered in favor of the plaintiff, the court shall also render judgment for reasonable attorney's fees in favor of the plaintiff against the defendant.

(e) If judgment is rendered in favor of the defendant and the court finds that the plaintiff's suit was frivolous and brought in bad faith, the court may render judgment for reasonable attorney's fees in favor of the defendant against the plaintiff.

SECTION 11. CONSTRUCTION.

(a) Nothing in this Act shall be construed as creating or recognizing a right to abortion.

(b) It is not the intention of this Act to make lawful an abortion that is currently unlawful.

SECTION 12. RIGHT OF INTERVENTION.

The [*Legislature*], by joint resolution, may appoint one or more of its members, who sponsored or cosponsored this Act in his or her official capacity, to intervene as a matter of right in any case in which the constitutionality of this Act is challenged.

SECTION 13. SEVERABILITY.

Any provision of this Act held to be invalid or unenforceable by its terms or as applied to any person or circumstance shall be construed so as to give it the maximum effect permitted by law, unless such holding shall be one of utter invalidity or unenforceability, in which event such provision shall be deemed severable herefrom and shall not affect the remainder hereof or the application of such provision to other persons not similarly situated or to other, dissimilar circumstances.

SECTION 14. EFFECTIVE DATE.

This Act takes effect on [*Insert date*].

COERCIVE ABUSE AGAINST MOTHERS PREVENTION ACT

HOUSE/SENATE BILL NO. _____

By Representatives/Senators _____

SECTION 1. TITLE.

This Act shall be known as the "Coercive Abuse Against Mothers Prevention Act."

SECTION 2. LEGISLATIVE FINDINGS AND PURPOSES.

(a)　The [*Legislature*] of the [*Insert name of State*] finds that:

　(1)　Research indicates that violence against pregnant women is a serious problem. Many women report that they were coerced into abortions and have suffered grievous physical, emotional, psychological, and spiritual harm as a result.

　(2)　Reproductive healthcare facilities are often the only and last opportunities of hope for victims of coercive abuse and, as such, are in a unique position to help these women.

　(3)　More cases of coerced or attempted coerced abortions are reported if women are informed of their rights and given information concerning treatment and protection options.

　(4)　More women receive treatment for coercive abuse if they are informed of their rights and given information concerning treatment and protection options.

　(5)　Coercive abuse is a serious women's health issue because it violates a woman's rights to physical and emotional health, freedom of conscience and to freely choose either to continue her pregnancy or to have an abortion.

(b)　Based on the findings in subsection (a), it is the intent of the [*Legislature*] to:

　(1)　Prohibit actions intended to coerce or otherwise force a woman to abort her unborn child; and

　(2)　Empower all mothers in the State of [*Insert name of State*] to exercise their freedom of conscience in choosing life for their unborn children, free of violent and abusive coercion.

SECTION 3. DEFINITIONS.

As used in this Act only:

(a) **"Abortion"** means the act of using or prescribing any instrument, medicine, drug, or any other substance, device, or means with the intent to terminate the clinically diagnosable pregnancy of a woman with knowledge that the termination by those means will with reasonable likelihood cause the death of the unborn child. Such use, prescription, or means is not an abortion if done with the intent to:

    (1) Save the life or preserve the health of the unborn child;

    (2) Remove a dead unborn child caused by spontaneous abortion; or

    (3) Remove an ectopic pregnancy.

(b) **"Abuser"** means any person who coerces, forces, attempts to coerce, or attempts to force a woman into having an abortion.

(c) **"Coercion"** occurs when, with purpose to restrict a pregnant woman's freedom of action to her detriment, any person engages in conduct defined in Section 3(d) of this Act.

(d) **"Coercing an abortion"** or **"forcing an abortion"** occurs when a person knows of or suspects the pregnancy of a woman and engages or conspires with another to engage in any conduct described below, that is intentionally and purposely aimed at causing or directing the pregnant woman to have an abortion and solely conditioned upon the pregnant woman disregarding or refusing the person's demand that she seek an abortion:

    (1) Committing, attempting to commit, or threatening to commit physical harm to the woman, unborn child, or another person;

    (2) Committing, attempting to commit, or threatening to commit any act prohibited by any statute of this State, [*or insert specific citation(s) or reference(s) to state's criminal and civil codes*] [*including any common law tort not codified in a State statute*];

    (3) Revoking, attempting to revoke, or threatening to revoke a scholarship awarded to the woman by a public or private institution of higher education;

    (4) Discharging, attempting to discharge, or threatening to discharge the woman or another person from employment, or changing, attempting to change, or threatening to change her or the other person's compensation, terms, conditions, or privileges of employment;

    (5) Denying, attempting to deny, or threatening to deny any social assistance for which a pregnant woman or another person has applied, has been approved for, or has been receiving and for which she or the other person is otherwise eligible; and

(6) Denying, removing, or threatening to deny or remove financial support or housing from a dependent.

The terms **"coerce"** and **"force"** do not include or encompass constitutionally protected speech, conduct, or expressions of conscience.

(e) **"Course of conduct"** means a pattern of conduct composed of a series of two or more separate acts evidencing a continuity of purpose.

(f) **"Dependent"** means [*Insert definition*] as defined in [*Insert citation(s) to appropriate federal or state law*].

(g) **"Mandatory reporter"** means any individual who provides healthcare services, including a physician, surgeon, physical therapist, psychiatrist, psychologist, medical resident, medical intern, hospital staff member, licensed nurse, nurse's aide, any emergency medical technician, paramedic, and any employee, staff member, or volunteer at a reproductive healthcare facility.

(h) **"Physician"** or **"attending physician"** means any person licensed to practice medicine in this State. The term includes medical doctors and doctors of osteopathy.

(i) **"Pregnant woman"** means any female, including those who have not reached the age of eighteen (18) [*or minors*], who is in the reproductive condition of having an unborn child in her uterus.

(j) **"Reproductive healthcare facility"** or **"facility"** means any office, clinic, or other physical location licensed by the State to provide surgical or medical abortions, abortion counseling, abortion referrals, contraceptives, contraceptive counseling, sex education, or gynecological care and services.

(k) **"Solely"** means the conduct described in Section 4 of this Act must be such that it would not have occurred but for the woman's pregnancy. This does not preclude the possibility that an actor may have multiple motives for engaging in the conduct described in Section 4 of this Act.

(l) **"Threat"** means at least one statement or a course of conduct by an individual that would cause a reasonable person to believe that the individual is likely to act in accordance with the statements or as implied by a course of conduct. A threat does not include constitutionally protected speech or any generalized statement regarding a lawful pregnancy option, including, but not limited to, an emotional expression by a family or household member of the pregnant woman.

(m) **"Unborn child"** or **"pre-born child"** means the offspring of human beings from conception until birth.

SECTION 4. COERCED OR FORCED ABORTION PROHIBITED; CRIMINAL PENALTIES AND CIVIL REMEDIES.

(a) Prohibition: It shall be illegal to coerce or force a pregnant woman to have an abortion.

(b) Criminal Penalties and Civil Remedies:

  (1) Anyone who is guilty of engaging in conduct described in and proscribed by this Section is, in addition to any other crimes described in [*state's criminal/penal code*], guilty of a [*Insert appropriate penalty/offense classification*].

  (2) If a violation of this Section is committed by the father or putative father of the unborn child against a pregnant woman who is less than eighteen (18) years of age, and the father or putative father is eighteen (18) years of age or older, the father or putative father is guilty of a [*Insert reference to a higher penalty/offense classification*].

  (3) A pregnant woman injured by reason of an abuser's violation of this Act may bring a civil suit for the recovery of damages for such injury, including wrongful death on behalf of an aborted child as provided for in [*Insert citation(s) or other reference(s) to state's Wrongful Death Act*], whether or not the abuser is criminally prosecuted or convicted and whether or not the pregnant woman has an abortion. In such civil suit, the pregnant woman shall be entitled to recover, in addition to any other damages, her reasonable attorney's fees and costs if she is the prevailing party.

  (4) Any minor [*or woman*] who is threatened with coercion, as defined in Section 3(d) of this Act, may apply to a court of competent jurisdiction for relief. The court shall provide the minor [*or woman*] with counsel, give the matter expedited consideration, and grant such relief as may be necessary to prevent such coercion.

  (5) If a minor is denied financial support by the minor's parent(s), guardian, or custodian because of the minor's refusal to have an abortion, the minor shall be considered an emancipated minor for the purposes of eligibility for public assistance benefits. Any public assistance benefits may not be used to obtain an abortion.

SECTION 5. REPRODUCTIVE HEALTHCARE FACILITY REQUIREMENTS; CRIMINAL PENALTIES, CIVIL REMEDIES, AND PROFESSIONAL SANCTIONS.

(a) Sign Postage Requirements:

  (1) A reproductive healthcare facility shall conspicuously post signs visible to all who enter so as to be clearly readable, which state: "It is against the law for anyone, regardless of his or her relationship to you, to force you to have an abortion. You have the right to contact any local or state law

enforcement or social service agency to receive protection from any actual or threatened physical, emotional, or psychological abuse. It is against the law to perform, induce, prescribe for, or provide you with the means for an abortion without your voluntary consent."

(2) Such signs must be posted in the waiting room(s), consultation room(s), and procedure room(s).

(3) The continued posting of such signs shall be a condition of licensure of any reproductive health-care facility under [*Insert reference(s) to state abortion facility licensure law or other administrative requirements*]. The display of such signs does not discharge the duty of a reproductive healthcare facility to have a physician orally inform the pregnant woman of information required by Sections 5(b)(5) and 5(c) of this Act.

(b) Mandatory Reporting Requirements:

(1) **Requirement:** A mandatory reporter must report every instance of alleged or suspected coerced abortion as defined in and proscribed by Sections 3 and 4 of this Act. The mandatory reporter may not use his or her discretion in deciding what cases should or should not be reported to the appropriate law enforcement or state agency.

(2) **Standard:** The standard to be applied to a mandatory reporter in determining a reportable suspicion is reasonability in good faith.

(3) **Procedure:** If a mandatory reporter has cause to believe that a pregnant woman is or was a victim of conduct defined in and proscribed by Sections 3 and 4 of this Act, the mandatory reporter shall make a report no later than the forty-eighth (48th) hour after such coercion, force, attempted coercion, attempted force, threatened coercion, or threatened force has been brought to his or her attention or suspicion. A mandatory reporter may not delegate the responsibility to report such coercion, force, attempted coercion, attempted force, threatened coercion, or threatened force to any other person, but must personally make the report. A mandatory reporter must make a report to [designated local or state law enforcement agency and/or other appropriate social services agency].

(4) **Content of Report:** The person making the report must identify the name and address of the pregnant woman, and, in a case of a minor, the name and address of the person who is responsible for the care or custody of the minor. The person making the report must also report any pertinent information he or she may have relating to the alleged or suspected coercion, force, attempted coercion, attempted force, threatened coercion, or threatened force.

(5) The attending physician shall orally inform the pregnant woman that no one can force her to have an abortion.

(6) It shall be unlawful for any reproductive healthcare facility to willfully and knowingly continue to employ a mandatory reporter who has violated Sections 4 or 5(b) of this Act.

(c) Private Counseling Requirements:

(1) In a private room, the attending physician shall orally ask the pregnant woman if she is being coerced or forced to have an abortion. If it is reasonably suspected that the woman is being coerced or forced into having an abortion, the physician shall inform the woman that such coercion is illegal, that the woman may have legal remedies, and that a request or demand by the father to have an abortion does not relieve his financial support responsibilities.

(2) The attending physician shall also provide the pregnant woman with information about assistance, counseling, and protective services offered by social programs and local or state law enforcement agencies, as well as access to a telephone where she can make a private call and to an alternate exit from the facility [*so that, if necessary, she can exit the abortion facility without being seen or confronted*].

(d) Required Reflection Period:

(1) No person shall perform an abortion upon a pregnant woman who is known or suspected to be a victim of conduct defined in and proscribed by Sections 3 and 4 of this Act within twenty-four (24) hours of when this fact or suspicion arises and informing the woman of her rights as provided in Sections 5(b)(5) and 5(c) of this Act.

(2) The mandatory twenty-four (24) hour reflection period may be waived if, in the physician's best medical judgment, an abortion is necessary to prevent the death of the woman or to prevent substantial and irreversible injury to a major bodily function.

(e) Criminal Penalties, Civil Remedies, and Professional Sanctions:

(1) Any mandatory reporter who has reason to believe a woman is or has been a victim of conduct defined in and proscribed by Sections 3 and 4 of this Act and willfully and knowingly does not report such coercion, force, attempted coercion, attempted force, threatened coercion, or threatened force as required by this Act is guilty of a [*Insert appropriate penalty/offense classification*].

(2) Any person who performs an abortion which is inconsistent with Section 5(d) of this Act is guilty of a [*Insert appropriate penalty/offense classification*].

(3) Any person who performs, induces, or assists in performing or inducing an abortion on a woman, and is unaware that the woman is or has been a victim of conduct defined in and proscribed by Sections 3 and 4 as a result of a willful, knowing, or purposeful failure to comply with the requirements of Section 5(c) of this Act is guilty of a [*Insert appropriate penalty/offense classification*].

(4) A pregnant woman injured by reason of a facility's violation of this Act may bring a civil suit for recovery of damages for such injury, including wrongful death on behalf of an aborted child as provided for in [*Insert citation(s) or reference(s) to state's Wrongful Death Act*], whether or not the

attending physician or the facility is criminally prosecuted or convicted and whether or not the pregnant woman has an abortion. In such a civil suit, the pregnant woman, if she is the prevailing party, shall be entitled to recover, in addition to any other damages, her reasonable attorney's fees and costs.

(5) Initial and continuing adherence to the requirements of Section 5 of this Act shall be a condition of licensure for any reproductive healthcare facility under [*Insert reference(s) to state abortion facility licensure law or administrative requirements*].

(6) A woman receiving an abortion inconsistent with any provision of this Act cannot be prosecuted or held civilly liable.

SECTION 6. DUTIES OF LAW ENFORCEMENT [OR OTHER DESIGNATED SOCIAL SERVICES OR PUBLIC AGENCY].

(a) Upon the request of the complainant (including a pregnant woman, a woman who was coerced or forced into having an abortion and later reports the coercion or force, or any woman whose rights under this Act were denied by any physician or facility), a law enforcement agency [*or designated social or other public services agency*] investigating a violation of this Act shall notify the complainant not less than twenty-four (24) hours before initially contacting the person(s) alleged to have violated Sections 4 or 5 of this Act.

(b) This Act does not preclude or prohibit an alleged perpetrator from being charged with, convicted of, or punished for any other crime committed while also violating this Act.

(c) A court of competent jurisdiction may order that a term of imprisonment imposed for violating this Act be served consecutively to a term of imprisonment imposed for any other crime committed while also violating this Act.

SECTION 7. CONSTRUCTION.

(a) This Act does not create, recognize, endorse, or condone a right to an abortion.

(b) It is not the intention of this Act to make lawful an abortion that is currently unlawful.

SECTION 8. SEVERABILITY.

Any provision of this Act held to be invalid or unenforceable by its terms, or as applied to any person or circumstance, shall be construed so as to give it the maximum effect permitted by law, unless such holding shall be one of utter invalidity or unenforceability, in which event such provision shall be deemed severable herefrom and shall not affect the remainder hereof or the application of such provision to other persons not similarly situated or to other, dissimilar circumstances.

SECTION 9. RIGHT OF INTERVENTION.

The [*Legislature*], by a joint resolution, may appoint one or more of its members who sponsored or cosponsored this Act in his or her official capacity to intervene as a matter of right in any case in which the constitutionality of this Act is challenged.

SECTION 10. EFFECTIVE DATE.

This Act takes effect on [*Insert date*].

CHILD PROTECTION ACT

HOUSE/SENATE BILL NO. _____

By Representatives/Senators _____

SECTION 1. TITLE.

This Act may be cited as the "[*Insert name of State*] Child Protection Act."

SECTION 2. LEGISLATIVE FINDINGS AND PURPOSES.

(a) The [*Legislature*] of the State of [*Insert name of State*] finds that:

  (1) Children are increasingly being preyed upon, victimized, and coerced into illegal sexual relationships by adults.

  (2) [*Insert name of State*] law requires [*caretakers, healthcare facilities, healthcare providers, teachers, and other specified individuals*] to report suspected incidents of sexual crimes against children. [*Insert reference(s) to appropriate state statute(s)*].

  (3) However, many of these suspected criminal acts go unreported, and perpetrators are not investigated or prosecuted.

  (4) [*Insert name of State*] may better prevent future sexual crimes against children by investigating, prosecuting, incarcerating, and treating those who prey upon and victimize children.

  (5) To prevent future and continuing sexual crimes against children, all suspected crimes of this nature must be reported to state investigators and agencies that are specifically trained and equipped to professionally, thoroughly, and compassionately investigate cases of suspected crimes against children, relieving mandatory reporters of any investigatory responsibility.

  (6) The physical, emotional, developmental, and psychological impact of sexual crimes on child victims can be severe and long-lasting.

  (7) The societal costs of these crimes are also significant and affect the entire populace.

  (8) The collection, maintenance, and preservation of evidence, including forensic tissue samples, furthers [*Insert name of State*]'s interest in protecting children from sexual crimes and provides the State with a necessary tool for successful investigations and prosecutions.

(9) Parents and guardians have both the right and responsibility to be involved in medical treatment decisions involving their children, and no one has the right to knowingly or willfully impede or circumvent this right.

(10) There are documented cases of individuals other than a parent or guardian aiding, abetting, and assisting minor girls to procure abortions without their parents' or guardians' knowledge, consent, or involvement. This includes transporting children across state lines to avoid [*Insert name of State*]'s parental [*involvement, consent, or notice*] requirements for abortion.

(11) Such actions violate both the sanctity of the familial relationship and [*Insert name of State*]'s parental [*involvement, consent, or notice*] law for abortion.

(b) Based on the findings in subsection (a), the [*Legislature*]'s purposes in promulgating this Act are to further the important and compelling state interests of:

(1) Protecting children from sexually predatory adults;

(2) Ensuring that adults who are involved in illegal sexual relationships or contact with children are reported, investigated, and, when warranted, prosecuted;

(3) Relieving medical professionals and other mandatory reporters of suspected sexual crimes against children from any responsibility to personally investigate an allegation or suspicion. Mandatory reporters must simply report allegations, suspicions, and pertinent facts. Trained law enforcement or social services personnel will then be responsible for any investigation and for the ultimate disposition of the allegations or cases;

(4) Reducing the physical, emotional, developmental, and psychological impact of sexual crimes on child victims;

(5) Reducing the societal and economic burdens on the populace that result from sexual crimes against children;

(6) Providing law enforcement officials with the tools and evidence necessary to investigate and prosecute child predators; and

(7) Protecting and respecting the right of parents and guardians to be involved in the medical decisions and treatment of their children and preventing anyone from knowingly or willfully subverting or circumventing these rights.

SECTION 3. DEFINITIONS.

As used in this Act only:

(a) **"Abortion"** means the act of using or prescribing any instrument, medicine, drug, or any other substance, device, or means with the intent to terminate the clinically diagnosable pregnancy of a woman with knowledge that the termination by those means will with reasonable likelihood cause the death of the unborn child. Such use, prescription, or means is not an abortion if done with the intent to:

    (1) Save the life or preserve the health of the unborn child;

    (2) Remove a dead unborn child caused by spontaneous abortion; or

    (3) Remove an ectopic pregnancy.

(b) **"Abuse"** means [*Insert specific language from existing state statutes concerning the reporting of child abuse, child sexual abuse, or similar offenses*] or [*the involvement of a child in any sexual act with a parent, guardian, or another adult; any sexual activity involving a child under the age of twelve (12); the aiding or toleration of a parent, guardian, or caretaker of the child's sexual involvement with any other adult; the child's involvement in pornographic displays; or any other involvement of a child in sexual activity constituting a crime under the laws of this State*].

    [*Drafter's Note: Depending on the specific provisions and prohibitions of the state's criminal/penal code or other statutes, a more definitive exclusion of sexual acts or conduct between two (consenting) children may be appropriate in light of recent federal court decisions. Please consult AUL for specific drafting assistance.*]

(c) **"Adult"** means one who has attained the age [*of eighteen (18) or the legal age of majority in this State*].

(d) **"Caretaker"** means any person legally obligated to provide or secure adequate care for the child, including a parent, guardian, tutor, legal custodian, foster home parent, or anyone else providing the child with a residence.

(e) **"Child"** or **"children"** means anyone under the age of [*eighteen (18) or, if appropriate, the state's age of consent for sexual activity*].

(f) **"Mandatory reporter"** means any of the following individuals or entities performing their occupational duties:

[Insert specific categories and definitions of mandatory reporters from existing state statutes or administrative rules defining "mandatory reporters" for child abuse, child sexual abuse, or similar offenses].

[Add "reproductive healthcare facility" (as defined in (h) below) to the list of mandatory reports under state law.]

(g) **"Physician"** means a person licensed to practice medicine in the State of *[Insert name of State]*. This term includes medical doctors and doctors of osteopathy.

(h) **"Reproductive healthcare facility"** means any office, clinic, or any other physical location that provides abortions, abortion counseling, abortion referrals, contraceptives, contraceptive counseling, sex education, or gynecological care and services.

(i) **"Sexual abuse"** means *[Insert specific language from existing state statutes concerning child sexual abuse or similar offenses]* or *[any sexual conduct, sexual contact, or sexual penetration as defined in [Insert appropriate reference(s) to state criminal/penal code provision(s) or other statutory provision(s)] and committed against a child by an adult or involving a child under the age of twelve (12)].*

SECTION 4. MANDATORY REPORTER REQUIREMENTS.

A mandatory reporter must report *[in writing]* every instance of alleged or suspected abuse, sexual abuse, or sexual crimes against a child as defined by *[Insert appropriate reference(s) to state criminal/penal code or other statutory provision(s)] [and this Act]*. The mandatory reporter may not use his or her discretion in deciding what cases should or should not be reported to the appropriate law enforcement or state agencies.

SECTION 5. MANDATORY REPORTING PROCEDURE.

If a mandatory reporter has cause to believe that a child has been abused, sexually abused, or has been the victim of a sexual crime as defined in *[Insert appropriate reference(s) to state criminal code or other statutory provision(s)] [and this Act]*, the mandatory reporter shall make a *[written]* report no later than the forty-eighth (48th) hour after such abuse, sexual abuse, or crime has been brought to his or her attention or after he or she suspects such abuse, sexual abuse, or crime. A mandatory reporter may not delegate the responsibility to report such abuse, sexual abuse, or crime to any other person, but must personally make the report. The mandatory reporter must make a report to *[Insert name of designated local or state law enforcement agency and/or other state or local agency responsible for investigating suspected or alleged abuse or crimes against children]*.

SECTION 6. CONTENTS OF THE REPORT.

The person making the report must identify the name and address of the child, as well as the name and address of the person(s) who is responsible for the care or custody of the child. The person making the report must also file any pertinent information he or she may have relating to the alleged or suspected abuse, sexual abuse, or crime.

SECTION 7. FAILURE TO REPORT.

Any mandatory reporter who has cause to believe that a child has been abused, sexually abused, or has been the victim of a crime as defined in [*Insert appropriate reference(s) to state criminal/penal code or other statutory provision(s)*] [*and this Act*] and does not report such abuse, sexual abuse, or crime as provided by this Act shall be subject to [*Insert reference(s) to appropriate civil remedy, fine, or other penalty*].

SECTION 8. MAINTENANCE OF FORENSIC SAMPLES FROM ABORTION PERFORMED ON A CHILD.

(a) Any physician who performs an abortion on a child who is less than [*fourteen (14)*] years of age at the time of the abortion procedure shall preserve, in accordance with rules and regulations adopted by the [*state Attorney General or other appropriate law enforcement agency charged with the collection and preservation of evidence*] pursuant to this Act, fetal tissue extracted during such abortion. The physician shall submit such tissue to the [*Insert name of proper state agency such as state Department of Public Safety, state Bureau of Investigation, or the state Crime Laboratory*].

(b) The [*state Attorney General or other appropriate law enforcement agency charged or familiar with the forensic collection and preservation of evidence*] shall adopt rules and regulations prescribing:

   (1) The amount and type of fetal tissue to be preserved and submitted by a physician pursuant to this Section;
   (2) Procedures for the proper preservation of such tissue for the purpose of DNA testing and examination;
   (3) Procedures for documenting the chain of custody of such tissue for use as evidence;
   (4) Procedures for proper disposal of fetal tissue preserved pursuant to this Section;

(5) A uniform reporting form [*or instrument*] mandated to be utilized by physicians when submitting fetal tissue under this Section which shall include the name and address of the physician submitting the fetal tissue and the name and complete address of residence of the parent or legal guardian of the child upon whom the abortion was performed; and

(6) Procedures for communication with law enforcement agencies regarding evidence and information obtained pursuant to this Section.

(c) **Penalties.** Failure of a physician to comply with any provision of this Section or any rule or regulation adopted thereunder:

(1) Shall constitute unprofessional conduct for the purposes of [*Insert appropriate statutory reference(s)*]; and

(2) Is a [*Insert appropriate criminal offense/penalty classification*] and a [*Insert appropriate higher offense/penalty classification*] upon a second or subsequent conviction.

SECTION 9. PROHIBITION ON INTENTIONALLY CAUSING, AIDING, ABETTING, OR ASSISTING A CHILD TO OBTAIN AN ABORTION WITHOUT PARENTAL [*INVOLVEMENT, CONSENT, OR NOTIFICATION*].

(a) No person shall intentionally cause, aid, abet, or assist a child to obtain an abortion without the [*consent or notification required by [insert reference(s) to state parental involvement for abortion statute(s)]*].

(b) **Penalties.** A person who violates subsection (a) of this Section shall be civilly liable to the child and to the person or persons required to [*give consent/receive notice under [insert reference(s) to state parental involvement for abortion statute(s)]*]. A court may award damages to the person or persons adversely affected by a violation of subsection (a) of this Section, including compensation for emotional injury without the need for personal presence at the act or event, and the court may further award attorneys' fees, litigation costs, and punitive damages. Any adult who engages in or consents to another person engaging in a sexual act with a child in violation of the provisions of [*Insert appropriate reference(s) to state criminal/penal code provision(s)*], which results in the child's pregnancy, shall not be awarded damages under this Section.

(c) It shall not be a defense to a claim brought under this Section that the abortion was performed or induced pursuant to consent to or notice of the abortion given in a manner that was otherwise lawful in the state or place where the abortion was performed or induced.

(d) An unemancipated child does not have capacity to consent to any action in violation of this Section.

(e) A court of competent jurisdiction may enjoin conduct that would be in violation of this Section upon petition by the Attorney General, a prosecuting or [*district*] attorney, or any person adversely affected or who reasonably may be adversely affected by such conduct, upon a showing that such conduct:

   (1) Is reasonably anticipated to occur in the future; or
   (2) Has occurred in the past, whether with the same child or others, and that it is not unreasonable to expect that such conduct will be repeated.

SECTION 10. RIGHT OF INTERVENTION.

The [*Legislature*], by joint resolution, may appoint one or more of its members who sponsored or cosponsored this Act in his or her official capacity to intervene as a matter of right in any case in which the constitutionality of this law is challenged.

SECTION 11. SEVERABILITY.

Any provision of this Act held to be invalid or unenforceable by its terms, or as applied to any person or circumstance, shall be construed so as to give it the maximum effect permitted by law, unless such holding shall be one of utter invalidity or unenforceability, in which event such provision shall be deemed severable herefrom and shall not affect the remainder hereof or the application of such provision to other persons not similarly situated or to other, dissimilar circumstances.

SECTION 12. EFFECTIVE DATE.

This Act takes effect on [*Insert date*].

STATE OF THE STATES: WHERE ARE WE NOW?

CURRENT STATE LAWS:

All 50 states have statutory rape and other laws that make sexual contact with a minor a crime, though there is significant variation in the laws from state to state.[4] The age of consent (for sexual intercourse) ranges from 16 to 18 years of age, with 32 states setting the age of consent at 16 years.[5] In two-thirds of the states, statutory rape is a reportable offense regardless of the relationship between the victim and the rapist. In the remaining states, reporting of statutory rape is only mandated when the perpetrator is someone who is responsible for the care of the child.[6]

In terms of who must report suspected cases of sexual abuse and statutory rape, it is ordinarily anyone who encounters the victim in his or her professional capacity. These mandatory reporters often include teachers, legal professionals, and clergy and universally include certain healthcare providers.[7] While some states allow these mandatory reporters to exercise discretion in the cases they report, a majority of states do not.[8]

CASE STUDY: SUCCESS IN TEXAS

In 2001, then-Texas Governor Rick Perry signed into law a measure strengthening mandatory reporting laws for healthcare providers and employees of reproductive healthcare facilities (i.e., abortion clinics). One of the main provisions of the law stripped much of the discretion that these individuals exercised over what cases of suspected sexual abuse they reported. Since that time, healthcare providers and employees at reproductive healthcare facilities have been required to report all cases of suspected sexual contact involv-ing clients under 17 years of age unless the partner is less than three (3) years older (than the victim). Moreover, all sexual contact that involves a child under fourteen (14) years of age must be reported regardless of the age of the sexual partner.[9]

During the debate over this legislation, Planned Parenthood complained that this new law would result in a flood of frivolous claims of sexual assault and statutory rape. They contended that real cases would be lost in the shuffle of the bureaucracy, and children would suffer adverse consequences. More than a decade later, however, that has not proven to be the case.

In 2000, there were 6,925 confirmed allegations of sexual abuse of children in Texas.[10] After the implementation of the new mandatory reporting requirements, confirmed allegations rose fairly steadily. By 2006, however, the number of confirmed allegations of sexual abuse of children had fallen back near 2000 levels (to 7,176).[11] Clearly, strong reporting requirements protect children and lead to more sexual predators and child rapists being identified and prosecuted. Moreover, in the wake of recent scandals involving Planned Parenthood clinics across the nation, the need for stricter mandatory reporting laws and harsher penalties for violation of these laws are clear.

[4] U.S. Dept. of Health and Human Services, 2003 *Child Abuse and Neglect State Statutes Series Statutes at a Glance: Mandatory Reporters of Child Abuse and Neglect* (U.S. Dept. of Health and Human Services 2003).

[5] *See* Glosser et. al, *supra* note 4 at 6-7.

[6] Id. at ES-2.

[7] *See* U.S. Dept. HHS, *supra* note 16 at 1.

[8] *See* Glosser et. al., *supra* note 4 at 12-13.

[9] Cynthia Daillard, *Statutory Rape Reporting and Family Planning Programs: Moving Beyond Conflict*, The Guttmacher Report on Public Policy, *available at* http://www.guttmacher.org/pubs/tgr/07/2/gr070210.html (last visited August 29, 2017).

[10] Texas Dept. of Family and Protective Services, 2000 Data Book 54 (State of Texas 2000).

[11] Texas Dept. of Family and Protective Services, 2006 Data Book 54 (State of Texas 2006).

PARENTAL INVOLVEMENT ENHANCEMENT ACT

HOUSE/SENATE BILL NO. _____

By Representatives/Senators _____

[*Drafter's Note: The requirements detailed below may be enacted individually or collectively, depending on the needs of the individual state. Each substantive Section contains a drafter's note indicating when enactment of the enhancement would be appropriate. For assistance in drafting a complete overhaul of a state's parental notice or consent law, please see AUL's Parental Consent for Abortion Act or Parental Notification of Abortion Act.*]

SECTION 1. SHORT TITLE.

This Act may be cited as the "Parental Involvement Enhancement Act."

SECTION 2. LEGISLATIVE FINDINGS AND PURPOSES.

(a)   The Legislature of the State of [*Insert name of State*] finds that:

   (1)   Immature minors often lack the ability to make fully informed choices that take into account both immediate and long-range consequences.

   (2)   The medical, emotional, and psychological consequences of abortion are sometimes serious and can be lasting, particularly when the patient is immature.

   (3)   The capacity to become pregnant and the capacity for mature judgment concerning the wisdom of an abortion are not necessarily related.

   (4)   Parents ordinarily possess information essential to a physician's exercise of his or her best medical judgment concerning the child.

   (5)   Parents who are aware that their minor daughter has had an abortion may better ensure that she receives adequate medical attention after her abortion.

   (6)   Parental consultation is usually desirable and in the best interests of the minor.

(b)   Based on the findings in subsection (a), the [*Legislature*]'s purposes in enacting this enhancement to the State of [*Insert name of State*]'s parental [*consent or notice*] law are to further the important and compelling State interests of:

(1)   Protecting minors against their own immaturity;

(2)   Fostering family unity and preserving the family as a viable social unit;

(3)   Protecting the constitutional rights of parents to rear children who are members of their household;

(4)   Reducing teenage pregnancy and abortion; and

(5)   In light of the foregoing statements of purpose, allowing for judicial bypasses of the parental [*consent or notice*] requirement to be made only in exceptional or rare circumstances.

SECTION 3. DEFINITIONS.

[*Drafter's Note: These are recommended definitions, but some may not be compatible with a state's existing parental involvement law. In drafting specific legislation, care should be taken to select only those definitions that are compatible with existing state law or with the intent of the legislation.*]

As used in this Act only:

(a)   **"Abortion"** means the act of using or prescribing any instrument, medicine, drug, or any other substance, device, or means with the intent to terminate the clinically diagnosable pregnancy of a woman with knowledge that the termination by those means will with reasonable likelihood cause the death of the unborn child. Such use, prescription, or means is not an abortion if done with the intent to:

(1)   Save the life or preserve the health of the unborn child;

(2)   Remove a dead unborn child caused by spontaneous abortion; or

(3)   Remove an ectopic pregnancy.

(b)   **"Actual notice"** means the giving of notice directly, in person or by telephone.

(c)   **"Coercion"** means restraining or dominating the choice of a pregnant woman by force, threat of force, or deprivation of food and shelter.

(d)   **"Consent"** means, in the case of a pregnant woman who is less than eighteen (18) years of age, a notarized written statement signed by the pregnant woman and her mother, father, or legal guardian declaring that the pregnant woman intends to seek an abortion and that her mother, father, or legal guardian consents to the abortion; or, in the case of a pregnant woman who is an incompetent person, a notarized written statement signed by the pregnant woman's guardian declaring that the guardian consents to the performance of an abortion upon the pregnant woman.

(e) **"Constructive notice"** means notice by certified mail to the last known address of the parent or guardian with delivery deemed to have occurred forty-eight (48) hours after the certified notice is mailed.

(f) **"Department"** means the Department of [*Insert appropriate title*] of the State of [*Insert name of State*].

(g) **"Emancipated minor"** means any person less than eighteen (18) years of age who is or has been married or who has been legally emancipated.

(h) **"Incompetent"** means any person who has been adjudged a disabled person and has had a guardian appointed for her under the [*state Probate Act or other appropriate state law*].

(i) **"Medical emergency"** means a condition that, on the basis of the physician's good-faith clinical judgment, so complicates the medical condition of a pregnant woman as to necessitate the immediate abortion of her pregnancy to avert her death or for which a delay will create serious risk of substantial and irreversible impairment of a major bodily function.

(j) **"Neglect"** means the failure of a parent or legal guardian to supply a minor with necessary food, clothing, shelter, or medical care when reasonably able to do so or the failure to protect a minor from conditions or actions that imminently and seriously endanger the minor's physical or mental health when reasonably able to do so.

(k) **"Physical abuse"** means any physical assault or injury intentionally inflicted by a parent or legal guardian on a minor.

(l) **"Physician," "attending physician,"** or **"referring physician"** means any person licensed to practice medicine in this State. The term includes medical doctors and doctors of osteopathy.

(m) **"Pregnant woman"** means a woman who is pregnant and is less than eighteen (18) years of age and not emancipated, or who has been adjudged an incompetent person under [*Insert citation(s) or other reference(s) to state statute(s) relating to petition and hearing; independent evaluation, etc.*].

(n) **"Sexual abuse"** means any sexual conduct or sexual penetration as defined in [*Insert citation(s) or other reference(s) to appropriate section(s) of the state criminal/penal code or other appropriate law(s)*] and committed against a minor by a parent or legal guardian.

SECTION [4]. NOTARIZED CONSENT.

[Drafter's Note: This enhancement is appropriate for a state with a parental consent law that does not already require notarized consent.]

(a)   No person shall perform an abortion upon a pregnant woman unless, in the case of a woman who is less than eighteen (18) years of age, he or she first obtains the notarized written consent of both the pregnant woman and one of her parents or her legal guardian; or, in the case of a woman who is an incompetent person, he or she first obtains the notarized written consent of her guardian.

(b)   The physician shall keep the notarized written consent of the parent or legal guardian in the medical file of the pregnant woman for five (5) years past the majority of the pregnant woman, but in no event less than seven (7) years.

SECTION [5]. NOTARIZED WAIVER OF NOTICE REQUIREMENT.

[Drafter's Note: This enhancement is appropriate for a state with a parental notice law that permits the person(s) entitled to notice to waive the requirement.]

(a)   Notice is not required if the physician obtains a notarized written statement by the pregnant woman's parent or legal guardian, dated not more than thirty (30) days before the abortion, waiving the right of the parent or legal guardian to notice of the pregnant woman's abortion.

(b)   The physician shall keep a copy of the notarized written statement of the parent or legal guardian waiving their right to notice in the medical file of the pregnant woman for five (5) years past the majority of the pregnant woman, but in no event less than seven (7) years.

SECTION [6]. PROOF OF IDENTIFICATION AND RELATIONSHIP TO PREGNANT WOMAN – CONSENT.

[Drafter's Note: This enhancement is appropriate for a state with a parental consent law that does not require the consenting parent or guardian to provide identification or proof of the parent or guardian's relationship to the pregnant woman.]

(a) The physician shall obtain from the parent or legal guardian entitled to consent:

    (1) Government-issued proof of the identity of the parent or legal guardian; and

    (2) Written documentation that establishes that the parent or legal guardian is the lawful parent or legal guardian of the pregnant woman.

(b) The physician shall keep a copy of the proof of identification of the parent or legal guardian and the written documentation that establishes the relationship of the parent or legal guardian to the pregnant woman in the medical file of the pregnant woman for five (5) years past the majority of the pregnant woman, but in no event less than seven (7) years.

(c) A physician receiving parental consent under this Section shall execute for inclusion in the medical record of the pregnant woman an affidavit stating: "I, (Insert name of physician), certify that according to my best information and belief, a reasonable person under similar circumstances would rely on the information presented by both the pregnant woman and her parent or legal guardian as sufficient evidence of identity and relationship."

SECTION [7]. PROOF OF IDENTIFICATION AND RELATIONSHIP TO PREGNANT WOMAN – WAIVER OF NOTICE REQUIREMENT.

[Drafter's Note: This enhancement is appropriate for a state with a parental notice law that permits the person(s) entitled to notice to waive the requirement.]

(a) In lieu of the notice required by this Section, the physician shall obtain from the parent or legal guardian entitled to notice:

    (1) Government-issued proof of the identity of the parent or legal guardian;

    (2) Written documentation that establishes that the parent or legal guardian is the lawful parent or legal guardian of the pregnant woman; and

    (3) A signed statement by the parent or legal guardian that the parent or legal guardian has been notified that an abortion is to be performed on the pregnant woman.

(b) The physician shall keep a copy of the proof of identification of the parent or legal guardian and the written documentation that establishes the relationship of the parent or legal guardian to the pregnant woman in the medical file of the pregnant woman for five (5) years past the majority of the pregnant woman, but in no event less than seven (7) years.

(c) A physician receiving parental notice under this Section shall execute for inclusion in the medical record of the pregnant woman an affidavit stating: "I, (Insert name of physician), certify that according to my best information and belief, a reasonable person under similar circumstances would rely on the information presented by both the pregnant woman and her parent or legal guardian as sufficient evidence of identity and relationship."

SECTION [8]. NOTICE OF POST-EMERGENCY.

[Drafter's Note: This enhancement is appropriate for states with parental consent or parental notification laws.]

(a) *[Consent or Notice]* shall not be required under *[Insert appropriate reference(s) to the state parental involvement law]* if the attending physician certifies in the minor or incompetent woman's medical record that a medical emergency exists and there is insufficient time to *[obtain the required consent or provide the required notice]*. However, the attending physician shall, within twenty-four (24) hours after completion of the abortion, notify one of the parents or the legal guardian of the minor or incompetent woman in the manner provided in this Section that a medical emergency abortion was performed on the minor or incompetent woman and of the circumstances that warranted invocation of this Section.

(b) Unless the minor or incompetent woman gives notice of her intent to seek a judicial waiver pursuant to *[Insert appropriate reference(s) to the state parental involvement law]*, the attending physician shall verbally inform the parent or legal guardian of the minor or incompetent woman within twenty-four (24) hours after the performance of a medical emergency abortion that an abortion was performed on the minor or incompetent woman. The attending physician shall also inform the parent or legal guardian of the basis for the certification of the physician required under paragraph (a) of this Section, and provide details regarding any additional risks to the minor or incompetent woman. The attending physician shall also send a written notice of the performed abortion by certified mail to the last known address of the parent or legal guardian, restricted delivery, return receipt requested.

(c) If the minor or incompetent woman gives notice to the attending physician of her intent to seek a judicial waiver pursuant to *[Insert appropriate reference(s) to the state parental involvement law]*, the physician shall file a notice with any judge of a court of competent jurisdiction that the minor has given such notice and shall provide the information the physician would have been required to provide the parent under subsection (b) of this Section if the minor or incompetent woman had not given notice of her intent to seek a judicial waiver.

(d) The court shall expeditiously schedule a confidential conference with notice to the minor or incompetent woman and the physician. If the minor or incompetent woman is able to participate in the proceedings, the court shall advise the minor or incompetent woman that she has the right to court-appointed counsel and shall, upon her request, provide the minor or incompetent woman with such counsel. If the minor or incompetent woman is unable to participate, the court shall appoint counsel on behalf of the minor or incompetent woman.

(e) After an appropriate hearing, the court, taking into account the medical condition of the minor or incompetent woman, shall set a deadline by which the minor or incompetent woman must file a petition or motion pursuant to [*Insert appropriate reference(s) to the state parental involvement law*]. The court may subsequently extend the deadline in light of the medical condition of the minor or incompetent woman or other equitable considerations. If the minor or incompetent woman does not file a petition or motion by the deadline, either in that court or in another court of competent jurisdiction with a copy filed in that court, the court shall direct that the court clerk provide the notice to a parent or legal guardian.

SECTION [9]. VENUE.

[*Drafter's Note: This enhancement is for any state that does not restrict the venue in which a minor may file a petition for judicial waiver of the state's consent or notice requirement.*]

The pregnant woman may petition a [*circuit*] court in the county in which the pregnant woman resides for a waiver of the [*consent or notice*] requirement.

SECTION [10]. BURDEN OF EVIDENCE FOR BYPASS.

[*Drafter's Note: This enhancement is for a state that wishes to define or to provide a heightened evidentiary requirement (i.e., "clear and convincing evidence") in judicial waiver proceedings.*]

(a) If the court finds, by clear and convincing evidence, that the pregnant woman is both sufficiently mature and well-informed to decide whether to have an abortion, the court shall issue an order authorizing the pregnant woman to consent to the performance or inducement of an abortion without the [*consent or notification*] of a parent or guardian and the court shall execute the required forms. If the court does not make the finding specified in this subsection or subsection (b) of this Section, it shall dismiss the petition.

(b) If the court finds, by clear and convincing evidence, that the pregnant woman is the victim of physical or sexual abuse by one or both of her parents or her legal guardian, or that [*obtaining the consent or providing the notification*] of a parent or legal guardian is not in the best interest of the pregnant woman, the court shall issue an order authorizing the pregnant woman to consent to the performance or inducement of an abortion without the [*consent or notification*] of a parent or guardian. If the court does not make the finding specified in this subsection or subsection (a) of this Section, it shall dismiss the petition.

SECTION [11]. JUDICIAL BYPASS STANDARDS.

[*Drafter's Note: This enhancement is for states that want to enact specific standards for courts to use when evaluating judicial waiver petitions.*]

(a) If the pregnant woman claims to be mature and well-informed at a proceeding held pursuant to [Insert appropriate reference(s) to the state parental involvement law], the pregnant woman must prove by clear and convincing evidence that she is sufficiently mature and capable of giving informed consent without [obtaining consent from or giving notice to] her parent or legal guardian based on her experience level, perspective, and judgment.

(b) In assessing the pregnant woman's experience level, the court may consider, among other relevant factors, the pregnant woman's age and experiences working outside the home, living away from home, traveling on her own, handling personal finances, and making other significant decisions. In assessing the pregnant woman's perspective, the court may consider, among other relevant factors, what steps the pregnant woman took to explore her options and the extent to which she considered and weighed the potential consequences of each option. In assessing the pregnant woman's judgment, the court may consider, among other relevant factors, the pregnant woman's conduct since learning of her pregnancy and her intellectual ability to understand her options and to make an informed decision.

(c) In assessing whether, by clear and convincing evidence, [obtaining the consent or providing notification] of a pregnant woman's parent or guardian is not in her best interest, a court may not consider the potential financial impact on the pregnant woman or the pregnant woman's family if the pregnant woman does not have an abortion.

SECTION [12]. MENTAL HEALTH EVALUATION.

[Drafter's Note: This enhancement is for any state that wants to better protect minors from their own immaturity or coercion or abuse by others.]

(a) Prior to court proceedings addressing a petition for judicial waiver, the court may require the pregnant woman to participate in an evaluation and counseling session with a mental health professional from the *[state Health Department]* or a staff member from the *[state Department of Social Services]*, or both. Such evaluation shall be confidential and scheduled expeditiously.

(b) Such evaluation and counseling session shall be for the purpose of developing trustworthy and reliable expert opinion concerning the pregnant woman's sufficiency of knowledge, insight, judgment, and maturity with regard to her abortion decision in order to aid the court in its decision and to make the state's resources available to the court for this purpose. Persons conducting such sessions may employ the information and printed materials referred to in *[Insert citation(s) to state informed consent law, if applicable]* in examining how well the pregnant woman is informed about pregnancy, fetal development, abortion risks and consequences, and abortion alternatives and should also endeavor to verify that the pregnant woman is seeking an abortion of her own free will and is not acting under coercion, intimidation, threats, abuse, undue pressure, or extortion by any other persons.

(c) The results of such evaluation and counseling shall be reported to the court by the most expeditious means, commensurate with security and confidentiality, to assure receipt by the court prior to a hearing on the pregnant woman's petition.

SECTION [13]. DISCLOSURE AND CONSENT FORM.

[Drafter's Note: This enhancement is appropriate for states with parental consent laws. It is based on the consent form developed by the Texas Medical Board.]

(a) A form created by the *[Insert appropriate state department or agency]* shall be used by physicians to obtain the consent required prior to performing an abortion on a minor who is not emancipated.

(b) A form is not valid and consent is not sufficient, unless:

(1) A parent or legal guardian initials each page of the form, indicating that he or she has read and understands the information included on that page;

(2) A parent or legal guardian signs the last page of the form in front of a person who is a notary public;

(3) The minor initials each list of risks and hazards, detailed in Sections (c)(4)(a)-(d) below;

(4) The minor signs a "consent statement," described in Section (c)(6) below; and

(5) The physician signs the declaration described in Section (c)(7) below.

(c) The form shall include, but is not limited to, the following:

(1) A description of the minor's rights, including her right to informed consent;

(2) A description of the parent or legal guardian's rights under [*Insert name of State*] law;

(3) A detailed description of the surgical and/or medical procedures that are planned to be performed on the minor;

(4) A detailed list of the risks and hazards related to the surgical and medical procedures planned for the minor, including, but not limited to, the following:

    a. Risks and hazards that may occur in connection with any surgical, medical, and/or diagnostic procedure: potential for infection; blood clots in veins and lungs; hemorrhage (heavy bleeding); allergic reactions; or death.

    b. Risks and hazards that may occur with a surgical abortion: hemorrhage (heavy bleeding); a hole in the uterus (uterine perforation) or other damage to the uterus; sterility; injury to the bowel and/or bladder; a possible hysterectomy as a result of complication or injury during the procedure; and failure to remove all products of conception that may result in an additional procedure.

    c. Risks and hazards that may occur with a medical/non-surgical abortion: hemorrhage (heavy bleeding); failure to remove all products of conception that may result in an additional procedure; sterility; and possible continuation of pregnancy.

    d. Risks and hazards of the particular procedure planned for the minor: cramping of the uterus or pelvic pain; infection of the female organs (uterus, tubes, and ovaries); cervical laceration; incompetent cervix; and emergency treatment for any of the above named complications.

(5) A description of additional information that must be provided by the physician to the minor under [*Insert name of State*] law, including, but not limited to [*Insert information required by the state's informed consent law, if applicable (e.g. the probable gestational age of the unborn baby; the availability of medical assistance benefits; the father's responsibilities, etc.)*]

(6) A "consent statement" which must be signed by the minor. The consent statement must include, but is not limited to, the following points, which must be individually initialed by the minor:

    a. That the minor understands that the doctor is going to perform an abortion on her which will end her pregnancy and will result in the death of her unborn child;

    b. That the minor is not being forced to have an abortion, and that she has the choice not to have the abortion and may withdraw consent prior to the abortion;

    c. That the minor gives permission for the procedure;

    d. That the minor understands that there are risks and hazards that could affect her if she has the planned surgical or medical procedures;

    e. That the minor has been given the opportunity to ask questions about her condition, alternative forms of treatment, risk of non-treatment, the procedures to be used, and the risks and hazards involved;

    f. That the minor has been given information required under [*Insert citation(s) to the state's informed consent law, if applicable*]; and

    g. That the minor has sufficient information to give informed consent.

(7) A **"physician declaration,"** which must be signed by the physician, stating that the physician or his or her assistant has, as required, explained the procedure and the contents of this form to the minor and her parent or legal guardian and has answered all questions. Further, to the best of the physician's knowledge, the patient and her parent or legal guardian have been adequately informed and have consented to the procedure.

(8) A **"parental consent statement"** stating that the signing parent or legal guardian:

    a. Understands that the doctor signing the "physician declaration" is going to perform an abortion on the minor, which will end her pregnancy and result in the death of her unborn child;

    b. That the parent or legal guardian has had the opportunity to read this form or have it read to him or her and has initialed each page;

    c. That the parent or legal guardian had the opportunity to ask questions to the physician or the physician's assistant about the information in this form and the surgical and medical procedures to be performed on the minor;

    d. That the parent or legal guardian believes that he or she has sufficient information to give informed consent; and

    e. That, by the parent or legal guardian's signature, the parent or legal guardian affirms that he or she is the minor's father, mother, or legal guardian.

(9) A page for the parent or legal guardian's signature that must be notarized by a notary public.

(10) Any additional information that must be provided to a woman under the laws of [Insert name of State] in order for a physician to obtain her informed consent prior to performing an abortion.

SECTION [14]. CONSTRUCTION.

(a) Nothing in this Act shall be construed as creating or recognizing a right to abortion.

(b) It is not the intention of this law to make lawful an abortion that is currently unlawful.

SECTION [15]. SEVERABILITY.

Any provision of this Act held to be invalid or unenforceable by its terms, or as applied to any person or circumstance, shall be construed so as to give it the maximum effect permitted by law, unless such holding shall be one of utter invalidity or unenforceability, in which event such provision shall be deemed severable herefrom and shall not affect the remainder hereof or the application of such provision to other persons not similarly situated or to other, dissimilar circumstances.

SECTION [16]. RIGHT OF INTERVENTION.

The [*Legislature*], by joint resolution, may appoint one or more of its members who sponsored or co-sponsored this Act, as a matter of right and in his or her official capacity, to intervene to defend this law in any case in which its constitutionality is challenged.

SECTION [17]. EFFECTIVE DATE.

This Act takes effect on [*Insert date*].

Patient Protection Project

Protecting the Vulnerable

Forty-two states currently prohibit committing suicide by taking a doctor-prescribed overdose of barbiturates (sleeping pills) – or "suicide by physician," as it should be called to remove all euphemisms. But suicide advocates are aggressively seeking to overturn these protective laws and replace them with dangerous laws legalizing suicide and providing little to no protection for vulnerable Americans nearing the Patient Protection. Over the past several years, more than half the states have considered legislative or ballot measures to legalize suicide.

Federal courts entered the debate over legalized suicide in 1996 when two appeals courts struck down state laws in New York and Washington prohibiting assisting in suicide. The U.S. Supreme Court reversed those decisions in 1997, holding that committing suicide with the aid of a doctor's prescription is not a "fundamental right" under the U.S. Constitution.[12] In doing so, the Court also affirmed the states' authority to legislate and regulate in this area.

Undeterred by their earlier failure to have a constitutional right to suicide recognized by the federal courts, suicide advocates have more recently challenged suicide prohibitions in several state courts, including New Mexico, New York, Massachusetts and Connecticut. For the most part, these lawsuits have largely failed.

Nonetheless, legalized suicide advocates have taken their agenda to the state legislatures, as demonstrated by the dramatic increase in the number of states that have considered measures to legalize the practice since 2015. But, with a small number of exceptions, most states have already passed laws prohibiting suicide by physician, and some have also passed resolutions or other legislation forming task forces or directing state agencies to consider ways to improve upon end-of-life care, to study pain management, to encourage the use of palliative care, and/or to improve care for the terminally ill and vulnerable.

To assist in combating the drive toward legalizing suicide by medicalized means or otherwise, Americans United for Life offers the Suicide by Physician Ban Act and the Joint Resolution Opposing Suicide by Physician, which reaffirm a state's opposition to suicide by prescription or otherwise and counter those asserting that suicide and death are America's answers to illness, disease, disability, or suffering.

The lack of regard for human dignity and the right to life have been eroding patients' rights in other ways besides the drive to embrace suicide. Over the last few decades, services that were once considered basic "humane care" have been redefined as "medical treatment." Today, the American Medical Association (AMA), which defines "life-sustaining treatment" as including but not limited to "mechanical ventilation, renal dialysis, chemotherapy, antibiotics, and artificial nutrition and hydration," argues that "[e]ven if the patient is not terminally ill or permanently unconscious, it is not unethical to discontinue all means of life-sustaining medical treatment in accordance with a proper substituted judgment or best interests analysis" (emphasis added). In other words, the AMA endorses broad discretion for healthcare providers to withhold or withdraw life-sustaining care.

In addition, "futile care theory" is rapidly penetrating hospital care protocols. This theory provides that a healthcare provider or healthcare institution may unilaterally withhold medical treatment because the healthcare provider or healthcare institution believes that a patient's quality of life is not worth continuing or it is simply not cost effective to do so, regardless of the wishes of the patient or the patient's family.

The redefinition of "humane care" and the promulgation of "futile care" protocols are imperiling patients. Patients need strong, protective laws requiring unwilling healthcare providers and institutions to continue the life-sustaining care they need pending transfer to a willing healthcare provider or institution. In the wake of the tragic case of British infant Charlie Gard, who died after hospital officials and courts refused to allow his parents to transfer him to other facilities that would have provided him the care he sought, it is essential that this standard be instituted in America before it is too late.[13] AUL offers the *Charlie Gard Act* to preserve little Charlie Gard's memory and to empower states to protect patients from having life-sustaining care withdrawn or withheld against their will.

Finally, patients deserve protection from misguided treatment or a lack of information about their treatment options. A dearth of knowledge among medical professionals is one of the most commonly cited barriers to good pain management for suffering patients.[14] Across America, 75 million people suffer from severe pain – both chronic and acute – daily.[15] These pain patients are often debilitated by their conditions and experience compromised quality of life. In the worst cases,

some even fall into depression and consider suicide – by prescriptive means (where legal) or otherwise. However, studies repeatedly confirm that 95 percent of pain sufferers could find relief for their symptoms with the proper use of pain medication.[16]

A disparity exists between the care needed to manage the pain of many patients, especially those in nursing homes and hospitals suffering from terminal illness or otherwise in the last stages of life, and the services rendered by America's healthcare providers. Many of these professionals admit that they do not feel comfortable with the training received in their professional schools regarding pain management and end-of-life care. Because textbooks are notably silent on these topics and because school curricula do not address how to manage patient pain, professionals enter the field of medicine ill-equipped to handle these patient needs and lacking the confidence to adequately address severe pain symptoms.

Better education and training for healthcare providers is needed to help patients receive adequate care. For example, a physician's fear of causing patient addiction to powerful medications or losing a license for over-prescribing pain medications are among the reasons that many doctors will often hesitate to prescribe effective palliative medicine. Notably, many states have laws that protect doctors from civil suits for prescribing effective dosages of pain medication.

Likewise, poor education perpetuates presumptions including that certain opiates will hasten death. In fact, such opiates, when properly monitored and titrated, may actually prolong life by lessening the burden on distressed bodies that cannot cope with pain.

Many state medical licensing boards have begun to address this problem by adopting the Model Guidelines (1998) and Model Policy (2004) for the Use of Controlled Substances for the Treatment of Pain suggested by the Federation of State Medical Licensing Boards. The provisions of AUL's *Pain Medicine Education Act* are largely adopted from these guidelines and policies. In addition, the Joint Commission on Accreditation for Health Care Organizations (JCAHO) requires protocols for addressing patient pain as part of its accreditation standards. While these are positive steps, their impact has not inspired better medical or professional school education for healthcare providers in proper pain management. Instead, state legislatures have tried to address these concerns.

In 2000, the California legislature passed a bill requiring that pain management and end-of-life care be added to medical school curricula. In 2006, the New York legislature approved $4.6 million in grants to undergraduate institutions and medical schools to create programs for palliative care education and training. (Unfortunately, Governor Pataki vetoed the bill.) While so many suffer, state legislation that furthers the rights of each patient to quality care and pain management through better education for healthcare providers is necessary.

[12] *See Washington v. Glucksberg*, 521 U.S. 702 (1997), *rev'g Compassion in Dying v. State of Washington*, 79 F.3d 790 (9th Cir. 1996) (finding that Washington's prohibition of assisted suicide does not violate the Due Process Clause of the Fourteenth Amendment); and *Vacco v. Quill*, 521 U.S. 793 (1997), *rev'g* 80 F.3d 716 (2d Cir. 1996) (holding that the New York ban on assisted suicide does not violate the Equal Protection clause of the Fourteenth Amendment).

[13] Rachel del Guidice, *Pro-Life Leaders Rally to Support Charlie Gard*, The Daily Signal, July 6, 2017, available at, http://dailysignal.com/2017/07/06/pro-life-leaders-rally-support-charlie-gard/ (last visited Aug. 14, 2017).

[14] D.E. Hoffmann, *Pain Management and Palliative Care in the Era of Managed Care: Issues for Health Insurers*, 26 Journal of Law, Medicine & Ethics 267 (1998).

[15] Gureje O, Von Korff M, Simon GE & Gater R. *Persistent Pain and Well-Being: A World Health Organization Study in Primary Care*, 280 J. Amer. Med. Assoc. 147 (1998).

[16] Jeffrey Wishik, *Chronic Pain: Medical and Legal Aspects*, 53-DEC R.I. B.J. 23, 23 (2004).

SUICIDE BY PHYSICIAN BAN ACT

HOUSE/SENATE BILL NO. _____

By Representatives/Senators _____

SECTION 1. TITLE.

This Act may be known and cited as the "Suicide by Physician Ban Act."

SECTION 2. LEGISLATIVE FINDINGS AND PURPOSES.

(a)　The [*Legislature*] of the State of [*Insert name of State*] finds that:

(1)　"In almost every State—indeed, in almost every western democracy—it is a crime to assist a suicide. The States' assisted suicide bans are not innovations. Rather they are longstanding expressions of the States' commitment to the protection and preservation of all human life." *Washington v. Glucksberg*, 521 U.S. 702, 710 (1997).

(2)　"Indeed, opposition to and condemnation of suicide—and, therefore, of assisting suicide—are consistent and enduring themes of our philosophical, legal and cultural heritages." This almost universal tradition has long rejected a right to suicide with the aid of a physician, and the State of [*Insert name of State*] "continues to explicitly reject it today, even for terminally ill, mentally competent adults." *Washington v. Glucksberg*, 521 U.S. 702, 711 and 723 (1997).

(3)　The State of [*Insert name of State*] "has an unqualified interest in the preservation of human life, ... in preventing suicide, and in studying, identifying, and treating its causes." *Washington v. Glucksberg*, 521 U.S. 702, 729-30 (1997).

(4)　The State of [*Insert name of State*] "has an interest in protecting vulnerable groups—including the poor, the elderly, and disabled persons—from abuse, neglect, [coercion,] and mistakes." A ban on suicide by physician reflects and reinforces the well-supported policy "that the lives of the terminally ill, disabled and elderly people must be no less valued than the lives for the young and healthy, and that a seriously disabled [, *terminally ill, or elderly*] person's suicidal impulses should be interpreted and treated the same way as anyone else's." *Washington v. Glucksberg*, 521 U.S. 702, 731-32 (1997).

(5) The State of [*Insert name of State*] has an interest in protecting the integrity and ethics of the medical profession, including its obligation to serve its patients as healers, as well as to the principles articulated in the Hippocratic Oath to:

    a.   Keep the sick from harm and injustice.

    b.   Refrain from giving anybody a deadly drug if asked for it, nor make a suggestion to this effect.

(6) More specifically, the State of [*Insert name of State*] recognizes the close link between suicide by a doctor's prescription and euthanasia where a "right to die" easily becomes a "duty to die." A prohibition of suicide by physician is the only reasonable means to protect against foreseeable abuses. *Washington v. Glucksberg*, 521 U.S. 702, 734-35 (1997); *Vacco v. Quill*, 521 U.S. 793, 808-09 (1997).

(7) The State of [*Insert name of State*] also recognizes the distinction between a patient refusing life-sustaining medical treatment (not to include the withdrawal of artificial nutrition and hydration), where he or she dies from the underlying fatal disease or pathology; and a patient ingesting or administering a lethal medication prescribed by a physician, where the medication is the cause of death. *Vacco v. Quill*, 521 U.S. 793, 801 (1997).

(8) The State of [*Insert name of State*] further recognizes the importance of palliative care and pain management and emphasizes the distinction in the "legal principles of causation and intent" between pain management intended to alleviate pain and suicide by a doctor's prescription intended to cause death. *Vacco v. Quill*, 521 U.S. 793, 801-03 (1997).

(b) Based on the findings in subsection (a), it is the purpose of this Act to:

(1) Provide protection for our most vulnerable citizens by explicitly prohibiting suicide by a doctor's prescription within the State of [*Insert name of State*]'s criminal code.

(2) Reinforce and reflect the intended purpose of our medical professions to preserve life and act as healers.

SECTION 3. DEFINITIONS.

As used in this Act only:

(a) **"Aid in dying"** means the act or instance of a person providing the means or manner for another to be able to commit suicide.

(b) **"Deliberately"** means to consider carefully; done on purpose; intentional.

(c) **"Healthcare provider"** means any individual who may be asked to participate in any way in a healthcare service, including, but not limited to, the following: a physician; physician's assistant; nurse; nurses' aide; medical assistant; hospital employee; clinic employee; nursing home employee; pharmacist; pharmacy employee; researcher; medical or nursing school faculty member, student, or employee; counselor; social worker; or any professional, paraprofessional, or any other person who furnishes or assists in the furnishing of healthcare services.

(d) **"Person"** means any natural person and, when appropriate, an "organization" to include:

   (1) A public or private corporation, company, association, firm, partnership, or joint-stock company;

   (2) Government or a governmental instrumentality; or

   (3) A foundation, institution, society, union, club, or church.

(e) **"Physician"** means a person licensed to practice medicine in the State of [*Insert name of State*]. This term includes medical doctors and doctors of osteopathy.

(f) **"Suicide"** means the act or instance of taking one's own life voluntarily and intentionally.

SECTION 4. CRIMINAL PENALTIES.

(a) Any person who deliberately advises, assists, or encourages another to commit suicide or provides aid in dying is guilty of [*Insert appropriate degree of felony*].

(b) Any physician or healthcare provider who

   (1) Prescribes any drug, compound, or substance to a patient with the intended purpose to enable the patient to end the patient's life; or

   (2) Performs or participates in any medical procedure for the intended purpose to assist in ending the patient's life or to enable the patient to end his or her own life is guilty of [*Insert appropriate degree of felony*].

SECTION 5. CIVIL PENALTIES AND FINES.

(a) Any person, physician, or healthcare provider who intentionally or knowingly violates this Act shall be liable for damages.

(b) If any person violates Section 4 of this Act and death results, any surviving family member, other beneficiary, executor, or administrator of the decedent's estate may bring an appropriate action under [*Insert reference(s) to state's wrongful death statute(s)*].

(c) Any physician or other healthcare provider who violates Section 4 of this Act shall be considered to have engaged in unprofessional conduct for which his or her [*certificate or*] license to provide health-care services in the State of [*Insert name of State*] shall be suspended or revoked by [*Insert name of State Medical Board or other appropriate entity*].

SECTION 6. CONSTRUCTION.

Nothing in this Act shall be construed to prohibit a physician or healthcare provider from

(a) Participating in the execution of a person sentenced by a court to death by lethal injection.

(b) Following a patient's clear, expressed, and documented wishes to withhold or withdraw life-sustaining treatment [*not necessarily inclusive of withdrawing artificial nutrition and hydration*].

(c) Prescribing and administering palliative care or pain medication treatment options intended to relieve pain while the patient's illness or condition follows its natural course.

SECTION 7. RIGHT OF INTERVENTION.

The [*Legislature*], by joint resolution, may appoint one or more of its members, who sponsored or cosponsored this Act in his or her official capacity, to intervene as a matter of right in any case in which the constitutionality of this Act, or any portion thereof, is challenged.

SECTION 8. SEVERABILITY.

Any provision of this Act held to be invalid or unenforceable by its terms, or as applied to any person or circumstance, shall be construed so as to give it the maximum effect permitted by law, unless such holding shall be one of utter invalidity or unenforceability, in which event such provision shall be deemed severable herefrom and shall not affect the remainder hereof or the application of such provision to other persons not similarly situated or to other, dissimilar circumstances.

SECTION 9. EFFECTIVE DATE.

This Act takes effect on [*Insert date*].

STATE OF THE STATES: WHERE ARE WE NOW?

LAWS AGAINST SUICIDE BY PHYSICIAN

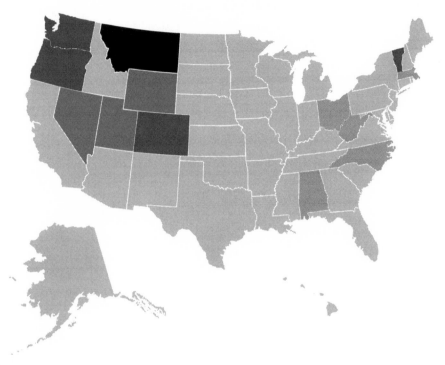

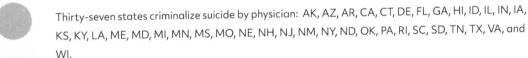

Thirty-seven states criminalize suicide by physician: AK, AZ, AR, CA, CT, DE, FL, GA, HI, ID, IL, IN, IA, KS, KY, LA, ME, MD, MI, MN, MS, MO, NE, NH, NJ, NM, NY, ND, OK, PA, RI, SC, SD, TN, TX, VA, and WI.

Five states prohibit suicide by physician under common law of crimes or judicial interpretation of its homicide statutes: AL, MA, NC, OH, and WV.

Three states have left the legal status of suicide by physician undetermined: NV, UT, and WY.

Four states and the District of Columbia permit suicide by physician: CO, OR, VT, and WA.

One state permits a physician to enable suicide by recognizing a statutory "consent" defense for those "aiding" a suicide: MT.

JOINT RESOLUTION OPPOSING SUICIDE BY PHYSICIAN

JOINT RESOLUTION NO. _____

By Representatives/Senators _____

WHEREAS, [*Insert name of State*] has an "unqualified interest in the preservation of human life," and this State's "prohibition on assisted suicide, like all homicide laws, both reflects and advances its commitment to this;" [17]

WHEREAS, neither this State's constitution nor the U.S. Constitution contains a right to suicide or to assist another in committing suicide and, thus, no individual has the right to authorize another to kill him or her in violation of federal and state criminal laws; [18]

WHEREAS, suicide is not a typical reaction to an acute problem or life circumstance, and many individuals who contemplate suicide, including the terminally ill, suffer from treatable mental disorders, most commonly clinical depression, which frequently goes undiagnosed and untreated by physicians; [19]

WHEREAS, in Oregon, forty-six (46) percent of patients seeking prescriptions to enable their suicide changed their minds when their physicians intervened and appropriately addressed suicidal ideations by treating their pain, depression, and/or other medical problems; [20]

WHEREAS, palliative care continues to improve and is nearly always successful in relieving pain and allowing a person to die naturally, comfortably, and in a dignified manner without a change in the law; [21]

WHEREAS, the experiences in Oregon and the Netherlands explicitly demonstrate that palliative care options deteriorate with the legalization of medical means to enable suicide; [22]

WHEREAS, [*Insert name of State*] rejects abuses of palliative care through "futility care" protocols and the use of "terminal sedation" without life-sustaining care as seen in the Liverpool Care Pathway; [23]

WHEREAS, a physician's prescription for suicide relies on the physician's judgment—to include prejudices and negative perceptions—that a patient's life is not worth living, ultimately contributing to the use of "futility care" protocols and euthanasia; [24]

WHEREAS, [*Insert name of State*] rejects the "sliding-scale approach" which claims certain "qualities of life" are not worthy of equal legal protections;[25]

WHEREAS, the legalization of suicide by physician prescription sends a message that suicide is a socially acceptable response to aging, terminal illnesses, disabilities, and depression and subsequently imposes a "duty to die";

WHEREAS, the medical profession as a whole opposes suicide by physician because it is contrary to the medical profession's role as healer and undermines the physician-patient relationship;[26]

WHEREAS, suicide by a doctor's prescription is significantly less expensive than other care options, and Oregon's experience demonstrates that cost constraints can create financial incentives to limit care and offer assisted suicide;[27]

WHEREAS, as evidenced in Oregon, the private nature of end-of-life decisions makes it virtually impossible to police a physician's behavior to prevent abuses, making any number of safeguards insufficient;[28] and

WHEREAS, a prohibition on enabling or assisting suicide, and specifically suicide by physician prescription, is the only way to protect vulnerable citizens from coerced suicide and euthanasia.[29]

NOW THEREFORE, BE IT RESOLVED BY THE [*LEGISLATURE*] OF THE STATE OF [*INSERT NAME OF STATE*]:

Section 1. That the [*Legislature*] strongly opposes and condemns suicide in every form, including suicide accomplished by a physician's prescription, because the [*Legislature*] has an "unqualified interest in the preservation of human life" [*and because "its ban on suicide insists that all persons' lives, from beginning to end, regardless of physical or mental condition, are under the full protection of the law."*] [30]

Section 2. That the [*Legislature*] strongly opposes and condemns all forms of suicide, including suicide by physician, because anything less than a prohibition leads to foreseeable abuses and eventually to euthanasia by devaluing human life, particularly the lives of the terminally ill, elderly, disabled, and depressed whose lives are of no less value or quality than any other citizen of this State.

Section 3. That the [*Legislature*] strongly opposes and condemns all forms of suicide, including suicide by physician, for terminally ill, mentally competent adults because enabling suicide by medical means eviscerates efforts to prevent the self-destructive act of suicide and hinders progress in effective physician interventions including diagnosing and treating depression, managing pain, and providing palliative and hospice care.

Section 4. That the [*Legislature*] strongly opposes and condemns all forms of suicide, including suicide by physician, because enabling suicide by medical means undermines the integrity and ethics of the medical profession, subverts a physician's role as healer, and compromises the physician-patient relationship. For these reasons and others, the medical community summarily rejects it.

Section 5. That the Secretary of State of [*Insert name of State*] transmit a copy of this resolution to the Governor, the [*Insert name of State*] [*Department of Health and Human Services*], and the [*Insert name of State*] Medical Association.

[17] *Washington v. Glucksberg*, 521 U.S. 702, 728 (1997).

[18] *See id.* at 735 (upholding Washington's ban on assisted suicide and finding there is no constitutional right to assisted suicide under the Due Process Clause of the Fourteenth Amendment); *Vacco v. Quill*, 521 U.S. 793, 808-09 (1997) (upholding New York's statute prohibiting assisted suicide as consistent with the U.S. Constitution in that it did not violate the Equal Protection Clause of the Fourteenth Amendment); *Sampson v. State*, 31 P.3d 88, 95 (Alaska 2000) (finding Alaska's manslaughter statute prohibiting assisted suicide constitutional in that it does not infringe upon their constitutional rights to privacy, liberty, and equal protection); *Donaldson v. Lungren*, 2 Cal. App. 4th 1614, 4 Cal. Rptr. 2d 59, 63-5 (Cal. Ct. App. 1992) (finding no constitutional right to assisted suicide under the California Constitution); and *Krischer v. McIver*, 697 So. 2d 97, 104 (Fla. 1997) (upholding the constitutionality of Florida's statute prohibiting assisted suicide).

[19] New York State Task Force on Life and the Law, WHEN DEATH IS SOUGHT: ASSISTED SUICIDE AND EUTHANASIA IN THE MEDICAL CONTEXT 77-82 (May 1994) available at http://www.health.state.ny.us/nysdoh/provider/death.htm (last visited December 12, 2016).

[20] Linda Ganzini et al., *Physicians' Experiences with the Oregon Death with Dignity Act*, 342 NEW ENG. J. MED. 557, 557 (2000).

[21] Herbert Hendin & Kathleen Foley, *Physician-Assisted Suicide in Oregon: A Medical Perspective*, 106 MICH. L. REV. 1613, 1634-35 (2008).

[22] Id. at 1615-20 (noting only 13 percent of patients received palliative care consultations after the Oregon law went into effect).

[23] *See id.* at 1634-35; Kate Devlin, *Sentenced to death on the NHS*, TELEGRAPH, September 2, 2009 at http://www.telegraph.co.uk/health/healthnews/6127514/Sentenced-to-death-on-the-NHS.html (last visited December 12, 2016).

[24] *See Washington v. Glucksberg*, 521 U.S. at 732 (1997).

[25] Id. at 729.

[26] Id. at 731; *see also*, American College of Physicians, Ethics Manual, *available at* http://www.acponline.org/running_practice/ethics/manual/ethicman5th.htm#patients (last visited June 29, 2015) ("The College does not support legalization of physician-assisted suicide or euthanasia. After much consideration, the College concluded that making physician-assisted suicide legal raised serious ethical, clinical, and social concerns and that the practice might undermine patient trust; distract from reform in Patient Protection care; and be used in vulnerable patients, including those who are poor, are disabled, or are unable to speak for themselves or minority groups who have experienced discrimination."); *Royal College of Physicians cannot support legal change on assisted dying – survey results*, May 9, 2006, *available at* http://www.rcplondon.ac.uk/news-media/press-releases/rcp-cannot-support-legal-change-assisted-dying-survey-results (last visited December 12, 2016).

[27] Susan Donaldson James, *Death Drugs Cause Uproar in Oregon, Terminally Ill Denied Drugs for Life, But Can Opt for Suicide*, ABC News, Aug 6, 2008 *available at* http://abcnews.go.com/Health/story?id=5517492&page=1 (last visited December 12, 2016).

[28] Hendin & Foley, *supra* note 10 at 1637-38.

[29] *Glucksberg*, 521 U.S. at 733-34.

[30] Id. at 728-29.

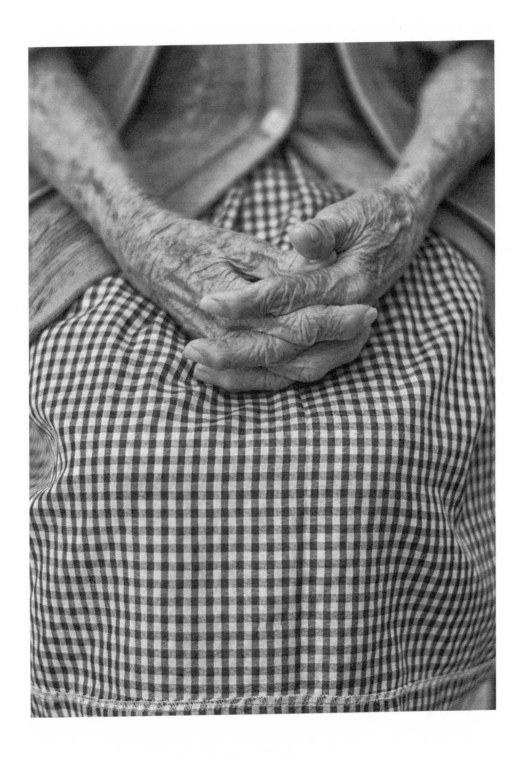

CHARLIE GARD ACT

HOUSE/SENATE BILL NO. _____

By Representatives/Senators _____

SECTION 1. TITLE.

This Act may be known and cited as the "Charlie Gard Act."

SECTION 2. LEGISLATIVE FINDINGS AND PURPOSES.

(a) The [*Legislature*] of the State of [*Insert name of State*] finds that:

    (1) Over the last few decades, services that were once considered basic "humane care" have been redefined as "medical treatment," and may, therefore, be rejected by individuals in their advance planning documents or by their surrogates when they are incapacitated. For example, food and water supplied through a feeding tube has been redefined by some as "medical treatment," with the term "artificial nutrition" coined to analogize the process to "medical treatment" rather than "humane care."

    (2) In some circumstances, life-sustaining care may be withheld or withdrawn at the discretion of healthcare providers or healthcare institutions.

    (3) The American Medical Association (AMA), which defines "life-sustaining treatment" as including but not limited to "mechanical ventilation, renal dialysis, chemotherapy, antibiotics, and artificial nutrition and hydration" has stated that "[e]ven if the patient is not terminally ill or permanently unconscious, it is not unethical to discontinue all means of life-sustaining medical treatment in accordance with a proper substituted judgment or best interests analysis."

    (4) "Futile care theory" is rapidly penetrating hospital care protocols. This theory provides that a healthcare provider or healthcare institution may unilaterally withhold medical treatment because a healthcare provider or healthcare institution believes that a patient's quality of life is not worth continuing or it is simply not cost effective to do so, despite the wishes of the patient or patient's family.

    (5) "Futile care theory" contradicts "choice" and "patient autonomy;" instead, it is akin to euthanasia in that it replaces the ethic that all humans are equal and worthy of protection with one where doctors decide which lives are worth saving and sustaining.

(6)   The tragic case of British infant Charlie Gard, whose parents' repeated requests for treatment or transfer of their child went unheeded until his death because of the hospital's belief that further treatment would be "futile," is a warning to us that the standard of practice must be clarified to insist that attending physicians and staff respect parents' treatment decisions for their minor children.

(6)   Patients or their [*Insert appropriate term(s), e.g. "healthcare agent," "surrogate," or "proxy"*], whose desire that life-sustaining care be continued or provided is refused by a healthcare provider or institution benefit from state laws requiring the provision of life-sustaining care pending transfer to a willing provider or institution.

(7)   The law in the State of [*Insert name of State*] does not explicitly require healthcare providers or healthcare institutions to provide or continue to provide life-sustaining care pending transfer to a willing provider or institution.

(b)   Based on the findings in subsection (a), the purpose of this Act is to require healthcare providers or healthcare institutions that decline to honor a patient or patient's [*Insert appropriate term(s), e.g. "healthcare agent," "surrogate," or "proxy"*]'s request for the provision or continuation of life-sustaining care to provide continuing life-sustaining care to the patient until a transfer can be effected and to make reasonable efforts to assist in the transfer of the patient to a willing healthcare provider or healthcare institution.

SECTION 3. DEFINITIONS.

As used in this Act only:

(a)   **"Healthcare institution"** means any public or private organization, corporation, partnership, sole proprietorship, association, agency, network, joint venture, or other entity that is involved in providing healthcare services, including but not limited to hospitals, clinics, medical centers, ambulatory surgical centers, private physician's offices, nursing homes, or other institutions or locations wherein healthcare services are provided to any person.

(b)   **"Healthcare provider"** means any individual who may be asked to participate in any way in a healthcare service, including, but not limited to a physician, physician assistant, nurse, nurse aide, medical assistant, hospital employee, clinic employee, nursing home employee, or any other person who furnishes or assists in the furnishing of healthcare services.

(c) **"Life-sustaining care"** means health care including, but not limited to mechanical ventilation, renal dialysis, chemotherapy, antibiotics, and nutrition and hydration that, in reasonable medical judgment, has a significant possibility of sustaining the life of a patient.

SECTION 4. DUTY TO PROVIDE LIFE-SUSTAINING CARE.

(a) If a patient, a patient's [*Insert appropriate term(s), e.g. "healthcare agent," "surrogate," or "proxy"*], or a patient's advance directive directs the provision or opposes the withdrawal of life-sustaining care that, in reasonable medical judgment, has a significant possibility of sustaining the life of a patient, a healthcare provider or healthcare institution shall ensure the provision [*or continuation*] of the directed life-sustaining care.

(b) A healthcare provider or healthcare institution that is unwilling to provide directed life-sustaining care under paragraph (a) may transfer the patient to another healthcare provider or healthcare institution capable of and willing to provide the directed life-sustaining care, but the unwilling provider or institution shall ensure the provision of the directed life-sustaining care until the patient is transferred. Any transfer of a patient under this subsection must be done promptly upon agreement by the receiving provider or institution to admit the patient.

(c) Upon the request of a patient or resident or a prospective patient or resident, or of a patient or prospective patient's [*Insert appropriate term(s), e.g. "healthcare agent," "surrogate," or "proxy"*], a healthcare provider or healthcare institution shall disclose in writing any policies that relate to the services a patient or resident may receive involving resuscitation or life-sustaining measures, including any policies related to treatments deemed to be "ineffective," "futile," or inappropriate.

SECTION 5. RIGHT OF INTERVENTION.

The [*Legislature*], by joint resolution, may appoint one or more of its members, who sponsored or cosponsored this Act in his or her official capacity, to intervene as a matter of right in any case in which the constitutionality of this Act or any portion thereof is challenged.

SECTION 6. SEVERABILITY.

Any provision of this Act held to be invalid or unenforceable by its terms, or as applied to any person or circumstance, shall be construed so as to give it the maximum effect permitted by law, unless such holding shall be one of utter invalidity or unenforceability, in which event such provision shall be deemed severable herefrom and shall not affect the remainder hereof or the application of such provision to other persons not similarly situated or to other, dissimilar circumstances.

SECTION 7. EFFECTIVE DATE.

This Act takes effect on [*Insert date*]

PAIN MEDICINE EDUCATION ACT

HOUSE/SENATE BILL NO. _____

By Representatives/Senators _____

SECTION 1. TITLE.

This Act may be known and cited as the "Pain Medicine Education Act."

SECTION 2. LEGISLATIVE FINDINGS AND PURPOSES.

(a)   The Legislature of the State of [*Insert name of State*] finds that:

(1)   One goal of medicine is to relieve suffering.

(2)   Inadequate pain relief is a serious public health problem in the United States, especially for those with chronic pain, the terminally ill, or those who are otherwise in the final stages of life. Approximately [*Insert number based on studies or other evidence*] percent of chronic pain patients in this State do not receive adequate treatment for their pain symptoms.

(3)   Clinical experience demonstrates that adequate pain management leads to enhanced functioning and increased quality of life, while uncontrolled pain contributes to disability and despair.

(4)   Every person experiences pain, suffers, and dies at some point in his or her life. Diagnosis and treatment of pain is integral to the practice of medicine and appropriate pain management for each patient is the responsibility of the treating physician.

(5)   Inappropriate pain management and treatment may result from a healthcare provider's lack of knowledge and professional training.

(6)   All healthcare providers should become knowledgeable about assessing patients' pain and effective methods of pain treatment, as well as statutory requirements for prescribing controlled substances.

(7)   Some healthcare providers are ill-informed about current and effective management techniques for patients' pain symptoms, in part, because this topic is not adequately addressed in the normal course of professional schools' curricula.

(8)   With proper management techniques, chronic pain may be reduced in an overwhelming majority of suffering patients.

(9)   Controlled substances, including opioid analgesics, may be essential in the courses of treatment for all types of pain and are, therefore, necessary to the public health.

(10) Healthcare professionals' education has not provided appropriate training in the use of opioid medications for chronic pain.

(11) Patient pain should be assessed and treated promptly, and the quantity and frequency of doses should be adjusted based upon, among other medically relevant factors, the intensity and duration of the pain and the treatment outcomes being sought.

(12) Tolerance and physical dependence are normal consequences of sustained use of opioid analgesics and are not the same as addiction.

(13) The [*Legislature*] recognizes that some types of pain cannot be completely relieved.

(b) Based on the findings in subsection (a), the [*Legislature's*] purposes in promulgating this Act are to further the important and compelling societal interests of:

(1) Expanding the opportunities for medical students, residents, and other healthcare providers to gain experience in treating severe pain symptoms in suffering patients.

(2) Ensuring the best possible medical care for all patients suffering from intractable and chronic pain.

(3) Improving the quality of life for all chronic pain sufferers, especially those in the last stages of life, by ensuring that each patient undergoes a peaceful, natural, and, as much as possible, pain-free end-of-life experience.

(4) Reducing patient requests for physician-assisted suicide by addressing issues that may lead to depression and despair which are the root causes and the most-cited motivations for physician-assisted suicide.

(5) Broadening patient autonomy by presenting the greatest number of possible options for treatment through consultation with knowledgeable physicians.

SECTION 3. DEFINITIONS.

As used in this Act only:

(a) **"Addiction"** means a primary, chronic, neurobiological disease with genetic, psychosocial, and environmental factors influencing its development and manifestations. It is characterized by behaviors that include impaired control over drug use, craving, compulsive use, and continued use despite harm. Physical dependence and tolerance are normal physiological consequences of extended opioid therapy for pain and are not the same as addiction.

(b) **"Classroom instruction"** means education conducted with a licensed instructor present, either by lecture or discussion, as an integrated part of a healthcare provider school course curriculum.

(c) **"Clinical instruction"** means education conducted through interaction with patients suffering from severe chronic or acute pain in hospital-based sites, non-hospital-based ambulatory care settings, and palliative care sites and hospices and under the supervision of a licensed healthcare provider. This can include standardized patient experiences.

(d) **"Double effect"** is a doctrine justifying palliative sedation and requiring three standards for ethical medical treatment: (1) the treatment itself is not morally wrong; (2) the intended benefit to the patient is not achieved by the secondary and unintended effects of the treatment; and (3) proportionality exists between the intended effects and the unintended secondary effects.

(e) **"Healthcare provider"** includes the following professionals:

   (1) **"Nurses"** mean licensees of the [*Insert name of the State Board of Nursing*], including advanced practice nurses.

   (2) **"Nurse-practitioners"** mean licensees of the [*Insert name of State Board(s) licensing nurse-practitioners*].

   (3) **"Pharmacists"** mean licensees of the [*Insert the name of the State Board of Pharmacy*].

   (4) **"Physicians"** mean licensees of the [*Insert name of the State Board(s) licensing medical doctors and doctors of osteopathy*].

   (5) **"Physician's assistants"** mean licensees or registrants of the [*Insert the name of the State Board regulating physician assistants*].

(f) **"Intractable pain"** means a state of pain, even if temporary, in which reasonable efforts to remove or remedy the cause(s) of the pain have failed or have proven inadequate.

(g) **"Opioid"** means a strong pain medication derived from opium or synthesized to behave like opium derivatives. Examples of opioids include, but are not limited to, morphine, codeine, oxycodone, methadone, and fentanyl.

(h) **"Pain"** is an unpleasant sensory and emotional experience associated with actual or potential tissue damage or described in terms of such damage.

   (1) **"Acute pain"** is the normal, predicted physiological response to a noxious chemical, thermal, or mechanical stimulus and typically is associated with invasive procedures, trauma, and disease. It is generally time-limited.

(2) **"Chronic pain"** is a state in which pain persists beyond the usual course of an acute disease or healing of an injury, or that may or may not be associated with an acute or chronic pathologic process that causes continuous or intermittent pain over months or years.

(i) **"Palliative care"** means:

(1) The active, total care of a patient whose disease or medical condition is not responsive to curative treatment or whose prognosis is limited due to progressive, far-advanced disease; and

(2) The evaluation, diagnosis, treatment, and management of primary and secondary pain, whether acute, chronic, persistent, intractable, or associated with the end-of-life, the purpose of which is to diagnose and alleviate pain and other distressing signs and symptoms and to enhance the quality of life.

(j) **"Palliative sedation"** means the administration of sedatives to a terminally ill, conscious patient whose pain cannot be otherwise relieved to alleviate suffering, but with the effect of inducing unconsciousness. The intent of administering the drug is to relieve pain, not to produce unconsciousness or to accelerate death.

(k) **"Physical dependence"** means a state of adaptation that is manifested by drug class-specific signs and symptoms that can be produced by abrupt cessation, rapid dose reduction, decreasing blood level of the drug, and/or administration of an antagonist. Physical dependence by itself does not equate with addiction.

(l) **"Tolerance"** means a physiologic state resulting from regular use of a drug in which an increased dosage is needed to produce a specific effect or a reduced effect is observed with a constant dose over time. Tolerance may or may not be evident during opioid treatment and does not equate with addiction.

SECTION 4. REQUIREMENTS FOR HEALTHCARE PROVIDER EDUCATION.

(a) **Objectives.** The instruction required by this Act is designed to meet the following objectives:

(1) That students will become more comfortable addressing the needs of patients experiencing chronic or severe pain.

(2) That students will be trained in the most current methods regarding the use of controlled substances, especially opioid analgesics.

(3) That students will realize the importance of developing a pain treatment plan for each patient in chronic or severe pain and learn methods and techniques necessary for developing such a plan.

(4) That students will learn objective methods for evaluating pain symptoms in patients.

(5) That students will understand the differences between addiction to opioid analgesics and tolerance and dependence on opioid analgesics.

(6) That students will understand the principle of double effect, especially with regard to palliative sedation.

(7) That students will understand the extreme unlikelihood of opioid administration hastening death when properly monitored.

(8) That students will understand relevant laws applicable to prescription of controlled substances.

(9) That students will become aware of differences in diverse cultural approaches to pain management and end-of-life care and become comfortable working with patients who may express preferences different than those of the student's own intuitions.

(b) **Curriculum.** The curriculum in each school educating healthcare providers and receiving public funds shall include at least eight (8) hours of classroom instruction and at least four (4) hours of clinical instruction on pain management. The curriculum shall be designed to accomplish all objectives listed in Sections 4(a)(1) through 4(a)(9) of this Act. In developing a curriculum for pain management education, it is recommended that faculty educators are trained in or consult the Education for Physicians on End-of-Life Care (EPEC) Curriculum created by the Institute for Ethics at the American Medical Association.

(c) Procedures for evaluating and monitoring pain. Students shall be instructed in the following seven-step method for pain treatment:

(1) **Evaluation of the patient.** A medical history and physical examination must be obtained, evaluated, and documented in the medical record. The medical record should document the nature and intensity of the pain, current and past treatments for pain, underlying and co-existing diseases or conditions, the effect of pain onphysical and psychological function, and history of substance abuse. The medical record should also document the presence of one or more recognized medical indications for the use of a controlled substance.

(2) **Treatment plan.** A written treatment plan should state objectives that will be used to determine treatment access, such as pain relief and improved physical and psychosocial function, and should indicate if any further diagnostic evaluations or other treatments are planned. After treatment begins, the physician should adjust drug therapy to the individual medical needs of each patient. Other treatment modalities or a rehabilitation program may be necessary, depending on the etiology of the pain and the extent to which the pain is associated with physical and psychosocial impairment.

(3) Informed consent and agreement for treatment. The physician should discuss the risks and benefits of the use of controlled substances with the patient, persons designated by the patient,

or the patient's [*surrogate, guardian, or other appropriate term*] if the patient is without medical decision-making capacity. The patient should receive prescriptions from one physician and one pharmacy whenever possible. If the patient is at high risk for medication abuse or has a history of substance abuse, the physician should consider the use of a written agreement between physician and patient outlining patient responsibilities, including:

a. Urine/serum medication levels screening when requested;

b. Number and frequency of all prescription refills; and

c. Reasons for which drug therapy may be discontinued (e.g., violation of agreement).

(4) **Periodic Review.** The physician should periodically review the course of pain treatment and any new information about the etiology of the pain or the patient's state of health. Continuation or modification of controlled substances for pain management therapy depends on the physician's evaluation of progress toward treatment objectives. Satisfactory response to treatment may be indicated by the patient's decreased pain, increased level of function, or improved quality of life. Objective evidence of improved or diminished function should be monitored and information from family members or other caregivers should be considered in determining the patient's response to treatment. If the patient's progress is unsatisfactory, the physician should assess the appropriateness of the continued use of the current treatment plan and consider the use of other therapeutic modalities.

(5) **Consultation.** The physician should be willing to refer the patient as needed for additional evaluation and treatment in order to achieve treatment objectives. Special attention should be given to those patients with pain who are at risk for medication misuse, abuse, or diversion. The management of pain in patients with a history of substance abuse or with a comorbid psychiatric disorder may require extra care, monitoring, documentation, and consultation with or referral to an expert in the management of such patients.

(6) **Medical records.** The physician should keep accurate medical records including:

a. The medical history and physical examination;

b. Diagnosis, therapeutic, and laboratory results;

c. Evaluations and consultations;

d. Treatment objectives;

e. Discussion of risks and benefits;

f. Informed consent;

g. Treatments;

h. Medications (including date, type, dosage, and quantity prescribed);

i. Instructions and agreements; and

j. Periodic reviews.

Records should remain current and be maintained in an accessible manner and readily available for review.

(7) Compliance with controlled substance laws and regulations. To prescribe, dispense, or administer controlled substances, the physician must be licensed in the State and comply with applicable federal and state regulations. Physicians are referred to the Physician's Manual of the U.S. Drug Enforcement Administration [*and any relevant documents issued by the State Medical Board*] for specific rules governing controlled substances as well as applicable state regulations.

(d) **Hours Requirements.** The following requirements apply to the core curriculum of any healthcare provider education program and are in addition to any course content required in elective courses or courses required for discrete areas of medicine. A board issuing a license or certification to any healthcare provider under [*Insert relevant reference(s) or citation(s)*] shall require that each applicant for initial licensure complete at least:

(1) Eight (8) hours of classroom instruction, and
(2) Four (4) hours of clinical instruction. The requirements of this subsection shall not apply to those seeking licensure from the [*State Board of Pharmacy*].

(e) **Application.** The licensure requirements of this Act shall apply to any student beginning healthcare provider education after [*Insert appropriate date*].

SECTION 5. PAIN MANAGEMENT REGULATIONS ENCOURAGED.

[*Drafter's Note: Include this Section when the State Medical Board has not already adopted pain management regulations or similar standards.*]

The [*Legislature*] strongly encourages [*Insert name of State Medical Licensing Board*] to adopt pain management regulations based on the Pain Management Model Policy of the Federation of State Medical Licensing Boards and the provisions of this Act.

SECTION 6. SEVERABILITY.

Any provision of this Act held to be invalid or unenforceable by its terms, or as applied to any person or circumstance, shall be construed so as to give it the maximum effect permitted by law, unless such holding shall be one of utter invalidity or unenforceability, in which event such provision shall be deemed severable herefrom and shall not affect the remainder hereof or the application of such provision to other persons not similarly situated or to other, dissimilar circumstances.

SECTION 7. RIGHT OF INTERVENTION.

The [*Legislature*], by joint resolution, may appoint one or more of its members, who sponsored or cosponsored this Act in his or her official capacity, to intervene as a matter of right in any case in which the constitutionality of this Act or any portion thereof is challenged.

SECTION 8. EFFECTIVE DATE.

This Act takes effect [*Insert date*].

Appendices
and resources

DEFENDING LIFE 2019
Evaluation Criteria

MAX POSSIBLE
100
POINTS

States receive credit for an enforceable law only, not for laws enacted but later enjoined by a court or otherwise deemed unenforceable. The 2019 state ranking reflects all legislative and litigation activity through August 15, 2017, except for successful ballot measures which are reflected as of the date of the general elections, November 6, 2018.

I. WOMEN'S PROTECTION PROJECT

20 PTS

A. Enforcement of Abortion-Related Laws

1. Provides for criminal penalties for violations of one or more abortion laws
2. Provides for civil penalties for violations of one or more abortion laws
3. Provides for professional sanctions for violations of one or more abortion laws

B. Laws Ensuring Fully Informed Consent

1. Basic informed consent requirements (e.g., mandatory counseling as to risks of procedure and gestational age of unborn child)
2. Reflection period (of any length)

C. Coercive Abuse Prevention

Maintains a law criminalizing coercive abuse in the context of a woman's abortion decision, requiring the posting of signs on coercive abuse, requiring that a woman be informed that no one may coerce her into undergoing an abortion, or imposing similar requirements

D. Health and Safety Requirements for Abortion Facilities

1. Requires facilities performing abortions to meet specified health and safety standards
2. Requires facilities performing abortions after the first trimester to meet specified health and safety standards

E. Abortion Reporting

1. General reporting (e.g., demographic information, information about gestational age of the unborn child and abortion method used, etc.)
   a. Requires information on all abortions
   b. Requires information on surgical abortions only
2. Complication reporting

F. Specific Informed Consent for Drug-Induced Abortion

1. Requirement that a woman be informed about the efficacy of and risks associated with drug-induced abortion
2. Requirement that a woman be told that a drug-induced abortion can be reversed.

G. Parental Involvement for Minors

1. Maintains enforceable parental involvement law
   a. Parental consent law
   b. Parental notice law
2. Maintains any legal enhancement of parental involvement requirement(s)

H. Child Protection Act

1. Abortion facility personnel are mandatory reporters of abuse
2. Requirement to retain forensic evidence from minor's abortion
3. Penalizes efforts to circumvent parental involvement laws

II. INFANTS' PROTECTION PROJECT

A. Unborn Infants' Dignity Act

1. Treats the bodily remains of unborn infants with dignity and respect
   a. Maintains specific law mandating the dignified disposition of bodily remains of aborted infants and prohibits treatment as medical waste
   b. Prohibits the sale, purchase, or transfer of the bodily remains of aborted infants
2. Authorizes a fetal death certificate, certificate of stillbirth, or similar document
   a. Applies before 20-weeks gestation
   b. Applies only after 20-weeks gestation
3. Bans experimentation on bodily remains of aborted unborn children

B. "Missouri Preamble" or Similar Legislative Declaration

Has adopted a law or legislative declaration that each life begins at conception; that unborn children have protectable interests in life, health, and well-being; that parents have protectable interests in the life, health, and well-being of their unborn children; and/or that all state laws shall be interpreted to extend every protection to unborn children (not prohibited by the U.S. Constitution and Supreme Court jurisprudence).

C. Ban on Partial-Birth Abortion

Bans the use of the partial-birth abortion procedure

1. At any stage of pregnancy
2. Only after viability

D. Prenatal Nondiscrimination Act

1. Bans abortions performed for sex-selection
2. Bans abortions performed for reason of genetic abnormality

E. Perinatal Hospice Information Act

Requires that families be informed about the availability of perinatal hospice care following a life-limiting fetal diagnosis

F. Born-Alive Infant Protection Act

1. Provides protection at any stage of development
2. Provides protection after viability and/or only protects child from "deliberate acts" by physician

G. Unborn Wrongful Death Act

1. Allows wrongful death lawsuits when a pre-viable or viable unborn child is killed
2. Allows wrongful death lawsuits only when a viable unborn child is killed

III. DEFUNDING ABORTION PROVIDERS

(State Funding Limitations)

A. Public/taxpayer funding of abortion

1. Consistent with federal Hyde Amendment
2. In cases of rape, incest, fetal abnormalities, and/or threats to woman's life or health
3. Public funding in most cases (e.g., "medical necessity")

B. Enacted a law or otherwise taken action to defund (or partially defund) abortion providers (including Planned Parenthood)

C. Law opting out of federal abortion mandate (in healthcare law)

D. Prohibition on use of state funds for abortion counseling and/or referrals

E. Prohibition on use of state facilities for abortions

F. Prohibition on abortion (insurance) coverage for state employees

IV. OTHER ABORTION-RELATED LAWS

10 PTS

A. State Constitutional Right to Abortion or Freedom of Choice Act (FOCA)

1. Has no state FOCA and does not recognize state constitutional right to abortion
2. Has state FOCA and/or recognizes state constitutional right to abortion

B. Other Abortion Bans/Limitations

1. Enforceable pre-Roe ban or a "delayed enforcement" ban
2. Ban on post-viability abortions

C. Physician-Only Law for Performance of Abortions

D. Support for Pregnancy Resource Centers (PRCs)

1. Provides direct funding to PRCs and/or offers "Choose Life" license plates (with proceeds going to PRCs or alternatives)
2. Enacted pro-PRC resolution in 2017
3. State legislature enacted anti-PRC statute, regulation, or resolution in 2017

V. LEGAL RECOGNITION OF UNBORN AND NEWLY BORN

A. Unborn Victims of Violence/Fetal Homicide

1. Recognizes unborn child at any stage of gestation as potential homicide victim
2. Recognizes unborn child later in gestation (but before viability) as potential homicide victim
3. Recognizes unborn child after viability as potential homicide victim

B. Protection for Unborn Children from Nonfatal Criminal Assaults

C. Prohibition on Wrongful Life & Wrongful Birth Lawsuits

1. Wrongful life lawsuits
   a. Prohibits or limits wrongful life lawsuits
   b. Allows wrongful life lawsuits
2. Wrongful birth lawsuits
   a. Prohibits or limits wrongful birth lawsuits
   b. Allows wrongful birth lawsuits

VI. BIOETHICS

A. Human Cloning

1. Bans all forms of human cloning
2. Affirmatively permits any type of human cloning

B. Embryo/Stem Cell Research

1. Destructive embryo research (DER)
   a. Bans at least some forms/methods of DER
   b. Expressly allows any form of DER
2. Encourages, promotes, or funds any ethical alternative to DER (e.g., adult stem cells, iPS, or cord blood)

C. State Funding of Destructive Embryo Research and/or Human Cloning

1. Prohibits or restricts state funding of DER and/or human cloning
2. Funds DER and/or human cloning

D. Assisted Reproductive Technologies (ART)

1. Requires informed consent for IVF procedure and/or for storage/disposition of unused embryos
2. Imposes some regulation on human egg harvesting

VII. PATIENT CARE AND SUICIDE

5 PTS

Suicide by Physician

1. Statutory prohibition on assisted suicide
2. Common law prohibition of assisted suicide
3. Requires physicians to counsel patients on how to commit suicide and to provide prescriptions for patients who decide to commit suicide
4. Law or judicial decision permitting medicalized suicide

VIII. HEALTHCARE FREEDOM OF CONSCIENCE

15 PTS

A. Protects Individual Healthcare Freedom of Conscience

1. Provides protection for healthcare providers for all procedures/services
2. Provides protection for healthcare providers for abortion and specified procedures (e.g., sterilization and contraception)
3. Provides protection for healthcare providers for abortion only
4. Affirmatively compels any healthcare provider (including pharmacists) to provide or participate in any procedure/service in violation of his or her conscience

B. Protects Institutional Healthcare Freedom of Conscience

1. Provides protection for public, private, and religious healthcare institutions for all procedures/services
2. Provides protection for public, private, and religious institutions for abortion and other specified procedures/services (e.g., sterilization and contraception)
3. Provides protection for private and religious institutions for abortion and other specified procedures/services (e.g., sterilization and contraception)
4. Provides protection for public, private, and religious institutions for abortion only
5. Provides protection for private or religious institutions for abortion only
6. Affirmatively compels any healthcare institution (including pharmacies) to provide or participate in any service in violation of its conscience

AUL MODEL
Legislation

Americans United for Life, the legal architect of the pro-life movement, maintains the nation's most comprehensive catalogue of model legislation protecting human life from conception until natural death. AUL legal experts have carefully crafted each piece of model legislation to advance legal protection for life and to withstand judicial scrutiny.

AUL's model legislation covers the full spectrum of life issues: abortion, protection for unborn children in contexts other than abortion, emerging biotechnologies, the end-of-life, and healthcare freedom of conscience. Copies of AUL's model legislation, legislative policy guides, and additional information are available at AUL's website, *www.aul.org.*

RESOURCES RELATED TO UNSAFE:

Joint Resolution On Epidemic of Substandard Abortion Practices and Abortion Industry Efforts to Mainstream Dangerous Abortion Facilities provides statistics on and state-specific evidence of dangerous abortion care and medically substandard abortion facilities; criticizes the Supreme Court's decision to ignore such evidence in *Whole Woman's Health v. Hellerstedt* (2016); and calls on Congress to reject any federal legislation that prioritizes "mere access" to abortion over women's health and safety.

THE WOMEN'S PROTECTION PROJECT:

Enforcement Module provides options for the criminal, civil, and administrative enforcement of all abortion-related statutes and details enhanced inspection requirements for abortion facilities.

Women's Late-Term Pregnancy Health Act prohibits abortions at or after 20 weeks and is based on concerns both for women's health and the pain experienced by unborn children.

Women's Right to Know Act provides a woman, at least twenty-four (24) hours before an abortion, with detailed information regarding her medical and psychological risks; her child's gestational age, development, and pain capability; and the abortion procedure itself.

Coercive Abuse Against Mothers Prevention Act prohibits coercing a woman to undergo an abortion, as well as requires abortion facilities to post signs concerning coercion and to report suspected cases of coercive abuse.

Women's Health Protection Act requires abortion facilities to meet medically appropriate health and safety standards designed specifically for such facilities and based on the abortion industry's own treatment protocols. State laws based on and similar to the Women's Health Protection Act have been upheld by federal courts.

Abortion Reporting Act requires abortion providers to report demographic information about women undergoing abortions and mandates that any medical provider treating abortion-related complications report information about those complications to state officials.

Drug-Induced Abortion Information and Reporting Act requires abortion providers to inform women about the efficacy and dangers of drug-induced abortion and mandates that women be told that drug-induced abortions can be reversed. It also requires the reporting of complications related to drug-induced abortions.

Parental Involvement Enhancement Act strengthens state parental involvement laws with, among other elements, requirements for notarized consent forms and for identification and proof of relationship for a parent or guardian providing the requisite consent, as well as more stringent standards for judicial bypass proceedings.

Child Protection Act strengthens requirements that abortion facilities report all cases of suspected statutory rape and sexual abuse, mandates the collection of forensic evidence for certain abortions performed on minors, and prohibits a third-party from aiding or abetting a minor in circumventing her state's parental involvement law.

THE INFANTS' PROTECTION PROJECT:

Unborn Infants Dignity Act ensures that every mother of a deceased unborn infant is given the opportunity to ensure that her child is treated with dignity and respect and that the bodies of aborted infants are not exploited for scientific or pecuniary gain.

"Missouri Preamble" provides that each life begins at conception; that unborn children have protectable interests in life, health, and well-being; and that parents have protectable interests in the life, health, and well-being of their unborn children. Further, the Act provides that all state laws shall be interpreted to extend every protection to unborn children not prohibited by the U.S. Constitution and Supreme Court jurisprudence. It is based on a 1986 Missouri law.

Partial-Birth Abortion Ban Act bans the unnecessary and barbaric partial-birth abortion procedure and is modeled after the federal Partial-Birth Abortion Ban Act, which was upheld by the Supreme Court in *Gonzales v. Carhart* (2007).

Prenatal Nondiscrimination Act bans abortions performed solely for reasons of sex-selection or genetic abnormalities such as Down syndrome.

Perinatal Hospice Information Act ensures that every woman considering an abortion after receiving a life-limiting fetal diagnosis is aware of the availability of perinatal hospice.

Born-Alive Infant Protection Act protects all infants born alive during abortions or attempted abortions and includes appropriate enforcement mechanisms and penalties.

Unborn Wrongful Death Act permits a wrongful death claim in the death of an unborn child, at any stage of development or gestation, remedying both the lack of wrongful death laws in some states and the lack of comprehensive protection provided by most state laws.

DEFUNDING ABORTION PROVIDERS:

Defunding the Abortion Industry and Advancing Women's Health Act prohibits the use of public funds, facilities, and personnel for the performance of abortions or the provision of abortion counseling and/or referrals.

Federal Abortion-Mandate Opt-Out Act prohibits insurance providers operating within the state health insurance Exchanges (required under the federal healthcare law) from offering coverage for abortion.

Abortion Coverage Prohibition Act prohibits health insurance coverage for abortion.

Employee Coverage Prohibition Act prohibits the use of state taxpayer funds to pay for health insurance coverage of abortions for state employees.

Exchange & Private Insurance Coverage Prohibition Act prohibits insurance providers operating within the state health insurance Exchanges (required under the federal healthcare law) from offering coverage for abortion and prohibits other health insurance coverage for abortion.

Abortion Subsidy Prohibition Act prohibits the use of public funds, facilities, and personnel for the performance of abortions or the provision of abortion counseling or referrals for abortion and avoids the funding of abortion and abortion providers through state and federal family planning programs.

Joint Resolution Calling for Investigation and De-funding of Planned Parenthood and Other Abortion Providers calls on state authorities to look into the practices of abortion providers and to freeze any state funding allocated for abortion providers, as well as voicing the state legislature's support for similar efforts at the federal level.

OTHER ABORTION LEGISLATION:

State Constitutional Amendment enunciates a state policy to protect the life of an unborn child from conception until birth that will guide the interpretation of existing and future state laws; prevents any branch of state government from manufacturing a "right" to abortion under the state constitution; and prohibits state funding of abortion to the extent permitted by federal law.

Joint Resolution Proposing Constitutional Amendment Returning Determinations on Abortion Law and Policy to the American People enables the American people and their elected representatives to express their continuing conviction that, more than 40 years after *Roe v. Wade*, the U.S. Supreme Court's abortion decisions are erroneous and should be overturned, restoring self-government on this issue to the American people.

Women's Ultrasound Right to Know Act requires abortion providers to offer a woman the opportunity to view an ultrasound of her unborn child prior to any decision to undergo an abortion.

Parental Consent for Abortion Act mandates parental consent prior to a minor's abortion.

Parental Notification for Abortion Act requires parental notice before a minor's abortion.

Joint Resolution Honoring Pregnancy Resource Centers honors pregnancy resource centers for their life-affirming work.

LEGAL RECOGNITION AND PROTECTION OF THE UNBORN:

Crimes Against the Unborn Child Act criminalizes fatal and nonfatal assaults against an unborn child and specifically recognizes an unborn child as a potential crime victim.

Pregnant Woman's Protection Act extends state law allowing the use of force to defend another to women who use force to protect their unborn children from third-party violence.

BIOETHICS AND BIOTECHNOLOGIES:

Human Cloning Prohibition Act prohibits all forms of human cloning.

Destructive Human Embryo Research Act prohibits destructive embryo research.

Prohibition on Public Funding of Human Cloning and Destructive Embryo Research prohibits state funding for any form of human cloning or destructive embryo research.

Real Hope for Patients Act provides options for states to encourage ethical stem cell research.

Assisted Reproductive Technologies Disclosure and Risk Reduction Act regulates assisted reproductive technologies – the "gateway" to unethical embryo research – by requiring detailed informed consent requirements, imposing data collection and reporting requirements, and placing limits on the creation and transfer of embryos in a single reproductive cycle

Egg Provider Protection Act protects women from the health risks and exploitation associated with human egg harvesting.

Embryo Adoption Act provides a legal adoption procedure for human embryos.

PATIENT PROTECTION:

Suicide by Physician Ban Act prohibits assisted suicide.

Joint Resolution Opposing Suicide by Physician reaffirms the state's opposition to assisted suicide and provides information to counter any momentum achieved by those asserting that suicide and death are America's answers to illness, disease, disability, or suffering.

Pain Medicine Education Act establishes an educational curriculum for pain management and provides guidelines for evaluating, monitoring, and treating pain.

Charlie Gard Act protects a patient from having life-sustaining care withdrawn or withheld against his or her will.

HEALTHCARE FREEDOM OF CONSCIENCE:

Healthcare Freedom of Conscience Act provides comprehensive protection for the freedom of conscience of individual healthcare providers, institutions, and payers.

Pharmacist Freedom of Conscience Act provides comprehensive protection for pharmacists' freedom of conscience.

Ensuring Compliance with Healthcare Freedom of Conscience Act requires healthcare institutions receiving taxpayer funding to certify that they are knowledgeable of state and federal laws protecting freedom of conscience and have policies in place to abide by those laws, providing an incentive to protect – not coerce or discriminate against – healthcare professionals' conscience rights.

Joint Resolution Calling for Rescission of HHS Coercive Mandate & Affirming Freedom of Conscience reaffirms the state's opposition to the federal "HHS Mandate" (requiring many employers to purchase health insurance coverage for their employees that covers life-ending drugs and devices) and its commitment to protecting healthcare freedom of conscience.

ABOUT
Americans United for Life

Americans United for Life is the legal architect of the pro-life movement. We are accumulating victories, building momentum, and advancing a culture of life in America. As the nation's premier pro-life legal team, we work through the law and legislative process to one end: Achieving comprehensive legal protection for human life from conception to natural death. We hold the unique distinction of being the first national pro-life organization in America, incorporated in 1971, two years before the infamous *Roe v. Wade* decision.

AUL's legal team has been **involved in every abortion-related case before the U.S. Supreme Court** since *Roe v. Wade*, including AUL's successful defense of the Hyde Amendment before the high court. AUL's legal expertise and acumen set the bar in the pro-life community for the creation of effective and defensible pro-life laws. At the state, federal, and international levels, AUL works to advance life issues through the law and does so through measures that can withstand judicial obstacles and ultimately be enforced. AUL knows that reversing *Roe v. Wade* can be accomplished through deliberate, legal strategies that accumulate victories, build momentum, and restore a culture of life.

A LEADER IN THE STATES:

AUL works at the state level to craft tailored strategies and legislative tools that will assist state and local officials as they defend and protect life. **In all 50 states**, AUL's team has worked with governors, legislators, and pro-life leaders to ensure that everyone is welcomed in life and protected in law. AUL drafts legislation and provides in-depth legal analysis and expert testimony on critical life issues being debated in the states.

An example of success: since 1985 AUL has spearheaded efforts both to educate about and to pass fetal homicide laws, protecting unborn victims of violence. As a result, 39 states – and counting – now have fetal homicide laws.

A LEADER IN PRINT:

Comprehensive analysis and state-by-state insight are extraordinary resources that AUL makes available to pro-life leaders, attorneys, and officeholders nationwide. *Defending Life,* an annual guide which details the life initiatives underway in all 50 states, analyzes important issues, provides model legislation, and compares the 50 states in the well-publicized "Life List," which ranks the states based on their progress on the full spectrum of life issues.

Defending Life has been unparalleled in pointing the way to protecting women now, to limiting the abortion license created by the Supreme Court, and to preparing the ground to overturn Roe.

A LEADER AROUND THE WORLD:

AUL is also defending life around the world. Though human rights belong to all human beings, anti-life forces seek to develop a body of international law that provides for a "right to abortion" that agenda-driven U.S. judges will, in turn, impose upon America. Joining with pro-life lawyers around the world, AUL fights this at the United Nations, in international courts, and in other countries. Our groundbreaking Latin American counterpart to *Defending Life, Defending the Human Right to Life in Latin America*, was published in Spanish and in English in 2011. AUL attorneys regularly consult with pro-life allies in other countries to assist them in passing and defending pro-life laws.

A LEADER AMONG LEADERS:

AUL experts write for news outlets and speak at events nationwide. You can find AUL on television, in print, and on informative websites every day. AUL has been innovative in getting its message out through on-line events and inventive media strategies.

AN AWARD WINNING VIEWPOINT:

The national vantage point of AUL's operation makes it uniquely qualified to recognize and honor pro-life leadership for accomplishments at state, federal, and international levels, often achieved in partnership with AUL's team. Among the leaders who have accepted AUL's honors for their consistent and effective efforts to protect life are the legendary Rep. Henry Hyde, Rep. Chris Smith, Gov. Haley Barbour, and U.S. Speaker of the House John Boehner.

AUL's work promotes a culture of life through the law. For assistance on legislation, questions about litigation, or to have AUL host a briefing for legislators and policy makers in your state, please contact:

AMERICANS UNITED FOR LIFE
2101 Wilson Boulevard, Suite 525
Arlington, VA 22201
(202) 289-1478 | Info@AUL.org | www.AUL.org

AUL'S PROVEN
Track Record of Success

With more than 40 years of pro-life legal leadership, AUL has a distinguished record of accomplishments, but a few key victories stand out as representative of AUL's unique contributions to pro-life success.

1. WINNING THE HYDE AMENDMENT CASES BEFORE THE U.S. SUPREME COURT.

In 1980, AUL won an historic victory for the Hyde Amendment in the celebrated U.S. Supreme Court case, *Harris v. McRae,* and its companion case, *Williams v. Zbaraz.* AUL's attorneys were counsel for both cases, and AUL attorney Victor Rosenblum argued *Zbaraz* before the Court. These monumental court decisions upheld federal and state prohibitions on public funding of abortion except in cases where the life of the mother is implicated, resulting in as many as two million human lives saved since 1980.

2. ESTABLISHING FETAL HOMICIDE LAWS IN 39 STATES.

A fetal homicide law recognizes an unborn child as a potential victim of criminal violence. AUL's legal experts laid the intellectual groundwork to implement these laws nationwide. At the time of the *Roe* decision in 1973, only three states enforced these protective laws. Today, 39 states have fetal homicide laws in place, and 30 of these states protect the child beginning at conception.

3. DEFENDING LIFE, REDUCING ABORTIONS STATE BY STATE.

According to scholar Dr. Michael J. New, AUL's crucial work in helping pass and enact parental involvement laws, informed consent laws, and limits on taxpayer funding of abortion has reduced abortions across the country by an estimated 25 percent since 1992 (when the Supreme Court's decision in *Planned Parenthood v. Casey* opened the door to more significant regulations of abortion). In 2006, AUL decided to make its legal knowledge accessible to pro-life legislators and activists across the country and published the first edition of *Defending Life,* which instantly became known as the "pro-life playbook."

4. A LEADING ROLE IN THE FIGHT AGAINST SUICIDE BY PHYSICIAN.

In 1980, AUL published an important book on "Death, Dying and Euthanasia" and has continued to be involved in every significant case, at the state and federal level, concerning suicide by physician, including the extensive role AUL played in *Baxter v. Montana* in 2009.

5. SUCCESSFULLY PROTECTING LIFE OVERSEAS.

In 1979, AUL played a pivotal role in amending the Irish Constitution to protect life by precluding abortion. At a pro-life conference in Ireland, AUL was consulted about abortion and the role *Roe v Wade* played in the United States. AUL also engaged in an extensive educational and media campaign to educate the Irish people who eventually amended their constitution. As a result, Ireland remains one of the strongest pro-life nations in Europe and a target of the international pro-abortion Left. Its pro-life constitution was challenged before the European Court of Human Rights in a case in which AUL served as a consultant. The Court held that Ireland was required to amend its laws to provide for abortion when the mother threatened suicide (to conform its laws to a decision of the Irish Supreme Court that had so interpreted the constitution). Pro-abortion forces began an effort to pass such a law. AUL consulted several times with Irish politicians opposed to such a law during their visits to the U.S. and worked with Irish pro-life groups and attorneys on the matter.

If you are interested in supporting AUL's life-saving work financially we will accept your donations by mail, on our website www.AUL.org, or over the telephone. For more information about making a donation, email Info@AUL.org.

Americans United for Life *Defending Life 2019*

AUL.org

Made in the USA
Middletown, DE
14 May 2019